*Race Relations
in Virginia &
Miscegenation
in the South
1776-1860*

The University of
Massachusetts Press

Amherst 1970

JAMES HUGO JOHNSTON

Race Relations in Virginia & Miscegenation in the South
1776-1860

Foreword by Winthrop Jordan

Standard Book Number 87023-050-6
Library of Congress Catalog Card
Number 78-87833

Set in Baskerville and Bulmer types
and printed in the United States of America
by Kingsport Press, Inc.
Designed by Richard Hendel

Foreword

I N 1937, WHEN James Hugo Johnston completed the University of Chicago doctoral dissertation which is here published in substantially its original form, it was both less fashionable and less feasible than it is now to publish one's dissertation. There would be little purpose in resurrecting most such older dissertations. Yet it seems to me that *Race Relations in Virginia and Miscegenation in the South* constitutes a clear exception, and I am delighted that the University of Massachusetts Press has undertaken to make this work more widely available.

Professor Johnston completed this study at a time when Negro history—now black history—was not, to put the matter as gently as possible, a widely popular topic. He was fortunate to be able to approach his topic in an atmosphere largely free of the tensions now affecting everyone—black and white—writing on the history of race relations. Some readers today will find his discussion of relations between the races too genial, too gentle, and lacking in appropriate moral outrage. Without in any way denying the legitimacy of that outrage, I would point to the advantages which derive, in part, from composition in the emotionally neutral key. Professor Johnston was able to shun such all-encompassing, generalizing images as the "Benevolent Massa," the "Fawning Sambo," the "Rapacious Oppressor," and the "Vigilant Revolutionary." Relations between the races during slavery times were far more varied and complicated than this, as Johnston's approach and his factual material make abundantly clear. The point needs emphasis: race relations in Vir-

ginia were characterized by variety and complexity, and historical accounts and meditations which ignore these factors run
contrary to the facts.

It is precisely the attention to and respect for the "facts"
which give this study its special value. Professor Johnston examined thoroughly one of the best—and still least exploited—
collections of manuscript materials pertaining to slavery: the
petitions of ordinary citizens to the Virginia governors and
legislatures from the late eighteenth century to the Civil War.
What seems to me especially valuable at this stage in the development of black history is that Professor Johnston has included
extensive quotations from these materials, long paragraphs
which convey in rich detail the tone of human relationships.
The book affords a good introduction to historical source materials which ought to be further examined for the light they
can shed upon slave life in Virginia.

In his treatment of miscegenation, Professor Johnston again
demonstrates the complexities of what needs to be regarded as a
centrally important aspect of race relations. He makes clear that
sexual relations did not uniformly involve white men and black
women and that sometimes genuine affection was felt by both
parties. He details relationships ranging from lifetime attachments to the better known instances of outright rape of helpless
female slaves. There is dramatic tragedy inherent in so many of
these instances of our past which Professor Johnston has dredged
to the surface: as, for example, in the trial of Peggy and Patrick,
two slaves who killed her master because he had "generally kept
her confined, by keeping her chained to a block, and locked up
in his meathouse" and who had threatened that he "would beat
her almost to death, that he would barely leave the life in her,
and would send her to New Orleans" unless she "consented to
intercourse with him." Peggy was her master's daughter. Professor Johnston does not editorialize upon this incident; evidently he felt that the circumstances themselves were sufficient
commentary upon the slave system. What he *has* provided in
the second half of this book is a unique compilation of details
concerning the hidden world of interracial sex. He has even
uncovered solid evidence of "passing," that silent phenomenon
which speaks so eloquently as to how tragic—and how silly—

America's race relations have always been. He knows, as the reader should also, that the details he has uncovered constitute merely a visible portion of the iceberg of actual events.

In commending this book I ought to state frankly two reservations. Professor Johnston states that the first Negroes to arrive in Virginia were treated as servants, not slaves. Many other historians have made the same assertion, without adequate evidence. We simply lack the information necessary to determine whether those first Africans were slaves or servants. On the crucial early years of race relations in America there is very little information available, and in all probability no more is going to be uncovered.

Secondly and more generally, Professor Johnston discusses the persistence of slavery in terms of "the universal and characteristic control of economic forces over moral forces in the determination of human action" and he suggests that "many analogies may be found between the relation of the master and slave and the relation between the propertied class and the poor." Fair enough. These formulations are probably correct, but they omit precisely the dimension upon which this book is focussed. It was *racial* distinction—and still is—which made black people slaves and white people exploiters. More accurately, it was the white man's perception of physical difference which made racial slavery a possibility. Many Southern whites, especially before 1830, would have been delighted to be rid of slavery if they could at the same time have gotten rid of Negroes. Many yearned, as do many white Americans today, to have blacks simply go away. Virtually all whites then (and most now) were unwilling to have blacks both in America and at the same time free.

Having said this, it seems fitting to conclude by saluting the author upon publication of his valuable dissertation. Professor Johnston is now emeritus, having actively served Virginia State College for many years as head of the History Department, as Dean, as Vice-President, and as Acting President. It is especially fitting that his long and valuable career be capped by publication of his important contribution to Negro history.

Berkeley, California, 1969   WDJ

Preface

T HIS VOLUME is a study in the social history of Virginia and other Southern states in the period extending from the American Revolution to the outbreak of the Civil War. My chief sources are to be found in the Archives of Virginia. It has been my privilege to examine more than twenty-five thousand manuscript petitions to the legislature of Virginia, now preserved at Richmond. In many cases these are voluminous documents. The petitions deal with every phase of the life of the state. They were sent to the legislature from all sections of the state and included many petitions from counties in the present state of West Virginia. Of these petitions approximately one-tenth relate to varied phases of the life of slaves and free Negroes.

Certain features of the slave code are responsible for many of the petitions addressed to the legislature of Virginia. For example, in 1785 an act was passed which provided that any slave brought into the state and remaining for twelve months would be thereby set free.[1] Because of this act we find numerous petitions asking that individuals be permitted to bring in slaves from states to the north of Virginia. These documents recite the benefit that slave labor has been to the state and the valuable qualities of the slaves in question. After 1800 many reactionary laws seem to be in response to the prayers of petitioners who described conditions making such laws necessary. Harsh laws concerning slaves and free Negroes brought, in turn, protests from humani-

[1] William W. Hening, *Statutes at Large of Virginia* (Richmond, 1823), IV, 132.

tarians and antislavery workers, and the Archives bear abundant evidence of the sincerity of the efforts of these workers. The growth of antislavery sentiment threatened the slave system and compelled the owners of slaves to defend the right to their property. Many petitions coming from antislavery men demonstrate the strength of the antislavery movement and the pro- and antislavery petitions portray the slavery conflict in Virginia. The number of documents pertaining to slaves is greatest in the period from 1828 to 1833. The causes of the increase of the petitions in these years will appear in later chapters of this work. From 1833 to 1860 the petitions concerning the Negro become increasingly rare.

The factor which was productive of most of the petitions referred to in this study was an act, passed on January 25, 1806, which provided that "all slaves emancipated after May 1, 1806, must leave the state within twelve months after the act of emancipation, or be sold for the benefit of the literary fund."[2] This act made for great hardships among the Negro people, for it caused the separation of families. Because of its passage hundreds of petitions were addressed to the legislature by Negroes asking to be exempted from the penalty of the law. In these documents individuals were forced to show that their residence would not be injurious to the state, and this collection of human documents bears remarkable testimony for the persons in whose behalf they were sent. The legal form in which most of the petitions were drawn indicates that they were written by white lawyers, but in many cases it appears that they were written by the Negro petitioners. In most cases it appears that the petitioner was at least able to sign his own name, but it often happened that the man of necessity signed with his mark. Whereas the author may have been a hired attorney or a legal friend of the Negro petitioner, it is always true that the memorial is endorsed by white men who wished to see the Negro obtain the desire expressed in his petition. In many cases a hundred or more names testify that the Negro has told the truth and that he possesses all of the fine virtues claimed for him in his memorial.

In addition to the legislative documents I have examined the

[2] Ibid., XVI, 252.

executive papers of the governors of Virginia, using the letters sent to the executives in the period from 1774 to 1833. In this large collection the most valuable source has been the reports of the trial courts in cases in which Negroes were condemned for capital crimes. In all such capital cases the execution of the criminal could not legally be carried out until the governor of the state had reviewed the evidence. The evidence as now preserved presents the voluminous testimony presented to the courts in these cases. In addition to the official records, to the executive, were sent many letters containing requests for mercy for the condemned men and often describing conditions which were not mentioned in the evidence.

Much has been written about slavery, but in many cases the writing has been done by men of violent anti- or proslavery opinion or, if written since the Civil War, I have found it difficult to secure sources unbiased by prejudiced views of propagandists. In this work some may claim that conclusions as here indicated are weakened because the white advocate appears to be pleading for his client or the evidence is based upon unusual cases, for the exceptional cases are always the ones that become matters of record. However, there are considerations which seem to make the sources here used more valuable than much that is already familiar. These documents were not intended for the use of the abolitionists, and, when written, they were not intended for use outside the state of Virginia. They seem to be a record of the thought and life of the people of Virginia as they themselves saw and understood the Negro and the slave system.

Again, there should be much value in this study, not only because of the sources from which it is derived but also because much of the material here made available comes from the humble Negro slave: a people about whom much has been written and concerning whom it is sometimes claimed that a great war was fought; a people because of whom it is also claimed ruin came to a large part of this nation, but who, while all these things transpired, are usually portrayed as inarticulate.

It may possibly appear that this work is too largely a collection of documents and that the narrative is obscured by lengthy quotations from the sources. I regret that this should be true, but the temptation to give the documents and thus permit these people to speak for themselves has been hard to resist. The student who uses these sources develops an attitude that leads him to feel that at best what he may write may be unfair to those so long dead, that the silent ones should now have full opportunity to make themselves heard, and that no present-day writer can tell the story so effectively as they if they can be made to speak for themselves. Much has been omitted. The publication of the documents in the Virginia Archives will fill many volumes. In many cases fifty or more pages of manuscript relate to a single individual mentioned in this work. It will be realized that much remains to be published, and the student will find a fertile field for investigation in the Archives office at Richmond.

Many persons have helped to make this work possible. To my friends I am grateful. It is my sincere hope that my efforts may prove worthy of those who have aided in the completion of the task, that my friends may be generous if errors of judgment have been made, and that I shall retain the friendship of those to whom I am indebted.

JHJ

Chicago, Illinois, 1937

Contents

I

The Relation of the Negro to the White Man in Virginia

ONE

Friendly Relations

I N THE ENGLISH COLONIES of the mainland of North America racial institutions were formed in the seventeenth century. As then established they were to be handed down to the generations of men who were to govern America. There is reason to believe that in the early years of this century the Negroes brought into Virginia were regarded as servants and not as slaves and that the condition and treatment of the black and white servant were very similar.[1]

Seventeenth-century discipline for servants or slaves was harsh and the lot of the laboring man in colonial times is not to be envied.[2] The development of America demanded an abundant supply of manual labor and in the South the Negro furnished the needed workman. The slave code, by which the Negro workman was controlled, evolved as it was demonstrated that the code, with all its severe characteristics, made it possible to gain profits through the production of staple crops.

While in the seventeenth century the slave appears to have been debased and the conditions of his life were hard, when we approach the period of the American Revolution we find that a class of Negroes had developed that no longer looked, thought, or acted like African savages. In the first hundred years of American slavery the Negro had assimilated much of the life, customs,

---

[1] James C. Ballagh, *White Servitude in the Colony of Virginia* (Baltimore, 1895), p. 91; Helen T. Catterall, *Judicial Cases Concerning American Slavery and the Negro* (Washington, 1926), I, 53–63.

[2] Marcus W. Jernegan, *Laboring and Dependent Classes in Colonial America* (Chicago, 1931), pp. 3–44.

and civilization of the Englishman. Newspapers of the time advertise men and women who may be purchased only on condition that exceedingly high prices are offered for them. Such slaves are said to possess industrial skill, intelligence, and personal characteristics that distinguish them from their fellows.[3] The process of adjustment of the African to American life took place at a time when important changes were transpiring in the economic life of the colonies, and the Negro profited because of these changes. Authorities have shown that by 1750 many Virginia planters were convinced that there existed an overproduction of the great staple crop. The price of tobacco had declined and consequently many planters were unable to pay their debts to British merchants. Since, as a consequence, the value of the Negro field hand had decreased, many men considered the natural increase of their slaves an embarrassment of riches. Then it was that enlightened agriculturalists began to make experiments with the diversification of crops and others attempted to establish manufactures.[4] Naturally changes in industrial life demanded an improved type of labor. Accordingly, masters began to employ slaves at more exacting and complex forms of labor, and many Negro slaves proved adaptable to the changing economic life of the colony. Thus was developed a class of Negro tradesmen, a class destined to play an important part in the life of Virginia until the end of the Civil War. Such workmen often proved more profitable as free or semifree workmen and by worthy lives and demonstrated mechanical skill rose out of the mass of their fellows. It is this class of Negroes upon whom attention will frequently be focused.

The fine characters and superior qualities of certain black men are demonstrated in the petitions of such men for emancipation or for the privilege of remaining in the state after they had won their freedom. The occupations of certain of the petitioners are signs of intelligence or aptitude superior to that of the field

[3] "Eighteenth-Century Slaves as Advertised by Their Masters," *Journal of Negro History*, 1 (April, 1916), 163–216; Jernegan, op. cit., pp. 25–45.

[4] Ibid., pp. 44–45; Johann Schoef, *Travels in the Confederation* (London, 1784), II, 44; *Virginia Magazine of History and Biography*, xv (October, 1907), 350, 352.

hand. Because of the advantages offered by certain occupations money might be obtained and accumulated more easily than in other forms of employment. Very prominent among these petitioners are the Negro barbers. Ben Godwin, of the town of Portsmouth, explains that his master, by will, bequeathed to him his freedom on condition that he should amass a sum of money sufficient to care for himself in his old age. Many citizens of this town certify that Godwin had accumulated the sum of $2,346 and "he has by his skill and attention engrossed the whole custom of the place" and "it is most earnestly believed his emancipation and residence within the state would produce a general good, but particularly in this town within which we venture to say there is not a single man but does not wish the application of Ben to prevail."[5] A similar petition comes from a barber of Fredericksburg. This man declares that "he has been enabled to collect together a sum of money to purchase his freedom from his master . . . who is willing to emancipate him."[6] Petitions for freedom are also sent to the legislature of the state by Negro blacksmiths. A slave in the employ of a physician residing at the Hot Springs explains that for twenty years his master was confined to his bed, without the use of his limbs, "during which time and until his master's death he served him faithfully as his blacksmith, besides rendering him valuable and important services as his body servant . . . ; and that he has paid $600 dollars for his freedom and $500 for his hire."[7] A petition coming from the city of Petersburg shows that Edward Stokes "is a blacksmith; and from his industry, frugality, and good behaviour is much encouraged in his calling, from the profits of which he has been enabled to lay up a considerable sum of money."[8] Jacob Prosser, a drayman of the city of Richmond, declares that "by the unusual satisfaction it has been his good fortune to render to commercial men of the

[5] Archives of Virginia, Legislative Papers, Petition 6315, Nansemond, Oct. 14, 1814. Hereafter Archives of Virginia, Legislative Papers, will be omitted and the petitions to the State legislature will be listed by number, county, and date (insomuch as this information is available).

[6] Petition 6541, Stafford, Dec. 13, 1815. See also Petition 7461a.

[7] Petition 11063, Allegheny, Dec. 29, 1836.

[8] Petition 10894, Dinwiddie, Feb. 13, 1835.

city . . . and with his own indefatigable labour and economy" he has been able to purchase his freedom.[9] In Fredericksburg a slave claiming "the profession of Butcher" explains that he is ready to purchase his freedom.[10] A miller of Fredericksburg makes a similar declaration.[11]

In the above examples it is to be noted that the petitions are sent by slaves residing in urban centers. Such residence in towns or cities made possible the slave's purchase of his freedom. Examples, also, are to be found in which the applicant declares that he is the overseer of a small farm and in such employment has been able to acquire the price of his freedom, but such examples are comparatively rare.[12] The rural slave was dependent upon the generosity of the owner's family. In most cases the slave could acquire money only by the service of the public, and fortune favored the slave mechanic of the towns.

It is also to be noted that many white men aided the slaves of other men to obtain their freedom. The case of James Lott is an example of this kind. His master, by will, emancipated this Negro,

> but a certain Cornelius Sharky, who took upon himself
> the administration of the estate, wanted the property
> and most unjustly exposed your petitioner to the claims
> of a creditor and he was sold. . . . Major Garland Carr,
> knowing the hardship of the case, generously advanced
> the money for which he was sold and waited with
> your petitioner until by his labour he had repaid him.[13]

Pompey Branch explains that he contracted with his master for his freedom. He was unable to make the payment in advance but he secured two white men who did so and "by great industry and economy he was enabled to pay the whole of the purchase money" and therefore asked to be set free.[14]

[9] Petition, Henrico, 1815.
[10] Petition 6031, Stafford, Dec. 3, 1812.
[11] Petition 5578, Dinwiddie, Dec. 6, 1810; 6217, Dec. 14, 1813.
[12] Petition 6644, Louisa, Dec. 21, 1815.
[13] Petition 5592, Albemarle, Dec. 10, 1810.
[14] Petition 5635, Isle of Wight, Dec. 10, 1810.

The slaveowner in many cases is found to have contributed money to his own slaves to help them to buy their freedom. Concerning a certain slave woman it is declared that

> having been found to be a remarkably steady and industrious woman . . . the extraordinary character of the said petitioner and her husband induced her master about two years ago when she was likely to be separated from her husband, in consequence of the removal of her master, who was nevertheless willing to sell her and her then youngest child Ellen, to encourage her in her endeavouring to raise money by subscription to purchase herself and her said child. The master subscribed a considerable sum for this purpose and many of your petitioners also subscribed. By this means and by her own indefatigable efforts and industry she has raised money sufficient for the purchase of herself and her child Ellen.[15]

Also, a certain citizen of Petersburg made it possible for his slave to purchase his freedom. Concerning this slave the owner informs the legislature of the State that "James is my miller, in which capacity he has acted for upwards seventeen years during which time he has conducted himself with respect to honesty, sobriety, and every other virtue generally found in human nature with so much zeal, that he has not only obtained my most unlimited confidence, but so far as I can judge that of all others that are acquainted with him . . . and I wish to see him liberated."[16]

Many other examples may be given of the purchase of freedom by slaves. In the course of this study it has not been possible to determine how many slaves purchased their freedom. A careful study of the records of the county courts would reveal many instances of freedom granted by will or deed but bought and paid for by the slave. However, this study has been confined to the examination of documents concerning slaves and free Negroes to be found in the archives at Richmond. It is as if by accident that the story of freedom by purchase appears in these records. The rec-

[15] Petition 6419, Loudoun, Dec. 6, 1815.
[16] Petition 5578, Dinwiddie, Dec. 6, 1810.

ords of the city of Petersburg seem to reveal that certain white men made a practice of assisting Negroes to buy their freedom.[17] Nevertheless it is true that I have found in the Archives of Virginia ninety-one cases in which it is asserted that the slave bought his personal freedom. Except in rare cases, the circumstance that both the slave and the slave's *earnings* were the property of the master precluded the opportunity of the slave to buy freedom. Concerning these ninety-one cases we seem to be justified in believing that the slaves in question were fine types of human beings. They possessed an unusual type of skill or for other reasons may be regarded as exceptional.

From the cases so far presented few general conclusions can be drawn. However, similar cases can be given.[18] Also the motives and racial attitudes of the men who assisted these slaves to gain freedom must be left for consideration in another portion of this investigation.

Many masters liberated their slaves because of the realization that the slave had made a valuable contribution to the masters' wealth. Whereas gratitude prompted the act of the master, the character and conduct of the slave is very similar to that of the men who bought freedom. The case of the slave Abraham is an example. About this man it is written:

> During the life time of his former master, by a series of
> most faithful, assiduous, and affectionate services he ob-
> tained the confidence and regard of his master, in-so-much
> that he was regarded as a clerk and assistant rather than
> in the unfortunate character of a slave, and during the
> life time of the said master was always entrusted with
> the care, account, and disposition of his money, effects,
> and other property That in testimony of these services
> your petitioner's master always expressed . . . a uniform
> intention to grant him his freedom.[19]

[17] Luther P. Jackson, "Free Negroes of Petersburg, Virginia," *Journal of Negro History,* xii (July, 1927) , 365–87.

[18] Petitions, Albemarle, Oct. 23, 1779; 2908; 5749; 5819; 6031; 6217; 6251; 6644; 7252; 7485; 8012; 8230; 8345; 10972; 11063; 11482; 15798.

[19] Petition 1393, James City, Nov. 22, 1785.

Another slave testifies that he served his master faithfully for twenty years, "ten of which he was on the tan yard, by which he was enabled to acquire a perfect knowledge of that business" and "his master gave him strong assurances that it was not his intention that he should remain a slave for life."[20] Fincastle Sterrett declares that "he was favoured with the highest confidence of his master." It appears that the owner of this man was engaged in extensive mercantile pursuits extending from Baltimore to New Orleans. The master entrusted him with large sums of money to "transport from one state to another." The slave was promised his freedom and "with an eye to that end his master allowed him to purchase real property and enjoy the benefits of it, and in no respect did he treat him as a slave."[21] In still another case it is certified that "we are happy to say that he, Godfrey, is not only considered by us a harmless, well conditioned, and honest man, but as a mechanic he is extremely useful to the public."[22] In the case of another slave it is said that "by his great exertions since his master's death he had extinguished his master's debts."[23] In aid of the petition of another slave the family of the deceased master give the following testimony: "Lest there should be objections to his remaining here . . . your petitioner's family having inherited a large part of the estate of the said John Campbell, . . . are willing to be security for the said Roger, that he shall never be a burden to the public and to give farther security if deemed necessary to support him during his natural life, as he believes that himself and his family are now enjoying the fruits of the labour of the said Roger."[24] Such documents might be multiplied. The character of the individuals here described seems to indicate that their liberty came as the reward of years of faithful service that had proved profitable to their owners. Many of the emancipators must have felt that they were paying just debts; that they and their families were now "enjoying the fruits of the labour" of the Negro slave.

[20] Petition 5839, Jefferson, Dec. 15, 1811.
[21] Petition 5880, Washington county, Dec. 10, 1811.
[22] Petition 6337, Brunswick, Oct. 21, 1814.
[23] Petition 6251, Dec. 17, 1813.
[24] Petition 7686, Jefferson, Dec. 11, 1821.

In the Archives of Virginia are to be found many examples of
heroic action performed by the slaves. Liberty came to many
slaves as a natural result of such conduct. Richard Pointer, a
slave, relates that "in 1778 when a large body of Indians made an
attack upon the home of his master . . . your petitioner was principally instrumental in repelling the first attack, by opposing
himself to a large number of them who had well nigh forced
open the door, and by that means gave time to the inhabitants
who were collected there to arm and defend themselves and defeat the attempt of the Indians."[25] In another instance the slave
declares that

> he was brought to this country when it was a frontier
> settlement and much infested with savages. He was then
> owned by a Mr. Henry Hambleton, whose family was
> attacked by the Indians and several of them butchered
> and made captive. Your petitioner is now able to prove
> that by his own intrepidity and valor he preserved and
> carried into the fort two of the small children, being
> closely pursued by the savages and beating them off
> with a butcher knife.

The accompanying note gives testimony in this man's favor.[26]
The owner of a certain Nelson Jackson testifies that this slave in
1838 "was intrusted with a team and wagon for service in Florida, the place of destination being distant about nine hundred

[25] Petition 3339, Greenbrier, Nov. 12, 1795; also see 10101, Scott, Dec.
8, 1832.

[26] Petition 7696, Lee, Dec. 12, 1821: "This day came Charles Hamble-
ton before the undersigned, a Justice of the Peace for the said County,
and made oath that he was one of the children then about thirteen
years of age rescued by the Negro Swann then owned by his father. And
his statement of the affair in his petition is substantially true only not
representing in character sufficiently honorable to the petitioner. The
affiant perfectly recollects that the Indians pursued the petitioner with
this affiant and the other child in his care, and came frequently with
tomahawks and knives drawn within ten steps of them, when the
petitioner would urge the children on and turn and beat them back
with his butcher knife till he got in the house and saved us."

miles." The Negro was there employed in the transport service of the United States Army. On the occasion of an attack by the Seminole Indians he defended two white teamsters who accompanied him and returned to camp, bringing the surviving, though severely wounded, man and the body of the other. The master declares, "I concluded to set him free not only in justice to himself but that his course through life and his reward may be referred to as an example for all men of color."[27] Caesar, a black man, declares that "he once had the good fortune, at the peril of his own life, to save that of his master . . . who was in danger of drowning."[28] The master of a certain Joe bears testimony that "the said Joe is as honest a man as ever lived in the state of Virginia, white or black, . . . that he was once in danger of losing his life from the attack of a mischievous and dangerous bull and the said Joe came promptly to his relief and saved his life as he verily believes at the risk of his own."[29] Wilson Miles Carey certifies that he "is possessed of a mulatto house servant of the name of London . . . who he conceives (under God) was the great means of saving his and his wife's life in a carriage with frightened horses."[30] In 1810 a petition is found to have been sent to the legislature by the mayor and two hundred and fifty citizens of the city of Petersburg. This document asks that a certain slave be set free because the man had exposed and made possible the capture of a white man who had attempted to burn the city. The citizens declare that they "have voluntarily raised a sum of money to purchase the Negro man Emanuel, as a reward for conduct so highly praiseworthy and exemplary."[31]

Among the examples of freedom won by heroic action should be included those of the service of the Negro in the American Revolution. For service of this kind the state promised freedom to

[27] Petition 14124, Dec. 6, 1844.
[28] Petition 6490, Wythe, Dec. 11, 1815; also see 11415, Cabell, Dec. 28, 1836; 12745, Giles, Dec. 18, 1841.
[29] Petition 9612, Bedford, Dec. 17, 1830.
[30] Petition 5712, James City, Dec. 11, 1815.
[31] Petition, Dinwiddie, Dec. 15, 1810. For additional examples see petitions 10101; 11415; 12744; 18123.

the slave.[32] The following documents offer examples of such heroic action:

> In the beginning of the late war which gave America freedom, your petitioner shouldered his musket and repaired to the American standard, regardless of invitations trumpeted up by British proclamations for the slaves to emancipate themselves by becoming the assassins of their owners. Your petitioner avoided the rock that too many of his colour were shipwrecked on. He was taught that the war was levied on Americans not for the emancipation of the blacks, but for the subjugation of the whites, and he thought that the number of bondmen ought not to be augmented. Under these impressions he did actually campaign in both armies— in the American army as a soldier, in the British as a spy; which will fully appear reference being had to certificates of officers of respectability. In this double profession your petitioner flatters himself that he rendered essential service to his country.[33]

The accompanying note gives one of many excellent testimonials contributed to this man by officers who knew of his value to the American cause.[34]

---

[32] Hening, op. cit., xi, 308; St. George Tucker, *A Dissertation on Slavery, with a Proposal for the Gradual Abolition of It in the State of Virginia* (New York, 1796), p. 19.

[33] Petition, Oct. 9, 1792.

[34] Unclassified Petitions: "Be it known by all to whom it may concern: That Saul, formerly the property of Thomas Mathews, Esquire, during the different invasions of the state by the British army in the late war, left his residence in the city of Norfolk and joined the troups of this state, under my command, and when under my authority acted in such a manner as to merit my particular approbation and in my opinion to deserve the applause of his country. In many instances he was more serviceable than if he had been white. From his colour he had the opportunity of visiting the camps of the enemy from which he brought me much valuable information respecting their numbers, and was not only serviceable to me and my command but useful to different officers in the Southern states with whom I had the honor to correspond

In the Revolution slaves were employed in the naval as well as the military forces of Virginia. The following petition offers an example of naval service.

> During the late war, the slave Pluto was in the service of the Commonwealth, a mariner on the armed boat Patriot . . . , that at the period of the engagement between that vessel and the "Lord Howe," a British Privateer, the said Negro slave was one of the crew, and in the course thereof displayed a degree of courage and ardour, that drew the attention of the captain and his officers and such as in their opinion, and he presumes to hope that of your Honourable Body also, might entitle him to his freedom. The said Pluto prays the consideration of the Honourable the Legislature in his behalf for exertion in its defense that he may be exempted from a longer continuance in slavery.[35]

Unfortunately no record of the number of Negroes serving in the Revolution is known to exist. However, the question of such service by slaves became the subject of consideration by the high command of the American army,[36] and many references to such service are found in the Archives of Virginia. A petition dated October 23, 1779, declares that "William Beck, a mulatto slave,

---

and from whence they often got information that could not else be so easily assertained. As may be assertained from letters from Gen. Green, the Marquise de la Fayette, Baron Steuben, Gen. Wayne, Gen. Muhlenberg, the last of which was personally acquainted with some of Saul's services. Independent of his service as a spy, when unemployed in that way he was always employed with the flankers in advance with his picquet.

"It would be presumptious for me to say how Saul should be rewarded by his country but I can with truth declare that his service was as meritorious and more so than could be expected of a slave, and I venture to say that he who has done so much in the cause of freedom deserves to share a part of it.

"J. Parker"

[35] Petitions 3113, Nov. 4, 1793, and 3623, Nov. 22, 1796.

[36] George H. Moore, *Historical Notes on the Employment of Negroes in the Army of the Revolution* (New York, 1907).

during his service behaved in a most exemplary manner while under Col. Charles Lewis in several campaigns to the Northward."[37] A letter of May 10, 1791, declares that "Negro Hill served the United States in the late war for the term of three years, in the 15 Virginia regiment, with fidelity and credit."[38] Jack Thomas, a slave, certifies that "he served in the Northampton brig belonging to the state of Virginia, as Boatswain's mate from the year 1776 to the year 1779."[39] A certain slaveowner asks to be paid for a slave who "sometime in the month of July 1776, made his elopement and afterwards . . . entered the service of the United States in the 14th Virginia regiment, under the fictitious name of William Ferguson, and served until discharged from thence by Col. William Davies."[40] The slave David, alias David Baker, explains that "sometime in the year one thousand seven hundred and eighty-one your petitioner was delivered up as a free man and substitute for Laurence Baker, his former owner."[41] Other examples of Negro slaves who served as substitutes for white men are to be found.[42] In 1838 an interesting petition was sent to the State legislature by sixteen free Negroes of the town of Fredericksburg in which it is stated that their ancestors served in either the Revolution or in the War of 1812.[43] Occasions for heroic action come rarely in the lives of men; however, certain slaves were faced by circumstances of this description, and freedom came to many of those who faced danger bravely.

In many instances far simpler reasons than heroic action

[37] Petition, Albemarle, Oct. 23, 1779.

[38] Executive Papers, Archives of Virginia, Letters Received, May 10, 1791. Hereafter Archives of Virginia, Letters Received will be omitted and the Executive Papers will be identified by the date of the document.

[39] Petition 3613, Nov. 22, 1796.

[40] Petition 2034, Oct. 22, 1789.

[41] Petition 3290, Nov. 26, 1794.

[42] Executive Papers, May 11, 1781; Aug. 21, 1791; Nov. 22, 1781; Feb. 18, 1782; March 5, 1782; May 6, 1782.

[43] Petition 12130. For additional references to the service of the Negro in the Revolution see petitions 1622; 1957; 2324; 2503; 5775; 6375; 7323; 7414; 7467; 7947.

brought freedom to the slaves. Common acts of friendship, sometimes extending throughout the long lifetime of the master and
the slave, in which both the master and the slave shared the experiences of life together, resulted in emancipation; for the slave
had become the loyal and respected friend of the master and the
master could not hold the friend in bondage. In this class of man-
umissions a very prominent place is held by "body servants."
Such men were a selected group who, because of their nearness to
the household, had many opportunities to demonstrate their
worth. A servant of this description declares that "at an early period of his life he was purchased by the late Captain John T.
Price . . . in whose immediate and particular service he remained until the death of the former; that in health and in sickness and in all the vicissitudes of life your memorialist was a dutiful and faithful servant to his master."[44] Another slave explains
that

> having been nearly of the same age of his late master
> and brought up in the same family, he was so fortunate
> as to attract his regard and for eighteen years he faith-
> fully served him; the partiality which had commenced
> in early life, he had the good fortune to strengthen and
> increase by his fidelity and gratitude. . . . For many
> years his master had uniformly declared that he should
> never be the slave of another, and that he should be
> emancipated.[45]

The widow of the deceased master gives a fine testimonial to this
man.[46] A slave in the employ of Benjamin Harrison describes

[44] Petition 6531, Henrico, Dec. 13, 1815.

[45] Petition 6596, Frederick, Dec. 18, 1815.

[46] "The slave of her late husband had belonged to her father's estate,
was about the same age, and brought up in the same family, had
belonged to his late master for about eighteen years and had always
been treated by him with less the spirit of a master than a friend. . . .
When her late husband in his last illness thought that his health was
impaired and turned his conversation on his affairs, his first thoughts
were naturally turned to his child; his next always reverted to the
emancipation of his favorite slave. His general fidelity was always
mentioned and he frequently dwelt on a particular occasion on which

himself as "a body servant," and the master expresses great confidence in and affection for this man.[47] Another body servant declares that when his master suffered a severe illness and was sent to the West Indies for the benefit of his health, he was entrusted with his care. Concerning this man, members of the family declare that "no man of colour is of better character or more meritorious."[48] The friends of the slave David Skurry, testify that

> we have for a number of years known David Skurry and
> can say that in point of character he has no superior.
> His late mistress, Mrs. Skurry, had a great confidence in
> him which was manifest on many occasions. He was her
> body servant. She attained to a great age and was
> lame from an early period of her life, being incapable
> of locomotion. She was eminent for her piety and with
> the assistance of David was a regular attendant on Di-
> vine worship. He accompanied her on horseback, took
> her out of her gigg, and carried her in his arms to a seat
> in the house appropriated to the worship of God. He
> performed similar services for her when she visited any
> of her many friends or acquaintances.[49]

Other examples of this type of personal services and its reward may be offered.[50]

Certain other cases found in the Archives seem to indicate a relation between the master and slave deeper than mere friendship. A certain William T. T. Mason petitions the legislature in behalf of a slave girl that he desires to liberate and have remain in his family. If she is not permitted to remain in the state he fears that she will be "thrown destitute on the world, and in all proba-

---

in travelling through the wilderness this humble dependent had manifest a remarkable firmness and constancy in circumstances of no inconsiderable peril and a sincere attachment that made the deepest impression."

[47] Petition 6348, Buckingham, Oct. 25, 1814.
[48] Petition 6333, Hanover, Oct. 21, 1814.
[49] Petition 11197, Amelia, Jan. 28, 1836.
[50] Petitions 7529, 7627, 8378.

bility reduced to the utmost wretchedness and misery."[51] The reader can not doubt the fine motives that prompted the author of the following petition:

> Your petitioner, Mary Austin, of Hanover County, begs leave to represent to the General Assembly that she is possessed of a Negro woman aged about fifteen years named Amanda. That the said Amanda, whilst an infant, had her mother taken away from her and was affected with a long and painful illness, during which time your petitioner from motives of duty and humanity nursed her. That your petitioner during her attentions to the said Amanda formed, perhaps unfortunately, a strong and from its continuance, it seems, a lasting attachment for her. And it is now the inclination and intention of your petitioner to endeavour to form in the said Amanda till the age of eighteen habits of industry and virtue. Your petitioner knowing that without interposition of the General Assembly she can make no disposition of the said Amanda, consistently with the laws of the State and impressed with feelings the most abhorrent and distressing of leaving the said Amanda in slavery at the death of your petitioner, therefore, hopes that the General Assembly will see no injury to the State which compares with the happiness of your petitioner in this particular which will forbid the emancipation of the said Amanda.[52]

The evidence given above seems to show that many Negro slaves possessed excellent characters; that many slaves by great labor and economy bought their freedom; that certain occupations made it especially easy for many slaves to obtain freedom; and that the slaves residing in the cities possessed advantages that the rural slaves did not enjoy and because of these advantages were able more easily to procure freedom. It has appeared also

[51] Petition 6602, Prince William, Dec. 18, 1815.
[52] Petition 6922, Hanover, Dec. 2, 1817.

that white men, including the masters of certain slaves, made it possible for slaves to purchase freedom; that freedom came to many slaves as the reward of faithful service that had proved profitable to the master; and that heroic action on the part of certain slaves sometimes resulted in emancipation. It is also true that emancipation came to many slaves because of the respect, attachment, and affection of the master for his property.

A controlling motive in all these documents is the desire of the slave for freedom. The study of these papers makes it clear that these men wanted to be free. In this collection of petitions there are found four hundred and sixty-two cases in which individual slaves asked the state for freedom. This comparatively small number must signify that there were large numbers of other slaves similarly circumstanced who wanted freedom and who won it but who never applied to the state government to secure their freedom. There were always other ways by which freedom might be secured. The records of the county courts give much evidence that large numbers of slaves were set free by will and deed. Most of these cases never reached the state legislature. The cases here reported seem to refer to men who could not procure their freedom in their local communities. Of the 58,023 free Negroes in the state of Virginia in 1860, it is fair to believe that, while many of them were the children of free parents, many of them had won freedom by purchase, by heroic action, or by faithful service. To the number of the free Negroes in the state should also be added the unknown number who had moved out of the state according to the law.

It is interesting to observe the peaceful methods by which these men won their freedom. The testimony of their masters and the certificates of hundreds of their neighbors give these slaves the character of faithful, honest, industrious servants, and in many cases the statement is made that their going out of Virginia would be a loss to the state The significance of this record is not only that the number of such slaves who won freedom was large but that the men in question possessed the attributes that should be the pride of all good citizens. While it is not my purpose to establish the doctrine that all Negroes of the slave period were honest, industrious, and faithful, it is a pleasure to make known this group, possibly of chosen men, who were no doubt superior to many of their fellows. It is most often true that a people is not judged by the mass. In an historical sense only the chosen few are ever able to make themselves remembered. Judged on this basis, this group of chosen men bear gallant testimony for their people.

TWO

Violent Relations

I N THIS CHAPTER we shall consider another type of Negro slave. These slaves are the men condemned for the murder of masters or overseers or for participation in insurrections. In the appendix an index is given for such crimes as are recorded in the Archives of Virginia. In the period from 1800 to 1833 in Virginia, there are found to be eighty-eight cases in which Negro slaves were condemned for murder or attempted murder of white men. These cases do not include instances in which Negroes were condemned for participation in insurrection. In this same period there are recorded twenty-seven additional cases in which the slave is condemned for attempted poisoning, and fifteen cases of arson are reported. Omitting the arson cases there were one hundred and fifteen cases of violent slave crimes reviewed by the governors of Virginia in this period of thirty-three years. This record should make possible some observations concerning masters and slaves.

In these criminal cases similar motives are found to have prompted each of the crimes. The slave objected to correction or resisted the master or overseer who attempted to whip him or the slave feared the prospect of sale to the lower South. The case of the slave women, Sall and Creasy, may serve as an example. The following is the principal evidence given at the trial of these women:

> Jordan Martin . . . saith, that on the 2nd of April 1806 being at the house of John Lockado, this deponent asked the said Lockado if he had heard anything of Martha Morrisett, who the said Lockado informed him

had been missing for some time; upon being informed
of the fact this deponent in company with Charles
Clarke and the said Lockado went in search of the said
Martha Morrisett. That in their search near the margin
of the James River, near Mrs. Morrisett's plantation,
they found some blood on the ground, and upon min-
utely examining, found several pieces of flesh and a
small bone, supposed to be a part of the skull bone. The
ensuing morning this deponent with the said Clarke
collected a company of men, and with long poles
searched the river near where they had discovered the
blood from the body but they found nothing. About 12
o'clock of the same day, the company proceeded to take
up Sall and Creasy, Jim Strode and Jinny; and examined the said Jinny at the house respecting the supposed murder . . . but could get no information; that
they proceeded to the river, at the place aforesaid, and
examined Creasy respecting the facts, whereupon, she
replied . . . "I could not help it. It was not my fault.
I ought not to be blamed,". . . she then proceeded to
tell that she in company with Jinny was ploughing,
when her mistress came to her and attempted to
correct her, and after a while left her; during which
time she went to Sall and said that her mistress was so
hard to please, she must run away; upon which Sall advised her not to run away but to kill her, for that she
could do it; she then returned to her ploughing; shortly
after her mistress again attempted to correct her, whereupon, she attempted to prevent her by taking hold of
her arm and pushing her off; while she held her, Sall
came up and knocked her mistress down with the end of
an axe and gave her five or six blows, and then covered her up with some pine bushes, and at night she
and Creasy with the assistance of Jim Strode and Sall
carried her to the river, and Sall and Creasy proceeded
to cut her up in pieces and threw the pieces in the river.
After this confession, upon further search by the company two or three pieces of calico which were acknowledged by the said Creasy to be a part of their

mistress gown was found, also one leg of the deceased
was found. Jinny, a Negro slave, . . . saith, that she
and Creasy were ploughing in the field together, and
she heard Creasy say in the morning, that her mistress
had put her to laying off corn ground, when she knew
very well she could not do it; and that if her mistress
came out there to beat her she would kill her; . . . that
her mistress came to the field in the evening and just
before she came up to the spot where they were
ploughing her (Jinny's) plough handle broke, and she
set off to the house to get it mended, that she had not
gone more than 30 or 40 yards when her mistress
reached the spot where Creasy was; upon which her
mistress struck Creasy; whereupon Creasy seized her,
and her mistress called Sall; upon which Sall came up
and struck her mistress upon the forehead and knocked
her down and gave her several blows with the axe and
killed her.

. . . It is the opinion of the court that the prisoner
at the bar is guilty. . . . Therefore, it is demanded of
the prisoner if she had anything to say, wherefore the
court should not pronounce sentence of death against
her and order execution thereof to be made; to which
she answered that she was pregnant and therefore
prayed that her sentence might be suspended until she
was delivered. . . . It was ordered that she be remanded to jail . . . there to remain until the 2nd Friday in July next.[1]

Such evidence offered at slave trials may be given at great
length. The case of a certain Negro blacksmith relates that his
master ordered him to bring a rope with which he was to be tied
before being whipped. The slave demanded to know why he was
to be whipped and the master refused to tell him until he was
tied. "When the master picked up a bar of iron, the slave wrested

[1] Executive Papers, Archives of Virginia, Letters Received, *Commonwealth* v. *Sall and Creasy*, Chesterfield, April 14, 1806. Hereafter Archives of Virginia, Letters Received, will be omitted and Executive
Papers will be identified by the date of the document.

it from his hand and struck him on the head with it and knocked him down."[2] In another case, the overseer of a certain slave told him that he would whip him. The slave objected to being whipped and

> when the master picked up a stick, the slave picked up an axe. . . . The overseer attempted to strike the Negro with the stick. Several passes passed between them . . . at last each struck about the same time. . . . The witness finding himself severely wounded attempted to retreat.[3]

William Wilson testifies that in preparing to whip a Negro boy,

> he ordered the head man of the Negroes to get some switches, which he refused to do. Upon which the witness got two of his neighbors to assist him; that they caught the head man Tom and carried him off to whip him; that he (the witness) sent the prisoner off to grind his axe, and when he heard Tom holler, the prisoner ran up and struck Tom Bowles with his axe, and said, G____ d____n you, I will kill the whole of you.[4]

In the case of a slave who had permitted a horse to become injured, when the master proposed to tie and whip the offender, a fellow slave expostulated with the master. The master struck the protesting slave several times and knocked him down. The slave that was to have been whipped then fell upon his master and killed him.[5] In another instance,

> Jim . . . a slave, told the overseer that some of the Negroes must go home to shell corn. The overseer replied in an angry manner, "They must go, you say?" "Yes," answered Jim, "I suppose they must go"; and after four

[2] Executive Papers, *Commonwealth* v. *Henry,* Boutetout, Feb. 3, 1819.

[3] Executive Papers, *Commonwealth* v. *Charles,* Amelia, Sept. 25, 1828.

[4] Executive Papers, *Commonwealth* v. *Tom,* Powhatan, Sept. 21, 1818.

[5] Executive Papers, *Commonwealth* v. *Allen,* Washington, Oct. 19, 1827.

or five repetitions in this manner, the overseer told Jim
he would teach him better manners. And they being in
the tobacco house, stripping tobacco, the overseer first
picked up one stick and broke it over Jim, and then
another; on which Jim took hold of the overseer and
after some scuffling Jim broke loose and went out of
the house . . . leaving the overseer dead.[6]

In another case the evidence shows that the slave had attempted
to keep liquor away from the master. The prisoner testified that

there was no peace on the plantation. On the night of
the crime . . . he came to the house of his master; his
master met him with a club, with which he suspects his
master intended to kill him; on receiving a blow the
prisoner fell against the house, but recovering himself
he wrested the club from his master and afterwards
struck him three or four times with the club. He waited
until he was convinced he was dead and then he left
him.[7]

Another master testifies that "for an offence committed by a
Negro woman (the wife of the prisoner and the property of the
witness) he had stricken her three or four times with a whip; the
said slave, Auck, sitting a few steps from the place at the moment, he was struck down . . . and remained insensible for sometime afterward." Fanny, a slave witness, declares, "She saw Auck
a few moments before he struck her master, and he spoke to his
son, and said, 'come my boy, see if I can carry you home,' and he
immediately struck his master down as has been stated."[8] Still another master tells how his Negro overseer attempted to murder
him; he relates that

[6] Executive Papers, *Commonwealth* v. *James,* Campbell, Jan. 14,
1828.

[7] Executive Papers, *Commonwealth* v. *Sam,* Montgomery, Sept. 2,
1809.

[8] Executive Papers, *Commonwealth* v. *Edward,* Prince Edward, July
31, 1797.

it came into my head, upon seeing a fire in Abraham,
my Negro overseer's house, that he had been stealing my
potatoes, and upon examining the fire I found it full
of potatoes, roasting, which I took out. . . . Upon
Abraham's return I charged him with the theft, which
he denied and swore it was a lie. After some little conversation, he, the said Abraham, came up to me and
forcibly took the potatoes from me and in taking them
from me did, as he believes, endeavor to cut off . . . his
this deponent's head with the scythe blade, and did actually make a stroke at his head, which being fended
off struck him on the knee by which he was wounded
to the bone. After this he called for his gun, which being brought to him but finding it was unloaded, he re-
treated to the door of his house and made the door
fast after him. Abraham came to the door and after repeated blows broke the doors down, swearing he would
kill him.[9]

In another instance slave witnesses testify that

several times in the past years they heard Billy and
Archer planning their master's death with several of the
other Negroes. . . . The witnesses said they would
have nothing to do with it. That the reason the witnesses did not inform their master was that Rachel two
years ago informed him of their intention to kill him,
and he whipped her for it, and told her if she or any of
the other Negroes ever told him such a thing again, he
would give them one thousand lashes for he was afraid
of none of them, and if they chose to do it let them do so.[10]

Among these crimes should be included cases of Negroes, going
South in the coffles of slave traders, who rebelled and murdered

[9] Executive Papers, *Commonwealth* v. *Abraham,* Chesterfield, Oct. 7,
1803.
[10] Executive Papers, *Commonwealth* v. *Tom et als.,* Lunenburg,
March 20, 1827.

their captors.[11] Also, cases are to be found in which Negroes who had escaped from their masters lived in freedom in the swamps and defied those who attempted to re-enslave them.[12]

[11] Executive Papers, Nov. 20, 1799; Sept. 19, 1801; March 13, 1802; Dec. 29, 1810; Oct. 14, 1820.

[12] Executive Papers, Jan. 4, 1819; Jan. 24, 1823; April 6, 1825:

"An American Pirate

"Some two or three years ago, a certain Jermiah Delk, a respectable citizen of the Isle of Wight County, owned a Negro man slave. . . . This fellow was so unmanageable and artful that he could do nothing with him and he sold him to Maj. Charles Gee . . . and it was with much difficulty that he managed to get hold on him. And after he had done so he was so artful as to make his escape from him in a short time and return to this neighborhood, where he has remained ever since until a few months ago . . . when he was caught . . . by some Negroes, who had been induced by a reward offered for him to become intimate with him, and by some means got him to lay by his gun which he always carried, to wrestle with him, when they took him and delivered him to Major Gee. After he was taken he was so desperate and ferocious as to abuse in the most gross manner every gentleman who met with him. Major Gee I understand carried him to Petersburg, and delivered him to Mr. Seth Masom of that place, who I understands now owns him. He put him in jail. The jailor, who no doubt had been apprised of his character, turned him out, or what amounted to the same thing carelessly let him get out, and he went immediately to the neighborhood where he has procured another gun and has been committing depredations ever since. He is no doubt connected, harboured, and furnished with arms and everything he wants by some desperately mean white people, who I no doubt he furnishes with plunder in return. You will no doubt wonder that he has been permitted to go at large so long, but the people near him are absolutely afraid to take any means to apprehend him, for were they to do so, and fail, he might do them immense damage, or perhaps waylay them and murder them; armed and protected as he is, he lives in the islands of the Black-Water River, where he has the facility of canoes, and a perfect knowledge of the river, and on Sunday last, as before observed, four respectable young men, one married and three single went down the river a few miles, on a trip of pleasure and on their way down found a dead hog, just prepared for cooking, which they took in. They were immediately hailed and the hog demanded of them. They told him to come up and

It is also true that this description of slave crime should not close without mention of many instances of poisoning or attempted poisoning. Here we find ingenious attempts at vengeance. While arsenic is the most frequently used instrument of death, concoctions of "rat's bane," "mixtures of leaves and heads of reptiles," "hemlock," "Jamestown week, poke root, and powdered glass," "Powdered scopions ashes, four snake heads, and spiders beaten together in buttermilk" found their way from the kitchens to the masters' tables. Also in these documents interesting evidence of the role played by the conjurer is to be found. Cases of arson are also frequent.

Many of the slaveowners must have suffered because of the fear of violence at the hands of their slave property. In 1813 a native of western Virginia who is described as one of "the commoner class of men," declared that "this very class of men [the masters] are afraid to lie down at night lest their throats would be cut or their houses burned before morning by their Negroes."[13] We are not prepared to subscribe to this sentiment as it is here applied to all the owners of slaves. The contrast between the men as here described and the men portrayed in the former chapter is very apparent. However, the testimony leads the reader to wonder if there were not many plantations on which the sentiment of a certain slave woman would hold true when she affirmed that "she would rather be in hell than where she was."[14] Southern communities could not overlook or forget the testimony produced at slave trials. The owners of slave property must have questioned their own safety when they thought of condemned slaves who had dared to say: "He would be damned if he did not kill his

---

he should have it. . . . He pursued them in his canoe; they saw him deliberately take aim, prime his gun and fire at them, the married man who is in very moderate circumstances and has a family is supposed by his attending surgeon to be mortally wounded. To issue a warrant against this fellow would answer no purpose as he would very easily by his spies and confederates, always evade search, and so desperate is his character was he surrounded by 50 armed men, he would not be taken alive. . . . I beg you therefore, to have him outlawed and offere a hansome reward for him, as this is the only way he will ever be taken."

[13] Executive Papers, April 3, 1813.
[14] Executive Papers, April 10, 1812.

master, if he ever struck him again";[15] or "His master had whipped him, but he should not live to whip him again";[16] or "I told Dick he had killed me and he replied, 'Damn you, that is what I intended to do' ";[17] or the slave that rejoiced as he dug his master's grave, "I have killed him at last";[18] or the prisoners who had declared that "they would kill him whenever he beat them more than they could bear";[19] or "He attempted to whip him . . . when he defied him by raising his axe and telling him to come on, if he thought proper";[20] or "Their master had attempted to whip Patrick . . . and it took five persons to hold him. That Patrick said that he was not done yet, that he was a good Negro when he was let alone, but if he was raised he was the devil";[21] or another prisoner who told the witness that "the deceased had made his son whip his wife, and that he would kill them both";[22] or the case of the slave who conceived that "if their master were dead, there would be a better one";[23] or that "she was justified in what she had done from the ill treatment of her mistress toward her";[24] or again "If she, the witness, were a man, she would murder her master";[25] or "If old mistress did not leave her alone and quit calling her a bitch and a strumpet, she would

[15] Executive Papers, *Commonwealth* v. *Dick,* Southampton, July 22, 1812.

[16] Executive Papers, *Commonwealth* v. *Will,* Prince Edward, Oct. 15, 1810.

[17] Executive Papers, *Commonwealth* v. *Dick,* Goochland, Dec. 15, 1812.

[18] Ibid.

[19] Executive Papers, *Commonwealth* v. *Tom,* Lunenburg, March 20, 1827.

[20] Executive Papers, *Commonwealth* v. *George,* Goochland, April 21, 1818.

[21] Executive Papers, *Commonwealth* v. *Patrick,* Louisa, June 30, 1821.

[22] Executive Papers, *Commonwealth* v. *Daniel,* Lancaster, May 14, 1831.

[23] Executive Papers, *Commonwealth* v. *Davey,* Gloucester, Dec. 7, 1801.

[24] Executive Papers, *Commonwealth* v. *Sarah,* Albemarle, Jan. 12, 1803.

[25] Executive Papers, *Commonwealth* v. *Jinny,* Amherst, Sept. 20, 1824.

take an iron and split her brain out";[26] or another slave who declared "His master talked of carrying him off and selling him, but he would let the old fellow know";[27] or "He would kill Capt. Peter Land or any other man who came after him and no man should carry him out of the country."[28]

The preservation of the evidence has made these men audible and these, the criminal slaves, must be considered as witnesses for their people. Like their good fellows they are character witnesses for the thousands who lived, died, and will never be heard.

From the record given above it is evident that there were slaves who resisted the discipline of the slave system. Such evidence is not confined to any section of the state, for as much crime occurred in the white western section, proportionately, as in the more populous counties of the east. The crimes committed in such resistance were individual affairs; a master or overseer was oppressive and the slave violently resisted the oppressor. The way in which master and slave reacted to such a situation depended on their individual characteristics; so each crime tells a different story. Since slave crimes arose from the discipline of the slave system, however, the crimes were rooted in the system. Not all the masters were oppressive, and not all the slaves were rebellious, but where crimes occurred, oppressive conditions were responsible for the murderous act. One can not tell how many of the criminals, if they had had different masters, would have been able to purchase their freedom peaceably, or how many of those slaves who purchased it would have become murderers had their masters been cruel. The chances of life were against the criminals. They may well have been good men, but they faced death because of the cruelty possible under the system. It is evident that in the slave days not all the slaves were docile, humble servants. In thirty-three years, one hundred and fifteen of them died in Virginia because they were found guilty of violent crimes.

[26] Executive Papers, *Commonwealth* v. *Caty,* Brunswick, Dec. 23, 1803.

[27] Executive Papers, *Commonwealth* v. *Jack,* Bedford, March 30, 1804.

[28] Executive Papers, *Commonwealth* v. *Mingo,* Princess Anne, Jan. 4, 1804.

The evidence given above has described the violent crime of individual rebels. However, these same sources reveal many attempts and plots to bring about the freedom of the slaves by concerted action. For our purpose any uprising of five or more slaves, acting in concert, may be regarded as an insurrection.[29]

A summary of Virginia slave insurrections will show that after the Revolution, the first serious event of this nature is reported from Northampton county. Here in 1792 three slaves were ordered transported outside the territory of the United States and seven other slaves were ordered soundly whipped for their part in an insurrection.[30] In 1793 one slave was ordered executed as the leader of an attempted insurrection in Warrick county.[31] In the familiar insurrection of Gabriel in 1800 twenty-five slaves were ordered to be executed; one committed suicide while being carried to the jail; and an unknown number were sent out of the state.[32] In 1802 slaves were imprisoned in various parts of the state. Of those so imprisoned the number ordered executed was as follows: one in Brunswick, one in Caroline, one in Princess Anne, one in Hanover, one in Nottoway, one in Norfolk, one in Dinwiddie, one in Isle of Wight, and one in Westmoreland was shot while attempting to make his escape. Thus nine men were condemned or executed in that year. Others were sent out of the state.[33]

Since 1802 as leaders or participants in insurrections the number of slaves ordered executed in various counties of Virginia was as follows: in 1805 in Stafford, two;[34] in 1808 in Westmoreland,

[29] James C. Ballagh, *A History of Slavery in Virginia* (Baltimore, 1895), p. 92.

[30] Executive Papers, May 17, 1792.

[31] Executive Papers, Nov. 25, 1793.

[32] Executive Papers, Sept. 28, 1800; Stanislaus M. Hamilton (ed.), *The Letters and Writings of James Monroe* (New York, 1920), III, 217; Archives of Virginia, Legislative Papers, Petition 4294. Hereafter Archives of Virginia, Legislative Papers will be omitted and the document identified by number, county, and date (insomuch as this information is available).

[33] Executive Papers, Jan. 19, 1802; Feb. 3, 1802; Feb. 21, 1802; April 26, 1802; May 5, 1802; Dec. 2, 1802; May 13, 1802; May 17, 1800.

[34] Executive Papers, Feb. 6, 1805; Petition 4940, Stafford, Dec. 10, 1805.

one;[35] in 1810 in Isle of Wight, one;[36] in 1812 in Montgomery, one; and in Mason, two;[37] in 1813 in Fauquier, one; and in James City, three;[38] in 1816 in Spotsylvania, four;[39] in 1829 in Mathews, two;[40] in 1831 in Southampton, twenty-eight (and an unknown number met death at the hands of the men sent to suppress the rebellion).[41] Thus a total of eighty-four slaves appear to have met their death or to have been sentenced to die because of participation in attempts at insurrection in Virginia. In addition to this number there were many other slaves who received milder punishment for their share in these uprisings.

The evidence submitted to the governors of the state in time of insurrection offers much evidence of the character of the Negro leaders of insurrection. In 1800 Gabriel Prosser and Jack Bowler were the leaders. Gabriel was twenty-four years of age and Jack Bowler twenty-eight; both of these men are described as "intelligent Negroes."[42] Their fitness for leadership is to be seen in the skill with which they concealed their plot. "They organized as many as a thousand men in Henrico county" and they must have labored under great difficulty in maintaining secrecy among so large a following. The extract which follows, taken from the voluminous testimony of the rebels, reveals the plans and methods used by the slave leaders in this affair:

> Communication of Ben, Alias, Ben Woolfolk
> The first time I ever heard of the conspiracy was from Mrs. Ann Smith's George; . . . the second persons that gave me information was Samuel, alias Samuel Bird, the property of Mrs. Jane Clarke. They asked me to come over to their house on Friday night, it was late, before I could get there, the company had met and dispersed. I inquired where they had gone, they answered,

[35] Petition 5554, Westmoreland, Dec. 26, 1809.

[36] Executive Papers, June 6, 1810.

[37] Executive Papers, April 2, 1812; Oct. 28, 1812.

[38] Executive Papers, April 23, 1813; March 31, 1813.

[39] Executive Papers, March 10, 1816; Feb. 26, 1816.

[40] Executive Papers, July 18, 1829.

[41] William S. Drewry, *Slave Insurrections in Virginia, 1830–1865* (Washington, 1900), pp. 195–96.

[42] Ibid.

to see their wives. I went after them and found George, he carried me and William (the property of William Young) to Sam Birds, after we got there he (Sam) enquired if he had any pen and ink. He said no, he had left it at home. He brought out his list of men and he had Elisha Price's Jim, James Price's Moses, Sally Price's Bob, Drury Wood's Emanuel; after this George invited me to come and see him the next night, but I did not go. The following Monday night, William went over and returned for me with a ticket, and likewise one for Gilbert. The Thursday night following both George and Sam Bird came to see me, Bowler's Jack was with them. We conversed until late in the night upon the subject of the meditated war. George said he would try to be ready by the 24th of August and the following Sunday he went to Hungary Meeting house to enlist men. When I saw him again he informed me that he had enlisted 57 men there. The Sunday after he went to Manchester where he said he had recruited 50 odd men. I never saw him again until the sermon at my house, which was about three weeks before the rising was to take place. On the day of the sermon George called on Sam Bird to inform how many men he had. He said he had not his list with him but he supposed about 500. George wished the business to be defered sometime longer. Mr. Prosser's Gabriel said the Summer was almost over and he wished them to enter upon the business before the weather got too cold. Gabriel wished to bring on the business as soon as possible. Gabriel porposed that the matter should be refered to his brother Martin to decide upon. Martin said there was this expression in the bible "Delay breeds danger." At this time he said the Country was at peace, the soldiers had been discharged, and the arms all put away. There was no patrolling in the Country and that before he would any longer bear what he had borne, he would turn out and fight with his stick. Gilbert said he was ready with his pistol, but it was in need of repair. He gave it to Gabriel who was to repair it for him.

I spoke to the company and told them I wished to
have something to say. I told them I had heard in the
days of old, when the Israelites were in servitude to
King Pharoah, they were taken from him by the power
of God, and were carried away by Moses. God had
helped them with an Angel to go with them, but I could
see nothing of that kind in these days. Martin said in
reply, I read in my Bible where God says if we will worship Him we should have peace in our lands. Five of
you shall conquer an hundred, and a hundred a thousand of our enemies. After this they went into a consul-
tation upon the time they should execute the plan.
Martin spoke and appointed for them to meet in three
weeks which was to be a Saturday night. Gabriel said he
had 500 bullets made . . . Smith's George said he had
done the same and would then go to make as many cross
bows as he could . . . Bowler's Jack said he had got 50
spiers, or bayonetts fixed at the end of sticks. The plan
was to be as follows: We were all to meet at the Briery
Spot, on the Brook . . . one hundred men were to
stand at the Brook Bridge Gabriel was to take one hundred men and go to Gregories Tavern and take the arms
which were there. Fifty men were to be sent to Rocketts,
to set that on fire, to alarm the upper part of the town
(Richmond) and induce the people to go down to the
fire. Gabriel and the other officers and soldiers were
then to take the capital and all the arms they could find,
and be ready to slaughter the people on their return
from Rocketts. Sam Bird was to have a pass as a free
man, and was to go to the nation of Indians, called
Catawbas, to pursuade them to join the Negroes to fight
the white people. As far as I can understand all white
men were to be murdered, except Quakers, the Methodists, and the Frenchmen, and they were to be spared
on account, as they conceived of their being friendly to
liberty, and also they had understood that the French
were at war with the Country for the money that was
due them, and that an enemy was landed at South
Key which they had hope would assist them. . . .

The above communication was put down precisely as delivered by Ben, Alias Ben Woolfolk. . . . Given under our hands this 17 day of September, 1800.

Gervas Stone

Joseph Seldon[43]

Whereas large numbers of Negroes seem to have been involved in the insurrection of 1800, the insurrection of 1802 is remarkable because of the wide extent of territory which it embraced. In this year between January 1 and June 22 the alarm of insurrection was sounded in the following counties of Virginia: Nottoway, Powhatan, James City, Brunswick, Norfolk, Halifax, Pittsylvania, Campbell, Charlotte, Princess Anne, Hanover, Goochland, Henrico, King and Queen, Nansemond, Mecklonburg, Dinwiddie; in Hertford and Bertie counties in North Carolina, and in the cities of Richmond, Petersburg, and Norfolk.[44] As indicated above ten Negroes were executed in this year, but we have no way of knowing the number of slaves involved in the plot. However, if each communication sent to the governor of the state is regarded as evidence of a part in the general plan of insurrection, this insurrection of 1802 appears to have been the most serious rebellion in the history of slavery in Virginia. The evidence seems to show that each of these events was a part of a general plan of insurrection. The plot had been conceived at least six months before the citizens of Nottoway county became alarmed. Certain slaves under arrest were shown to have travelled far as recruiters.[45] Written communication was carried on between the slaves, as evidenced by the following quotation, found in a letter sent from Hertford county, North Carolina, to certain citizens of Virginia:

Being fully impressed with the nature of the impending danger, we do most seriously entreat the people generally to be on their guard, and we would recommend to you to pursue the plan which led to the discovery among us. It is as follows: the officers throughout the

[43] Executive Papers, Nov. 10, 1800.

[44] Executive Papers, Jan. 1, 1802; Jan. 18, 1802; Feb. 3, 1802; March 10, 1802; April 2, 1802; April 26, 1802; May 5, 1802; May 13, 1802; May 17, 1802; June 8, 1802; June 10, 1802; June 12, 1802; June 22, 1802.

[45] Executive Papers, March 10, 1802; May 5, 1802; June 5, 1802.

counties at a certain time previously agreed upon, proceeded to make a general search in all the Negroes
houses and other suspected places; and in a cotton bar-
rel in one of the cabins the before mentioned letter was
found very cleverly concealed.[46]

Copies of communications, supposedly written by slaves, but
discovered and sent to the governor of Virginia, are given
below.[47]

[46] Executive Papers, June 5, 1802.

[47] Executive Papers, Jan. 18, 1802: "Mr. Jacob Martin my friend be
true and faithful to your trust . . . get your weapons all ready against
the night appointed . . . our travelling friend has got ten thousand in
readiness to the night . . . you need not be afraid to tell our friend
Pointer anything you want me to know . . . he will bring it safe to me.
. . . You will tell Capt. Saunders I must see him in the course of a week
as I will give him information how to do. . . . We have agreed to begin
at Judes Ferry and to put to death every man on both sides of the river
to Richmond, and I think we will get abundance of money and also
men enuf to destroy Richmond when joined to the army that will meet
us there on the appointed time. . . . I am your aid and assistance

"Frank Goode."

Executive Papers, May 14, 1802: "I can inform you that those negroes
at least some of them will not revolt they are so attached to them that
all persuasion will not do. I have offered them $25 each when Rich-
mond shall be ours. I have brought under our banner 100 or there
about who is determined to fight for us. . . . Keep everything silent
until that fatal night which will show the world that slavery will not
longer exist in Virginia. The plans you laid down was good. You say
that you have 60 under you armed with scythe blades, etc. I have 20
armed with muskets and rest with old swords and clubs. I think you say
you will set fire to Todds lane, and while the people are there set fire
up the town good. I will devide my men into 4 divisions. I will
command 25. Peter the bearer the second, Bob the third, and Henry the
4th. I will be stationed by or near the capital. Peter near the Eagle
Tavern behind their houses. Bob near the market bridge on the right
and Henry on the left. When the houses burn or the alarm is given we
shall set fire to the alley opposite the Bell tavern. You lay off your men,
conduct everything with mercy and we trust in God if we succeed. We
will be very rich. We are moulding balls every night. I am

"J. B.

"N.B.   I have a small keg of powder."

The leaders in this insurrection were the slaves Author, alias
Will Farrow; Caesar, alias John Price, both of Richmond, and
Corry, a slave, Hanover County. They planned to take the cities
of Richmond and Petersburg and expected to use the methods
anticipated by Gabriel. "All white men between eight and eighty
were to be put to death and not a white woman on earth to live."
These leaders and their lieutenants must have been men of courage and some ability. They could read and write. They made use
of forged passes and their agents travelled over the country attending all possible "religious meetings" and "drunken frolics."
They hoped to incite the slaves in all the counties of the state.[48]

In the confession of the slave Lewis we find preserved an ex-
hortation of the insurrectionist, Will Farrow, to a group of his
people:

> Black men if you have a mind to join me, now is your
> time for freedom. All clever men that will keep secret
> these words I give to you is life. I have taken it upon
> myself to put the country at liberty. This lies on my
> mind for a long time. Mind men I have told you a
> great deal. I have joined with me both black and white.
> That is the common or poor white people. Mulattoes
> will join with me to free the country although they are
> free already. I have got eight or ten white men to
> lead me in the light of the magazine. They will be be-
> fore me and will hand out the guns, pistols, powder,
> shot and other things that will answer our purpose. The
> Negroes that can not have guns must make use of clubs.
> Black men I mean to loose my life in this way if they
> will take it. I have been under great exertions. I have
> escaped. Now I will live at a palace. . . . If you make
> known these words to black or white people from
> county to county, these words will make against you at
> the day of your death. I think that this is the only way
> that we black people can take the country of Virginia.
> . . . The white people have had the country long
> enough.[49]

[48] Executive Papers, May 5, 1802.
[49] Executive Papers, May 5, 1802.

In 1810 there appeared in the Isle of Wight county a Negro who might be considered as a forerunner of John Brown. This man's name is not known, but in 1789 he had been condemned for a felony by the courts of the county and for his crimes had been transported to the West Indies. He made his escape from the island of St. Croix and for a time lived in the city of New York. From this place he came back to Virginia, armed with free papers which he had written himself. It is said that the purpose of his return was to incite the slaves to rebellion. This man is described as "remarkable for his volubility and information." The account continues: "From the turpitude of his disposition [he] is equal to the commission of any crime; his avowed intention in coming here is to disseminate discontent and excite insurrection among the Negroes." After he had remained for five months in the county, the man was put in the county jail, upon which it is reported that "since his imprisonment he has had frequent conferences with Negroes through the windows of the Jail, recommending an attempt at emancipation, representing it as a matter of facility."[50] Apparently the efforts of this insurrectionist were of little avail. Several slaves were imprisoned because of his efforts, but their fate is not known.

Nat Turner, the leader of the insurrection of 1831, is the most familiar of all the slave leaders. William S. Drewry gives him the character of a man of courage.[51] According to report he was a slave preacher, a foreman of his master's plantation, a skillful mechanic, and an ardent lover of nature. By some of his fellows he was considered a conjurer as well as a moral instructor. With little or no assistance he taught himself to read and write, and because of his demonstrated ability, seems to have been humored by his owners. At his trial he testified that he had been well treated. As their leader he was both feared and respected by the slaves of the county.[52] Although in 1831 he was only thirty-one years of age, it is said that he began his plans for the rebellion in 1825 and that for six years had worked toward his aim. It seems that he considered it possible to conquer the county of South-

[50] Executive Papers, June 16, 1810; May 10, 1810.
[51] Drewry, op. cit., p. 116.
[52] Ibid.

ampton and with his followers take refuge in Dismal Swamp, where other Negroes had hidden and defied capture.[53] Hidden with his followers in this retreat he expected that other slaves would join him, and with increasing numbers he would gradually overcome the white people of the State. While these apparently impractical aims may have been his objectives, it is the conclusion of his biographer, who, so far, has given most consideration to Nat Turner, that "all his efforts he believed would call attention of the world to his race."[54] If this was his aim, the man succeeded famously.

The brief account here given must not, by any means, be considered as a complete record of the slave insurrections in the state of Virginia. The record could be continued after the day of Nat

[53] Executive Papers, Sept. 4, 1831; June 4, 1809; June 24, 1823; April 6, 1829.

"By the Governor of the Commonwealth of Virginia
"A PROCLAMATION
"Wheras the slave Nat, otherwise called Nat Turner, the contriver and leader of the late insurrection in Southampton, is still going at large; Therefore, I, John Floyd, Governor of the Commonwealth of Virginia, have thought proper, and do hereby offer a reward of five hundred dollars to any person or persons who will apprehend and convey to the jail of Southampton County, the said slave Nat: And I do hereby require all officers civil and military, and exhort the good people of the Commonwealth to use their best efforts to cause the said fugitive to be apprehended, that he may be dealt with as the law directs.
"Given under my hand as Governor, and under the Lesser Seal of the Commonwealth, at Richmond, this 17th day of September, 1831.
"John Floyd"
Executive Papers, Sept. 17, 1831: "Nat is between 30 and 35 years old, 5 feet 6 or 8 inches high, weighs between 150 and 160 lbs. rather bright complexion, but not a mulatto . . . broad shouldered . . . large flat nose . . . large eyes . . . broad flat feet . . . rather knocked kneed . . . walks brisk and active . . . hair on top of head very thin . . . no beard except on the upper lip and tip of chin . . . a scar on one of his temples . . . also one on the back of his neck . . . a large knot on one of the bones of his right arm, produced by a blow."
[54] Drewry, op. cit., p. 113.

Turner.[55] At a later time reference will be made to the constant fear and the ever recurring rumor of uprising. The correspondence of the governors of the state is most impressive evidence that the fear of the people of the state was not always idle. But while the effects of slave insurrections are left to further consideration, it may be pointed out that Gabriel, Farrow, Bowler, Turner, and other rebels, like the slaves considered in former chapters, may be regarded as leaders among their people. These men were exceptional characters. All the slaves were not insurrectionary. The evidence makes it clear that rebellion had little appeal to many slaves. All the odds of wealth and of government were against these slaves, even as the odds were against John Brown. So much of hopelessness faced the rebel slaves that they appear more mad, perhaps more foolhardy, than John Brown. But these were men who wanted to be free, and for them slavery was more than an individual matter. While other slaves gained freedom by worthy conduct and manly living and while others rebelled when faced by personal injury, these men were plotters against a system that oppressed a people, and they appear to have made the supreme sacrifice in futile efforts to free their people.

If we combine the number of Negroes ordered to be executed for violent crimes and the number who are known to have been executed for participation in rebellion, we find that there are a total of more than two hundred such executions. Or, for this period of approximately thirty years, six Negroes were executed each year for crimes of violence. These men offer a vivid contrast to the peaceful, inoffensive, humble Negroes described in the first chapter, but, in each of these groups of humble men and violent rebels, the fact seems to be clear that these were slaves who did not want to be slaves. Their reactions were controlled by the circumstances that surrounded them. Fortune favored those that won freedom by peaceful means.

It may also be observed that Virginians had found that rebellious leadership might be developed among the humble slaves. In 1800 James Monroe wrote that "unhappily while this class of people exist among us, we can never count with certainty on its

[55] Ibid., p. 179; Petitions 12812, Jan. 11, 1840; Jan. 1, 1843.

tranquil submission. The fortunate issue of the late attempt should not lull us into repose."[56] A letter to the governor of the state, May 31, 1810, declares that

> from evidence of this witness as well as from other cir-
> cumstances I am convinced that the Negro preachers are
> more dangerous than any other description of blacks.
> He, the witness, charged two of these Christians with
> reproving him and others for not attending their
> meetings more regularly; and with stating that if the
> Negroes had attended as they ought to have done, the
> great and important object which they (the preachers)
> had long in view, would before this time have been ac-
> complished, and that all, by this time, would have been
> over.[57]

There is much evidence of the influence of religious leaders on insurrections. The editor of the Richmond *Enquirer,* August 30, 1831, writing on the subject "The Banditti," declared that "the case of Nat Turner warns us. No black man ought to be permitted to turn a preacher throughout the country."[58] After the affair in Southampton county, Governor Floyd wrote to the governor of South Carolina, "I shall in my annual message recommend that laws be passed . . . to prohibit Negroes from preaching, and absolutely, to drive from the State the free Negroes."[59] Following his advice an act was passed by the legislature of 1832 which was intended to prevent Negro preachers from instructing or preaching to their people.[60]

In this chapter it has been shown that many of the slaves, possessing violent tempers rebelled against harsh discipline. The harsh features of the slave system furnished the motives for crimes of violence. Crimes of this nature were individual affairs.

[56] Hamilton, op. cit., III, 245.

[57] Executive Papers, May 30, 1810.

[58] Charles H. Ambler, *Life and Diary of John Floyd* (Richmond, 1918) , p. 86.

[59] Ibid., p. 80.

[60] William W. Hening, *Statutes at Large of Virginia* (Richmond, 1823) , VII, 108.

Oppressive masters and rebellious slaves might be found in any section of the state. The acts of these rebellious slaves are an evidence of slave character and demonstrate that all the slaves were not humble and contented with their lot as slaves. The records show also that repeatedly the slaves plotted concerted insurrection. The spirit of insurrection was ever present. The leaders of insurrections appear to have been courageous and daring spirits and possessed many of the qualities of leadership. All the slaves were not rebellious and repeated examples are found in which the slave exposed the plots of fellow slaves. However, in the period studied, it appears that an average of six Negro slaves were condemned each year for violent crimes. The persistent spirit of rebellion manifested by these slaves could not be ignored by the governing classes. The effects of these violent slave crimes will be described in a later chapter.

THREE

Free Negro Relations

EVIDENCE CONCERNING the emancipated slave—his condition, attainments, and influence on the other elements of society—will form the principal subject matter of this chapter. The Negro who remained in the state of Virginia after he had been emancipated continued to be an important problem in the life of the commonwealth.

It is not difficult to discover testimony that the free Negroes were undesirable members of society. As indicated above, the period of the Revolution was marked by great liberality toward the Negro. However, even in this period of enthusiasm for the doctrine of the rights of man, protests are to be found against the misuse of liberty extended to the Negroes. On January 3, 1783, a petition from Accomac county recites that manumission of slaves should be ended because "of the great number of Negroes who have joined the enemy from this country, the great damage done this place under the sanction of the British, the great number of relations and acquaintances they still have among us, and from the harbours the houses of such manumitted Negroes would probably afford them and outlying slaves."[1] In June of the same year a second petition to the legislature, again enumerating many evils resulting from liberties extended to the slaves, is discovered. The petition reads as follows:

---

[1] Archives of Virginia, Legislative Papers, Petition 766, Accomac, Jan. 3, 1783. Hereafter Archives of Virginia, Legislative Papers will be omitted and the petition identified by number, county, and date (insomuch as this information is available).

Whereas many persons have suffered their slaves to go
about to hire themselves and pay their masters for their
hire, and others under the pretense of putting them free
set them out to live for themselves and allow their masters such hire as they can agree on, by which means
the slaves live in a very idle and disorderly manner, and
in order to pay their masters their due hire are frequently stealing in the neighborhood in which they reside, or which tends to worse consequences, encourage
the neighboring slaves to steal from their masters
or others, and they become the receivers of or traders of
those goods, having time to go at large, and also give
great discontent to the slaves who are not not allowed
such indulgences; it being generally believed that those
slaves are not labouring efficiently to pay their masters
hire and also clothe themselves.[2]

In the following year the claim is again asserted that "the free
Negroes are agents factors and carriers to the neighboring towns,
for the slaves, of stolen property, by them stolen from their masters."[3] In 1785 after a lengthy exposition of the legal and Biblical
basis of the rights of the slaveowners, the petitioners declared
that the present tendency toward emancipation among slave
owners will be followed by dire results

in the production of want, poverty, destitution and
ruin to the free citizens. Neglect, famine, and death to
the helpless black infant and superanuated parent. The
horrors of all the rapes, murders, outrages which a vast
multitude of unprincipled, unpropertied, vindictive,
and remorseless banditti are capable of perpetrating.[4]

In 1800 under the influence of Gabriel's insurrection, still another petition declares that "it is notorious that the law for
freeing Negroes hath tended to bring upon us our disturbed and

[2] Petition 788, Henrico, June 3, 1783.

[3] Petition 1197, Hanover, Nov. 16, 1784.

[4] Petition 1354, Brunswick, Nov. 10, 1785; 1395, Pittsylvania, Nov. 10,
1785.

distressed situation."[5] The protest against free Negroes continued after 1800, but the volume of such protests multiplied after the insurrection of 1831. These protests will be described in a later part of this study.

The Negroes against whom these accusations are made are the same Negroes whose virtues were described in the first chapter. The burden of complaint seems to be that the free Negroes were idle and indolent, that they stole or received stolen property from slaves or from vicious white men, that they excited slaves to rebellion, or that they aroused discontent among the slaves by living among them.[6] It is not my purpose to prove these charges false or true. Numerous examples of free Negroes who were guilty of one or another of these charges can be found, but more important than the proof or disproof of these individual cases is the fundamental contradiction of such evidence. On the one hand are documents, signed by more than a hundred citizens, who declare that all the free Negroes are worthless and that they should be exiled from the State; on the other hand are documents, again signed by more than a hundred citizens, who certify that a particular Negro, by the name of John, Tom, or Harry is a skillful workman and an honest man, whose exile would inflict loss upon them and upon the commonwealth. The number of such Johns, Toms, and Harrys may be multiplied and it is my belief that actual evidence on the lives of these simple individuals gives more authentic testimony on this controversial question than the rhetorical generalizations often prompted by local agitation or fears of proslavery or antislavery petitions.

The fact that many of the men who had secured their own freedom devoted their best energies and their earnings to the purchase of members of their families is among the facts revealed by a study of the petitions to the legislature. For example, in 1790 Benjamin Bilberry having "by his unremitting labours" purchased his wife Kate, "humbly prays the legislature of Virginia, that no policy may restrict your Honours from suffering him to enjoy the sweet reflection of having spent the whole labours of his life in bestowing freedom on one equal by nature

[5] Petition 4153a, King and Queen, Dec. 5, 1800.
[6] Petitions 4864, 5723, 6478, 6820, 6996a, 8025.

(whose laws alone he is acquainted with) to himself and whom he has chosen to be the partner of his earthly care."[7] Also, in 1809, Patience, the former wife, and Philemon, Elizabeth, and Henry, the children, "of a free black man, named Frank, late of the county of Amelia," petition the legislature of the state, declaring that "he had acquired his freedom either by purchase or by the voluntary and liberal act of his master, that when he became a free man, his industry and propriety of conduct enabled him to raise a sufficient sum of money to purchase his wife and children above named, after which he lived in peace and quietude with his family around him, honestly pursuing his usual industry for their support and comfort . . . ; that since the death of the said Frank his wife and children are still liable to be held in slavery."[8]

In 1811 the state granted Samuel Johnston his freedom and permission to reside in the town of Warrentown.[9] In 1815 Johnston declares that "your petitioner since his emancipation pursuing that line of conduct by which he was enabled to accumulate money enough to buy his wife, whose name is Patty, his daughter, whose name is Lucy, and his son, named Samuel, all of whom are now held by your petitioner as his slaves; the end to which all the anxious labours and privations of your petitioner have been directed will be attained, if your Honourable Body will be graciously pleased to pass a law permitting your petitioner and his family to remain in this Commonwealth . . . as free persons."[10]

Judith Hope, of the city of Richmond, the daughter of Caesar Hope, who was emancipated on October 29, 1799, petitioned the legislature for her freedom in the year 1819. She certified that "her late father having by a long life of labour accumulated some small property, both real and personal, having two children in

[7] Petition 555, Henrico, Nov. 11, 1790.
[8] Petition 5483, Amelia, Dec. 16, 1819.
[9] Petition 5674b, Fauquier, Dec. 13, 1811.
[10] Petition 6580, Fauquier, Dec. 16, 1815. This man seems to have had great difficulty in liberating his children. His petitions making the same repeated request are to be found in the following: Petitions 7555a, 1820; 7893, 1822; 8001, 1823; 8267, 1824; 8642a, 1826; 9109a, 1828; 10835, 1835; 11580, 1837.

his old age who were in bondage . . . published his will in writing, by which he directed the late Edmund Randolph, Esq. to purchase with a portion of the estate both your petitioner and her brother, and to have them emancipated."[11]

Benjamin Godwin, who was set free by an act of 1814, in 1829 declared that "since the passage of the act, he has purchased and set free Elizabeth Godwin, whom he is anxious to emancipate."[12] In 1835 Arthur Lee, a free Negro, declares that

> he has paid Colonel Brown $500 dollars for hire and
> $600 for his freedom, and has moreover purchased his
> wife and child of Mr. Henry Massie, and since the pur-
> chase has had born to him three other children. All this
> he has done by great industry and good conduct, and is
> anxious to remain in the State as a free man.[13]

In 1845 a petition from Frank Allen, "emancipated about twenty-five years prior to this date" recites that "he, the said Frank purchased her [his wife] soon after the death of her said master and they have lived together . . . on the land every since."[14] Oscar Taliaferro in a petition sent to the legislature in 1847 certifies that

> the wife of your petitioner is a slave. . . . Your peti-
> tioner, when he accumulated the fund, was animated
> with the hope of being able to procure the freedom of
> his wife as well as his own. It was this which stimulated
> him to work while others rested, and to deny himself in-
> dulgences which others enjoyed.[15]

Many other cases are found in which it is recorded that the petitioner has purchased members of his family and wishes to set

[11] Petition 7361a, Henrico, Dec. 21, 1819; see also Yorktown, Oct. 29, 1779.
[12] Petition 9287, Norfolk, Dec. 10, 1829.
[13] Petition 11063, Allegheny, Dec. 28, 1835.
[14] Petition 14494, Richmond, Feb. 14, 1845.
[15] Petition 15698, Henrico, Dec. 15, 1847.

them free.[16] According to the census of 1830 there were in the
United States 319,509 free Negroes. These free Negroes owned
14,002 slaves.[17] In the state of Virginia there were, in 1830, 952
free Negroes who owned 2,242 slaves. In almost all of these cases
the slaves so owned were the wives or the children of their owners. For these slave wives and children the owners were taxed,

[16] Petitions 2908, 5635, 5674B, 5774A, 5891, 5870, 5880, 5921, 6090,
6208A, 6329, 6581, 6630, 6644, 7180, 7446, 7555A, 7681, 8793, 8001, 8012,
8267, 8293, 8642A, 8834, 9109A, 9131, 9352, 9466, 10111, 10253, 10580,
10649, 10716, 10835, 10894, 12200, 12223, 12483, 13802, 14494, 15664,
16729, 17254, 17466, 19231, 19280. Cases are also found in which free
Negroes bought and liberated slaves that were not relatives, 6581.

[17] *Slaves Owned by Free Negroes in 1830**

STATE	TOTAL NUMBER OF FREE NEGRO SLAVEOWNERS	TOTAL NUMBER OF SLAVES OWNED
Alabama	43	195
Arkansas	1	3
Connecticut	1	1
Delaware	9	21
District of Columbia	133	242
Florida	15	92
Illinois	7	11
Kentucky	120	162
Louisiana	967	4382
Maine	1	1
Maryland	643	1456
Mississippi	17	74
Missouri	2	4
New Hampshire	3	3
New Jersey	16	22
New York	21	41
North Carolina	191	636
Ohio	1	6
Pennsylvania	23	50
Rhode Island	3	3
South Carolina	474	2794
Tennessee	68	144
Virginia	952	2242

* Carter G. Woodson, *Free Negro Owners of Slaves in the United
States in 1830* (Washington, 1925).

and to these slave children all of the laws that made up the slave code were applicable. The death of the father and owner left many of these slaves in a precarious situation. If the free man failed to secure the freedom of his children prior to his death, he might leave them to free relatives, but if he died intestate his children reverted to the state and were accordingly sold for the benefit of the literary fund. Such free Negro slaveowners had the best motives for industry, thrift, and sacrifice, and the legion of names that attest to the truth of their petitions proves that by their "indefatigable labour and unremitting toil" they paid for their children. These men were slave buyers and investors in their own flesh.

In spite of the conditions that circumscribed the lives of the free Negroes, an overwhelming mass of evidence seems to make it clear that these people loved their native state. The following are examples of a sentiment that finds expression over and over again: "Your petitioner was born in this Commonwealth, has a wife and children residing therein, and all the friends, connections, and protectors he has on earth are residents of this state";[18] another asks "that he be permitted to spend that short remainder of his days in the land of his birth, . . . for he not only would be compelled to withdraw himself from a spot which is endeared to him by many pleasing reflections, but he would have to tear himself from his wife, with whom he has long lived, and, become a wanderer in a distant state";[19] another,

> your Honorable Body will perceive the limited space of
> action of your petitioner and to which he has formed at-
> tachments that nothing but death can destroy. Your
> petitioner states that he has not only formed local
> attachments (which is common to all mankind) but he
> has formed personal friendships and partialities for both
> white and black of Virginia. The former he views as his
> protectors in the land of his birth, and the others . . .
> as his associates, friends, and relations;[20]

[18] Petition 6315, Nansemond, Oct. 14, 1814.
[19] Petition 10972, Albemarle.
[20] Petition 11063, Allegheny, Dec. 28, 1825.

and also, "So many are the difficulties which emigration presents
. . . so frought with peril to the welfare and happiness of her
child and herself, would be the attempt to seek those blessings to
which they are entitled, in a strange land, in the midst of
strangers, cut off from the society and the aid of relations and
friends as almost to shut from their view the prospect of freedom
which is held out to them";[21] and again, "or he must be banished
from the place of his nativity, which place is likewise endeared to
him by the very circumstance that it is the place of his nativity."[22]
Similarly, the slave Caesar prays that "it may not be in the power
of anyone to tear him from a country he holds dear, because it is
his native country, and because its sacred laws have protected
him; poor, friendless, and held in slavery, against considerable
wealth and power"; [23] and still another slave recites that "he
knows no other state or government than that of Virginia; consequently his little interest, the happiness of his human existence,
every emotion of hope or liberty in life, and all the affections of
the time and sense, are contained in his petition."[24] In yet another
instance:

> Your petitioner hopes that your Honourable Body will
> relieve him from the austerity of a law the ultimate de-
> termination of which is either to expell him from his
> native state and soil, or take from him the liberty
> he has attained by his good conduct when a slave; both
> of which he thinks to be incompatable with the natural
> rights of man or the genius of liberty. First that he be
> driven from his native state as a fugitive and vagabond,
> after having worn out his juvenile days in the service
> of Virginia, to take refuge in an unknown land and
> country . . . an asylum precarious and uncertain.[25]

It is apparent that the sentiment of love for the state is very
closely connected with dread of separation from relatives and

[21] Petition 5839, Jefferson, Dec. 5, 1811.
[22] Petition 6177, Cumberland, Dec. 7, 1815.
[23] Petition 6327, Louisa, Oct. 21, 1814.
[24] Petition 6494, Wythe, Dec. 11, 1815.
[25] Petition 7660, Monongalia, Dec. 8, 1821.

loved ones. However, an additional cause for attachment to Virginia was the fear of the hardships of life in a strange land. Economic opportunities for the Negro in the North were limited. Northern white labor did not propose to admit the competition of free Negroes. James Madison claims that

> even the state of Massachusetts, for example, which displayed most sympathy for the people of colour . . . prohibitions are taking place against their becoming residents. They are everywhere regarded as a nuisance.[26]

Examples are to be found of free Negroes who went to the North and attempted to settle there, but because of the hardships to be endured, returned to their native place.[27] But, old Virginia held a place in the hearts of these people that developed because of a variety of causes. With all the limitations and proscriptions on the life of the free Negroes, there were for them some of the things that make life worthwhile. Individuals might with thrift, industry, and always with tact accumulate property in houses and lands. If the state would only relax the rigor of the law that made for the separation of husbands and wives, there were love and the simple joys of the home, wife and children. If we are to believe the words of the petitioners, the affections of these men and women were the supreme things in their lives. In these cabins there was love; with love, the absence of many things did not matter.

These whom I have attempted to describe to you were not a debased people. In their homes they developed some of the things that are considered high and holy. They were interested in religious matters, and they established their own churches.[28] A petition from the congregation of the First African Baptist Church of the city of Richmond in 1823 gives a list of the mem-

[26] Gaillard Hunt (ed.), *The Letters and Other Writings of James Madison* (New York, 1900–10), III, 240.

[27] Petitions 6011, 6143, 12483, 19231.

[28] Luther P. Jackson, "The Religious Instruction of Negroes, 1830–1860," *Journal of Negro History,* xv (Jan., 1930), 72–113.

bers of the church, most of whom were prosperous free Negroes.[29]
Their petition tells why they wanted to control their own
church, and many white citizens, including the mayor, the chief
of police, and the pastors of several of the white churches give
their opinion that they should have a separate church. From this
church Lott Carey was sent as the first Negro missionary to Africa. However, even before the establishment of this church, free
Negroes and slaves are known to have established churches in Petersburg, Norfolk, and in Charles City county. After legislation
had been adopted to stop preaching by Negroes, we find petitions
from the Richmond congregation in 1834 and from the Petersburg congregation in 1839, asking that Negro preachers be permitted to bury their own dead. It is claimed that because of the
difficulty in finding white ministers to perform this service "many
coloured human beings are interred like brutes."[30]

The following petition from free people of the city of Fredericksburg shows the interest of one free Negro group in the education of their children.

> The undersigned humbly beg leave to represent to
> your honourable body that they are free people residing
> within the jurisdiction of the corporation of Fred-
> ericksburg and natives of the State of Virginia . . . ;
> that some of them [are] descendants of soldiers of the
> Revolution . . . others having been personally engaged
> in aiding the efforts of their country in the late war with
> England . . . ; that many of them are possessed of
> property, real as well as personal and have therefore an
> abiding interest in preserving the peace and good order
> of the community. They beg leave further to represent
> that so general has become the diffusion of knowledge
> that those persons who are so unfortunate as not to be
> in some slight degree educated are cut off from the ordi-
> nary means of self-advancement and find the greatest
> difficulty in gaining a livelihood. In consequence of this
> condition of things and of the prohibitary statutes of

[29] Petition 7987, Henrico, Dec. 3, 1823.
[30] Petitions 10733, Henrico, Dec. 17, 1834; 12164, Dinwiddie, Jan. 8,
1839.

Virginia on the subject, the undersigned have been compelled to send their children abroad for education. The
expense attendant upon this course, though being
heavy to persons of small means, is the least important
part of the evils growing out of it. The residence of
their children in the North not merely deprives them of
the fostering care of their parents, but unavoidably ex-
poses them to the risk of having their minds poisoned
by doctrines alike inimical to the good order of society
and destructive of their own interests.

Moved by these considerations, your petitioners
humbly beg leave that an act may be passed authorizing
a school in the corporation of Fredericksburg, for the
instruction of free people of colour, resident therein
. . . subject nevertheless to such conditions and restrictions as to your honourable body may seem necessary
and proper, and your petitioners will ever pray. . . .

Edward D. Baptist	Shelton Phillips
William O. Baptist	Thornton Fox
Adolph Richards	Walter Wilkins
James Wilkins	Francis Dannes
Strackley Simmons	Henry Lucas
Washington Simmons	Alexander Duncan
Lawson Phillips	Fielding West
William Thronton	William Maine[31]

The life of a certain Christopher McPherson affords an illus-
tration of the fact that free Negroes occasionally attained a position high in the respect of the white citizens of the state. The Archives of Virginia contain a large collection of documents
concerning this man. The study of these documents makes it very
clear that McPherson was a respected and honored citizen of
Richmond in the early nineteenth century. McPherson owned a
fine home. He owned also a carriage and horses and in this outfit
his wife and two daughters were driven about the town. The
owner claimed that he needed the carriage because his advancing
years made it difficult for him to get to his work which took him
to many parts of the city. However, in 1810, the City Council evi-

[31] Petition 12130, Spotsylvania, March 16, 1838.

dently decided that this was not the proper style of life for a Negro; hence the Council passed an ordinance which made it possible for Negroes to ride in carriages only in the capacity of maids or coachmen. In his protest against this action, McPherson produced many excellent testimonials from some of the most distinguished citizens of Virginia, but the ultimate suggestion of these men was that it would be best for McPherson and his family to live elsewhere than in the State of Virginia. McPherson sent to the legislature an outline of his life. This document indicates that he was a man of high attainments, who had performed many useful services. The document is given below.[32] The last we hear of this man indicates that he had become insane.

[32] Petition 5633, Henrico, Dec. 10, 1810:
"Christopher McPherson
"Outlines Of The Life Of Christopher McPherson, Born in Louisa County, Virginia, As Well As Can Be Recollected.
1770 I went to school in Goochland, near the Courthouse. . . . Remained 1-¾ years
1772 Went behind the counter at the Elk Horn Store, at Petersburg
1776–7 Schooling children, etc.
1778 TO 1781 Clerk for the Commercial Agent for the State; during this time and at the seige of Yorktown was clerk for one of the Commissaries Genl. and otherwise rendered essential service for the Continental Army
1782–3 Clerk for David Ross, Esquire
1784 Principal storekeeper for D. Ross Esquire. till the end of the year 1787 when the store was closed. Whilst there 8 or 10 white gentlemen were under my direction (I mustered in this time . . . which I disliked)
1788 TO 1799 Was principal clerk to David Ross, Esq. Whilst 2 to 6 gentlemen were under me. (in the Summer of 99 I quited Mr. Ross) Twas I think in 1797 that a riot was passing in the road by my door near Columbia, of a number of slaves. . . . I turned out with my sword, to suppress it, without expecting any help. Major John Quarle's certificate goes to prove that with my help mischief was prevented.
1799 (Winter) Enrolled for Congress . . . till Spring 1800
1800 (Spring) Mr. Jefferson by letter introduced me to Mr. Madison . . . I sat at table noon and evening with Mrs. Madison, his lady, and company, and enjoyed a full share of the conversation.
1800 Clerk for W. W. Hening . . . Investigating British claims,

In comparison with Christopher McPherson most of the free people lived much simpler lives. They were not all good, prosperous, or contented. While many may have found a measure of happiness, into the experience of others came many of the problems which perplex life of the present day. We find in these records suits at law in which certain free men attempted to defraud other free men of valuable real estate.[33] Although there were many contented homes and fine examples of the family virtues, there were also desertions and petitions for divorce.[34] Unfortu-

---

etc. Nominated by Mr. James Ross, brother to D. Ross, Esq. his principal Executor, by will, as per probate from the Court of Fluvanna County. Clerk in the Office of High Chancery.

1801 Clerk to Col. Carrington, as supervisor, and in the office of H. Chancery.

1802 Clerk in H. C. C. and for others . . . and I then invented an Index for the Court docket of the H. C. C. . . . which Index . . . twas said by several Attrs. expedited the business every session to about three days more business than would have been done without it. (Querie) What did this save to the public at large? I was witness for a man of colour. . . . When my oath was taken by the jury in the District Court, in preference to the opposite oaths of two white witnesses.

1803 TO 1810 Clerk for all the principal offices both under the General and State Government, and for Judges, Lawyers, Merchants, etc. I have paid voluntarily out of my own pocket near one hundred dollars toward improving the two streets on which I live, donation toward building a Seminary of Learning in the suburbs of the city . . . thirty dollars. Throughout the whole course of my life I have been considered by numerous white acquaintances as one of their number . . . and they have uniformly treated me as such.

   "(Color is nothing. . . . Worth is all with liberal minds) I can prove all the above by very many substantial witnesses. . . .

                                        "Christopher McPherson."

[33] Executive Papers, Archives of Virginia, Letters Received, June 14, 1832. Hereafter Archives of Virginia, Letters Received, will be omitted and the document identified by the date.

[34] Petition 11772, Fauquier, Jan. 3, 1838. This is a case of desertion. The husband is said to have expressed sympathy for Nat Turner. It became dangerous for him to remain in the state and he went to the city of Philadelphia and requested his wife to follow him. She refused to leave and petitioned for a divorce.

nately, too, are recorded murders in which the cause of the crime was the fact that the murdered man had stolen the avenger's wife.[35] One case is recorded in which a Negro danced with another man's wife and then announced to the assembled company that the woman "had feet like lead," whereupon the husband murdered the man.[36]

How much of real property the free Negroes acquired is not known. It remains for some student to examine the records of the towns and counties. However, in the records here studied we find copies of wills of free Negroes and receipts for taxes showing that individuals of this class acquired considerable real estate.[37] It is also true that many freedmen offered the proof of acquisition of property as evidence that in the event that their children were set free they would not be a burden upon society. In the case of Samuel Johnston, as cited above, in his petition of 1820 he was able to show that the property acquired by him, in addition to the value of his wife and children, was assessed at $3,600.[38] In 1816 Hembro and Dilsey Galego, in a petition asking for the emancipation of their son, show that the parents were emancipated in 1807 and that "since the said emancipation your petitioners have followed an honest livelihood and have possessed themselves of some valuable real and personal property, which has been acquired by honest industry, as the annexed certificates will prove."[39] This property included lots on what is now Broad Street, Richmond, Virginia. In 1810 it developed that two free Negroes, Uriah Tyner of North Carolina, and Major Elbeck of Pennsylvania, had settled in the city of Petersburg contrary to the law forbidding the emigration of such free Negroes from other states. Each of these men had been permitted to marry and live in peace in the said city for more than ten years, when suddenly, for reasons unknown, the magistrates decided to enforce the law and expel the Negroes. Tyner petitioned the legislature for permission to remain in the city, and in his petition, among other things, proved that "he had acquired the good will

[35] Executive Papers, Sept. 8, 1788.
[36] Petition 7545, Pittsylvania, Dec. 13, 1820.
[37] Petition 7180, Dec. 10, 1818; see Appendix.
[38] Petition 7555a, Fauquier, Dec. 14, 1820.
[39] Petition 6329, Henrico, Oct. 21, 1816.

of the inhabitants, by whom he was deemed a very useful man; that by his persevering industry he has been enabled to purchase a home and a lot in the said town, in fee simple, exclusive of personal property."[40] In like manner Elbeck proved that he had succeeded "in the purchase of several lots of ground in the said town, and in erecting buildings and making improvements thereon . . . believing himself entitled to all the rights and privileges . . . to which other free people of colour are entitled."[41] In each of the above cases more than one hundred citizens, including the mayor and other officials of the city, endorsed the petitions. In 1824 Robert Trout, a native of one of the western counties, when ordered out of the state, petitioned that he be allowed to remain for one year, in order that he be enabled to settle his affairs; he declared that

> he hath acquired some property which he can not have
> the benefit of unless some indulgence is afforded him.
> Your petitioner therefore humbly prays that he may
> have the benefit of legislative interference, that one year
> be allowed him to make sale of his property and col-
> lect his dues, without which he will sustain considerable
> loss.[42]

Other petitions of this description may be given which certify that the freedman owned 700 acres or 180 acres of land, and in other cases that "he had sufficient property not to be chargeable to the State."[43]

[40] Petition 5681, Dinwiddie, Dec. 15, 1810.

[41] Petition 5681a, Dinwiddie, Dec. 15, 1810.

[42] Petition 8279, Pocahantas, Dec. 9, 1824: "We the sinors dou herre by certify that we have been acquainted with Robert Troute a man of Coller upwards of Twenty years and dou be leve him to be an honeste sober uprite and well dis posed man of Couller and that he is not In Clined to Stir up mischieft with those that air Slaves in this Neighborhood and we dou be lieve if aney man of Coller Should be in titled to the bennefitt of Legislative aid he is . . . given under our hands. This day and date written."

[43] Petitions 4428a, 5635, 5880, 6208, 6313, 6630, 6719, 7686, 8644, 8649, 8834, 8836, 8837, 8982, 9078, 9400, 9566, 9615, 10235, 10361, 10649, 10839, 11389, 15236, 15413, 15964, 17254, 17527.

It is my sincere belief that more adequate study will reveal that the free Negro had acquired considerable property.

Possibly it would be of interest to compare the condition of the freedman with the condition of the poor white rather than with the governing class, in which case it will be observed that the poor white man is often described as shiftless, idle and indolent: terms often thought to apply exclusively to the free Negroes. The period described in this study is characterized by hardships for and limitations on all poor men, black or white. Society was controlled by and for the governing agriculturalists. Even the best and richest Virginia plantation owners had their economic difficulties. Each year the lands were becoming more and more exhausted. Prices declined; debts accumulated; and young men left the state. But the planters owned the better lands. On their acres they had become entrenched through the generations. Poor men or new men took what was left, which most often meant arid or unproductive fields. Too often the poor man sank to the dregs of poverty. Often the records of the courts reveal the poor white man and the poor Negro as allies in vice.[44]

As a part of the poor, free Negroes shared the vices of the poor, but in addition to natural difficulties the freedman faced restrictions imposed by custom, law, and prejudice. The attainments or failures of the free Negroes should be studied in the light of such restrictions.

The white workman hated the Negro as an economic rival; for the Negro, slave or free, monopolized much of the labor of the state. "Sundry free people of Colour, residing in the Borough of

[44] Executive Papers, Aug. 15, 1806: "A list of Names, Etc. of Sundry Persons, United for the Purpose of Stealing, Plundering, etc.

"Edward or Ned, and his brother, whose Christian name I do not know, both white men, live near Occoquan Mills on this side of Alexandria.

Thomas Bowles, a Free Negro lives in Dumfries

David Arton, a free Negro lives in the Federal City

John Leanard, a white man, lives in the Federal City

William Coleman, a free Negro, lives in Richmond

Nellie Bullet, a free Negro woman, lives near Dumfries

John Bedford, a free Negro, lives in Falmouth

Jerry·Tyler, a free Negro man, lives in Fredericksburg"

Norfolk, in behalf of themselves and the rest of that class of the community" explain in a petition:

> We have nothing to apprehend from the better order of men . . . but there are many wanton and malignant in their disposition and if no white person is present . . . the oath of the complaint alone subjects us to corporal punishment. We pray that this may become a subject of consideration. That as mechanics we are necessitated to keep accounts and our oaths can not be admitted.[45]

In 1831 a group of white mechanics of Culpeper county asked the state to pass a law "forbidding any Negro to be apprenticed to a trade."[46] In the same year white mechanics of the city of Petersburg petitioned the legislature that a law be passed forbidding any Negro to pursue a trade without the supervision of a white overseer.[47] In 1851 white mechanics of the city of Norfolk asked the state to stop all free Negroes from working at any trade. This petition declares that such a policy will "destroy jealousy between slave holders and non-slaveholders" and if not enacted "non-slaveholders will finally demand the expulsion of all slaves."[48]

The slave system made necessary certain laws which hindered the progress of the freedmen. In 1791 a petition from a group of free Negroes of the city of Norfolk asks that black persons be not prohibited from serving as pilots on the Chesapeake Bay.[49] In 1810 Henry Jackson, evidently a free Negro of a very fine type, if he is judged by the testimonials given to him, asked the legislature that he be granted special permission to serve as a pilot "as his father had done for many years before his time."[50] Also, when the ownership of firearms was prohibited to free Negroes protests were filed. The following is an example:

[45] Petition 5391, Norfolk, Dec. 7, 1809.
[46] Petition 9789, Culpeper, Dec. 9, 1831.
[47] Petition 9860, Dinwiddie, Dec. 20, 1831.
[48] Petition 177707, Norfolk, Nov. 12, 1851.
[49] Petition 2628, Norfolk, Nov. 12, 1791.
[50] Petitions 5636, and 6769, Norfolk.

The petition of Joseph Ruff humbly represents that he is one of that unfortunate class in Virginia, who neither possesses the common privileges of a freeman nor has the protection and security of the slave. He has for many years been a peaceful, industrious citizen of the county of Bedford, where by his honest labour he has raised in credit a considerable family. He owns a small farm in the mountains (on which he resides) where the ownership of a gun is not only desirable for the purpose of obtaining such wild fowl as the country affords, but is indispensably necessary for the protection of his crop.[51]

For obvious reasons the ownership of dogs caused complaint on the part of those who attempted to regulate the activities of free Negroes. As a result the legislature received many petitions asking that such ownership be prohibited.[52]

The evidence also shows that many efforts were made to prevent free Negroes from engaging in certain forms of trade because of the general belief that the slaves sold stolen goods to the freedmen. A petition coming from Powhatan county asks that restrictions be placed on the amount of grain sold by free Negroes.[53] The inhabitants of Charles City county wished to stop Negroes from serving as millers.[54] The people of Loudoun county wished to stop them from using market carts.[55] Citizens of Charlotte county asked that free Negroes be stopped from owning, possessing, or raising stock, horses, or hogs.[56] Citizens of Fairfax and Prince William counties wished to prohibit them from using the Potomac fisheries.[57] And certain citizens of the city of Rich-

[51] Petition 10397, Bedford, Dec. 9, 1833; for similar petitions see 12744 and 13054.

[52] Petitions 9780, 12834, 15837, 18781.

[53] Petition 12113, Powhatan; see also petitions 11441, 12932, 13700, 14003, 14163.

[54] Petition 9960, Charles City, Dec. 27, 1831.

[55] Petition 12575, Loudoun, Jan. 13, 1836.

[56] Petitions 12657, Fairfax, April 6, 1839; 11125, Prince William, March 2, 1839.

[57] Petition 5725, Charlotte, Dec. 20, 1810.

mond wished to stop free Negroes from driving to work in private carriages.[58] A free man of the city of Petersburg declared that because of his skill as a brickmason his services were in demand outside the limits of his city; he therefore asked permission to travel over the state and contract for work where ever it might be found.[59] A free Negro residing in Goochland county protests that for more than fifteen years he has kept a tavern, but the state now prohibits his engaging in this business.[60]

The free Negroes felt the pressure of economic and legal restrictions, but in addition they lacked security of person and property. There were provisions in the law for their protection and there were always staunch white defenders of the liberties of the Negroes, but, in spite of the law, theirs was a precarious freedom. Many instances are recorded in which avaricious white men stole free Negroes and sold them into slavery.[61] The records of the county of Hampshire tell the story of the plot of a band of slave catchers to steal the free wife and children of a slave. In this instance the Negroes discovered the plot. They were armed and prepared and when four white men appeared defended themselves. As a result of the fight which followed one of the white men was killed. For this crime the guilty slave was sentenced to death.[62]

[58] Petition 5633, Henrico, Dec. 10, 1810.
[59] Petition 15733, Henrico, Dec. 22, 1847.
[60] Petition 14182, Goochland, Dec. 13, 1844.
[61] Executive Papers, Aug. 28, 1792; Dec. 13, 1792; Petition 785, Bedford, 1799; Executive Papers, Dec. 30, 1805; Dec. 11, 1811; Petitions, 7077, Henrico, Dec. 17, 1817; 8920, Accomack, Dec. 17, 1827; 10398, Princess Anne, Dec. 9, 1833.
[62] Executive Papers, Jan. 29, 1823: "On the fifteenth of October, last, a certain Joseph Stafford of this county, undertook to sell a woman of colour and her children to a man from one of the Southwestern states. This woman was the wife of the condemned Negro, Peter, had been reputed free, and acted as such for many years, and whose name stands recorded free on the records of this county. Nor did any of the heirs of her late master, who liberated her, eight in number, ever pretend to claim her as a slave save his son Joseph. He, however, being it is presumed tempted with a pretty large sum of money, undertook to sell her and her children as stated above and by special agreement as we

Carelessness in matters of legal form and sometimes lack of understanding of legal matters resulted in disaster for the free Negro. The case of the Negro woman, Sarah Green, given in the Appendix, may serve as an example.

As time went on and restrictions on free Negroes increased, it is found that they were thrown into jail and held in confinement many months because of the inability to prove that their "free papers" were authentic.[63] Suspicions against free Negroes increased with the passing years, and it became constantly more difficult for them to maintain their liberty. Provisions were made whereby freedmen without visible means of support might be forced again into slavery.[64] An effort was made to change the law in suits for freedom, whereby the expense of the trial would be placed on the Negro.[65] At the same time a constant agitation on the part of the colonizationists propagated the doctrine that all free Negroes were worthless and dangerous and had to be sent out of the state.

On the other hand, certain of the free Negroes gave full justification for suspicion and agitation. Free men were found implicated in insurrections. They were punished when found harboring runaway slaves.[66] Free papers were written or forged by free Negroes.[67] Pamphlets written by Northern abolitionists were found in the possession of these people, and such works were distributed by them.[68] Also free Negroes were known to have assisted the escape of slaves.[69] While these things were happening

---

understand was to deliver them at a certain place in the state of Maryland. In order to do which he or the purchaser, it is not known which, hired two or three men to seize them in the night and convey them to the place agreed on; but in this attempt one of the men was shot with a musket ball and died the next morning."

[63] Petitions 4590a, 5432, 7097, 8537, 8920, 9124, 9835.

[64] Petitions 18033, 18059, 18334.

[65] Petition 17500, Fairfax, Jan. 14, 1857.

[66] Executive Papers, Dec. 19, 1806.

[67] Petitions 8631, 10751; Executive Papers, July 3, 1820; April 17, 1827; Petition 10751, Culpeper, Dec. 19, 1834.

[68] Petition 19231, Rockbridge, Jan. 12, 1856.

[69] Executive Papers, April 17, 1823; Petition 7679, Amelia, Dec. 11, 1821.

in Virginia certain free Negroes were serving at the North as most effective antislavery agitators.

Existence under the difficulties which surrounded the free Negroes must have robbed life of much of its joy, or perhaps, it made life an adventure, the more joyous because of its perils. In every case it called for adjustments to surroundings and to fellow men, without which adjustment the outcome would have been poverty, a return to slavery, exile from the state, or perhaps death.

In this chapter we have been concerned with the life of the Negro after he had won freedom. It is not fair to judge the entire people by the conduct of these free men and leave out the mass that could never be free. It is without doubt true that the men who made much progress as free men had not been rebellious when they were held as slaves. It is also very significant that the leaders of insurrections were slaves and not free Negroes. Possibly, it is a fair supposition that life in Virginia was possible for free Negroes only on condition that they were ever submissive and humble, and that they hid all pretense to a station in life higher than that allotted to them.

But the character of the men who prospered under this system remained slavish, and there are manifestations of traits of character, developed under the limitations of the system, that are out of all harmony with the ideals of liberty. For instance, it is true that repeated examples are found in which slaves were the first to reveal the insurrectionary plots of their fellow slaves. There are to be found letters (written by slaves) which afford interesting examples of this type of conduct. The following are examples found among the papers of Governor James Monroe:

White pepl be ware of your lives there is a plan now
forming and intended to be put in execution this
harvest time they are to commence and use their scithes
as weapons until they can get posession of other weapons their is a great many weapons hid for the purps
and be you all assured if you do not look out in time
many of you will be put to death this plan is to kill all
before them wemin and children their has been expressis
going in every direction for some days to see all the

Negroes they could this hollerday to make the arrange-
ments and to conclude what time it is to commence and
at what places they are to assemble watch the conduct
of your Negroes and you will see an alteration I am a
confident of the leaders and can not give my name I am
also a greater friend to some of the whites and wish to
preserve their lives. I am a favorite servant of my master and mistis and love them dearly.[70]

The following is found in the Executive Papers for 1812:

my Dar mstor Structon wats Richmon town on 25
nite of dis mont all the niggros will rise on that nite to
meet in this place tha mean fost to salt the Cappitols
and take all the arms. that got powder nuff and has got
many guns and cut lash hide thro all Dese Pine woods
Rounde town but tha will not lead me into it that wish
me to gine them but I Got Good master and love all the
white Peoples tha made me swarn that I would not tell
what they told me Befor tha told me the Cecret and
after I will not gine them my life was to be stroyd if I
told that Dar sir I warnt this known so my name is to
come to lite or Darth will be my fate By the Blacks But
will put all on gard to prepare for that fatell nite the
Sceen of the Play Hous will not be compared with the
sceen of the nite of the 25 without your Gards is Duble
and the Drums and fifs is Ratline thro the Streets_____
live with muncur at Vandu _____ is Rupting the nig-
gers and telling them tha all will be free that is another
Inglish man in Petersburg Doing the same thing thare
is naw a Cask and Powder Plant under the Bank to
blow it up and that will not spar man woman noe
children in tha place if tha get upper hand of you all
I dont sleep one nite since I here this _____ Nur Yull
Scuse my bad Riting I poor Black man that wish you
well and if it come to push will fend you will all my
mite But take that man live at muncur offic who call
him Hart and carry for the offis the Head of the Black

[70] Executive Papers, June 7, 1802.

call him self Generall Wayne who kill all the Indians
this from your Dar well wisher

> Poor Black
> Sam.[71]

In 1800 Mosby Sheppard in a letter to the governor explained
how he had been informed of the intended insurrection of Gabriel:

> I will recite to you the manner in which I got this in-
> formation. I was sitting in the Compting room with the
> door shut, and no one near except myself, they knocked
> at the door, and I let them in . . . they shut the door
> themselves . . . and then began to recite what I have
> before recited.[72]

For their part in revealing the plans of Gabriel, Tom and Pharoah Sheppard were bought by the state and were emancipated,
and in 1810 Pharoah Sheppard asked the legislature to permit
him to emancipate his son on the strength of the service he had
rendered to the state.[73]

Other examples abound. In 1801 a certain W. Claiborne wrote
to the governor:

> Last night my white family lodged upstairs were alarmed
> by a number of Negroes going around about the house
> the greater part of the night. No information of this was
> given to me last night by my white family upstairs. But
> this morning I was taken by a mulatto servant girl into
> the dining room, who told me the negroes were about
> to do mischief to the whites.

The insurrection of 1816 was revealed by a slave girl named Lucy
Powell.[74] For this service she was emancipated and the state pro-

[71] Executive Papers, Nov. 18, 1812.

[72] Executive Papers, August 30, 1800.

[73] Petition 5675, Henrico, Dec. 14, 1810; Executive Papers, Feb. 28, 1801.

[74] Executive Papers, Feb. 18, 1801.

vided her a pension of one hundred dollars per year. The pension was paid until 1849.[75] A slave called Lewis revealed the plot of 1802; in 1805 his master asked the state to pay the value of the slave on the grounds that while in the custody of the commonwealth he had "been suffered to escape."[76]

The most easily understood explanation of the slaves' activity in revealing plots and plans of their fellows is found in the fact that the state considered this type of conduct as meritorious service, and having rendered such service the slave expected the reward at the expense of his fellows. The conduct of the informers seems to have been profitable. Nat Turner's insurrection appears to have been an exception in that it was begun before suspicion had been aroused or the plot revealed.

In addition to the fact that plots were revealed, it is also true that many slaves refused absolutely to have any part in insurrections. When in 1813, the slave Aaron was on trial for plotting an insurrection, testimony to the following effect was given against the defendant by the slave John: "When he had returned from Ohio with his master, Frank, a slave came to him while he was lying asleep in a kitchen and attempted to secure his aid as a recruit to the rebellion." The following conversation is said to have taken place:

After some observation had passed between them on common topics and the said Aaron said we have something on hand we want to know of, and being asked what he wanted with him, he replied that there was company forming or about to be made up to go through the country in order to become men of our own. This deponent then asked him how he expected to become men of their own, to which the said Aaron answered, we will go through the country and cut and slash and by that means we will become men of our own. This deponent then replied, that him and his company were fools and that he would join no such com-

[75] Petition 7109, Spotsylvania, Dec. 29, 1817; Executive Papers, March 1, 1816..
[76] Petition 4880, Goochland, Dec. 2, 1805.

pany and upon this deponents expressing the same
language a second time, he said the said Aaron proposed
to give him twelve dollars if he would join them. This
deponent then replied that for twelve dollars and for
twelve more and twelve to the back of that he would not
join no such company. This deponent then lay down
and went to sleep again and was again awakened by
the said Aaron who asked him to go out with him,
and they went out—then said Aaron, come Johnny wont
you join us, and upon his answering in the negative the
said Aaron then offered him sixteen dollars to join
him. This deponent said he would not join him if he
was to give him as many dollars as there was leaves on
the trees from the mouth of the Kanawha River to
that place. The said Aaron then said if you will not
join with us, there is someone I have a spite against and
he would be damned if he did not have revenge before
he stopped. This deponent then said he had a wife and
eight children and if he ever died he was determined
to die in defense of his country. The said Aaron said
he would never die in defense of the white people, and
the said Aaron after some further observations on the
subject told the deponent that he was a white folks
negro.[77]

We can not know how much this man's anxiety, lest he himself
be implicated, influenced his testimony, but the fact remains that
in the insurrections of 1800, 1802, 1816, and 1831 many Negroes
were freed of the charges made against them and in the Southampton affair many slaves manifested loyalty to their masters.
This loyalty to the master class seems to indicate much of contradiction in the reaction of the Negro to the slave system. While
many slaves appeared to have wanted freedom other slaves appeared to have been friends of the system that enslaved them.
The explanation of this contradictory situation seems to lie in
the importance of the individual situations. They pursued that

[77] Executive Papers, *Commonwealth* v. *Aaron*, Kanawha, Oct. 28,
1818.

course of action that seemed to offer the most of practical reward. There were personal profits in humble, inoffensive loyalty. Rebellion for all Negroes was dangerous but for the freedmen it was both dangerous and perhaps foolish. Loyalty to the master class was the only assurance of the continuance of the liberties that had been won. And in most cases it had been the loyal, humble slave that had been emancipated. Certain petitions affirm interestingly that this or that man was a good Negro because he was accustomed to telling of the misconduct of the other slaves. Such recommendations are to be found as the fact that "he did not associate with slaves," or that the individual in question "had a peculiar aversion to people of his own colour," and that the slave "hated abolitionists."[78] Without doubt, the tattler was to be found among the loyal humble slaves. After emancipation many a freedman could not forget the white men who had liberated them. He had won white friends and his continuance in a state of freedom depended upon his retaining the friends he had already won. The free Negro adjusted his conduct accordingly. Also, economic progress depended on white men—not on slaves. The freedman had to labor for white men or he had to sell his produce to white men. Success of his labors depended upon the confidence he could win among white men. The more white friends he gained, the more he prospered. Moreover, the free Negro knew that many white men hated him; that he was of a suspected class; that someone was always ready to attribute every local evil to him. There was, also, the ever increasing agitation to drive the free Negroes out of the state. The freedman adjusted himself to both economic and social conditions and the process of adjustment made many of them "white folks' Negroes."

Freedmen who could not so adjust themselves were sold again into slavery or were driven out of the state. It is not in the province of this study to describe the men who left the state. Hundreds of slaves left by way of the underground railroad, but free Negroes, too, found it to their advantage to move into the North or to Canada. Literature of the abolitionists was found in the homes of freedmen, and freedmen are known to have hurried from the state because of the suspicion that they were guilty of

[78] Petitions 7903, 6011, 16642, 19279.

distributing antislavery literature.[79] It is possible that certain of these men concealed their sympathies for the slave and that they learned to deceive white men to the end that they might remain in the state.

It is very true that men like James Madison felt that the sympathies of the free Negro were always for the slave, and the idea persisted that the free Negroes incited the slaves to insurrection.[80] There is also evidence that it was dangerous for Negroes to reveal the plots of the slaves. The slave Lewis, the informer in 1802, was permitted to escape from the state possibly because of his plea that his confession would be the cause of his death at the hands of fellow slaves. The following is his testimony:

> Question—"Why did you suppose that these words will
> kill you?" Answer: "Because I spoke against my colour;
> the black men will kill me. The white men whip openly,
> but the blacks kill stilly. I prefer being hanged than
> being poisoned, if for my confessing the whole truth,
> my life is spared, a strict watch must be kept over me.
> My life is now in your hands."[81]

In 1824, a free Negro applied for permission to remain in the state of Virginia. He had come to Virginia from the state of Louisiana, in which state he had been emancipated for exposing an insurrection of the slaves. He claimed that the Negroes of his native state would not let him live among them and he felt that his conduct should give assurance that he would not be dangerous to the people of Virginia.[82]

The prospect of profit and the process of adjustment in relation to the white people of the state offer an explanation of the conduct of "proslavery" Negroes. While their own personal liberty was precious to them, there are instances in which they bought and sold other Negroes and held them as slaves in the

[79] Archives of Virginia, Executive Letter Book, 1823–1830 (Governor Giles), p. 333; Petition 12812, Loudoun, Jan. 11, 1840.

[80] Stanislaus M. Hamilton (ed.), *Letters and Writings of James Monroe* (New York, 1920), III, 315.

[81] Executive Papers, May 5, 1802.

[82] Petition 8194, Henrico, Dec. 3, 1824.

same sense as did the white masters. As already indicated, the great majority of slaves held by Negro masters were members of the master's family, but all the slaves were not relations of their masters. Examples are found in which Negro masters of Virginia slaves owned large numbers of such slaves.[83] These men were sent into the fields to labor for the profit of the Negro owner and these Negro slaveowners thought and acted as the white planters thought and acted. First, the free Negro slaveowner had done what he could to convince his white neighbors that he was not dangerous to the existing slave system; next, they had themselves become convinced that it was to their profit to use the labor of slaves. They, the Negro slaveowners, lived in a land in which the slave system was considered profitable and just and they, too, wanted the profits. In their efforts to rise above their situation they were tempted to make use of what was supposedly the sole profitable labor system of the existing economic order. Also, while these people were seeking economic gain, the ownership of slaves was a demonstration to their white neighbors that they could be regarded as trusted members of society. A Negro who himself owned slaves was not to be regarded as an insurrectionist. Slaveownership was a part of a protective device developed by men who used every means to prove that they were safe. How far the zeal of these free Negroes might carry them is shown in service offered by these men to the Confederacy. The following instance might be duplicated in other Southern localities in the first days of the Civil War.

A newspaper, published in the city of Petersburg in the month of July, 1861, describes a meeting in the Court House

[83] *Examples of Virginia Negro Slaveowners, 1830**

NEGRO OWNER	COUNTY	NUMBER OF SLAVES
William Daniel	Cumberland	32
William Brockenborough	Hanover	46
Curtis Carter	Richmond	22
Benjamin O. Taylor	King George	71
Thomas A. Morton	Powhatan	45
Littleton Waller	Wythe	28

  * Woodson, op. cit.

square, on which occasion the former mayor of the city, with appropriate oratory, presented colors to a local company of free Negroes, about to set out to assist the Confederate army in the defense of the lower Chesapeake Bay. The Negro leader of the company came forward to receive the colors and is quoted as responding in the following manner:

> We are willing to aid Virginia's cause to the utmost extent of our ability. We do not feel that it is right for us to remain here idle, when white gentlemen are engaged in the performance of work at Norfolk that is more suitable to our hands, and of which it is our duty to relieve them. There is not an unwilling heart among us . . . we promise unhesitating obedience to all orders that may be given us. . . . I could feel no greater pride, no more genuine gratification, than to be able to plant it first upon the ramparts of Fortress Monroe.[84]

The manifold effects of slavery on the minds and characters of the masters often have been declared deplorable. Here we seem to have demonstrated the deplorable effects of the system on the character of black masters—perhaps we have the clearest explanation of many human evils for which the slave states are condemned. But, in fairness to the Negro, the few Negroes who aided the cause of the Confederacy should be contrasted with the 104,387 recruited in slave territory who are known to have served in the Union army.[85] These were men who found no profit in slavery, but who fought bravely, with Negro soldiers enlisted at the North, to free other Negro slaves.

However the slave system may have circumscribed their lives or debased their characters in the days before the War, the free Negro, as described in this chapter, had in many cases attained a position of economic well-being that such Negroes are seldom thought to have possessed. These attainments are, in turn, the proof of like abilities and capacities, possessed by hundreds of

[84] Luther P. Jackson, "Free Negroes of Petersburg, Virginia," *Journal of Negro History*, xii (July, 1927), 387.

[85] Fred A. Shannon, *The Organization and Administration of the Union Army* (Cleveland, 1928), ii, 160.

other Negroes held in slavery. By 1860 the African had been transformed into an American Negro. He had adjusted himself to an American environment and had made much of what Americans call progress. The present-day status of the Negro people is not solely the story of progress since the proclamation of Abraham Lincoln. Building on the heritage of Africa, Negroes learned much of the American way of living in the days of slavery. They are building today on what their fathers were before the Civil War.

In this study no effort has been made to indicate the economic or political significance of the Negro slave. My efforts have been confined to a description of the Negro people. In Part II a similar effort will be made to describe the characteristics of the white people who owned the slave and who governed the state. The history of the state of Virginia was profoundly affected by the relations between these races. What the governing class did or failed to do, in the period between 1830 and 1860, was in a large measure determined by the black people already portrayed.

II

*The Relation of
the White Man to
the Negro in
Virginia*

FOUR

The Humanitarians

THE DOCUMENTS preserved in the Archives of Virginia present as vivid a picture of the antebellum white man as they do of the Negro of that day. I believe that as we know both white and black men better, we shall be enabled to interpret more justly the history of the period.

The history of Virginia, and of other Southern states, in many respects was the result of the contact of black and white men. Human traits of character and human reactions of the two races toward the system that surrounded them are the background of legislation and administration in the slave period. What the lawmakers did was the result of what they were and of what the slaves were. In an active manner white men governed; in a passive manner black men governed. Both black and white were the makers of the history of the state. If mistakes in acts or policies were made, they were human errors.

It is very obvious that all white men did not believe that the Negro should be held as a slave. However, the study of the slaves as made in previous chapters has revealed so many white men as advocates of the slave that such men cannot be regarded as exceptional characters. If we are to understand the history of the slave period, we must give due consideration to these friends and defenders of the slave.

The preservation of the slave system made necessary a harsh slave code. In a day when all laws seem harsh as compared with present-day legal standards, the slave code seems excessively cruel. To a present-day reader it appears that many slaves were executed for petty offenses. It may be noted that in such instances the governor and council were given the power to pardon the culprit or to commute the sentence, in which case the slave would be transported outside the limits of the territory of the United States. The table given below is a typical example of slave convictions for each year of the period from 1780 to 1830.[1]

There were many who objected to the severity of the slave code, and in the correspondence of the governors are included many letters asking mercy for the slave. The following is quoted from a letter relative to a certain slave, the property of Miles Carey:

[1] *Slaves Sentenced to be Executed for Certain Crimes*

DATE	NAME	CRIME
1787	York	Stealing men's clothing
	Davy and	
	Simon	Stealing men's clothing
	James	Stealing meat
	Mark	Stealing an overcoat
	Dick	Stealing meat
	Ben	Stealing bacon
	Moses	Stealing bacon (value 2£)
	Moses	Killing a steer
	George and	
	Dick	Stealing meat (value 40 shillings)
	Arthur and	
	Charles	Stealing pork
1792	Cuff	Stealing
	James and	
	Ben	Stealing two bushels of Indian Corn
	Argyle	Stealing merchandise (value 5£)
	Bartlett	Stealing merchandise (value 9 shillings)
	Joe	Stealing Money (3£)
	Will	Stealing Money (15£)
	Isaac	Stealing four pieces of bacon
1830	Harry	Stealing tobacco
	Jim	Stealing wheat
	Harry	Stealing merchandise (value $7.00)
	Solomon	Stealing ($45.00)
	Jacob	Stealing merchandise (value $4.50)
	James	Stealing merchandise (value $21.00)

One Fitzhugh of this County had lost a small quantity
of bacon . . . the fellow's confession when taken up and
under terror of immediate punishment was produced
against him, and I would not have it understood that I
mean any reflection on the members of the court, as
they were good men (one of them a clergyman) and I
am convinced that they were convinced as men, if not as
judges, of the prisoner's guilt. . . .

But waiving every other consideration as the theft is
only trifling, one of thirty-five pounds of tobacco, I have
some hope you will step in between the sentence and
the execution of our rigorous, I have almost said, unjust
laws. For the sake of humanity I could wish something
short of death was substituted for small crimes and for
our reputation among other nations I could wish too
that the trial of slaves was still further emended and that
pregnant circumstances, as our law reads might not be
permitted to condemn a black man more than a white
one. . . .

I am persuaded if I have not forgot your character
since our youthful acquaintance that you will not think
your time mis-applied in performing this act of mercy.

Sam Kello[2]

The same humanitarian spirit is to be found in the following
communication:

Truly grieved am I when I contemplate the marked difference between the privileges of a slave and those of
free men. Had slaves the command of money and
were enabled to employ the ablest counsel, they would be
acquitted or condemned to the penitentiary when the
crimes have been capital.[3]

[2] Executive Papers, Archives of Virginia, Letters Received, Aug. 12,
1787. Hereafter Archives of Virginia, Letters Received, will be omitted
and the document identified by the date.

[3] Executive Papers, Nov. 23, 1814.

Still another humanitarian declares:

The wretched slave is badly situated at best, having no
sort of influence in society or before his judges. Shut out
from the blessings and enjoyment of the Great American
prerogative, trial by jury, he would find himself insu-
lated indeed from justice were he not from an intuitive
impulse of his feeling offered an invitation to approach
the white throne of mercy.[4]

Many similar complaints against the harshness of the slave
code may be presented.[5] No doubt local conditions and sentiment sometimes served to modify the severity of the law. In 1829
a letter from Staunton, Virginia, reports to the governor that in
the western section of the state

until recently our inferior courts have commuted the
punishment for larcenies by slaves, by whipping . . .
not knowing that whilst there had been a change in
punishment of free people of colour, slaves were still
punished by the common law. By many this has been
esteemed an oversight in the legislature and wants only
to be named to be corrected. Ought it not to be so.[6]

While many petitions ask for mercy for the slave because of the
harshness of the law, other letters give extenuating circumstances

[4] Executive Papers, Nov. 26, 1814.

[5] Executive Papers, June 25, 1796: "When the life of a human
creature is involved and at a time too when the general sentiment
sanctions the opinion that in all offenses except murder the punishment
is out of all proportion to the crime, more especially when applied to
slave, I feel a confidence little short of certainty that your liberality and
zeal for equal rights will on this awful occasion induce you to extend
mercy (that darling attribute of the Deity) to a man whose life the
tyranny of our laws has brought into jeopardy . . . that he is a slave
and not so much protected from the passions and prejudices of those
who have been used to exercise absolute authority over half the human
race, and therefore hard indeed if no appeal could be made to the seat
of mercy so wisely instituted by the government where cool and
dispassionate justice will preside."

[6] Executive Papers, Sept. 11, 1829.

as the cause of slave crime. A letter to Governor Randolph states that two slaves are about to be executed for "breaking into a smoke house and a mill and taking from those places a small quantity of bacon and meal" and that "the crime appears to have been perpetrated to satisfy hunger."[7] A letter from the city of Petersburg declares that "the needy and distressed situation of the slaves in general afforded an inducement to felony which it would here require more than common honesty to resist."[8] In still another letter it is declared that the slaves sentenced to die should receive pardon "because they were induced to steal by a white man."[9]

The efforts of the humanitarians to secure justice for the slaves extended not only to minor offenses but applied also to certain slaves who had murdered white men. The long letter which follows is typical of the humane spirit which characterized the members of the Quaker sect. The letter seems to offer a typical description of conditions that might develop on a slave plantation and affords a rather pathetic example of the desire of the slaveowner to be merciful to the guilty slave.

Hagley, March 20, 1824

Dear Cousin:

I imagine there has been laid before thee before now in an official way the case of the two slaves belonging to the estate of Edward Garland who lately murdered their overseer in Hanover and are in jail under sentence of death at this time for the crime. I have received no authentic statement of the particulars of each case as exhibited in proof at the trial. The uniform report, however, which has reached us in regard to the part acted by Thornton is that he never struck a blow in aid of King's death, and was no further accessory to it than by joining with Humphery in an agreement to perpetrate the meditated deed. If this is the fact as it is stated, no

[7] Executive Papers, Aug. 2, 1787.
[8] Executive Papers, Feb. 22, 1815; see also April 3, 1827.
[9] Executive Papers, Sept., 1786; May 10, 1784.

doubt thou hast been apprised of it through the medium
alluded to above. Presuming on its truth it is only necessary to void the circumstances with the poor creature's
general good conduct as testified to by the overseer himself in order to discover more than a slight reason to
conclude that he was not effectually ripe for the horrid
deed and that the bloody resolution was probably formed
through the influence of the other's persuasions with
the additional impulse of some sense of severity recently
practiced upon himself or some of his fellow servants.

It has been 9 or 10 months since a greater degree of discontent became obvious among the slaves of that place
than had before been the case. It went on to increase
to the end of the year and up through the commencement of the present till the time of the murder. It was
not till about 2 months past that Thornton first discovered anything of the kind. He then absconded with
several more and came to Goochland to make a complaint to their mistress of the hardships of their condition
under the overseer. He the overseer followed them up
to this county shortly afterwards. The conduct of Thornton upon the occasion perplexed and disturbed him to
such a degree that he tendered an offer to Betsy Garland
of giving up the business if she desired it saying that he
knew not what to think of the case now as this man had
always behaved himself with such uncommon propriety.
The unfortunate man I dare say was unconscious of
any cause in himself that had been operating to produce this state of things, that then existed or that to
which it too directly led. He had given proof of cruelty
and severity of disposition before he engaged at that
place, and when the strength of his authority became
weakened by Edward Garland's death he found himself
incapable of any conciliatory resources to supply the
wanted remedy. The consequence probably was that he
went on to exercise those of an opposite character
to an impudent degree until a stock of incurable ani-
mosity between him and the slaves was engendered.

It was Betsy Garland's wish, I know, to have accepted his offer to relinquish the business, but she was advised against it, and having no confidence in her own judgment pursued the course recommended. It was, however, like death, she said in a conversation to me on the subject, to think of beginning the year under such distressing circumstances. She has experienced much distress from the melancholy occurrence and is exceedingly desirous in the case of Thornton (That of Humphery being a hopeless one) will admit of any extension of mercy, that it may be obtained for him.

I well know the humanity of thy disposition would always incline thee as far as thy official duty deemed to allow to the side of this lovely and exalted attribute. But I have understood the courts have not recommended the case in this light to the executive department and that no petition has set on foot in favor of either of the criminals in any shape whatever. The probability I fear is that there will be none such before the term of life allotted them by their sentence has expired. Yet I would gladly hope if the case of Thornton be really as I suppose it is in relation to the murder it would be thought admissible by the executive to grant at least a respite from the infliction of the dreadful sentence till the ferment of mental excitement which a crime of this nature is peculiarly calculated to inspire shall have had a little time to subside and leave the public mind in a capacity to think, and set more dispassionately upon the case and propose, if it seem to be right, some commutation of the punishment.

At Elizabeth Garland's urgent request and in compliance with my own feeling I have ventured to offer this communication to thy attention. I shall rest satisfied that every relief in they powers to promote consistent with thy deliberate views of duty will receive thy ready aid towards its effectuation.

I hope I shall see thyself and thy family settled calmly at thy plantation e'er long. Sharing the sweets of private

life instead of the honors of a public one which I don't
doubt most of you admire quite as much.

I am with affectunate regard,

Thy friend and relation
Wm. H. Kearnts.[10]

In some instances the members of the courts that ordered the
execution of the slave often recommended the prisoner to the
governor as an object of mercy. In the case of the slave, Arch, the
justices declare that

> as members of the Court from the whole train of evi-
> dence we thought him guilty of the crime with which he
> stood charged, but as the law under which he stood
> condemned appeared to be a very harsh one and in-
> asmuch as it made that offense a capital one in a black
> man or a slave, which only inflicted a moderate corporal
> punishment on a free person, we could not help feeling
> considerable concern, that we were called upon to take
> part in the execution of a law which operated so un-
> equally and which is only to be justified by expedience.
> Since his conviction we have had opportunity of hearing
> the opinions of numerous persons, some of whom are
> well informed, and whose judgments merit respect, who
> think that this man might be pardoned and ought not to
> receive capital condemnation under the law.[11]

In another instance the court declared that the prisoner was
guilty according to the law but that he should be pardoned because the murderer had executed the command of a white man to
whom he was hired.[12]

[10] Executive Papers, March 20, 1824.

[11] Executive Papers, Sept. 12, 1797.

[12] "We take the liberty of imploring your Excellency in behalf of a
slave who is now under sentence of death in this jail. The reasons by
which we are induced to make this application to your Honourable
body are such as we think must have influence on every humane and
generous mind."

Many other letters are found in which the writer asks for mercy for a slave condemned to die for murder.[13]

The same humanitarian spirit that prompted men to acts of mercy toward the slave extended also to the free Negro. There are many instances in which free Negroes were stolen and forced into slavery. These victims of the slave system had their advocates. The case of a free girl carried into North Carolina and sold into slavery was reported to the governor of Virginia in 1792. In this instance a certain David Miller of Norfolk, Virginia, while on a journey to Charlestown, South Carolina, chanced to discover this girl. He addressed a letter concerning her to the mayor of Norfolk, stating that "the people who have the girl in their possession treat her in a most barbarous manner" and adding that "knowing your humanity and desire to do justice, makes me trouble you on this occasion." The mayor brought the case to the attention of the governor of the state, explaining that

> the enclosed letter will I hope sufficiently appologize for
> troubling your Excellency on such an occasion; your
> feelings I am certain must be hurt by the villainy of the
> persons who perpetrate the measure. I have done all

[13] Executive Papers, Oct. 25, 1799; Nov. 20, 1799; Sept. 19, 1801; March 13, 1802; Oct. 14, 1820; Jan. 28, 1823; Nov. 16, 1786:

"All the knowledge which the Court could ever obtain concerning his guilt and from which they were induced to pronounce sentence against him is derived solely from his own confession. At the same time the Court was so fully sensible of the hardships which the law seemed to lay them under in declaring him guilty that they unanimously recommended him to mercy. We beg leave further to observe, that before his examination by a Magistrate, he confessed the fact to his mistress and that it was by his discovery that the body of Muir was found. Without which it must always have remained uncertain whether or not the murder had been committed.

"His particular situation as a slave, at that time being in the service of a man so bloody minded and cruel as William Tanner, is known to be, must have left him no choice but the strictest obedience to any orders which were given him by his master, as his own immediate destruction must have followed his refusal. It does not appear that his being concerned in so atrocious and bloody a deed as murdering Muir, he did anything but what his master ordered him to do."

that lay in my power by sending the mother on to claim
the child but I had no acquaintance I could rely on near
the place she is, and considering it a matter of consequence conceived if you would be so good as to write a
letter to the Governor of North Carolina that he would
have justice done the poor Negro. . . . You will pardon
my freedom in writing you on this occasion but I felt so
much for the parent that I could not refrain.

> I am your Excell. Obt. Servt.
> Thomas Newton, Jr.[14]

The law of Virginia required that the state should pay to the
owners of slaves the value of all slaves executed by the state. In
certain cases letters to the governors indicate that the owners are
more anxious to have the state pay a high price for the slave than
they are interested in the execution of justice. While there are recorded complaints that the state failed to pay a just value for certain condemned slaves, it seems to be true that the state of Virginia was liberal in its efforts to protect the property rights of the
masters. Because of this liberality such statements as the following are recorded: "His master employed no attorney; and it is the
general opinion that he has much greater regard for the high
value set upon his negro than for his life.";[15] and "the obstinate
master is content with the valuation being eighty pounds . . .
fifty per cent more than his real worth";[16] and "that for some
time the said [master] has been offering the negro for sale without being able to procure a purchaser";[17] and again, "as to the
master I rather think him a pecuniary man and so no doubt he
will consider it a fortunate circumstance, the sentence of the law
upon his negro by which he gets an enormous price for his

[14] Executive Papers, August 28, 1792; Dec. 13, 1792. In the Appendix
to this work there is given a melodramatic recital of the adventures of
another free Negro who had been sold into slavery. The communication gives also a fine example of the gentle spirit of a Catholic defender
of the Negro.

[15] Executive Papers, Jan. 20, 1792.

[16] Executive Papers, Jan. 7, 1789.

[17] Executive Papers, Nov. 1, 1805.

blood.''[18] In 1832 citizens of Buckingham county petitioned the legislature to prohibit the policy by which the state paid masters the value of executed slaves. The petitioners declare that this policy encouraged masters to incite slaves to commit crime and also that certain masters put their own crimes on slaves.[19]

While many men are found who protested against the harshness of the slave code, other men are found who objected to cruelty of those entrusted with the administration of justice. The following communication gives an example of cruel treatment of a Negro prisoner. It is probable that such treatment was not the rule.

Petersburg, 8th Dec. 1789

Dear Sir:

I have your favor of the 29th Ulto. accompanying a letter to my care sent by Mr. E. Harrison, directed to the sheriff of Brunswick, for Robin's reprieve. I accordingly hired an express and sent up for fear of the letter's miscarrying. The man has returned and brought the sheriff's receipt and reports that it is impossible the poor fellow can survive until next month. I did not suspect it was a partial reprieve at the time I hired the man to carry it out. He says the man is ironed up against a wall standing, bear of clothes, exposed to the cold without a fire, in a melancholy situation, as well as in very great pain. There are holes bore through the legs and iron bolts through fastened outside with a key. From this information you may judge the situation he must be in. He is almost reduced to a skeleton from the cruel treatment he gets from the guard. Humanity has taken its flight, certainly from people of that county that are privy to the circumstances. Mr. Taylor is now here present says unless a reprieve can be immediately got the fellow had better be hanged at once as it will be easing him of a very tedious and lingering pain which is more terrible than death. He says the fellow has per-

[18] Executive Papers, Nov. 26, 1814.
[19] Executive Papers, Jan. 19, 1832.

fectly made his peace and he was constantly praying to
be hanged sooner than undergo the torture of his present
fate. Should the fellow be kept until the time of his
suspension and should not die within that time. Mr.
Taylor says he can not be worth within twenty pounds
of the price he was to give. The fellow must be inevitably frostbite should nothing else befall him. These
things considered there had better be something decisive
done. . . . Stegall, the man who took him up swears he
will put him to death on his being released. Being determined he shall lose his life.[20]

The study of slave crime and the administration of justice, in
spite of the testimony that has been given above, impresses the
student with the fact that the slaveholders were, in most cases,
sincere in their efforts to give full justice to the slave according to
the letter of the law. It appears that the slave under arrest received full measure of "due process of law" according to pre-Civil
War standards. This belief is attested by voluminous testimony
of witnesses at slave trials, both white and Negro. While in certain cases it is asserted that the verdict of the court submitted to
the governor, has been influenced by the intoxication of the justices and in others that the members of the court were "not on
speaking terms" because of local quarrels and so were influenced
against the defendant of the slave, and also, while local feuds
sometimes had their origin in decisions for or against the slave,
the student is led to believe that the Negro slave in Virginia may
have received, according to slave law and legal procedure, a more
full measure of "due process of law" than is possible in many of
the courts of certain states in the present day.[21]

It is also true that the executives of the state were apparently
disposed to listen to the appeals for mercy. A letter sent to the

[20] Executive Papers, Dec. 8, 1789; for additional protests against
cruelty on the part of local officials see Papers, Sept. 1, 1786; Jan. 7,
1780; July 25, 1824; Archives of Virginia, Legislative Papers, Petitions
1597c, 2882, 7560. Hereafter Archives of Virginia, Legislative Papers
will be omitted and the document identified by number, county, and
date (insomuch as this information is available).

[21] Executive Papers, Dec. 14, 1806; Dec. 18, 1823.

governor, March 23, 1823, mentions "the almost uniform interposition of the executive, on a recommendation to mercy by the court—an interposition that has nearly grown into a law, and a general understanding with the court, that such a recommendation will be effectual and on the faith of which only, they pronounce sentences of guilty."[22] By order of the executive, between January 25, 1801, and March 8, 1806, the state of Virginia sold to slave traders for transportation outside the limits of the United States fifty-seven slaves. For these Negroes the state received $15,268. Many of these slaves had been sentenced to death, but their sentences had been commuted because of the recommendation for mercy. The money value of these Negroes would have been lost to the state had they been executed and possibly the financial interest of the state may have operated for the benefit of the condemned slave, but the evidence seems to testify that the governing class in Virginia were sincere in their efforts to secure justice for the slave, in full accord with the law.

Nevertheless, while transportation may have been considered to have met the demands of mercy, it was harsh punishment and was so considered by the slave. One of his correspondents informs the governor that "transportation from this part of the country produces almost as strong an impression on the other slaves as hanging."[23]

So far, in this chapter, an effort has been made to describe the activities of those who defended the slaves. The humane sentiments of these men were characteristic of unknown numbers of fine Virginians, but it is not to be believed that all the owners of all the slaves on the plantations always protected or respected the legal rights of the slaves and that consequently the treatment of the slave was always kind and gentle. Like human beings everywhere, Virginia slaveholders were good and bad, gentle and passionate, just and unjust, sober and sometimes intoxicated. Luck or chance played an important part in the fortune of the slave. Instances of extreme cruelty are to be found, and sometimes slaves died from whippings at the hands of white men. It is to be expected that those who defended the slave in the courts would

[22] Executive Papers, March 23, 1823.
[23] Executive Papers, Sept. 20, 1811.

also prosecute the white men who murdered the slave. We shall
give two instances of the murder of the slave and shall examine
the evidence of sentiment adverse to such inhumanity.

Buckingham, July 5th, 1820

Sir:

Being the prosecutor for the Commonwealth in the
County of Charlotte, I deem it my duty to communicate
to you the circumstance of a most horrid murder which
has lately been perpetrated in that County; in order that
such steps may be taken by the Executive as may be
considered proper to secure the apprehension of the
offender. It appears that a negro man the property of
George Hamlet ran away on the morning of the 27th
of last month and returned home on the evening of the
same day about dark. Hamlet stripped him immediately
entirely naked, put his head between two fence rails, and
with switches and a paddle whipped and paddled him
from that time until about midnight occasionally pouring
on him hot water which immediately produced blisters;
after acting thus cruelly he took the negro from under
the fence and ordered him to get up, he made the attempt
but was not able to rise. Hamlet then with the same
paddle struck him several blows on the head which produced immediate death, after which he took the body
and removed it to a distant part of the plantation and
deposited it under a pile of rails with a view to burning
it. These facts I am told are proven by the overseer who
was prevented from affording the negro any assistance
or giving information of what was going on by Hamlet
who kept his gun constantly by him swearing that he
would shoot him if he moved. After the body was deposited under the pile of rails, the overseer finding an opportunity to get off gave information immediately to a
Magistrate who without delay took the necessary steps
to have Hamlet apprehended. He however made his
escape and is now gone at large.

I would have enclosed a copy of the inquest had I
considered it necessary. You have a description of Hamlet
below.

>Your most obt. svt.
>Samuel Branch.[24]

At an inquest held after the death of the slave Rachel, the jury
made the following report of its findings:

that one Isham W. Clements, late of the parish of St.
James Northam, in the said County of Goochland, not
having the fear of God before his eye, but being moved
and seduced by the instigation of the devil, did on the
13th of the present month (November) in the present
year 1828 did at sundry times both previous and subse-
quent to that time in and upon the aforesaid negro
woman slave, Rachel, then and there being in the peace
of God and of the said Commonwealth feloniously,
voluntarily, and of malice aforethought did assault—and
then and at divers times, with sticks, brush, and switches,
which the said Isham W. Clements then and there held
in his right hand the aforesaid negro woman Rachel, in
and upon the head of the said Rachel in various parts,
inflict the most cruel and severe wounds, also on the
back of the said slave woman, Rachel, were inflicted the
severest wounds, and in fact the said slave woman,
Rachel, was severely beaten, brused, and whipped from
the crown of her head to the soles of her feet, of which
beating, whipping and wounds the said woman Rachel
died on the morning of the 24th instant, November, a
little before the break of day, and so the said Isham
W. Clements there and then feloniously killed and murdered the said negro woman slave Rachel against the
peace and dignity of the Commonwealth.[25]

In the colonial period the murder of a slave by a master or overseer was punished as a capital crime and evidence shows that

[24] Executive Papers, July 5, 1820.
[25] Executive Papers, Dec. 8, 1828.

men were executed for such crimes.[26] Although certain citizens
protested "that the taking away of the life of this man will in all
probability stir up the negroes to contempt of their masters and
overseers, which may be attended with dangerous consequences
to this colony,"[27] the British governors appear as defenders of the
slave. Governor Spotswood writes that "in this dominion, no
master has such sovereign power over his slave as not to be liable
to be called to account whenever he kills him; that at the same
time, the slave is the master's property he is likewise the king's
subject."[28] That colonial juries were severe in their punishment
of such murders is shown in the following petition from the heirs
of a man condemned under colonial judicial procedure.

Southampton
Nov. 8, 1780

The petition of Ann, Thomas, Samuel, John, Sylvia, and
James Meacom declares:

That your petitioner Ann is the widow and relict of John
Meacom. Who at a court of Oyer and Terminer held at
the capital in the city of Williamsbur, in the month of
Dec. . . . was arrainged, tried, and convicted of the
murder of one of his slaves and soon after suffered a
fully ignominious death, that by such attainder and
conviction not only the blood of your petitioners becomes
corrupt and vitiated but the estate of the said John
Meacom is forfeited and hath by writ of inquisition
been taken into the hands of the Commonwealth, sold
and paid into the hands of the treasury, by which several
degrees of retributive justice your petitioners, some of
whom are very young and helpless, are exposed not

[26] Arthur P. Scott, "History of the Criminal Law in Virginia during
the Colonial Period," (unpublished Doctor's thesis, University of Chicago, 1916); St. George Tucker, *A Dissertation on Slavery, with a
Proposal for the Gradual Abolition of It in the State of Virginia* (New
York, 1796), pp. 50–51.

[27] Ibid., p. 142.

[28] R. A. Brock (ed.), *The Official Letters of Alexander Spotswood*
(Richmond, 1882), II, 202.

only to the obliquy and contempt of the unfeeling many
by reminding them of the ignomy of their unhappy
parent but left to contend with the horrors of the most
abject poverty and are likely to become a charge to their
few remaining friends or the parrish. From the known
justice and humanity of the honourable house your
petitioners are let to hope that the public suffering of
their unhappy parent will be sufficient sacrifice and
atonement to justice for the crimes and errors of his life
and that this house will not extend the punishment of
his already unhappy offspring by depriving them of the
means of subsistence as the total forfeiture and seizure
of all the property of their said father will most certainly
do, they being in every way innocent tho by the rigor of
the law involved in the punishment of their unfortunate
parent.[29]

After the Revolution there appears to have been a relaxation
of the severity of the law as it applied to white criminals. The
records show that before 1831 there had been twenty-one cases of
murder of slaves, but in no case is there evidence of the execution
of the criminal. When these crimes were committed they were declared to be unpremeditated and not malicious cases of murder.
In 1807 a man was sentenced to twelve years imprisonment. In
1808 another murderer was sentenced to five years imprisonment,
and in 1811 a woman was imprisoned for two years. The evidence in the cases here described is based on the proclamation of
the governor offering reward for murderers who had fled the
scene of their crimes and on petitions for pardon for men who
had been condemned to the state prison. Certain of these petitions seem to indicate a sentiment that tended to condone the
crime. A petition from citizens of Powhatan and Cumberland
counties declares concerning

their friend and countryman, Mathew Farley, that your
petitioners have been intimately acquainted with him for
many years, during which time he has acted in the different capacities of clerk of the church, singing master,

[29] Petition 544, Southampton, Nov. 9, 1780.

constable, and patroler. In each of which employments he has acquited himself with credit, to the general satisfaction of the public, and particularly to the neighborhood in which he lived. That he has always conducted himself as a good citizen and kind neighbor. His rich neighbors in particular have often experienced the effects of his benevolent disposition and so far from intending to take away the life of the slave (on whose account he now stands condemned) your petitioners are well assured he had not the least idea of it, but rather meant to give him a smart correction, as the slave had often discovered a stubborn, refractory, and ungovernable disposition.[30]

Another letter sent to the governor in 1814 indicates that the murderer of the slave sometimes went unpunished. This correspondent declared: "I am truly grieved as I contemplate the marked difference between the privileges of a slave and those that are free men . . . murder is surely of the first order of crimes, yet, I know two men who have escaped the punishment they deserved, one was condemned to the penitentiary for five years, and even a part of that time the eloquence of his counsel contrived to lessen the term of, while the other (who murdered a negro) was acquitted of the murder and the court of Caroline awarded to the owner of the negro (as the negro was hired to the man who beat him to death) one hundred pounds."[31]

It would seem to be probable that the twenty-one cases here disclosed by means of petitions and proclamations offering reward for runaway murderers may not include other instances of slave murder that were tried and settled in the county courts and which never came into the correspondence of the governor of the state. It is also true that if there were men that murdered slaves by whipping there must have been other men of like tempers, forgetful of the value of their property who whipped Negroes "nigh to death" but since the slave managed to live the law could not take action.

However, all the masters were not cruel to their slaves and in

[30] Executive Papers, Jan. 17, 1789.
[31] Executive Papers, Nov. 23, 1814.

every county and town there were those of humane sentiment. A
letter written in 1792 declares that

> the people are all stirred up over old John Bagwell
> whipping the negro wench nearly to death. Such a hard
> hearted rascal oughtn't be allowed to have black people.
> Mr. Wyatt told me the poor things back was all cut up
> like a piece of raw meat.[32]

In some communities men were imprisoned for the murder of
slaves, and the governor's proclamations offering reward for absconded white murderers make it evident that in these instances
both law and public opinion condemned the offender. The record of the state of Virginia might, without doubt, be duplicated
in all the slaveholding States; also, similar crimes against slaves
might be found to have been committed in northern states in the
period when slavery was sanctioned there. Anglo-Americans were
of like characteristics in whatever state they were located. Both
humane and cruel men might be found in any of the American
states. In all states humanitarians rebelled against cruelty in
whatever environment the unfortunate suffered cruelty. Fortunately certain states had freed themselves from a labor system
that made possible many inhumanities. However, men might
seek to protect the slave, but while there was slavery there could
be no security for the Negro. The records of the slave period
make evident the disaster for the slave that often followed the financial misfortune or the death of the master. A change of masters might mean for the slave other hardships than separation
from wife and children. Hardships were always possible as long
as all slave owners were not good and fortunate men.

Everywhere antislavery increased because men were humane.
Men had to defend mistreated slaves. They could not defend the
injured slave and fail to know that slavery itself was wrong. In
Virginia the antislavery movement developed among such men as
we have found protecting and defending the slaves. The work of
these men was not always a struggle against evil or cruel masters,
but it was rather a struggle against political and economic forces

[32] *Virginia Magazine of History and Biography,* XII (1904), 437.

that made many men forget humanity and justice since by exploiting black men there came into their possession profits, position, and many earthly rewards.

The following quotation is taken from a letter written in defense of a slave, by a writer who speaks in the language of the abolitionist:

> Why is it, sir, that the life of one man must be sacrificed for the commission of a crime, which if committed by another, but of a different color, will call only for confinement? Are not the lives of all men of whatever color, or condition, equally precious? The same image was originally stamped upon *all* men by the Great Creator. And God made man in his own likeness after his own image. And from whence, it might be asked, derived legislative authority to destroy that image unless it be for the commission of such crimes as the word of God declares to be worthy of death. It was only among the heathen that the life of a slave was thought less sacred than a free man, and has only obtained among Christians where they have degenerated from the precepts of the Gospel and fallen into the dark systems of heathen morals.[33]

The state of Virginia had its share of humanitarians, and among their number were as sincere and ardent abolitionists as might be found at any time or place in the United States.

[33] Executive Papers, Oct. 12, 1813.

FIVE

The Growth of Antislavery

M ANY FACTORS combined to cause the growth of anti-slavery in Virginia. Among these causes a very prominent place must be given to the work of certain distinguished men. Thomas Jefferson would be placed foremost among such men. In early life Jefferson decided that slavery was wrong and that the final abolition of the system was necessary. Possibly the chief significance of Jefferson, for this study, is that he devised a plan for the gradual abolition of slavery, and the essential features of this plan were to be advocated by other Virginians who hoped to show that abolition was practical.[1] Jefferson's plan was devised in 1778 at a time when he, with others, was employed in the revision of the laws of Virginia. At this time he exerted every effort to modify the law of slavery—to humanize the law just as at that time the laws which controlled free men were being modified and made more humane. Following the work of Jefferson came the efforts of St. George Tucker, at that time a professor at the College of William and Mary. He published a series of lectures in which he denounced the severity of the slave code, advocated the emancipation of the slave, and described what he believed to be a practical plan for emancipation of all the slaves of the State.[2] In turn, James Madison professed opinions similar to those of the above men and he, too, advocated a

[1] Thomas Jefferson, *Notes on the State of Virginia* (Trenton, 1803), pp. 252–57.

[2] St. George Tucker, *A Dissertation on Slavery, with a Proposal for the Gradual Abolition of It in the State of Virginia* (New York, 1796).

plan for the emancipation of the slaves.[3] The list of great men who advocated the final emancipation of the slaves can be extended at great length, and the value of the service of these men to the antislavery cause can not be overestimated.[4]

It also is true that the slave profited because of the propagation of the doctrine of the rights of man; thus, the spread of revolutionary philosophy must be considered as an important cause of the growth of the antislavery movement. In the period of the Revolution Castellux reported that "the planters of the South seem afflicted to have slavery and are constantly talking about abolishing it."[5] Travelers in this period are impressed with the fact that the South had developed a mild and humane system of servitude.[6] Many deeds of emancipation recorded between 1770 and 1810 state the conviction of the emancipator that all men are created equal.

Another force for the emancipation of the slave was the work of the Quaker sect and the early Methodist, Baptist, and Presbyterian churches. In these churches a fiery gospel of equality and freedom was preached. This gospel included the idea of freedom for the black man. Vast numbers of men were added to the antislavery cause from the membership of these churches.[7] In the testimony of the slaves taken on the occasion of Gabriel's insurrection it will be remembered that the Quakers, Methodists, and Frenchmen were to be exempted from slaughter "on account as

[3] Gaillard Hunt (ed.), *Letters and Other Writings of James Madison* (New York, 1900), III, 75–103.

[4] Beverly B. Munford, *Virginia's Attitude toward Slavery and Secession* (New York, 1909).

[5] Francois Jean Castellux, *Travels in North America in the Years 1780, 1781, and 1782* (London, 1787), II, 195; "The Diary of Langdon Carter," *William and Mary Quarterly*, XX (January, 1912), 182.

[6] Duc de la Rochefoucauld, *Travels through the United States of North America* (London, 1799), II, 43; Abbe Robin, *New Travels through North America in a Series of Letters* (Boston, 1784), p. 220; "Travellers' Impressions of Slavery in America, from 1750 to 1800," *Journal of Negro History*, I (October, 1916), 442–46.

[7] Luther P. Jackson, "Religious Development of the Negro in Virginia from 1760 to 1860," *Journal of Negro History*, XVI (April, 1931), 168–239.

they [the slaves] believed of their being friendly to liberty." The case of James Allen, a Methodist, appears to offer the example of a white man who gave his life to make possible the escape of a slave. In this instance Holloway's Charles, with the aid of Allen, made his escape from his master. Allen was taken into the woods to be whipped until he revealed the location of the missing Negro. He refused to speak and the testimony sent to the governor reveals the harrowing details of his torture and death.[8] The following letter is descriptive of conditions that are not usually thought to have existed in rural Virginia, but the letter shows the influence of the Methodist church on slavery.

King William County, Sept. 5, 1789

Sir:

According to the law I have appointed Paterrolers to
Kech our Negroes in order & to serch all Disorderly
houses after night & unlawful Meetings & where they find
a large quantity of Negroes assembled at night to take
them up and cary them before a justice which has been
done but we have a set of disorderly People who call
themselves Methodists and are joined by some of those
who call themselves Baptists, who make it a rule two or
three times a week to meet after dark & call in all the
Negroes they can gather & a few whites & free mulattoes
who pretend under the cloak of Religion to meet at a
School house where no one lives & there they pretent
to preach & pray with a sett of the greatest Roges of
Negroes in this County & they never break up Till about
two or three o'clock in the morning & those Negroes who
stays with them goes through the neighborhood and
steels everything they can lay there hands on & our
Negroes are not to be found when we are in want of
them, but are at such meetings & I have ordered the
Peterrolers to go to such unlawfull meetings & to take
up all the Negroes that they should find at such places

---

[8] Executive Papers, Archives of Virginia, Letters Received, Feb. 17, 1802. Hereafter Archives of Virginia, Letters Received, will be omitted and the document identified by the date.

which they have done & the masters of the Negroes has
approved of this plan very much, but these people who
are determined to encorige or Negroes to wrong & the
other day they sent to the Capt. of the Paterrolers that on
Friday night they wood have a Meeting & if they came
there & offered to toch a Negro That they wood protect
the Negroes & if they said a word would beat them, upon
this the Capt. of Paterrolers came & asked me what they
was to do. I told them to go for I am shore that no person
of credit that wood be there & therefore that they ought
to go by all means as they had sent them a Challenge
for it it was overlooked our Negroes wood next under the
same pretence disobey the orders of there Masters under
the pretence of Religion, but however the Paterrolers
went and one Mr. Charles Neale who's mother is the
head of the Crim Come down & at night the Paterrolers
went & discovered as usual a large Company of Negroes
& they went into the House & Mr. Charles Neale
through one of them out of the doore & said that they
should not take up one Negroe that was there, upon
which the Paterrolers finding themselves over Powered
was obliged to leave the place & went home & afraid to
act and will not without some protection. Now I shall
be much obliged to your Excellency & your Honorable
Board that you will inform me how I am to act on those
occasions. I hope your Excellency will order me to treat
Mr. Charles Neale & his party as they deserve for if there
is nothing done with those people we shall not have a
Negroe to Command & I am afraid that with a little
encorigement they themselves will drive away the Paterrolers & there will be an end to all such Power & as to
the Orders of the County think it will be at an end & we
shall have no Paterrolers if they are not protected for
these persons will be in danger therefore will refuse to
act in futur.

> I am Sir Yr Excellency
> Most obedient & Very
> Hbl. svt.
> Holt Richardson.[9]

[9] Executive Papers, Sept. 5, 1789.

Again, under date of June 5, 1792, Holt Richardson writes to the governor of the commonwealth reciting his difficulties with Negroes, Methodists, and "Paterrolers."[10]

Still another cause for the spread of antislavery sentiment in Virginia is to be found in the sectional differences which divided the people of eastern and western Virginia. Until 1830 the West was a section in which there were few slaves. The inhabitants of this region were descendants of liberty-loving pioneers who hated slavery. But the slaveholders controlled the government of the state and always were able to defeat the special interests of the people of the West. The resulting hatred of the slaveholders of the East served to make the West a powerful force for antislavery.[11] The testimony given in the accompanying note seems to indicate that the discontent existing among the people of the West might endanger the safety of the slaveowners.[12]

[10] Executive Papers, June, 1792.

[11] Charles H. Ambler, *Sectionalism in Virginia from 1776 to 1861* (Chicago, 1910); James C. McGregor, *The Disruption of Virginia* (New York, 1922).

[12] Executive Papers, April 2, 1813: "Being requested by Colo. Woods to relate the conversation which took place last May between Mr. Bane, Mr. Watkins, and Mr. Richardson respecting the right of suffrage, etc., Mr. Bane said that the population of the state would be much greater if the right of suffrage was extended to a greater length than it is, that it prevented some of the most useful citizens in this state, such as mechanics, and artists of every description whom he thought ought to be most encouraged of any other class of people, but they would not stay in this state being deprived of the privilege of voting for their representatives, etc. Although it did not injure them materially but the thought was degrading and they enjoyed this privilege. Mr. Watkins agreed with Mr. Bane and said that he believed it was himself that prevailed on Mr. Richardson to stay in this place, that he being accustomed to that privilege in other states and deprived of it here he was determined to move over to the state of Ohio. Mr. Bane went on to mention such characters as he thought was not entitled to vote, but such men as he, alluding to Mr. Richardson, was as well entitled to vote as him or any other man in the union, no matter how much land they possessed. But the memorial alluded to he knew would be suppressed by the members from the Eastern part of the State as was many others of the same kind, that they had the superiority over the members of this side of the mountains and it was their policy always to suppress such

Whereas we might expect to find radical abolitionists in the western portions of the state, it is not usually thought that white aids and instigators of Negro insurrections were to be found in the counties of the East. However, in 1816 in the county of Spotsylvania in a plot for a Negro uprising in which twenty Negroes were immediately placed in the county jail, it was discovered that the leader of the Negroes was a white man. The facts concerning this case are reported as follows:

> The slaves in this part of the county had been invited to the house of _____, a man generally thought to be in desperate circumstances; and under pretence of purchasing whiskey and some other articles of merchandise from him, they were to consult with him about the means of obtaining their freedom by force of arms on a day in June or July next to be by him appointed. They were to collect in great numbers on horse back at some place near his home, armed with scythes or any other weapons they could lay hands on; as soon as possible they were to proceed to Fredericksburg and take that place; from Fredericksburg they were to hasten with increased numbers to the city of Richmond; and with all imaginable expedition they were to seize the magazine, (by which we suppose they meant the armory) . All who were opposed to them were to be slain and as soon as they could supply them with arms, they were to drive the white people from the country and take possession of it themselves. They understood that there was a white man in Fredricksburg and another in Richmond whose names they

---

things, and at the same time these very men was afraid to lie down lest their throats would be cut or their houses burned before morning by their Negroes. Mr. Richardson, something warmly, observed that if any foreign enemy was to invade the United States that he would not suffer himself to be drafted but would volunteer his services if it was tomorrow at the hazard of all he possessed, but if the Negroes was to rise in an insurrection and destroy their masters, he would not turn out and risk his life for any set of men that would deprive him of his just right that he believed was granted to him by the constitution of the United States."

know not, chiefs in the conspiracy, who were to act the
same parts in those places, which was to act here.[13]

A description of the white conspirator is given in the note
below.[14]

Unfortunately little is known of the social attitudes of poor

[13] Executive Papers, Feb. 25, 1816.

[14] Executive Papers, March 1, 1816; March 10, 1816: "George Boxley,
the chief of the conspiracy in this neighborhood, is naturally a man of
restless and aspiring mind; wild and visionary in his theories, and
ardent in pursuit of his designs. At an early period of his life, without
any necessary qualifications, and with no great respectability of character, he offered his services to represent the County in the Legislature of
the State; but was prevailed on to resign his pretensions to that office in
favor of General Minor. During the late war with Great Britain, he
served as an ensign in the militia, and went on a tour of duty at
Norfolk; where he was considered a good drill officer. Whilst he was in
the service there, he solicited the appointment of adjutant to the
regiment, but was foiled by a more successful candidate. From that
period he became dissatisfied with the existing order of things; and
after his return, on many occasions expressed his disapprobation of
them. Subsequently to this transaction, and while the militia of this
county were in service near Fredericksburg, he acted for a short time as
adjutant under Major Crutchfield, but was displaced by that officer and
the post given to one, without doubt, deemed by him more respectable.
These repeated disappointments seemed to have embittered his mind.
On many occasions he has declared that the distinctions between the
rich and the poor were too great; that offices were given rather to
wealth than to merit; and seemed to advocate for a leveling system of
government. For many years he had avowed his disapprobation of the
slavery of the negroes, and wished that they were free.

"During the latter end of last summer or early in the beginning of
the fall, according to the testimony of the negroes, he began the
conspiracy. To facilitate the means of carrying it out he kept a shop for
selling whiskey, and some articles of merchandise. Under the pretense
of purchasing these, great numbers of negroes were received at this
house; and the horrible plot which has been detailed in our first
communication was formed; the detection of which we will now more
particularly relate."

The governor offered a reward of one thousand dollars for the
capture of Boxley but it appears he made his escape.

white men in this period, but there is evidence that among this class were to be found those whose hatred of the upper classes made them allies and aids to the Negro conspirators. The following incident is related by way of example: In July, 1821, a white country woman who came to Richmond to sell market produce made affidavit before the police of the city that

> she with her son who is nearly grown went to the market house in Richmond and there stayed in their coverd cart until morning. During the night an elderly white man with red whiskers and of ordinary stature who speaks a little broken, who she understands was a gardener in or about Richmond, at all events he had at market vegetables to sell and an old and very black Negro man who walked lame and seemed to be affected in the left hip, who also had vegetables to sell, one article of which she remembers was early cabbage, that this man and the Negro set up all night talking together generally in a whisper and at some times in a very low tone. She heard distinctly the white man say to the Negro, that they were all of Adam's race, or words to that import, and that you ought to be free. . . . That they might when they got a plenty of money seat themselves in the middle of Richmond and drink wine too. He said to the Negro—how many have you? The Negro answered that he had twenty on his list. The Negro also said to the white man, when you hear my horn blow something will be done. Between these remarks of the Negro and the white man they kept up a constant whispering which she could not hear. Late in the night after the foregoing conversation which she heard between these two, the white man said to the Negro—Go round and know what they say. Alluding to two other Negroes, that came with the aforesaid Negro who was a little distance from them. The Negro accordingly got up and went around to the cart where they were. He returned in a short time and commenced whispering again, but she could hear nothing more that they said.[15]

[15] Executive Papers, July 16, 1821.

In 1802 the mayor of Norfolk reported to the governor that he had found incendiary communications being carried by an Irishman to the city of Petersburg. These papers are said to have been used as "stoppers to a jug belonging to the Irishman."[16]

In the exciting days of the Nat Turner insurrection, among other interesting communications found and sent to the governor is a letter which seems to testify by its content and the often illegible hand of the author that the writer was one of the poor white allies of the Negro. The following is a copy of this illiterate effort:

Addressed to
Ben Lee, in great haste
mail speedily
Richmond, swift.

Chesterfield County
August 29, 1831

My old fellow
Ben—
    you will tell or acquaint every servant in richmond &
adjoining countys they all must be in a strict rediness—
that this occurence will go through Virginia with the
slaves & whites—if there had never been an association—
a visiting with free and slaves this would never had of
been. They are put up by the free about there liberation.
Ive wrote to norfolk, amelia, nottoway & sevel other
countys to different slaves bob & bill Miller bowler john
fergerson—& several other free fellows been at Mr.
Crumps—a great many gentlemens servants how they
must act in getting their liberation—they must set fire to
the city being at Shokoe hill then going through east
west north south set fire to the bridges. they are about to
break out in goochland & Mecklenburg & several countys
very shortly. now there is a barber here is this place—
tells that a methodist of edmonds has put a great many
servants up how they should do & act by setting fire to

[16] Executive Papers, May 14, 1802.

this town. I do wish they may succeed by so doing we
poor whites can get work as well as slaves or collored.
This fellow edmonds the methodist says that judge J. F.
is no friend to the free & your richmond free associates
that your mister Watkins Lee brokenberry Johnson
Taylor of Norlfol & several other noble delegates is bitterly against them all—servants says that billy hickman
has just put him up how he is to do to revenge the whites
—edmonds says so you all ought to get revenge—every
white in this place is sceared to death except myself & a
few others this methodist has put up a good many slaves
in this place how to do and i can tell you—so push on
boys push on.

> your friend
> Williamson Mann.[17]

In the files of Governor Monroe are to be found papers that involve men of a higher order in slave insurrections. The justices of
the peace of Nottoway county declare that

James Hall Munford who is one of the acting Justices of
peace for the county of Nottoway has been strongly
suspected of instigating the late insurrection of the slaves
of this County. For the want of sufficient testimony to
prove the fact it had been deemed unnecessary to prosecute him. . . . Your petitioners are convinced that the
facts are true from the testimony of two witnesses of
respectability and good character.[18]

Governor Monroe transmitted this intelligence to the members
of the General Assembly.[19]
In Lunenburg County a physician was accused of being an in-
stigator of an insurrection. This man is said to have

[17] Governor John Floyd, "Slaves and Free Negroes" (a scrapbook
collection of papers pertaining to the Nat Turner insurrection, the
Archives of Virginia).
[18] Executive Papers, Jan. 15, 1802.
[19] Executive Papers, Jan. 25, 1802.

been seen in company with several Negroes in a Negro quarter at a late hour of the night reading a paper to them. He told them that they were entitled to their freedom and he would be their head man, aid and assist them in obtaining it. He was seen a few days afterward and asked if he had said what was mentioned above. He answered that he did. When written to the next day on the same subject, the Doctor wrote for answer that his sentiments were the same.[20]

The results of the work of the antislavery agitators are difficult to estimate. It is not probable that many men in the large slave-holding counties held radical views on this subject. Most antislavery men believed that abolition should be accomplished by gradual and peaceful means. Possibly a measure of antislavery sentiment is to be found in the large number of those men who emancipated their slaves, but such a measure would take no account of men like Jefferson, who are known to have hated the institution of slavery but would not set their own slaves free. Again, the remarkable growth of the colonization society may be taken as indicative of the extent of antislavery opinion, but there is the common belief that many members supported this organization in the hope that it would eventually free the state of dangerous free Negroes. Moreover, the existence of antislavery newspapers at Richmond, Lexington, Staunton, and Wheeling may be regarded as proof of the extensive patronage of antislavery readers of these papers, but all such evidence would be inconclusive.

It is my opinion that a measure of the strength of the antislavery movement and of the sentiment for and against slavery is to be found in the efforts of the antislavery workers to accomplish their aims by legislative action.

Repeated petitions were sent to the state legislature, signed by a multitude of citizens, asking for the abolition of slavery. These petitions seem to reflect the teachings of Jefferson and Tucker, the philosophy of the Revolution, and the precepts of the revivalistic churches. In these documents it will be seen that the motives prompting the petitioners are the familiar principles, at a later

[20] Executive Papers, Feb. 5, 1802.

date, characteristic of the northern abolitionists. The words in which they are written might have been the language of William Lloyd Garrison. The following document is an example of such petitions:

To the Honourable Legislature of the State of Virginia. The petition of the undersigned electors of the said state, Humbly sheweth that your petitioners are clerly and fully persuaded that liberty is the birthright of all mankind, the right of every rational creature without exception who has not forfeited that right to the laws of his country, that the body of negroes in this state have been robbed of that right without any such forfeiture, and therefore ought in justice to have that right restored. That the glorious and ever memorable revolution can be justified on no other principle but what doth plead with greater force for the emancipation of our slaves in proportion as the oppression exercised over them exceeds the oppression formerly exercised by Great Britain over these states. That the argument "that they were prisoners of war when they were originally purchased" is utterly invalid for no right of conquest can justly subject any man to perpetual slavery much less his posterity. That the riches and strength of any country consists in the number of its inhabitants who are interested in the support of its government and therefore to bind the vast body of negroes to the state by the powerful ties of interest will be the highest policy. That the argument drawn from the difference of hair, features, and colour is so beneath the man of sense, much more the Christian, that we would not insult the Honourable Assembly by enlarging upon them. The fear of enormities which the negroes may commit will be groundless at least if the emancipation be gradual as the activities of the magistrates and the provisions of the house of correction where occasion may require will easily suppress the gross, flagrant idleness either of whites or blacks. But above all the deep debasement of spirit which is the necessary consequence of slavery incapacitates the

human mind (except in a few instances; from the reception of the noble and more enlarged principles of the
Gospel. And therefore, to encourage or to allow it we
apprehend to be most opposite to that catholic spirit of
Christianity which desires the establishment of the kingdom of Christ over all the world and produces in the
conduct every action consonant thereto. That of consequence, justice, mercy, and in truth every virtue that
adorns man or mankind do unanswerably plead for the
removal of this grand abomination, and therefore, that
we humbly entreat the Honourable, the Assembly as
their superior wisdom may dictate to pursue the most
prudential but effectual method for the immediate or
gradual extirpation of slavery and your petitioners as in
duty bound will ever pray.[21]

In 1795, two petitions, this time signed by four hundred and
twenty-two "inhabitants of various parts of the state" and by one
hundred and fifteen citizens, whose locality is unknown, ask
again that the State abolish slavery. The first of these petitions
reads as follows:

To the Speaker and House of Delegates in Virginia.
The petition of sundry inhabitants of various parts of
the state, respectfully sheweth,
That your petitioners from a full conviction that
slavery is not only a moral but a political evil, which in
all its forms, in all its degrees, is an outrageous violation
and an odious degradation of human nature, tending to
weaken the bonds of society, discourage trades and
manufactures, endanger the peace, and obstruct the
prosperity of the country. And commiserating the unhappy situation of a large part of our population within
the state, who by the laws now in force are held as personal property and they and their innocent offspring

---

[21] Archives of Virginia, Legislative Papers, Petition, Frederick and
Hampshire, 1786. Hereafter Archives of Virginia, Legislative Papers
will be omitted and the document identified by number, county, and
date (insomuch as this information is available).

liable to be kept in perpetual bondage and ignorance subject to the arbitrary will of those who hold them, as well as in respect to inhuman treatment, as an unnatural separation from the most near and dear connections in life, without appeal, and without redress. They therefore conceive themselves in duty bound to remind this house as the proper guardian of every description of men within the state of a subject so interesting, and which appears to them in a particular manner to call the attention and require the interposition of the legislature.

Your petitioners regret that several states in the American union where those inalienable rights of human nature to life, liberty, and the pursuit of happiness have been so clearly defined and successfully asserted should in contradiction thereto, and contrary to the divine command of "doing to others, as they would they should do unto them" suffer under sanction of law, so large a number of their fellowmen to remain in a state of abject slavery at a time too, when the living spirit of liberty seems to be diffusing itself through the world.

Your petitioners are aware of the objections that probably would arise to a general and universal emancipation, as well from interested motives, as the unfitness of individuals for freedom; they are not insensible that a people long destitute of the means of mental improvement, may in some instances, be sunk below the common standard of human nature and accustomed to move at the command of the master, or overseer reflection may in some degree be suspended, and reason and conviction have little influence on their conduct; They are also sensible of the effect of custom and prejudice arising from a habit of looking upon the African race as an inferior species of mankind and regarding them only as property. Believing, nevertheless, that "God is no respector of persons," "that he hath made of one blood all nations of men for to dwell on the face of the earth" and that "his mercies are over all his works," encouraged also by the gracious message of our Saviour as an excitement

of acts of humanity, and benevolence, viz: "Verily I say
unto you, inasmuch as ye have done unto one of the
least of these my children, ye have done it unto me."
Your petitioners therefore in discharge of the duty they
owe to the merciful Father of all the families of the
earth, with compassion for the sufferers, and a desire to
promote the true interest and prosperity of the country;
And also to remove as much as may the objections which
may come from motives of present interest or the unfitness of individuals for freedom, and at the same time
abolish an evil of great magnitude, they humbly propose
and pray that a law may be passed declaring the children
of slaves now born or to be born after the passing of such
act to be free as they come of proper ages to enjoy their
instruction to read, etc., and to invest them with suitable
privileges as an incitement to become useful citizens, and
also to restrain the holders from inhuman treatment of
those who may remain in bondage. Or that the House
may grant such other relief, as in its wisdom may seem
meet.

And your petitioner as in duty will ever pray.[22]

The second of these petitions is given in the note below.[23]

[22] Petition 3371-d, Nov. 16, 1795.

[23] Petition 3371-e, Nov. 16, 1795: "To the Honourable the General
Assembly of the State of Virginia,

"The petition of the underwritten electors of the said state of Virginia, humbly sheweth,

"That your petitioners are fully and clearly persuaded that liberty is
the birthright of mankind, the right of every rational creature without
exception, who has not forfeited that right to the laws of his country.
That the body of Negroes in this state have been robbed of that right
without any such forfeiture and therefore ought in justice to have that
right restored.

"That the glorious and ever memorable revolution can be justified on
no other grounds, but what do plead with still greater force for the
emancipation of our slaves, in proportion as the oppression exercised
over them exceeds the oppression formerly exercised over these states,
by Great Britain.

"That the objection 'we treat them well' is not of sufficient force, as

While the antislavery petitioners failed to secure the objects of their memorials and thus do not appear to have won the support of the majority of the lawmakers, they and their fellow agitators and sympathizers had won so large a following that they were not to be ignored. Accordingly, a petition is found to have been sent to the legislature, this time signed by one hundred and sixty-four citizens who felt it necessary to defend the slave system. This defense of slavery may be interpreted as evidence that the number of the antislavery people had grown so large as to endanger the holding of slave property. This petition of proslavery Virginians reads as follows:

To the Honourable the General Assembly of the state of Virginia
The remonstrance and petition of the free inhabitants of the County of Pittsylvania.
Gentlemen:
When the British parliament usurped a right to dispose of our property without our consent, we dissolved the union with our parent state, and established a constitution and form of government of our own, that our property might be secure in future; in order to effect this we risked our lives and fortunes, and waded through seas of blood. Divine providence smiled on our enterprise, and crowned it with success, and our rights to liberty and property are as well secured to us as they can be by any human constitution or form of government.
But not withstanding this, we understand an attempt

---

the kindest treatment of them, can be no equivalent for the loss of liberty.

"That the argument 'they were (several of them) prisoners of war when originally purchased' is utterly invalid, for no right of conquest can justly subject any man to perpetual slavery, much less his posterity.

"That the riches, the strength of any country consist in the number of its inhabitants who are interested in the support of its government and therefore to bind that vast body of Negroes to the state by the powerful ties of interest will be the safest policy."

is made by the enemies of our country, tools of the
British administration, and supported by certain deluded men among us to wrest from us our slaves by an
act of legislature for a general emancipation of them,
they have the address indeed to cover their design with
the veil of piety and liberality of sentiment. But it is
unsupported by the word of God, and productive of ruin
to the state.

It is unsupported by sacred scriptures under the old
testament dispensation, slavery was permitted by the
Deity himself. For this is recorded, Leviticus Chapt. 25,
Verses 44, 45 "Both they, bond men and bond maids,
which thou shalt have, shall be the heathen that are
round about you, of them shall ye buy bond men and
bond maids—Moreover, of the children of strangers,
that do sojourn among you, of them shall ye buy, and
their families that are with you which they shall beget
in your land, and they shall be your possessions and ye
shall take them as an inheritance for your children
after you, to inherit them for a possession, they shall be
your bond men forever." This permission to possess and
inherit bond men we have reason to believe was continued through the revolution of the Jewish government
down to the advent of our Lord and we do not find that
either He or his discipline abridged it. The freedom
which the followers of Jesus were taught to expect, was
a freedom from the bondage of sin and satan and from
the dominion of the lusts and passions. But as to *outward
condition* whatever that was before they embraced Christianity, whether bond or free it remained the same
afterwards. This St. Paul hath expressly told us, 1st
Cor. Chapt. 7, verse 20; where he is speaking directly to
this point, "Let every man wherein he is called therein
abide with God." Thus it is evident that the said design
is unsupported by Divine work.

It is also ruinous to the state. For it involves in it, and
is productive of want, poverty, distress, and ruin to the
free citizens. Neglect, famine, and death to the helpless

black infant and superanuated parent. The horrors and outrages of all the rapes, murders, robberies, and outrages which a vast multitude of unprincipled, unpropertiated, vindictive, and remorseless banditti are capable of perpetrating—inevitable bankruptcy to the revenues and consequently breach of public faith and loss of credit with foreign nations; and lastly sure and final ruin to this now free and flourishing country.

We therefore your remonstrants and petitioners do solemnly adjure and humbly pray that you will discuntenance and utterly reject every motion and proposal for emancipating our slaves; that as the act lately made empowering the owners of slaves to liberate them has been, and is still, in part productive of many of the above pernicious effects you will immediately and totally repeal it—and that as many of the slaves liberated by the said act have been guilty of thefts and outrage, insolence, and violence, distructive to the peace, safety, and happiness of society; you will make effectual provision for the government of them in the future.

And your remonstrants and petitioners will ever pray, etc. etc.[24]

A similar proslavery petition was sent to the legislature in 1800.[25] The Archives of Virginia contain many petitions of a similar character, and reference will be made to such documents as they appear in the period after 1830.

Factors outlined above caused the antislavery movement to prosper in Virginia; however, the study of this subject has caused me to doubt that these factors were the most significant motives that caused men to oppose the system of slavery. Among a people so many of whom were humane and generous this cause would be expected to prosper, but the subject matter presented in the first section of this work leads the student to believe that the Negro slaves, themselves, caused the antislavery movement to grow in this and other slave States. Such men as Benjamin Lundy, Levi

[24] Petition 1359, Pittsylvania, Nov. 10, 1785.
[25] Petition 5133, King and Queen, Dec. 2, 1800.

Coffin, and James Birney testify that they became abolitionists because of their personal contact with the slaves.[26] The slaves were the first and most effective abolitionists. Before 1860 more than fifty thousand Negroes had been emancipated in Virginia.[27] These men had been liberated by masters, by nature humane, because the slaves had proved their right to freedom. By faithful service in sickness and in health, by honesty and industry, and by demonstrated skill as farmers, carpenters, or blacksmiths they had become far more effective abolitionists than Jefferson, Lundy, or Garrison. The lives of these Negroes made converts to the cause of antislavery and taught many other men, who knew that slavery was wrong, that the Negro should be free. It was not always the inhumanity of the slave system that made for abolition; often it was the humanity of the slave that brought his freedom.

It is very significant that many acts of emancipation were accomplished by the will of the dead master. Freedom was largely a matter of personal relation between the master and the slave. Repeated acts of masters, faced by the perils of death, seem to indicate that the master remembered what that special slave had done and that the master could face his Maker with more confidence if he finally had done a gracious act that he, through the prosperous years of his life, had known was right and proper. The experience of Izard Bacon furnishes an example of the human faltering of the master and of the part played by the slave in his own emancipation.

Testimony Relative to the Will of Izard Bacon
It having been understood that Izard Bacon, (in his lifetime) and myself had conferred together on the subject of his liberating his slaves, and as I am (now) requested to state the purport thereof—
As well as I (now) recollect, it was about the year 1807

[26] William Birney, *James G. Birney and His Times* (New York, 1890), p. 103; Levi Coffin, *Reminiscences of Levi Coffin* (Cincinnati, 1880), p. 12; *Benjamin Lundy, The Life, Travels, and Opinions of Benjamin Lundy* (Philadelphia, 1847), p. 15.

[27] James C. Ballagh, *A History of Slavery in Virginia* (Baltimore, 1902), p. 144.

or 1808 that I received a verbal, or written communication from Izard Bacon, but am inclined to believe that it was the latter (and by his own servant) wishing to advise with me on the subject of liberating his slaves.

As soon as I could make it convenient, I went to see him accordingly. We conversed on the subject: he appeared seriously concerned on account of some difficulty in the way of effecting the object in his mind; (and I can not at this time determine whether the law had then been passed prohibiting emancipated slaves remaining in the state, or that it was expected such a law would take place.) However, to obviate the difficulty in the way of effecting the difficulty that existed, and to relieve his mind from the anxiety he (seemed) to labor under— I proposed to him making them over to some person (in whom he could confide) in trust, for that special purpose. He expressed an unwillingness to liberate them during his life; but the idea of leaving them in slavery made him miserable. A boy (who I suppose was in the habit of waiting on him) coming into the room (at that time) he expressed himself as touching his situation of being left a slave in a very moving and impressive manner, with tears in his eyes, that he should be miserable to leave him or them in slavery or words to that import. (It seemed to me that his attachment to his Negroes was so great at least for some of them that he could not well bear parting with them to go entirely off even if it could have been done without their aid.)

I do not recollect further of our conversation, other than I expected to have heard from him again on the subject as he appeared so earnest in securing the liberty of his slaves after his decease.

Given under my hand this 14th day of the 12th mo. 1816.

Saml. Parsons.[28]

While the humble slaves were often the instruments of their own emancipation, it is also true that Southern life was influenced by slave crime and insurrection and that the criminal

[28] Petition 6891, Henrico, December 14, 1816.

slaves influenced the antislavery movement. The faithful slave gained respect and sympathy for his fellows, but the rebellious spirit created grave fears that bloodshed and suffering would be inflicted on the South if the Negroes were forced to remain forever in bondage. The spirit of rebellion taught many citizens that there were slaves who wanted to be free. Had all the slaves been docile and content, it might have been possible to hold the Negro as a slave indefinitely, but the violent spirits made the slave system a problem that would not be silenced.

If we are to judge by the letters sent to the governors, the fear of servile insurrection was ever present. Quotations from such letters are given in the accompanying note.[29] Much of this type of

[29] Executive Papers: "Called upon not only from anxiety for my immediate acquaintances but likewise for my countrymen in general, I thus presume to address you . . . a dangerous insurrection is among our negroes meditated" (May 6, 1786) .

". . . the people of this county are very much alarmed with the apprehension of an insurrection of the slaves" (May 6, 1792) .

"The defenseless situation of most of the counties of this state and particularly those that have the blacks in greatest numbers, seem to claim the attention of the executive. The late insurrection on the Eastern shore of that class of people have alarmed the counties of Gloucester and Mathews and we entreat that the executive will put in our hands arms" (June 9, 1792) .

". . . some of them were whip'd and the rest discharged. This I think has had a good effect for we experience at the present time a very different behavior among them—How long it will continue, God only knows. To guard against future consequences, the sooner our militia is put upon a more respectable footing the better" (May 17, 1792) .

"This alone renders a well organized militia, ready on the spot, absolutely necessary, if it had no other effect than holding a terror to those who might contemplate the same combination that lately menaced the city of Richmond" (Dec. 17, 1802) .

"Our negroes are uncommonly impudent" (Feb. 14, 1808) .

"On Thursday last, I received information that the negroes in and about this place were preparing an insurrection" (Nov. 14, 1808) .

"It is pretty confidently believed that an insurrection among the slaves is intended" (Dec. 14, 1808) .

"We hasten to communicate to you the alarm of this Neighborhood" (Dec. 17, 1808) .

"I deem it my duty to apprize you of an alarm which exists with

evidence might be added to that which has already been given. The memoranda of the governor and Council tend to show that such rumors led to preventive action on the part of the executive. The following is the record of a meeting of the Council, May 30, 1810:

> The Governor submitted for the consideration of the
> Board a letter from Richard W. Byrd, Esquire, of the
> 30th ulto. giving information of an alarm prevalent at

us,—An insurrection among the blacks on Saturday night preceeding Whit-Sunday is much feared" (May 30, 1810) .

"The public mind has been very uneasy for some time owing to apprehensions from that unhappy and unfortunate source of danger" (June 16, 1810) .

"It is—my duty to apprize you of the danger that is contemplated by the slaves of this state" (June 11, 1811) .

"I have no hesitation in saying that a very dangerous rebellious conspiracy can be detected in this neighborhood" (1812) .

"We have no hesitation in believing, under all the circumstances, that an attack is meditated by the blacks . . . it is not an extravagant idea to conclude that the negroes are under the impression that it is now in their power to liberate themselves—From the most respectable information the spirit of rebellion is very obvious in this county and in places where the greatest humility and obedience has hitherto been observed" (April 10, 1812) .

"We are threatened by an insurrection of our negroes" (March 10, 1813) .

"A general uprising has lately been the subject of frequent conversations amongst them and the banks of this place have always been spoken of as the first object" (Sept. 16, 1814) .

"The mayor of this city informs me that recent circumstances have occured to alarm the citizens of this town and vicinity in relation to an intended insurrection of our black population" (March 23, 1820) .

". . . on the 11th of this month I received information that there was danger of an insurrection of the slaves . . . our activity and vigilance on this occasion will produce a good effect and put a stop to what no doubt was in some of the minds of the slaves and which otherwise might have matured into very serious consequences" (July 18, 1823) .

". . . it is very manifest, that there is of late an evident difference in the deportment of our black population, and we can not but ascribe this fact to their knowledge that we are unarmed" (Feb. 3, 1827) .

this time in the vicinity of Smithfield of an insurrection
of slaves generally of this state and North Carolina.
Whereupon it is advised that the Governor should cause
a circular letter to be addressed to the commandants of
the several regiments of militia east side of the Blue
Ridge, enclosing a copy of the letter from Mr. Byrd and
enjoining upon them forthwith to give publicity thereto
in their counties respectively; and also a circular letter to
the Major or Commandants of Battallions of militia
whose activity and vigilance shall be excited for the preservation of the public peace and safety by the exercise of
the power of performance of the duties enjoined upon
them by the law relating to patrols and that for greater
dispatch a sufficient number of copies of the said letters be
printed and forwarded by mail or by special messenger
as the governor may deem expedient.[30]

The following year a similar meeting of the Council decided
that

a circular letter be immediately dispatched to the commandants of regiments in those parts of the state most
exposed to these species of danger, requiring them immediately to instruct the majors or commandants of
battalions to exercise with utmost promptitude and
diligence the powers and duties enjoined upon them by
the law relating to the appointment of patrols, and it is
further advised that the Governor address letters to
General Mathews and Col. Magnion approbatory of the
steps they have taken on this occasion.[31]

In 1813 the mayor of the city of Richmond felt it to be necessary to deliver the following instructions to the grand jury in
that city:

Through our navigable waters he (the enemy) has
penetrated into the very heart of our country. Plunder
and devastation mark his steps; and evils inflicted on us

[30] Executive Papers, May 30, 1810.
[31] Executive Papers, Oct. 3, 1811.

of magnitude and are sufficient on reflection to fill the
mind with horror. This being the state of things, vigilance in those at the helm of government and in those
of all its ramified extensions is requisite. Then it is does
it behoove us to construe most strictly our laws as well
state as municipal and rigourously to give to them every
meaning they are susceptable of. We of the Southern
States are most pecularly bound to do, unfortunately
we have two enemies, the one open and declared; the
other nurtured in our very bosoms! Sly, secret, and vin-
dicative, in our families, and at our elbows listening in
with eager attention; and sedulously marking all that is
going on; they know where our strength lies and where
and in what point we may be easily assailed. The standard of revolt is unfurled wherever practicable these
deluded creatures, regardless of consequences have
flocked to it, and enrolled into military bands, we perhaps may have this sanguinary set of desperadoes to
contend with, employed in works of vicious kinds. You
very well know that in and about this city we have a
considerable portion of the black population, connected
and associated with the free people of colour. The laws
then respecting, them, from whom evils of most serious
kind may originate I think it is my duty to recommend to
your serious consideration, these construed strictly and
with rigour enforced may in a measure conteract the
designs of the enemy, and be the means of depriving
him of information.[32]

The minutes of the Council for July 18, 1827, not many
months before the outbreak in Southampton County show that,

Rumors of an insurrection having been received, but
no information so definite as to cause immediate steps
to be taken, at the request of Mr. Bates, the governor
submitted a proposition to vest in the governor a discre-
tionary power to arm such voluntary companies in such sec-

[32] Executive Papers, Sept. 8, 1813.

tions of Virginia as he may have reason to think the
emergency calls for.[33]

The fears of the slaveholders were increased by the successful
insurrections of slaves in the West Indian Islands. November 25,
1793, a letter to the governor of the state declares "that since the
melancholy affair at Hispaniola the inhabitants of the lower
country, especially of this county, have been repeated alarmed by
some of their slaves having attempted to raise an insurrection,
which was timely suppressed in this county by executing one of
the principal advisers of the insurrection."[34]

The following letter describes the fears of the citizens of Norfolk:

Norfolk, March 11, 1802

Sir:

I take the liberty of addressing you on a subject of
much importance to this place and that may become of
general concern.

It is known that when the trouble obliged the inhabitants of the French Islands to seek refuge in other countries that a number of them came to the United States,
and to this state came numbers, and particularly to this
place, bringing with them a number of slaves and others
forbidden by law to become residents of this state. From
motives of humanity I suppose, the police were induced
to take no notice of the evasion or violation of the law
on this occasion.

But, Sir, at this moment I cannot disguise my anxiety
in which I am joined by many of our most respectable
citizens. There are now a considerable number of persons
of the above description in this place, whose dispositions
I apprehend will be influenced by the accounts which
are daily arriving and being published concerning the
horrid scenes of St. Domingo. On this subject your excellency will more readily conceive the sensations which

[33] Executive Papers, July 18, 1827.
[34] Executive Papers, Nov. 25, 1793.

arise from apprehensions of this nature than I can describe. The situation of this place is such as a few fires
would reduce it to ashes. I am well assured that the
removal of those persons will be attended with some
difficulty, and should be managed with great delicacy,
so much so that I hope you will excuse my troubling
you with this letter. At the same time I beg this that you
will favor me with your advice. I should add that I do
not know of any circumstance at this time which indicates a disposition that is to be seriously apprehended.
I have the honor to be

Your obt. servant
John Cowper

P.S. Since writing the above a reputable citizen has informed me of a suspicious meeting of the blacks of this
place. I have not time to examine into the case before
the mail departs.[35]

In 1805 a petition to the state legislature from the citizens of
the city of Norfolk recites

that the peace and quiet of this Borrough require some
change in its character. . . . That in addition to these
causes of tumult and alarm, the black population of the
borrough hath received a very formidable accession
from the Island of St. Domingo.[36]

James Monroe was the governor of Virginia at the time of Gabriel's insurrection. His writings concerning the conspiracy and
the executions which followed it show that this insurrection had
a very important influence in the development of the colonization society. In a message to the State legislature December 5,
1800, Monroe writes that

unhappily while this class of people exists among us, we
can never count certainty on its tranquil submission.
The fortunate issue of the late attempt should not

[35] Executive Papers, March 11, 1802.
[36] Petition 4907, Norfolk, Dec. 8, 1805.

lull us into repose. It ought rather to stimulate us to the
adoption of a system which if it does not prevent the
like in the future, may secure the country from calam-
itous consequences.[37]

In a message to the next meeting of the legislature he again
points to the dangers of servile insurrection, declaring:

It is our duty on this occasion to remark, that the public
danger proceeding from this description of persons is
daily increasing. A variety of causes contributes to produce
this effect, among which may be mentioned the contrasted condition of the free Negroes and the slaves, the
growing sentiment of liberty existing in the minds of
the latter, and the inadequacy of the existing patrol
laws.[38]

In a letter to Thomas Jefferson, written in the same year, Monroe wrote:

The spirit of revolt has taken firm hold of the minds of
the slaves. . . . I am persuaded the day is not far distant
when this neglect [to legislate on the subject of coloniza-
tion] must have a definite regulation from the councils
of the country.[39]

As a result of the admonitions of the governor there were a series
of resolutions passed by the legislature. These resolutions will be
described below.

Thomas Jefferson, at this time at Monticello, was soon to go to
Washington to assume his duties as president; however, his spirit
having been moved by the large number of executions which followed the uprisings, he wrote to his friend Monroe in the interest
of those slaves that still remained in the jail at Richmond. The
following is quoted from his letter to the governor:

[37] Stanislaus M. Hamilton (ed.), *The Letters and Writings of James
Monroe* (New York, 1920), III, 243.
[38] Ibid., p. 329.
[39] Ibid., p. 348.

When to stay the hand of the executioner is an important question. Those who have escaped from immediate
danger, must have feelings which dispose them to extend
the executions. Even here Monticello where everything
has been perfectly tranquil but where familiarity with
slavery, and a possibility of danger from that quarter,
prepares the general mind for some severities, there is
strong sentiment that there has been hanging enough.
The other states and the world at large will forever
condemn us if we indulge a principle of revenge, or go
one step beyond necessity. . . . Our situation is indeed
a difficult one for I doubt if those people can ever be
permitted to go at large among us with safety. . . . Surely
the legislature would pass a law for their exportation,
the proper measure on this and all similar occasions.[40]

Monroe agreed with the humane sentiments of Jefferson, and
he accordingly recommended to the legislature the provision for
transportation of slaves guilty of insurrection. The legislature in
turn passed a resolution instructing the governor to communicate with President Jefferson to the end that lands might be secured to which "persons obnoxious to the laws or dangerous to
the peace of society" might be removed. "This resolution had
been produced by the conspiracy of the slaves and the idea of
such an acquisition was suggested by the motives of humanity."[41]
In reply Jefferson, writing to Monroe on November 21, 1801, discussed the relative merits of colonizing slaves on the western
lands or of negotiating with foreign powers concerning colonization of Negroes. Jefferson then made known his wish that if such
lands were secured, free Negroes and those that he hoped would
be emancipated might be sent in addition to those slaves guilty of
insurrection.[42] At the next meeting of the legislature it was
agreed that the proposed colony should be made a refuge for all
free Negroes in accord with the wishes of the president.[43] Jeffer-

[40] Paul G. Ford (ed.), *The Writings of Thomas Jefferson* (New York,
1914), VII, 457.

[41] Hamilton, op. cit., p. 329.

[42] Ford, op. cit., VII, 103.

[43] Hamilton, op. cit., III, 336.

son then discussed the matter with the British chargé d'affaires and offered to negotiate through the American minister at London for the use of lands in or near the colony of Sierra Leone, on the west coast of Africa. He believed that this location was most desirable because the Negro colonists there located had originally migrated from Virginia and other Southern States.

From his correspondence with Monroe it appears that Jefferson's desire to aid the antislavery cause was hampered by his political ambitions. It seems possible that peaceful emancipation of the slaves in Virginia might finally have been accomplished if her great statesmen had been able to give the full measure of their genius to the service of their state, but to do so meant the sacrifice of their ambitions for distinguished service to the nation. Jefferson makes repeated reference to his desire that his opinions be considered confidential.[44] He feared that his liberal sentiments might alienate political supporters in other Southern states.

However this may be, Virginians had been tremendously influenced by the insurrection of the slave Gabriel. The efforts of Monroe in behalf of colonization had their origin in this period. His efforts were cut short by his appointment as minister to France, but Jefferson continued to aid the cause. The legislature of Virginia adopted resolutions on the "subject of obtaining an Asylum for the slaves of Virginia" in the sessions of 1802, 1804, 1805, and 1816. These resolutions were forwarded to the president as in 1800. Until 1816 such negotiations were conducted in secret sessions, and the resolutions were not printed in the record.[45] In 1817 John Randolph presented the cause of the Virginia colonizationists in Congress. In 1819 James Madison advocated the sale of public lands for the effective support of colonization. In 1821 Liberia was purchased and the long disputed question of the location of the colony was now settled in accord with the wishes of Jefferson. There now remained the question of securing financial support for the scheme.

[44] Archibald Alexander, *A History of Colonization* (Philadelphia, 1846), p. 72; Ford, op. cit., I, 339; II, 357, V, 6; Hamilton, op. cit., III, 322.

[45] William B. Giles, *Political Miscellanies, Political Disquisitions* (Richmond, 1827), No. 3.

In this period the membership of the colonization societies in Virginia increased tremendously and the antislavery movement in the state became almost exclusively a colonization movement. The efforts of the Virginians had much influence in other states. Governor Giles declared: "It is highly probable that the American colonization society owes its origin to the proceedings of the [Virginia] general assembly."[46]

In the development of colonization, the slave Gabriel, President Jefferson, and Governor Monroe each played an important part. Gabriel and his insurrectionists were responsible for the first legislative action that promised the abolition of slavery; the plan for colonization was chiefly the work of Thomas Jefferson; Monroe was most effective in executing the ideas of Jefferson. The workers who followed Monroe in most cases accepted the principle that emancipation should be accompanied by transportation outside the territory of the United States. This doctrine is found in the content of numerous petitions sent to the legislature before 1830.[47] It is no doubt true that many of the petitioners saw in the efforts of the society only a practical means by which "worthless and dangerous" free Negroes might be gotten out of the state, but it is also true that humane and generous men who believed in the justice and right of emancipation joined in this movement. Many humane men saw in the efforts of the colonizationists the only practical method by which all the slaves would ultimately be set free, though many may have agreed with Editor Ritchie that emancipation could not be finally accomplished before the year 2000. In this period of agitation western men were writing books and editing papers denouncing the institution of slavery and the domestic slave trade and deploring the adverse economic effects of the institution.[48] Governor Giles, a proslavery advocate, believed that the motives of humanity were the chief force that actuated the colonizationists. He denounced the "fanatical abolitionists of Virginia," and affirmed that they were actuated "first of all by their humane sentiment" but that "they

[46] Ibid., p. 14.

[47] Petitions, 8304, 8591, 8783a, 8909, 9011, 9041, 9218, 9220a.

[48] Alice Adams, *Neglected Period of Anti-Slavery* (Boston, 1908); *Liberator*, June 7, 1824, pp. 130–31.

had found their most effective argument was the doctrine that the dissolute free negroes endangered the state." He declared also that

> it would be unjust to be put down the whole colored
> population as dissolute and burdensome, but the free
> people of colour are despised, and there is a rage about
> getting rid of them. . . . This being the most seductive
> inducement, it is accordingly the most used by the
> friends of the project, and to produce its greatest effect,
> it is greatly exaggerated. . . . One half at least may be
> considered honest labourers, whose labour adds to the
> wealth of the State and would more than compensate, in a
> pecuniary point of view, for the evils of the dissolute
> part of the population.[49]

While many motives entered into the actions of the colonizationists, the people of the state never forgot Gabriel, and there were many reminders that such conspirators were always to be expected. In 1805 Thomas Jefferson wrote concerning this subject:

> Interest is preparing the disposition to be just; and this
> will be goaded from time to time by the insurrectionary
> spirit of the slaves. This is easily quelled in its first efforts,
> but from being local it will become general; and when-
> ever it does it will rise more formidable after every defeat,
> until we shall be forced, after dreadful scenes and suffer-
> ing to release them in their own way, which such suffer-
> ings we might now model after our own convenience.[50]

In Virginia the antislavery movement prospered and grew because of the efforts of brilliant and idealistic statesmen, because of the propagation of the philosophy of the Revolution, because of the teachings of revivalistic churches, and because of sectional antipathies. In this Southern state are to be found examples of the most radical type of abolitionists and of white men who sometimes became abettors of slave insurrections. Among the poor whites are to be found allies of the black conspirators. In

[49] Giles, op. cit.
[50] Ford, op. cit., VIII, 340.

addition to the above considerations, the Negro must be regarded as a worker for his own emancipation. The lives of worthy black men taught the governing classes that the slaves should be set free. The insurrectionary slave is largely responsible for the growth of the colonization societies. The criminal slave created a fear of insurrection that was constant. While these fears existed, men knew that slaves wanted freedom, and because slaves dared to rebel, wise white men advised that the system of slavery be abandoned.

SIX

The Convention of 1829 &
Nat Turner's Insurrection

THE YEARS 1828 to 1832 mark the culmination of the efforts of Virginians to rid the state of slavery. In 1829 a convention was called at Richmond for the purpose of revising the constitution of the state. The call for the convention was the result of the success of the men of the western and the upper Piedmont regions in forcing recognition of their familiar demands for a just share in the government of Virginia. Since the Revolution the men of the eastern part of the state had maintained a political system that gave to the slaveholding section what they wanted and made possible the defeat of any measure that threatened the interests of the slaveholding agriculturists. All of the interests of the western men seemed to conflict with the interests of the men of the East and all reforms proposed by the West were defeated. Roads and internal improvements were not to be had and social legislation was not considered. However, in 1827 the westerners forced the legislature to submit to a popular vote the question of a call for a convention to revise the constitution of the state. In 1828 the voters decided in favor of the call for a convention to revise the constitution by a vote of 21,196 to 16,649. The convention accordingly met in October, 1829. The work of this convention affords one of the most interesting studies in the history of Virginia. This study seems to establish the fact that the slaveholders of the state exercised a power that defeated the will of the majority and thus preserved the slave system. The western reformers demanded the redistricting of the state and the substitution of universal white male suffrage for suf-

frage based on ownership of land and Negroes. Given these reforms, the West was confident that their ardent desire for internal improvements would then be obtained. In the decisions
reached in the convention the East profited by the superior political experience and the skill of their representatives. The many
eminent men chosen as the representatives of the East is an evidence of the fact that the people of that section realized that this
was a time of crisis and that they needed their ablest defenders.[1]
Among the eastern delegates were included the former presidents
Madison and Monroe and Chief Justice Marshall. There were
also seven delegates who had served in the United States Senate
and eleven delegates who had served in the House of Representatives. However, there were able men, though less distinguished,
who represented the West. For many weeks it was far from evident that the East could retain control of the state and preserve
the system that protected its cherished institutions. So close was
the division between the parties that on the day of the most crucial ballot forty-seven votes were cast by eastern delegates and
forty-seven by the western representatives, and the men of the
East won the final decision on the vote cast by the speaker.[1] The
constitution as finally adopted may be regarded as a compromise
between the two sections but a compromise that satisfied neither,
for the West felt that its purpose had been defeated and the East
was equally certain that too many concessions had been made.
The suffrage had in a measure been extended, and a few more
representatives would now be sent from the West to the General
Assembly but the control of legislation remained in possession of
the eastern planters.[2]

The chief interest of this convention for the purpose of our
study is its very important relation to the question of slavery in
Virginia. The great majority of the men of the western section

[1] Charles H. Young, *The Virginia Constitutional Convention of 1829*
(Richmond, 1902), Randolph-Macon Historical Papers, No. 3, pp.
106–10.

[2] *Journal of the Constitutional Convention of Virginia, 1829–1830*
(Richmond, 1830); Charles H. Ambler, Sectionalism in Virginia (Chicago, 1910); James C. McGregor, *Disruption of Virginia* (New York,
1922); Theodore M. Whitefield, *Slavery Agitation in Virginia, 1829–
1830* (Baltimore, 1930).

who went down in defeat at the convention of 1829 were the pro-
ponents of antislavery, and the decision made by the vote cast by
the speaker of the house was a verdict in favor of the preservation
of the institution of slavery. In former years the lawmakers had
repeatedly debated and legislated on the treatment of the slave
and the free Negro and on the question of colonization and the
domestic slave trade, but never before had there been so bright a
prospect that the institution would be abolished.

In all the debates of this convention a studied effort was made
to exclude the question of slavery from public discussion. The
East feared the effect of such discussion on the slave population,
and the West feared that such agitation might alienate support
which they hoped to gain for primary suffrage reforms. According to James Madison, "the question [of slavery] infected the
proceedings throughout."[3] Outside of the convention hall, in the
press and on the streets the slave question could not be silenced.
Although the legislative reformers were for the most part western
men, these men had allies in the East. Alexander Campbell, a re-
presentative of the West and at the same time an ardent antislavery man, writes:

> I attended one caucus held in the capital of Virginia,
> on the question of general emancipation, while the
> convention was in session, and heard several gentlemen
> of Eastern Virginia, men owning hundreds of slaves
> say that, if Virginia would agree to fix upon some agree-
> able time, after which all should be free, they would
> cheerfully not only vote for it, but would set all their
> slaves free, for they believed slavery to be the greatest
> curse, the most unendurable incubus on the prosperity
> of Virginia, that could be imposed on it—a burden
> from which neither they nor their fathers could rid
> themselves, but which they could not and would not
> longer endure.[4]

[3] Gaillard Hunt (ed.), *Letters and Other Writings of James Madison*
(New York, 1910), IV, 58–60.
[4] Alexander Campbell, *A Tract for the People of Kentucky* (Lexington, Ky., 1849), p. 2.

In the campaign which had preceded the convention Governor
Giles had declared, "I sincerely believe that the principle of slave
labor is in danger; and that nothing can save it but the wisdom,
the vigilance, the caution, the concert, and the courage of the
owners of slave property."[5] When the sessions of the convention
opened Editor Ritchie, of the Richmond *Enquirer,* the most in-
fluential newspaper in the State, was exerting all his genius for
the antislavery cause.[6] Before the convention had adjourned
John Randolph declared that if the West had won "all the slaves
of Virginia would have been free within twenty years."[7]

The future history of Virginia was to prove that in the convention of 1829 the planters of eastern Virginia had made an unfortunate and regrettable decision. No doubt there sat in all the sessions of the convention, many distinguished men whose
humanitarian instincts prompted them to join hands with the
men of the West, for they knew that slavery was a great wrong,
but these same humane men were also prompted to action by
powerful economic motives that were based upon their knowledge that their Negroes were valuable property, and by political
motives that made them court the favor of slaveholders in and
outside of Virginia. In this instance it appears to be demonstrated that economic and political motives are more effective
causes of historic action than humanitarianism or morality. In
1805 Thomas Jefferson had written that he

> had long since given up the expectation of an early
> provision for the extinguishment of slavery among us.
> There are many virtuous men who would make every
> sacrifice to effect it, many equally virtuous who persuade
> themselves either that the thing is not wrong, or that it
> can not be remedied, and very many with whom interest

[5] William B. Giles, *Political Miscellanies, Political Disquisitions*
(Richmond, 1827), No. 3, p. 5.

[6] Charles H. Ambler, *Thomas Ritchie, A Study in Virginia Politics*
(Richmond, 1913), p. 115.

[7] *Journal of the Constitutional Convention of Virginia, 1829–1830*
(Richmond, 1830), p. 858.

is morality. The older we grow the larger we are disposed
to believe the last party to be.[8]

Jefferson's estimate of the power of economic motives over the action of slaveholders was no doubt true in 1829; and as in 1805
with many men their "interest was morality."

The action of the slaves in the convention years gives evidence
that in their homes and at their work the planters had loudly
voiced their belief that the victory of the West would be followed
by the emancipation of the slaves. For two years we find little evidence of the spirit of insurrection, but in the referendum of 1827
and in the convention campaign of 1828 there was much talk of
the emancipation of the Negroes. The slaves knew what was
being said and the hope of freedom had been raised among them.
The spirit of insurrection appeared in many counties in 1829,
and the evidence indicates that this spirit was the result of the
mistaken belief that they, the slaves, had been denied what had
been given to them in the late election.

On July 13, 1829, a regimental commander wrote to the governor: "I have information from Gloucester County last evening
stating a contemplated insurrection of the slaves in this and adjoining counties." On July 15, a letter reported insurrection in
Mathews and Isle of Wight.[9] July 26, another letter reads: "At
this moment there is great excitement relative to the insurrection
in Hanover. The fears of every citizen are alarmed."[10] July 18, a
citizen of Richmond wrote: "The Mayor yesterday informed me
that much alarm pervaded the city in consequence of the report
of an insurrection."[11] July 21, a citizen of Essex county wrote to
the governor: "An insurrectionary spirit having exhibited itself
among the slaves of this and several adjacent counties . . . I have
to request that one hundred stand of arms for infantry, and sev-

[8] Paul L. Ford (ed.), *The Writings of Thomas Jefferson* (New York,
1914), VIII, 340.

[9] Executive Papers, Archives of Virginia, Letters Received, July 13,
15, 1829. Hereafter Archives of Virginia, Letters Received, will be
omitted and the document identified by the date.

[10] Executive Papers, July 26, 1829.

[11] Executive Papers, July 18, 1829.

enty-five cavalry swords and pistols be sent immediately."[12] August 13, citizens of Accomack county reported insurrection in that county and declared: "Cut off as we are by an arm of the sea from all communication with other parts of the state—places us in a very alarming and dangerous situation."[13] On August 27, from the same county it is written that "for some weeks the citizens of this and the adjoining county have been excited by the many evidences of discontent exhibited by our slaves."[14] The following letter offers explanation for the alarms of the citizens and for the spirit of insurrection among the slaves in the year 1829.

Mathews Ct. House,
July 18th, 1829

His Excellency, William B. Giles
Sir:

As rumours may be spread abroad calculated to misrepresent the fears existing here of a suspected insurrection among the slaves and unnecessarily to disturb the public tranquility, I have deemed it my duty to communicate to you such circumstances as are of any importance. About ten days ago information was communicated confidentially by a negro to a widow woman that it was expected generally among the slaves that they would be free in a few weeks. The first of August seemed to be the time agreed on as the period. It was not deemed at the time of such importance as to take any notice of it, but a conversation in a blacksmith's shop between several negroes being overheard by two white apprentice boys who had secreted themselves behind it confessedly in relation to the subject of a general emancipation of the slaves, an investigation was made into it, and a great many taken up. The evidence taken in and the confessions generally seem to concur in the general belief among the blacks which had been for some time entertained that the last convention election had exclusively

[12] Executive Papers, July 31, 1829.
[13] Executive Papers, August 13, 1829.
[14] Executive Papers, August 27, 1829.

for its object the liberation of the blacks, and that the
question had been decided by the result of this convention
election and that it had been kept secret from them
and that their free papers had been withheld improperly,
but were to be delivered at August Court. The tenor of
the evidence given in upon the Magistrates was that
they were to be free at the period above mentioned.
This does not seem, however, to have been the only
idea entertained of it by two of the blacks in custody
who were remanded to the jail to take their trial, one
of them is the blacksmith in whose shop this conversation
was carried on, and the other negro fellow who was heard
to use expressions in that conversation of a nature
declaratory of a purpose to rise this year or next. The
trial of these slaves was commenced today but the court
remanded them to jail and adjourned to Friday next for
the purpose of ferreting out more evidence. To what
extent this delusion has gone among the blacks is not
entirely known. The negroes who have been examined
on the subject as witnesses say that it is the general belief
among the slaves that they are emancipated. Those
among them who have entertained thoughts of asserting
their freedom by insurrection are probably few, but
that there are some of the latter description there is
very little doubt . . .

With great respect, I am very truly
Your obdt. servt.
Sm. Tompkins, Col. 61 Regt.[15]

The following is a memorandum of the governor and council
which shows that the discontent which has developed among the
slaves was a subject of executive consideration and action.

The executive has received sundry communications
from distant and different quarters of the state, which
speak of rumors and alarms of an intended insurrection
of the slaves on or about the 1st inst. But it is not believed
that there is great immediate danger of such an evil.

[15] Executive Papers, July 18, 1829.

Nevertheless it is considered expedient at this time to
arm a portion of the militia, in such parts of the Commonwealth as are most exposed to danger or are subject to
alarms of insurrection. This opinion is founded on the
following reasons, to wit:

The number of slaves is so great in some parts of the
Commonwealth as to give cause at all times for appre-
hending danger, or adopting measures or precaution.
There have existed rumors of an intended insurrection
on or about the 1st inst. which have spread widely and
disquieted the minds of many of the good citizens of the
Commonwealth. These rumors have been much talked
about by the slaves themselves and have probably increased the spirit of insurrection. Such a spirit has
certainly existed. It is believed, however, in a small degree,
in some of the counties. The militia are almost without
arms at this time. It is believed that a judicious distribution of arms may be made, that their preservation and
faithful return may be provided for, and that the placing
of some arms in the hands of the militia will quiet
the minds of the good people of the Commonwealth, and
at the same time have a tendency to check, or suppress a
spirit of insurrection among the slaves.[16]

At the conclusion of the convention of 1829, the delegates returned to their homes, believing that the question of the emancipation of the slaves of Virginia had been ended. Virginia citizens
had by a very, very narrow margin decided for slavery. Slave
property was now secure and the slaveholders hoped that the action of the convention might be regarded as final and that they
had heard the last of the agitation of an embarrassing question.

After the convention adjourned, if we are to believe Governor
Floyd,

while the slaves now appeared to be humble and obedient
and the state appeared to be at peace, there was, in
the years 1830 and 1831, a silent but effective agitation
for freedom carried on by Negro preachers and by free

[16] Executive Papers, July, 1829.

Negroes in and outside the state. By these men the Negro
slaves were incited to rise in rebellion, to strike for freedom carried on by Negro preachers and by free Negroes
in and outside the state. By these men the Negro slaves
were incited to rise in rebellion, to strike for freedom
denied to them by the convention of 1829, and the outcome of such agitation was the fatal Southampton
insurrection.[17]

In his first message to the legislature, after the insurrection of
1831 Governor Floyd claimed that

the most active incendiaries among us, in stirring up
the spirit of revolt, have been the negro preachers. They
have acquired great ascendency over the mind of their
fellows and infused all their opinions, which had prepared them for their fatal design. There is also reason
to believe, those preachers have a perfect understanding
in relation to these plans throughout the eastern counties—and have been the channels through which the
inflammatory pamphlets and papers brought here by
the agents and emissaries from other states, have been
circulated among the slaves. The facilities thus afforded
for plotting treason and conspiracy to rebel and make
insurrection, have been great. Through the indulgency
of the Magistracy and the laws, large collections of slaves
have been permitted to take place, at any time through
the week, for the ostensible purpose of religious worship,
but in many instances, the real purpose, with the preachers, was of a different character; the sentiment and sometimes the words of these inflamitory pamphlets, which
the meek and charitable of other states have seen cause
to distribute as firebrands in the bosom of our society,

[17] Charles H. Ambler, *The Life and Diary of John Floyd* (Richmond,
1918), p. 159 (Sept. 2, 1831): "No news from Southampton, though
even Prince William has its emissaries in it from among the free
negroes of the District of Columbia. He is a preacher. The whole of
that massacre is the work of these Preachers, as daily intelligence
informs me."

have been read. . . . The public interest requires that the
negro preachers be silenced, who full of ignorance, are
incapable of inculcating anything but notions of the
wildest superstition, thus preparing fit instruments in
the hands of the crafty agitators, to destroy the public
tranquility.[18]

Nat Turner, a preacher, was said to have agitated for his insurrection for many months before the outbreak, which fact must
have influenced the opinions of Governor Floyd.[19]

In 1830 Thomas Lewis, a free Negro, living in the city of Richmond was found to have received thirty copies of a pamphlet
called "Walker's Appeal." This pamphlet, written by David
Walker, a free Negro residing in the city of Boston, preaches the
doctrine of the equality of all men; it recites the successes of the
Negro insurrections in the West Indies and urges the Negroes of
the South to follow their example. The following memorandum
shows that this incident became the subject of consideration by
the governor and council:

Called the attention of the council to a pamphlet purporting to be printed in the city of Boston and which
has been put in circulation among the blacks of the city
of Richmond, the character and tendencies of which
are to excite to insurrection among the people of color.
On consideration of the above mentioned pamphlet, the
council advises that the governor shall transmit the same
to the legislature, and shall at the same time call their
attention to the propriety of providing more explicitedly
by law for preventing the introduction and circulation
of papers, writings or publications, and for the prohibition of pictures designed or having a tendency to produce
insurrection or insubordination among the people of
color.[20]

[18] *Journal of the Senate of Virginia, 1831,* pp. 9–10.

[19] William S. Drewry, *Slave Insurrections in Virginia, 1830–1865*
(Washington, 1900) .

[20] Executive Papers, 1830; see also David Walker, *Walker's Appeal, in
Four Articles* (Boston, 1830) ; Archives of Virginia, Executive Letter
Book, 1823–1830 (Governor Giles) , p. 33.

In 1831, copies of the *Liberator* were found in circulation in the homes of certain free Negroes.[21]

[It now becomes necessary to refer, once more, to the work of Nat Turner. It is not my purpose to glorify or to condone the slaughter or bloodletting committed by this Negro and his followers, but Nat Turner was an interesting character, and if we are to judge this man by the extent of the shelves in the Archives of Virginia containing the manuscripts which record the works of Turner, he was a most important historic personage.

The significance of the work of this man is that he forced the legislature of Virginia to open the debate on slavery, when it has been assumed that all such agitation had been ended with the conclusion of the convention of 1829. Moreover, this time the debate was not to be silenced by questions of political expediency or discussed only on the streets and in the caucus. Turner made slavery the most important problem before the lawmakers of Virginia, and this time Virginians in open sessions of the General Assembly advocated and pleaded for the final emancipation of the slaves. Nat Turner had made many distinguished men, who had defended slaveowners in the convention of 1829, decide by 1831 that they had made a great mistake and that it was now the part of wisdom to rectify their error. Other important results of the work of Turner will appear later in this chapter, but attention must be called at this point to the immediate effects of what he had done.[22]

No doubt many of the lawmakers who assembled at Richmond in December, 1831, did not know how a practical plan might be found for the settlement of their problem, but many must have agreed with Thomas Ritchie that something must be done. "What is to be done? My God! I do not know, but something must be done."[23]

Governor John Floyd was among those who, in the excitement of the days following the insurrection, decided that they knew what should be done. Thus, on November 31, 1831, the governor recorded in his diary:

[21] Executive Papers, Sept. 25, 1831.

[22] John W. Cromwell, "The Aftermath of Nat Turner's Insurrection," *Journal of Negro History*, v (April, 1920), 208–34.

[23] *National Intelligencer*, Jan. 10, 1832.

There are still demands for arms in the lower country.
I could not have believed there was half the fear amongst
the people of the lower country with respect to their
slaves. Before I leave this government, I shall have contrived to have a law passed, gradually abolishing slavery
in this state, or at all events to begin the work by prohibiting slavery on the West side of the Blue Ridge
Mountains.[24]

In a letter to the governor of South Carolina, Floyd describes at
length what appeared to him to have been the causes of the insurrection and indicates that he had determined on a very definite plan for gradual emancipation. He declared:

I am fully persuaded that the spirit of insubordination
which has, and still manifests itself in Virginia, had its
origin among and emanated from the Yankee population
among us, but especially Yankee pedlers and traders.

Their course has been by no means a direct one, they
began first by making them religious; their conversations
were of that character, telling the blacks God was no
respecter of persons; the black man was as good as the
white; that all men were born free and equal; that they
can not serve two masters, that the white people rebelled against England to obtain freedom, so have the
blacks the right to do.

In the meantime, I am sure without any purpose of
this kind, the preachers especially Northern, were very
assiduous in operation upon the population. Day and
night they were at work and religion became and is the
fashion of the times. Finally our females, and of the most
respectable, were persuaded that it was piety to teach
negroes to read and write, to the end that they might
read the scriptures. Many of them became tutoresses in
Sunday Schools and pius distributors of tracts from the
New York Society.

At this point more active operations commenced, our
magistrates and laws became more inactive; large assem-

[24] Ambler, *Life and Diary of John Floyd*, p. 159.

blies of negroes were suffered to take place for religious purposes. Then commenced the efforts of the black preachers. Often from the pulpits these pamphlets and papers were read, followed by the incendiary publications of Walker, Garrison and Knapp of Boston. Then too with songs and hymns of similar character were circulated read and commented on; we resting in apathetic security until the Southampton affair.

From all that has come to my knowledge, during and since the affair, I am fully convinced that the black preachers, in the whole country East of the Blue Ridge, were in the secret, that the plans as advocated by the Northern prints were adopted and acted upon by them, that their congregations, as they were called, knew nothing of the rebellion except a few leading intelligent men, who may have been head men in the churches. The mass were prepared by making them aspire to an equal station by such conversations as I have related as a first step.

I am informed that they had settled the form of government to be that of the white people, whom they intended to cut off to a man, with this difference, that preachers were to be their governors, generals and judges. I feel fully justified to myself, in believing the Northern incendiaries, tracts, Sunday Schools, religion, and reading and writing has accomplished this evil.

I shall in my annual message recommend that laws be passed to confine the slaves to the estates of their masters, prohibiting negroes from preaching, absolutely to drive from the state all free negroes, and to substitute the surplus revenue in our treasury annually for slaves, to work for a time on our railroads, etc. and then sent out of the country preparatory, or rather as a first step toward emancipation. The last point will of course be tenderly and cautiously managed, and will be urged or delayed as your state and Georgia may be disposed to cooperate.

In relation to the extent of the insurrection, I think it greater than will ever appear.[25]

[25] Ibid., pp. 80–90.

Never before 1831 had the prospect been so bright that Virginia would be free from the slave system. While the legislature was assembled the Petersburg *Intelligencer* had reported:

> The sentiment is gaining in Virginia, that the whole
> African race ought to be removed from among us. Many
> people feeling unwilling to die and leave their posterity
> exposed to all the evils which, from the existence of
> slavery in our state, they have themselves so long felt.
> Others are unwilling themselves longer to suffer these
> inconveniences.[26]

The Richmond *Whig* declared: "We affirm that in the heaviest slave districts of the state, thousands have hailed the discussions with delight, and contemplate the distant, but ardently desired result, as the supreme good which a beneficent providence could vouchsafe to their country."[27] The antislavery sentiment is best demonstrated by the number of petitions sent to the legislature of the state. At the session of 1831–1832, fifty-seven petitions were received, asking the state to adopt various modifications of the Jefferson plan for emancipation.[28] It is reasonable to estimate that these petitions were endorsed by ten thousand citizens. It is interesting also to note that these documents came from all parts of the state. There is much similarity in all of these petitions and but one of them will be given here. Though it will be found that the petitioners place much emphasis on the economic evils of the slave system, it should not be forgotten that all of these documents had been provoked by the rebellion of the slave, Nat Turner.

> A Petition from Hanover County
> To the General Assembly of the Commonwealth of
> Virginia. The memorial of the undersigned citizens of
> the county of Hanover, most respectfully sheweth:
>   Free and unrestricted by shackles, as the right of the

[26] *Niles Register,* March 31, 1832.

[27] Ibid., August 27, 1830.

[28] James H. Johnston, "Anti-Slavery Petitions Presented to the Virginia State Legislature by Citizens of Various Counties," *Journal of Negro History,* XII (Oct., 1927), 670–90.

citizens of the Commonwealth to ask redress for supposed
grievances, at the hands of the General Assembly, has
ever been considered; there has at all times existed among
us, a circumspection in the exercise of that right, which
has tended greatly to preserve the peace and harmony
of the community. It is from no reckless disregard to this
consideration that we now approach you, on a subject
of the liveliest and deepest interest to the future happiness and quiet of the state, as well as one of the most
delicate nature.

An evil has existed among us from almost the first
settlement of the Commonwealth of the heaviest and
most serious nature.

It has grown with us and in every moment of our advance; it bursts from every lip, "That if we wish peace
happiness, quiet and prosperity, this fatal, paralizing,
destroying mischief must be removed." Who requires to
be informed to what we allude? Do not all men know,
it is the existing curse of slavery to whose mischief we
refer. This is not the proper time or place for speaking
abstractly on this serious subject. We are done with the
past and should only look to and act for the future.

How and by whose means this heavy and alarming evil
has been brought on the country may amuse the philan-
thropist and fill the pages of the historian. It is for us
to consider the character and extent of this evil, and to
apply the most salutary, peaceful, safe, just and effica-
cious means for its removal.

For this subject we approach you as the lawgivers of
the land, with no moral or constitutional restrictions on
your powers in the accomplishment of this great purpose.
A purpose which when attained will be a blessing of
ever continuing effect on our country and the unhappy
and degraded race of Africans, whose presence deforms
our land. Great and enduring will such a work be, and
he who shall devise and have the fortitude and constancy
to execute a system for its accomplishment will forever
live as the first and most signal benefactor of his country.

Should the legislature require any facts or arguments

to convince them of the imperious necessity for taking
some decided measures on this subject, we must respectfully submit to them the following as deserving particular consideration.

We affirm that for the past forty years the black population including therein the free negroes and the mulattoes,
have been gradually but surely increasing in that part
of the State East of the Blue Ridge mountains in a
greater ratio than the whites in the same district of the
State. We affirm that from having in 1790 been a minority
in this district, in 1830 the black population considerably
outnumbered the whites, and to sustain these assertions
we submit the following facts.

By the census of 1790, there were of whites East of the
Blue Ridge Mountains | 314,523
There were of blacks | 289,425
Majority of white | 25,098
In 1800 there were of whites | 336,389
There were of blacks | 339,393
Majority of blacks | 3,004
In 1810 there were of blacks | 386,942
There were of whites | 338,553
Majority of blacks | 48,389
In 1820 there were of blacks | 413,928
There were of whites | 348,873
Majority of Blacks | 65,055
In 1830 there were of Blacks | 457,013
There were of whites | 375,935
Majority of blacks | 81,078

From these statements taken from the census made at
each of the periods above referred to, it appears that the
white population with a majority of 25,098 in 1790, has
been in the ten years thereafter overtaken by the blacks
who at the end of the period exceeded the whites 3,004,
and who now exceed them in number 81,078. It is
farther made manifest that from

1790 to 1800 the black increased	49,968
The whites increased	21,866
Gain of blacks in the first period	28,102
From 1800 to 1810 the blacks increased	47,549
The whites increased	2,164
Gain of blacks in second period	45,385
From 1810 to 1820 the blacks increased	26,986
The whites increased	10,320
Gain of blacks in third period	16,666
From 1820 to 1830 the blacks increased	43,085
The whites increased	27,062
Gain of blacks	16,023
Thus the gain of the blacks was	
In the first period	28,102
In the second period	45,385
In the third period	16,666
In the fourth period	16,023
Total gain in the black population in the last forty years	107,176

Your memorialists forbear to anticipate in detail the future relation of the black population and the relative relation of the white population in this region Virginia. It may be safely asserted, however, that the end of the next forty years, will find a difference much, very much, greater in favor of the blacks. This anticipation is already inducing many of our most industrious and enterprising people to seek new homes, in distant and stranger states, where they and their children may be exempt from the dangers and difficulties with which they are unfortunately beset in their native land, while others are making rapid preparations to follow their example unless some hope of relief is held out to them. We are conscious, yes deeply conscious, of the many difficulties that surround this subject; yet we dare hope that a patriotic people and an enlightened legislature may greatly diminish them. There is a deep and pervading feeling among us, on this subject, which we trust may in some degree forward our efforts. We know that there are many people who would

voluntarily surrender now, at a short time, all this
property owned by them, to the Commonwealth, providing
means were dedicated for their removal and comfortable
maintainance outside of the United States, for a reasonable period. Those voluntary offerings for the public
good would in a short time diminish considerably the
numbers and excite a well founded expectation of the
total eradication of the evil. To these individual contributions should be added an adequate and appropriate
application of public means, for the removal of others
from the Commonwealth. The public and individuals
thus acting in concert, much would be effected at no
distant day.

To many such a plan we are fully apprised would be ob-
jectionable on the ground of inadequacy of the means of the
state to attain the object. To such it may well be answered,
what stay to the impending and horrible evil do you propose? Will you wait until the land shall be deluged in blood
and look alone to the fatal catastrophe of the extinction
of the black race, as the only remedy? Or rather will you
begin, the great and good work by kind, gentle, gradual, and
sure means? Let one count the cost and see at once, what
we are to expend of our means to effect this high purpose.

In the last forty years, the actual increase of the blacks
has been 107, 588, at this rate 4,189 per annum. An
indiscriminate removal then of this annual increase,
would in the course of thirty years, so diminish the evil
that thereafter by the removal of one-half this number
for thirty years more, an almost entire destruction of the
mischief would be effected.

Your memorialists do not, however, anticipate such
rapid and happy measures. Let but the Commonwealth
raise a tax on the blacks, free as well as slave, a reasonable sum, sufficient to defray the expense of the removal
and maintainance for the time of such as individuals
may voluntarily surrender to the state and for the purchase of a hundred of the young and healthy of both sex
and for their removal and maintainance, in like manner,
and we do not doubt the most happy and satisfactory

effects from such a beginning and a final full triumph
over all difficulties.

But these measures your memorialists confidently believe
should be accompanied by some others. The first should be
a total prohibition of emancipation by individuals, but
upon condition of removal from the state. The second
should be the immediate classification of the free blacks
and requiring at stated periods their removal, and where
they are not possessed of sufficient means to defray the
expense of immigration, the same should be paid by
the public. Such measures as these promptly adopted
and faithfully and energetically carried out, would save
to the Commonwealth many of the best people and much
of her domain from waste and abandonment.

Your memorialists are slaveholders; this is the country of
their birth, and they are attached to it by every tie that
can bind a people to their native land and that of their
ancestors, they have everything of interest or of feeling
at stake in this their final appeal to you. Humanity must
weep over a continuance of our present condition while
patriotism, self interest and our own happiness and that
of our offspring call equally strong for the application
on some remedy to remove this most appalling increasing
evil. Relying with most ample confidence on the wisdom,
patriotism, and known discretion and elevated public
spirit of the General Assembly, we most earnestly entreat
its attention to the subject of this petition and that it
would adopt measures in relation thereto as may seem
best calculated to advance the happiness, the greatness,
and the peace of the state.[29]

Many other petitions of a similar character make it very clear
that the memorialists were "deeply sympathetic with their fellow
citizens of Southampton, in their sufferings and sorrows, and that
they were sincerely desirous to take the most effectual measures

[29] Archives of Virginia, Legislative Papers, Petition, Hanover, Dec. 14,
1831. Hereafter Archives of Virginia, Legislative Papers, will be omitted
and the petition identified by the number, county, and date (insomuch
as this information is available) .

to shield their beloved state from, and to guard our posterity against the repetition of such enormities and horrors."[30] The petition given in the note below was sent to the legislature by the women of Augusta and of Fluvanna counties and must have had much influence upon the deliberations of the lawmakers.[31]

[30] Petition 9886, Loudoun, Dec. 23, 1831.

[31] Petition, Augusta, 1831: "To the Honorable the General Assembly of the State of Virginia, the memorial of the subscribing females of the county of Augusta, humbly represents, that although it is unexampled, in our beloved state, that females should interfere in its political concerns, and although we feel all that timidity incident to our sex in taking this step, yet we hold our right to do so to be unquestionable and feel ourselves to be irresistibly impelled to the exercise of that right by the most potent considerations and the perilous circumstances which surround us. We pretend not to conceal from you, our fathers and brothers, our protectors by the investment with the political powers of the land, the fear which agitates our bosoms, and the dangers which await us, as revealed by recent tragical deeds, Our fears, we admit, are great; but we do not concede that they are the result of blind . . . cowardice; we do not concede that they spring from superstitious timidity of our sex. Alas! We are timid indeed; but we appeal to your manly reason, to your more mature wisdom to attest the justice, propriety, of our fears, when we call to your recollection the late slaughter of our sisters and little ones, in certain parts of our land, and the strong possibility that the slaughter was but a partial execution of a widely projected scheme of carnage. We know not, we can not know the night, or the unguarded moment, by day or by night, which is pregnant with our destruction, and that of our husbands, brothers, sisters, and children; but we do know that we are at any moment exposed to the means of extinction of all that is dear in life. The bloody monster that threatens us is warmed and cherished on our hearth. Oh! hear our prayers, and remove it, ye protectors of our persons, ye guardians of our peace.

Tell us not of the labors and hardships which we shall endure when our bondservants shall be removed from us. They have no terror for us. Those labors, hardships cannot be greater or so great as those we now endure. . . .

Our fears teach us to reflect and reason. . . . And our reflections and reasonings have taught us that the peace of our homes, the prosperity of future generations, call aloud and imperiously, for some decisive and efficient measure—and that measure can not be believed to be efficient,

|Thomas Jefferson Randolph, a grandson of Thomas Jefferson, presented to the legislature the resolution which represented the will of the antislavery workers. This resolution, in part, reads "that the children of all female slaves, who may be born in this state on or after July 4th 1840, shall become the property of the Commonwealth, the males at the age of 21, the females at 18 years."[32]

This resolution was ably supported by the allies of Randolph. James McDowell declared that the members of the legislature had reason to believe that there were Nat Turners in their own households.[33] However, the proslavery forces were not idle. Petitions from such citizens were sent to counterbalance the antislavery petitions. The following petition from citizens of Hanover county displays the zeal of men who had much at stake and who did not fail to defend, ably, their interests:

> To the honorable the General Assembly of Virginia.
> The memorial of the undersigned inhabitants and free holders of the county of Hanover, respectfully sheweth, that they have heard of the proceedings of the House of Delegates in relation to a subject in which the good people of this Commonwealth have the deepest interest, with concern and astonishment. Doctrines have been advocated and published to the world, and questions debated from day to day which fill the whole community with alarm—Under these circumstances with the privilege of freemen they will speak that plain language, which it is their right to use, and which they doubt not you will hear with respect. In doing this they feel the most perfect confidence that they will have the concurrence of an immense majority of their countrymen. The right to property amounting to one hundred million dollars has been questioned—and can it be suffered the people to tamely submit to one single act that can in the slightest

---

or of much benefit, if it have not, for its ultimate object, the extinction of slavery from amongst us."

[32] *National Intelligencer,* June 16, 1832.

[33] Charles H. Ambler, *Sectionalism in Virginia* (Chicago, 1910), pp. 190–98.

degree injure their title to that property. By what tenure they hold it they will now disdain to inquire. It is theirs and they will at every hazard they are prepared to, defend it. Abolition questions may present fine themes for declamation, but it is strange that it should be necessary to tell Virginia Legislature that the fortunes and lives of the people ought not thus to be sported with, and that a debate which may be productive of the most horrible consequences should have been arrested in its commencement.

It has been said that no abolition will be attempted unless full compensation be made to the owners of slaves. This notion of compensation is the most extraordinary that ever entered into the mind of man. Whence is this compensation to proceed? From the state? The State is the people. No contributions could be expected from that portion of the country where there are few or no slaves. The citizens of the West will require, and justly, too, that at least as much money as they pay into the public treasury shall be expended in the improvement of their part of the state. The slaveholders then are to pay themselves for their own slaves. A more simple plan will avoid the expense of collecting and direct the owner to surrender his property. The burden of purchasing the slave from himself must be borne of necessity by the slaveholder alone, and all hope of compensation be completely delusive, if compensation be begun with, it is evident that such an absurdity must soon cause it to be abandoned.

But could compensation be in any mode obtained, or if the rights of property are to be entirely disregarded, while this process of abolition is going on what safety will there be for the white inhabitants? Slaves while kept in subjection are submissive and easily controlled, but let any number of them be indulged with the hope of freedom, one must have but little knowledge of their nature, who is to be informed that they reject restraint and become almost wholly unmanageable. It is by the expectation of liberty, and by that alone, that they can be rendered a dangerous population. So long as we are true to ourselves there can be nothing to fear.

Should our slaves be taken from us what will be the
value of our lands? What labor is to supply that of which
the country is to be deprived? We can hope for no immigration so long as the most fertile lands of the West
are unoccupied, and who can doubt if our slaves were
gone that the immigration from our country would be
still greater than at present. That scare of desolation,
sketched from imagination by some of your orators, with
a patriotism that we do not understand, which we regard
as fiction, would then be reality.

In all countries and conditions of life there must be
evils, but we had thought our own were not greater than
those of other people. Our slaves are a cheerful and contended race, strongly attached to their owners, and will
continue so unless great pains be taken to prevent it.
Let no man persuade himself he is serving the cause of
humanity by weakening the bond between master and ˙
slave. Any blow aimed at the owners will fall with twofold
violence on the objects of this mistaken philanthropy.

But why these new apprehensions of the dangers of an
increasing slave-population—were they more numerous
than they can possibly be for centuries to come, without
arms and incapable of concert, an insurrection would
be immediately quelled, and few or many, no man can be
secure against the acts of a fanatic who has resolved to
throw away his own life—we can never believe so long
as the vast regions to the South West, which can be cultivated only by slave labor, are yet to be settled, we
have to fear the dangers of overabundant slave population—Any laws to exclude it from that part of the country, must be transient and ineffectual. No scheme of
emancipation has ever been suggested which was not
most evidently impractical. Every plan is either wholly
inefficient or beyond the utmost resource of the state,
and in all cases attended with incalculable dangers. In
our fears for our posterity let us not forget our own safety,
and resisting hazardous experiments, have confidence that
our descendants will be able to take care of themselves.
When emancipation takes place it must be by the slow
work of time. It may take generations for its accomplish-

ment and will most probably require little or not any
legislative interposition.

How unreasonable is the time chosen for your unfortunate debate. Those alarms, so much exaggerated, had
subsided, and you ought to have exerted yourselves to
confirm the tranquility of the country, have again disturbed
it. Your discussions have invited insurrection. The state
has yet to learn why the uniform and wise precautions of
your predecessors has been disregarded, and your proceedings conducted with open doors. We might have
expected some laws punishing with severity the authors
of incendiary publications. These publications have
proceeded from your own body. Your time might have
been usefully employed on reforming the police, in arming
the militia, and providing for the public safety! It has
been worse than wasted in debating schemes which have
rendered property insecure, impaired the credit of the
State, retarded the improvement of your country,
interrupted the domestic relations of life, and brought
distrust and danger to our firesides.

We therefore urge you as you regard the welfare of
the State to abstain from every attempt to provide for the
emancipation of the slaves, partial or general, immediate
or prospective, in any manner whatsoever, and to adopt
such a rule or to pass such an act as in future will assure
the people that should this delicate subject be again
approached, it shall be in silent session—and above all
to terminate your debates and return to your constit-
uents as speedily as possible.

The former memorial from this country was signed by
many of us with the belief that a matter of such deep
interest might safely be confided to the discretion of the
legislature. We wish our names may be considered as
withdrawn from that memorial.[34]

The men who signed such petitions (as the above) were the same
class who had controlled the convention of 1829. They were the

---

[34] Petition 10005, Hanover, Jan. 30, 1931.

plantation aristocracy of the state and were making their traditional defense of their right to property in slaves. In times past
and in the present instance politicians responded to the will of
the men of property.

The power of the planters to control the will of the lawmaker
seems demonstrated in the conduct of Governor John Floyd.
Governor Floyd was a native of Montgomery county, in the western section of Virginia. His traditions were those of the antislavery western men, and he, himself, in 1814 had defended a slave
accused of inciting an insurrection. There seems to be every reason to trust the sincerity of Floyd when in November, 1831, he
confided to his diary: "Before I leave this government, I shall
have contrived to have a law passed, gradually abolishing slavery
in this state." But when Floyd sent his first message to the legislature in December he appears to have changed his mind completely on the subject of emancipation. At this time his only recommendations are the proslavery demands for a more strict and
rigid policing of both slave and free Negroes and for the silenc-
ing of the Negro preachers. Floyd's good intentions were silenced
by the same baneful influences that had in earlier days hampered
the humane instincts of Jefferson and Monroe. The explanation
of his regrettable change of heart seems to be found in his aspira-
tion for high federal office. This man was ambitious to follow the
example of earlier and greater Virginians. To him it appeared
that there should be Virginia successors to the roles played in the
national government by the great statesmen of the past. Floyd
was one of a group of young and frustrated Virginians who had,
because of their disappointments at the hands of President Andrew Jackson, broken all relations with the distinguished leaders
of democracy. Floyd had allied himself with John C. Calhoun.
There had been visiting by Calhoun at the governor's mansion at
Richmond and a correspondence had been begun that no doubt
promised to be mutually beneficial to both Floyd and Calhoun.
Floyd hoped to make Calhoun the president of the United States
and trusted that he would profit in the political fortunes of the
great South Carolinian.[35] However, Floyd knew that the aristo-

[35] James M. Batten, *Governor John Floyd* (Richmond, 1903), Randolph-Macon Historical Papers, IV, 33.

crats of South Carolina could not be expected to tolerate an ally suspected to be an abolitionist. It will be recalled that in his letter to the governor of South Carolina, Floyd had promised that his emancipation program would "be tenderly and cautiously managed, and will be urged or delayed as your state and Georgia may be disposed to cooperate."[36] Obviously the aristocrats of South Carolina were not disposed to cooperate in a program for emancipation, but his South Carolina friends sent to Governor Floyd a pamphlet entitled "A South Carolinian; A Refutation of the Calumnies Circulated against the Southern and Western States Respecting the Institution and the Existence of Slavery among Them, to Which Is Added a Minute and Particular Account of the Actual Condition of Their Negro Population." This work was written by a certain Edwin C. Holland and was dedicated to the South Carolina legislature of 1822. It included a history of Negro insurrections in that state and outlined a policy which, if always pursued, it was asserted, would guard the state against rebellion of the slaves. This South Carolina plan seems to have been adopted by the governor of Virginia and is responsible for his recommendation to the lawmakers of the state. Governor Floyd made his political future safe with the powerful politicians in the lower South and his reactionary influence served to defeat the antislavery men in the Virginia legislature.

Once determined on the expedient policy, Floyd called to his assistance a very able professor of political economy at the College of William and Mary. This man, a certain Thomas R. Dew, at the request of the governor published *A Review of the Debates in the Virginia Legislature.* This work must have eased the conscience of Governor Floyd, for it served to assure the people of the state that the slave system was just, necessary, and profitable, and that their government had pursued the course of wisdom. In later years this, the work of Dew, furnished the soundest arguments advanced by proslavery Southern men against the attacks of the North. Many men who had doubted the justice or the expediency of the slave system read the work of Dew and became converts to proslavery. Lesser men were controlled by the combination of economic and political motives that had determined

[36] Ambler, *Life and Diary of John Floyd,* p. 266.

the action of Governor Floyd. Such men joined the owners of slaves and defeated the most determined effort ever made by Virginians for the emancipation of slaves.

\ Nat Turner forced Virginia to make a great decision. Virginians had now determined on their course of action. From 1832 to 1863 there could be no doubt that this state intended to preserve the system of black slave labor.

Nat Turner made an effort to free the slaves and to all appearances he had failed. However, the insurrection was of national significance, and if the insurrection is judged by its larger effects, Nat Turner's efforts were not a failure.

The question of slavery was now to be fought out in the North. The rise of Garrisonian abolition coincided with the affair in Southampton county, and after the insurrection most Virginians placed Garrison and Turner in the same class. Possibly it would be difficult to decide whether Garrison or Turner was the most effective abolitionist. The alarm of the people of Virginia directed attention to the efforts of Garrison, and while the people of the South united in efforts to silence Garrison, at the North, men divided and became abolitionists or allies of the slaveholders.[37]

A letter from the postmaster of Orange Court House, Virginia, September 25, 1831, describes the excitement and the anger of a Virginia community, occasioned by the finding of a copy of the *Liberator* in the mail sent to a certain free Negro of that place. The postmaster sent this copy of Garrison's paper to the governor with the accompanying letter:

> I regret that the sheet is so much soiled and mutilated. It
> was occasioned by the interest which it excited in our
> village; being so great as to produce a desire in everyone
> to read it. Any more contempt and indignation, I am
> convinced, was never envinced, by any people, at such an
> assassin like publication. . . . I beg leave, in behalf of
> our village citizens and neighbors, to state, that they
> look upon the authors, editors, and publishers of such

[37] W. P. Garrison and F. J. Garrison, *The Life of William Lloyd Garrison, Story of His Life Told by His Children* (New York, 1894) , I, 219–76.

fiend like publications—these manifestors of insurrections
as lost to humanity and fellow feeling, and that they
are prepared and would be ready instruments, at all
times, to head the insurrection banditti—of negroes, of
this, and our sister states—to engage in the murder of
our wives, our daughters, our infant sons and aged and
helpless parents! And to apply the incendiary touch, to
every cottage, mansion, or hamlet in our country. They
act not from motives of Philanthropy, as they would
have us believe, but from those of most appalling wickedness and avarice. . . . I know that our laws, happily,
do, and that they ought to protect the rights of the press,
and the means of disseminating knowledge; yet in times
like these, such seditious incentives to insurrection and
murder, ought with some discretion, to be prohibited.[38]

The author of the following letter, probably influenced both
by Garrison and Nat Turner, was no doubt a man of character
very similar to many of the men we have already found working
for antislavery in Virginia, but as abolitionists the citizens of the
North were to be far more successful than the men who had
worked for emancipation in Virginia.

Albany, N.Y., Sept. 16, 1831

To The Post Master at
Chancellorsville

Sir:

As our constitution says that all men are created
equal; and as God made of one flesh all the nations of
the earth; and as the Negroes are no worse when born
than the whites; and as there is no good prospect that a
voluntary release of the slaves will be effected to any
great degree—I hereby make known that for these and
other reasons, I will as an individual, use all honorable
means to sever the iron bonds that unite the slaves to

[38] Governor John Floyd, "Slaves and Free Negroes" (a scrapbook
collection of papers pertaining to the Nat Turner insurrection, the
Archives of Virginia), September 25, 1831.

their masters. And so long as this national ulcer (slavery) remains upon one of the republic, a dis-union is highly desirable. It is a disgrace to the United States. It is looked upon as such by most of Europe—What? A republic boasting of its equal rights, when a worse system of slavery is hardly (if at all) to be found! It is a shame.

Yrs Respectfully
Shadrack S. Gregory.[39]

The numbers of the men with convictions like those of Shadrack Gregory were destined to multiply; but it is also true that the Southampton insurrection aroused much sympathy for the slaveholders among northern citizens. The letters of a resident of Philadelphia, who styled himself "L.N.2," makes it very clear that there were proslavery men in the North who joined with the South and helped to make slavery, in the period between 1831 and the Civil War, a national issue.

The first of these letters reads as follows:

Philadelphia

To His Excellency the
Governor of Virginia

Sir:

I have no doubt in my mind, from all that I can learn, that the conspiracy and insurrection of the negroes in the South is much more extensive than some of you gentlemen in the South can form any idea. That it is openly encouraged by two friends, William L. Garrison and Isaac Knap, of Boston, in proof of which I send you an address and one number of a periodical paper published by them and circulated extensively through these United States. The negroes of this city are principally from the Southern States, many of them runaways from the South, and they are busily employed in distributing these pamphlets and papers.

I make this communication because, altho' I abhor slavery, I disapprove of the measures taken to abolish it.

[39] Ibid., September 16, 1831.

It is an evil but the villains who would encourage the slaves to rise upon and murder their masters are monsters much more to be dreaded.

> I am Sir,
> Your obt. Servt.
> L.N.2.[40]

A second letter reads as follows:

Philadelphia, Oct. 15, 1831

To His Excellency
The Governor of Virginia

Sir:

I view with great anxiety the proceedings of the negroes in this city. Urged on by the editor of the *Liberator* and his murderous companion Walker, they hold meetings here of the most dangerous character, as regards the safety of our Southern bretheren. The addresses of the incendiaries I have mentioned are read in the churches by their ministers and others and they are taught the horrible doctrines that it is no harm for slaves to kill their masters and possess themselves of their soil. Depend upon it sir that much mischief is hatching here and in spite of all the salutary laws you can pass pamphlets and papers will be distributed among your slaves. Why can not the Southern States hold a convention and demand of the State of Massachusetts to silence these dangerous men? If it is unlawful to incite the subjects, of a foreign place to insurrection; can it be right to allow their fellows to encourage their slaves to kill their masters, our own bretheren in another state? You will find hundreds of thousands of friends here ready to second any general measure of the South, but we do not think we have a right to originate anything in which you are so critically concerned without your approbation—It would not be safe for an individual to openly do anything here; the only reason why I

[40] Ibid.

do not use my name to this, is that my house would in
all probability be fired and some private injury done me
by those fiends.

If you wish further information, write a line to L.N.2.,
Philadelphia, and if I receive a solemn pledge that my
name shall not in any way be disclosed without my approbation, I will with pleasure give it.[41]

The last of the letters from L.N.2 reads as follows:

Philadelphia, Oct. 24, 1831

Sir:

My only objection to writing to you over my proper
signature is that it would undoubtedly subject my family and property to the unjust fury of the ignorant and
deluded blacks of this city and country. I am an enemy
of slavery. I wish all the world were free; but the way
to obtain freedom is not to murder unoffending men,
women and children. God grant that matters with you
will never be brought to that crisis, but should our
service be wanting, I for one, will throw a knapsack
upon my back and march to your assistance. In like
manner should my name be necessary, concealment will
no longer be resorted to whatever may be the danger
—On the first page of the 42nd. no. of the liberator,
you will perceive a list of his agents. Of these of Penna.
Jos. Casey, is a Mulatto he keeps a perfumery in So.
4th Street, and has a little education and some natural
smartness. He is said to be worth 30 or 40 thousand dollars: Jos. Sharpless (I blush to write it) is a white man.
He is an old man, belongs to the Society of Friends or
Quakers, and keeps a crockery store in 4th street: J. B.
Vashon, is a mulatto who formerly lived in Carlisle now
in Pittsburg, is a hair dresser, and fruitier; John Veck,
Carlisle, is a black barber. The rest I do not know
anything about.

Does not the simultaneous rising in the South show
that there is some common cause? Besides the free

[41] Ibid., October 15, 1831.

Blacks of this city, this fall for the first time claimed a right to vote at the general election—This was exactly what the liberator advised them to do.

If it would be a crime to instigate the subjects of a foreign country to insurrection, a fortiers, it would be so to incite to insurrection and murder the slaves of a sister state. Would not this paper, then, plainly having this tendency, be a libel, and if it is a libel is not every one guilty of a libel in the place where it is published? i.e. Circulated? I submit then to your Excellency's better judgment, whether you might not with propriety apply to the executive of this state to have the publisher of these libels prosecuted. I am of the opinion that there is justice and humanity and magnanimity enough in this city to procure a conviction.

I send you 12 papers, I this day got from Sharpless. You may lay them and this before the legislature if you wish.

I am very respectfully
L.N.2.

p.s. I would be glad to correspond with you further if I can be of any assistance.[42]

It is not in the province of this study to describe the progress of the antislavery movement at the north. However, it may be observed that the same characteristics are to be found in the national contest that have already been discovered in the antislavery struggle in Virginia. The same human traits of character—the good or the bad, the moral or the immoral, the humane or the cruel—are to be found among the citizens of the North as among the citizens of Virginia. These human and personal traits made northern men anti- or proslavery advocates as they had tended to make citizens of Virginia anti- or proslavery men. But the advantage was on the side of antislavery in the North, not because God made northern men more moral and humane but because they had so little to lose in the emancipation of the slaves. Apparently, it is easier to see what is just and to do

[42] Ibid., October 24, 1831.

what is right when the cause of justice is far removed. Without doubt, if the sugar, cotton, and tobacco fields had been located in New England, the slave system with all its unfortunate aspects would have been defended by the governing classes of that section; and if the staple crops had not been grown at the South, radical abolition would have prospered in Virginia and South Carolina and finally the southern white man would have freed the oppressed slaves of the New England plantations.

The cause of antislavery sentiment developed a new sectionalism after 1832. We now have the North against the South, rather than the western farmers against the tidewater planters. As the slavery contest grew more and more intense and as more deep-seated sectional hatred developed, two nations were apparently developed, but, on the contrary, in the slavery struggle nationalism was being developed in the heat of the conflict. Slavery, after it had become a great national issue, caused the North and the South to grow to be more alike, as they increased in hatred the one for the other. The two sections were now tied together in thought by a great human problem. The two sections of the nation now reacted to each other as the East and West, in Virginia, had reacted in an earlier time. The final victory of the North over the South was the reversal of the earlier victories of the eastern planters in Virginia over the farmers of the western section, but in the strife, the men of the sections learned to know each other better, to hate each other more, and finally the South learned to accept the adverse decision imposed not by a foreign power but by the will of the majority of their nation, even as in earlier days western farmers had accepted the will imposed by the planters. The history of early American democracy seems to be the record of many local sectional conflicts and the imposing of the will of victorious sections on disagreeing factions. The institution of slavery served the cause of nationalism, for Negro slavery made an issue so great in its appeal that it transformed a local issue into a national issue. In the transformation the people at issue manifested the same human equalities and frailties that had given life to local politics, but the outcome of the strife and the great war was to be a more nearly perfect American nation.

In all the struggles of these eventful years, the Negro slave was the prime cause of the conflict, but the evidence found in the Archives of Virginia makes it clear that the Negro was not a passive factor in a great conflict. David Walker, Nat Turner, and a legion of other Negroes made it impossible to silence antislavery agitation. The police laws of the Southern states may have been increasingly severe, and insurrection may have been well nigh impossible, but freedmen and runaway slaves made slave property precarious. Such men of the North returned to the South and as operators on the underground railroad carried out thousands of the slaves. When escaped slaves told the story of their bondage and liberation they became far more effective abolitionists than any white man could become. The Negro worker at the North carried forward what the slaves had begun at the South, and, in large measure, by their own efforts, they won freedom.[43]

This study has been an effort to portray the relations between the white and the Negro races in Virginia as they seem to have been in the slave period of American history. Americans have long since decided that the system of slave labor was wrong, but the relations between these races will for many years be regarded as a peculiar American problem. Racial attitudes which today are familiar are in many respects the result of conditions which existed prior to the Civil War, and much has transpired to confuse or to falsify the story of conditions under the slave regime. I will be happy if any slight contribution may be made to the honor of the men then living, or if this little work may help to clarify the thinking of men of today.

Primarily the records here used have revealed human, rather than racial, relations. In these pages we find portrayed the contacts of good white men and good black men, bad white men and bad black men, good white men and bad black men, good black men and bad white men—with human nature as it is. Life had to have its complications, and the racial problem became primarily a problem of the adjustment of variable black and white characters. Of necessity there were maladjustments, and many of the evils of the system could never have been avoided under such a

[43] W. E. B. Dubois, *The Negro* (New York, 1915), pp. 199–200; Carter G. Woodson, *A Century of Negro Migration* (Washington, 1916), pp. 18–61, 81–160; Carter G. Woodson, *The Mind of the Negro as Reflected in Letters during the Crisis* (Washington, 1926).

system. Here men lacked freedom of movement and could not always amicably adjust their relations. There could be no easy divorce of master and slave. The accidents of life and the whim of fortune, since all men are not equally good, often brought together men of boisterous passions, or the misfortune of the master brought disaster to the slave. There were many great forces of evil in the system, but the evil in slavery did not result because all slaveowners were peculiarly evil and peculiarly different from white men outside the slave country; nor could the system ever be free from great evils, for all the slaveowners were not superior types of men, in righteousness different from men outside the slave country.

The Virginia slaveholders had inherited in their slaves a valuable form of property, and with the inheritance of property they acquired all the respect for the rights of property that are manifest by other American property owners. In 1860, the slaves of Virginia were valued at three hundred seventy-five million dollars and the slaves of all the Southern States at three billion dollars. It would not have been human to expect the owners to give up this property of their own volition. However, it is to be noted that some did relinquish their rights in this manner, and that there were many who testified that they would like to give up their slaves but were too human to do so. We seem to have in the slaveholders the manifestation of the universal and characteristic control of economic forces over moral forces in the determination of human action. Possibly the ease with which many men had acquired their slaves and the rapidity of the change from the poor into the propertied class made for hardship on the part of the slave, but as long as the present economic order exists many analogies may be found between the relation of the master and slave and the relation between the propertied class and the poor.

The records here used testify also to the human qualities of the slaves. The slaves were not all of like character; there were many humble, faithful servants and there were many rebellious spirits. The activities of both the faithful servants and the rebels were characteristic human reactions to the slave system. All the slaves could not always be humble and faithful; it would not have been human to have done so. Where there is injustice it is human to rebel. However, all the slaves would not rebel, for the system often made possible relations between masters and slaves under which it would have been inhuman to rebel. It is in the humanity of the slave that abolition has its origin. The splendid characters of hundreds of Negro slaves taught white men that the slaves should not be held in bondage. But the rebel, also, was an emancipator, for his actions were characteristic human conduct, and the willingness to resist injustice kept alive antislavery agitation. Had all the Negroes been humble and accepted the lot of slaves, they would have remained in slavery indefinitely; for while the slave system was profitable, there could have been no excuse for freeing men who did not care to be free.

If it be true that the slaves helped to emancipate themselves, it must be true, also, that they were, in large measure, responsible for the destruction and the bloodshed of the Civil War and for the hatreds that followed the war. It is possible to conceive of a happier America, if there had been no war between the States, and if there had been no such war, it may have followed that all the slaves would have been free by the year 1900 or the year 2000, and that the Negro would have assumed a status similar to that of the free Negro in 1830. However, progress does not always appear to be made by gradual and peaceful methods, and there is always a place in history for Gabriels, David Walkers, and Nat Turners. These men hastened the day of emancipation, and they have their part in the making of America. The Negro race would differ from other races of men if it could point to no such characters and if it did not attempt to do them honor.

In the preceding pages I have made a studied effort to exclude the question of miscegenation. However, in documents as here used repeatedly the student is reminded that this question infused itself into the relations of the people. Sexual problems could not be ignored by the men of earlier days and they can not be excluded in any attempt to describe racial relations as then existing. I have therefore, devoted the third section of this work to this subject. As we continue the story it is my hope that the reader will remember that this is an historical work and that he will excuse me if I fail to give *the* answer to controversial questions.

III

Miscegenation

SEVEN

The Intermixture of Races
in the Colonial Period

WHAT THE colonial settlers did in regard to miscegenation was to be the model for those that governed the United States in the early years of our history. It is the purpose of this chapter to describe racial attitudes as they existed in the colonial period and the resulting social and legal policy that then became established and was to be continued until the emancipation of the Negro slave. This policy had in view a very definite aim: it was intended to prevent the increase of a mixed race. But it will be found that the intermixture of the races continued to increase, and an effort will be made to show the cause of this increase and its results for each of the three races.

The mixture of the races began to take place almost as soon as the first Negroes and white men came into contact in America. This was the experience of the Spanish and the French as well as the English colonists. When colonization brings two dissimilar races into contact, the fusion of the races is as a rule more often the result of the union of the men of the stronger race with the women of the weaker.[1] This was true in America where the scarcity of white women possibly operated to cause interracial alliances. No doubt, Shufeldt is correct when he claims: "The crossing of the two races commenced at the very out-start of the vile slave trade that brought them thither; indeed, in those days many a negress was landed upon our shores already impregnated

---

[1] James Bryce, *Relations of the Advanced and Backward Races of Mankind* (Oxford, 1903), p. 23.

by someone of the demoniac crew that brought her over."[2] Captain Daniel Elfrye, said by some to be responsible for the introduction of the first Negroes into Virginia, received a letter from the London Company, May 10, 1632, "condemning him for too freely entertaining a mulatto."[3]

The first Negroes were brought to Jamestown in 1619, and in 1630 we find the first recorded step taken in the matter of race intermixture. It was then ordered "that Hugh Davis be soundly whipped before an assemblage of Negroes and others for abusing himself to the dishonor of God and the shame of Christians by defiling his body in lying with a Negro, which fault he is to acknowledge next Sabboth day."[4] Again, in 1640 it is recorded that, "Robert Sweet is to do penance in church according to the law of England, for getting a negro woman with child, and the woman to be soundly whipped."[5] After the record of the above cases we find that in 1662 Virginia enacted its first law prohibiting intermarriages.[6] Similar laws were adopted in most of the colonies. Maryland adopted such a law in 1662,[7] Massachusetts in 1705,[8] North Carolina in 1715,[9] Delaware in 1721,[10] and Pennsylvania in 1725.[11]

The penalty for intermarriage was the same as that for illicit relations between the whites. The action taken by Virginia seems

[2] Robert W. Shufeldt, *The Negro, a Menace to American Civilization* (Boston, 1907), p. 60.

[3] Alexander Brown, *The Genesis of the United States* (Boston, 1897), p. 436.

[4] William W. Hening, *Statutes at Large of Virginia* (Richmond, 1823), I, 146.

[5] Henry E. McIllwaine (ed.), *Minutes of the Council and General Court of Virginia* (Richmond, 1924), p. 476.

[6] Hening, op. cit., II, 280.

[7] William H. Brown (ed.), Archives of Maryland (Baltimore, 1883), I, 534–35.

[8] *Acts and Resolves of Massachusetts Bay* (Boston, 1869), I, 578.

[9] William L. Saunders (ed.), *Colonial Records of North Carolina* (Raleigh, 1886–), XXIII, 64–65.

[10] *Laws of Delaware* (New Castle, 1797), I, 108–09.

[11] H. Mitchell and E. C. Flanders, *Statutes at Large of Pennsylvania* (Philadelphia, 1801), IV, 62–63.

to have been typical of the other colonies. The punishment inflicted on Hugh Davis and Robert Sweet shows the existence of a condition, and the experience common to the other colonies is followed by the enactment of the law. The Virginia act of 1662 reads as follows: "Whereas some doubts have arisen whether a child got by an Englishman upon a negro should be free or slave, be it therefore enacted by this present grand assembly, that all children born in this country shall be bound or free according to the condition of the mother, and if any Christian shall commit fornication with a negro man or woman, he or she so offending shall pay a fine double the fine imposed by the previous act."[12] This policy, by which the mulatto offspring of a Negro woman must remain slaves, was generally adopted by the other colonies.[13] However, one exception is found in the decision of a Connecticut court, which freed the son of a slave mother by a white father. The court declared, "that Abda had English blood in him, and therefore was born free."[14] Laws prohibiting intercourse but declaring that the mulatto offspring should follow the condition of the mother were of little effect in preventing the evil.[15] Peter Kalm pointed out that the existence in the colonies of large numbers of mulattoes proved that the laws were easily evaded or enforced with great laxity.[16] Turner reports one example of an effort to enforce the law against a white man in the Pennsylvania colony. The charge presented against this man was, "for that He . . . Contrary to the Lawes of the Government and Contrary to his Masters consent hath . . . got with child a certaine molato woman called Swart anna."[17] The fact that the testimony of the

[12] Hening, op. cit., II, 280.

[13] George W. Williams, *History of the Negro Race in America from 1619 to 1880* (New York, 1882), I, 534–35.

[14] William G. Fowler, "Historical Status of the Negro in Connecticut," *Historical Magazine and Notes and Queries,* III (January, 1874), 14–16.

[15] Philip A. Bruce, *Economic History of Virginia, in the Seventeenth Century* (New York, 1896), II, 109–11.

[16] Peter Kalm, *Travels in North America* (London, 1772), pp. 502–03.

[17] Edward R. Turner, *The Negro in Pennsylvania* (Washington, 1911), p. 30.

slave woman could not be taken against a white man helped to prevent the enforcement of these early prohibitory laws.[18] In the entire colonial period there was much indiscriminate mingling of the races.[19] An interesting letter written in 1746 shows what might be expected as an outgrowth of racial contact in slaveholding society. This author writes that "if the trustees [Georgia] allowed one thousand white settlers so many negroes, in a few years, you would meet in the streets so as in Carolina, with many mulatto children, and many Negro children, which in the process of time would fill the colony."[20]

The criminal character of many of the convict class sent to the colonies must have helped to increase the intermixture of races.[21] As a rule the Englishman had no thought of legal marriage with the Negro woman, but an example of an exceptional attitude on the part of an Englishman is found in the records of a petition in the Lancaster county of Virginia, 1697:

> In that year a malatress entered a petition in the Lancaster court praying that she should be set free. She claimed that she had been purchased by John Beeching from Mrs. Elizabeth Spencer in consideration of his tanning one thousand hides. He had caused her and her infant child to be baptized, and if the assertion of the petitioner was to be relied on, had promised to marry her, and evidence was offered that he was the father of her offspring and that he had lived with her without disguise. The jury to whom the question of her freedom was submitted, decided in her favor and against Mrs. Spencer, who was of one of the most powerful families in the colony.[22]

[18] Hening, op. cit., v, 245; *State* v. *Waters*, 3 Iredell, *North Carolina Reports*, pp. 438–41 (1843).

[19] Bruce op. cit., II, 111.

[20] Andrew D. Chandler, *Colonial Records of Georgia* (Atlanta, 1902), XXIV, 434.

[21] William Douglas, *A Summary, Historical and Political of the Planting, Progressive Improvements, and Present State of the British Settlements in North America* (Boston, 1755), II, 434.

[22] Bruce, op. cit., II, 110.

After the marriage of Pocahontas there seem to have been no more of such alliances with Indians, in Virginia, although there were those who advocated such unions.[23] The following letter written by a certain Peter Fountaine illustrates such opinion:

Westover, Virginia
March 30, 1757

Dear brother Moses:

. . . I shall only hint at some of the things which we ought to have done, and which we did not do at our first settling among them, and which we might have learned to have done long since from our enemies the French. I am persuaded we are not deficient in observing our treaties with them, but we got our lands by concession, and not by conquest, we ought to have intermarried with them, which would have incorporated them with us effectively, and made them stanch friends, and which is of still more consequence, made them good Christians; but this our wise politicians at home put an effectual stop to at the beginning of our settlement here, for when they heard that Rolfe had married Pocahontas, it was deliberated in council, whether he had not committed high treason in so doing, that is, marrying an Indian princess; and had not some troubles intervened which put a stop to the inquiry the poor man might have been hanged up for having done the most just, the most natural, the most generous and polite action that was ever done on this side of the water. This put an effectual stop to all intermarriage afterward. Our traders have indeed their squaws, alias whores, at the Indian towns where they trade, but they leave their offspring like bulls or bears to be provided for at random by their mothers. As might be expected, some of these bastards have been the leading men or war captains that have done us so much mischief. This ill-treatment was enough to create jealousy in the natural

[23] John Oldmixon, *The British Empire in America* (London, 1708), II, 232.

man's breast, and made the Indians look upon us as
false and deceitful friends, and caused all our efforts to
convert them to be ineffectual. But here, methinks, I
can hear you observe, What! an Englishman intermarry
with Indians? But I can convince you that they are
guilty of much more heinous practices, more unjustifia-
ble in the sight of God and man (if that, indeed may be
called a bad practice) , for many base wretches among
us take up with negro women, by which means the
country swarms with mulatto bastards, and these mulattoes, if but three generations removed from the black
father or mother, may, by the indulgent laws of the
country intermarry with white people, and actually do
every day so marry. Now, if, instead of this abominable
practice which hath polluted the blood of so many
among us, we had taken Indian wives in the first place,
it would have been some compensation for their lands.
They are a free people, and the offspring would not
have been born in a state of slavery. We should become
the rightful heirs to their lands and should not have
smutted our blood, for the Indian children when born
are as white as the Spaniards or Portuguese, and were
it not for the practice of going naked in summer and
besmearing themselves with bears grease, etc., they
would continue white.[24]

---

[24] Ann Maury, *Memoirs of a Huguenot Family* (New York, 1872) ,
pp. 349–50. Colonel Byrd seems to have held similar views on this
subject. He has the following to say concerning intermarriage with the
Indian: "They had now made their peace with the Indians, but there
was one thing wanting to make the peace lasting. The natives could by
no means persuade themselves that the English were heartily their
friends so long as they disdained to intermarry with them. And in
earnest, had the English consulted their own security and the good of
the colony, had they intended either to civilize or convert these gentiles,
they would have brought their stomachs to embrace this prudent
Alliance. The Indians are usually tall and well proportioned, which
makes full amends for the darkness of their complexions. Add to this,
that they are healthy and strong with constitutions untainted with
lewdness, and not enfeebled with luxury. Besides morals and all consid-

Possibly in some of the colonies there may have been legal marriages between the English and the Indians. In New York, for instance, Sir William Johnson had an Indian wife who bore him many children. To her he was very faithful, and his great influence over the Six Nations was, in part, due to his marriage relation.[25] It is claimed that through Sir William Johnson's influence, eighteen marriages with Indians were contracted by white settlers in his colony.[26] But, as a rule, marriages with the Indians were disdained.[27] The acts of the colonies that controlled intermarriage with the Negro, in most cases, applied equally to the Indian.[28]

It will be found that there developed, in the colonial period, much intermixture of the Indian and the Negro slave. This willingness of the Indian to intermarry with the Negro must have helped build up a sentiment that in the Englishman's point of view placed the Indian and the Negro slave in the same general

---

ered, I can't think the Indians were very much greater heathen than the first Adventurers, who, had they been very good Christians, would have had the Charity to take this only method of converting the Natives to Christianity. For, after all that can be said, a spritly lover is the most prevailing missionary that can be sent among these or any other infidels, Besides, the poor Indians would have had less reason to complain that the English took their Lands, if they received it by way of a marriage portion with their daughters. Had such affinities been contracted in the beginning, how much bloodshed had been prevented, and how populous would the country have been, and consequently, how considerable. Nor would the shade of the skin have been any reproach at this day; for if the Moor may be washed in three generations, surely the Indian might be blanced in two" (John S. Bassett [ed.], *The Writings of Colonel William Byrd* [New York, 1901], pp. 8–9) .

[25] Maury, op. cit., p. 350.

[26] James Grahame, *History of the United States of America, from the Plantation of the British Colonies till Their Assumption of National Independence* (Boston, 1845) , IV, 151.

[27] Almon W. Lauber, *Indian Slavery in Colonial Times, within the Present Limits of the United States* (New York, 1913) , pp. 207–08; Oldmixon, op. cit., I, 252; for an opposite view see Thomas Shourd, *History and Genealogy of Fenwick's Colony* (Bridgeton, 1876) , p. 6.

[28] Lauber, op. cit., pp. 250–58; Bruce, op. cit., II, 130.

class.[29] The Frenchmen made use of this English attitude to the great injury of the English frontier settlements. The French did not disdain to intermarry with the Indian woman, and they taught the Indians that since the English did disdain such unions, they regarded the Indians just as they did the Negro slaves.[30] In 1749 Sir William Johnson wrote to the governor of New York: "The French told the Six Nations, that we look upon them as our slaves or Negroes, which affair gave me a great deal of trouble at the time to reconcile."[31] While Indian intermixture may not in colonial or in future times have been on so large a scale or of equal social significance with Negro intermixture, it does have a large place in creating the class of mixed racial blood. The class commonly called the mulatto is the result, in many instances, of the union of the three racial elements.

The evidence used in this study shows also that race mixture was sometimes the result of the union of the Negro man and the white woman.[32] Such unions became the subject of special legislation at an early date, and the language in which the laws are written often shows the abhorrence of the lawmakers toward these unions. The Virginia law of 1691 reads as follows:

> . . . and for the prevention of that abominable mixture
> and spurious issue which may hereafter increase in this
> dominion with English, or white women, as well as by
> their unlawful accompanying with one another. Be, it
> enacted . . . that for the time to come whatsoever
> English or white man or woman being free shall inter-

[29] Lauber, op. cit., pp. 207–08; Clarence Alvord, *The First Explorations of the Trans-Allegheny Region* (Cleveland, 1912), p. 91.

[30] John F. D. Smyth, *Tour in the United States of America* (London, 1784), I, 190–91.

[31] John R. Brodhead (ed.), *Documents Relating to the Colonial History of the State of New York* (Albany, 1858–87), VI, 647.

[32] Bruce, op. cit., II, 109–11; Arthur W. Calhoun, *A Social History of the American Family* (Cleveland, 1917), I, 323–33; Edward B. Reuter, *The Mulatto in the United States* (Boston, 1918), pp. 128–30, 145; John H. Russell, *The Free Negro in Virginia, 1619–1865*, p. 60; Carter G. Woodson, "The Beginnings of Miscegenation," *Journal of Negro History*, III (October, 1918), 335.

marry with a Negro, mulatto, or Indian man or woman,
bound or free shall within three months thereafter be
banished and removed from the dominion forever . . .
and be it further enacted . . . that if any English or
white woman shall have a bastard child by a negro or
mulatto, she shall pay the sum of fifteen pounds sterling, within one month after the child is born, to the
wardens of the parish, where she shall be delivered of
such child, and in default of such payment, she shall be
taken into possession of the said church wardens and
disposed of for five years . . . and such bastard child
shall be bound out as a servant by the said church
wardens until he or she shall attain the age of thirty
years.[33]

The law of 1691 was re-enacted in 1696 and 1705.[34] The act of
1705, however, provided that the minister marrying a Negro and
a white woman should pay a fine of ten thousand pounds of tobacco.[35] One half of this fine went to the informer. This was a
heavy penalty, for it meant two-thirds of the minister's salary for
the year. In 1753 the law was re-enacted without any important
change.[36] But, in 1765 a new law was adopted that reduced the
mulatto child's term of apprenticeship to twenty-one years for
males and eighteen years for a female child. If children were
born to an apprenticed mulatto who had not completed her term
of service, such a child should also serve a term similar to that of
the parent.[37]

The Maryland colony also passed laws to prevent such marriages.[38] In September, 1664, an act was passed, the second section
of which reads as follows: "And for as much as divers free born

[33] Hening, op. cit., III, 86–88. (In the event that the woman was
already an indentured servant, she had to serve an additional term of
five years.)

[34] Ibid., p. 87.

[35] Ibid., p. 453.

[36] Ibid., VI, 375.

[37] Ibid., VIII, 134–35.

[38] Eugene I. McCormac, *White Servitude in Maryland* (Baltimore,
1904), pp. 76–81.

English women, forgetful of their free condition do intermarry with Negro slaves, by which means divers suits may arise touching the issue of such freeborn women, and a great damage doth befall the masters, be it further enacted . . . that whatsoever English woman, should intermarry with a slave from and after the last date of this present general Assembly, shall serve the master of the said slave during the life of her said husband, and that all issue of such freeborn English women shall be slaves as their fathers were."[39]

The above act was sometimes used for the purpose of enslaving the white woman. This is indicated by the act of 1681, which reads as follows: "And for as much as divers English or white women, sometimes by instigation, or conivance of their masters, mistresses or dames, and always for the satisfaction of their lascivious and lustful desires, and to the disgrace not only of the English but also of many other Christian nations, do intermarry with negroes or slaves, by which means divers inconveniences, controversies, and suits may arise, touching the issue of the children, of such freeborn women aforesaid, for the prevention whereof in the future, be it further enacted."[40]

It is then enacted that, on proof of instigation on the part of the master, the woman shall be set free and the woman's master shall be required to pay a fine of ten thousand pounds of tobacco, one-half of which went to the Lord Proprietor and the other half to the informer. The act of 1664 was then repealed. In 1715 a new law was enacted, by which a white woman who married a Negro was made a servant for seven years, and if there were a child born of such a woman it was bound out for thirty-one years.[41] In 1717 a law was enacted that any free Negro who married a white woman should become a slave for life.[42]

In this colony, as in Virginia, the preambles of the laws indicate a situation that already existed, and the laws were intended to stop as well as to prevent, in future cases, the union of white women and Negro men.

[39] Browne, op. cit., I, 533–34.
[40] Ibid., VII, 203–04.
[41] Virgil Marcy, *The Laws of Maryland* (Baltimore, 1811), I, 115–16.
[42] Ibid., p. 141.

Similarly, in 1718 North Carolina passed an act to control this same situation. A fine of fifty pounds sterling was placed on the white woman and a like fine on the minister officiating at such a marriage. One-half of the minister's fine went to the informer and one-half to the government of the colony. In case a mulatto child was born of such a white woman, the mother should serve two additional years and pay six pounds or be sold for six years of service. This child of such a union was bound out to serve until thirty-one years of age.[43]

In 1717 South Carolina enacted a law punishing white women with limited servitude for such offenses; the child, also, was bound out for limited service.[44] Pennsylvania in 1725 prohibited such marriages and placed a fine of one hundred pounds on the minister officiating at the ceremony.[45] Massachusetts in 1705 passed an act "for the better preventing of a spurious and mixed issue." In this colony the penalty was made whipping, and a fine was placed upon the minister performing such a service.[46] The acts of the colonial assemblies prove that the intermarriage of white women and Negro men was a problem faced by most of the colonies.

While much of intermixture may have existed prior to the passing of the laws prohibiting it, the records of the period show many instances of the violation of the law and the application of penalties for such violations. The manuscript records of Elizabeth City county, Virginia, give the following example:

> Whereas by the law it is provided that in case any
> English woman being free shall have a mulatto bastard
> child borne of her body, she shall pay fifteen pounds
> sterling or be sold for five years and such bastard to be
> sold as servants until they attain the age of thirty years
> and for as much as Ann Wall of this county a free
> English woman being convicted of having two mulattoe

[43] Saunders, op. cit., XXIII, 115–16.

[44] Thomas Cooper, *Statutes at Large of South Carolina* (Columbia, 1838), II, 19.

[45] H. Mitchell and E. C. Flanders, op. cit., IV, 62–63.

[46] *Acts and Resolves of Massachusetts Bay*, I, 5; see also, *Laws of Delaware*, I, 108–09; Chandler, op. cit., XVIII, 102.

bastards by a negro begotten and borne of her body contrary to ye law. It is therefore ordered that ye said Ann Wall doe serve Mr. Peter Hobson or his assigns (of Norfolk County) the term of five years from ye date hereof and her said two mulatto bastards to serve ye said Hobson in like manner until they attain each of them unto ye age of thirty years as ye said law directs ye same being in consideration of ye sum of one thousand pounds of legal tobacco and cask and payment of costs and sheriffs due ye said Ann Wall, and it is further ordered that in case ye said Ann Wall after she is free from her said master doe at any time presume to come into this county she shall be banished to ye Island of Barbadoes.[47]

The records of Henrico county, Virginia, contain the following presentment:

Henrico County June 1, 1692
Information
Maj'r Chamberlaynes woman servant Bridgett by name for bearing a base born child by a Negro.
Henrico county
Presented to ye grand jury for this County of Hen'co May 16; 1692 & here recorded
Tests: Hen. Randolph, Vo; Cur.[48]

Another example is found in the records of Warrick county, Virginia:

Our Sovereign Lord the King	On presentment for
agt.	having a mulatto
Anne Wood, Widow	Bastard Child

The said Anne Wood being dully summoned & solemnly called, came not but made default and thereupon

[47] County Records, Elizabeth City County, Virginia, Vol. 1684–1699, p. 83.

[48] County Records, Henrico County, Virginia, Vol. 1688–1697, p. 322.

came a jury, to wit, James Jones, Peter Sandifer, William
Whitaker, Robert Seymour, Moory Lucas, Robert Mal-
licote, Robert Brown, Richard McKentosh, Thomas
Cary junr., & Wm. Langston, who being duly elected &
sworn to the [sic] truth to speak upon their oaths do
say that the said Anne Wood is guilty of the offense laid
to her charge. Wherefore tis considered by the said Court
that she shall forfeit and pay the Sum of fifteen Pounds
to the Church Wardens of Warrick Parrish for the use
of the said Parish and that she pay the Costs of this
Presentment.[49]

Such evidence is to be found in many Virginia county records,
but the records do not show that the condition was peculiar to a
special locality.[50]

According to the law of 1691, in cases in which the woman offender could not pay the fine imposed, she was bound out by the
church wardens of the parish. The records of such indentures do
not appear to have been preserved with care. According to an
opinion of Judge Green, rendered in 1827:

These indentures were not recorded, and remained either in the hands of the masters, or church wardens, or
justices, and not in the hands of the servant; and where
ever left, were not likely to be preserved with care. Such
fugitive papers might naturally be expected to be lost
within thirty years.[51]

While the evidence in many of these cases may have been lost,
according to Bishop Meade, the application of the Virginia law
placed a burden upon the parishes.[52] The records of Bristol Parish, Virginia, bear out this testimony. Here we find it ordered on

[49] Arthur P. Scott, "History of the Criminal Law in Virginia during
the Colonial Period," p. 91. Unpublished Doctor's thesis, University of
Chicago, 1916.

[50] Ibid., p. 25.

[51] Gregory v. Baugh, 4 Randolph, Virginia Reports, p. 635 (1827).

[52] William Meade, Old Churches, Families, and Ministers in Virginia
(Philadelphia, 1867), I, 366.

July 24, 1724, that, "the church wardens bind out to Godfrey
Ragsdale two mulatto children named Doll and Biddle as the
law directs."[53] Again, October, 1728, "on motion of Edward Colwell that Peter a mulatto boy should bound to him, it is ordered
that the Church Wardens bind him to the said Colwell according
to the law."[54] And so on, through this the record of one parish
and extending over a period of six years, there are found to be
eight cases that afford examples of mulatto children bound out as
provided by the law.[55]

At the expiration of their term of servitude, the mulatto children of white mothers were, according to the law, to be free. An
example of the operation of this process is found in a record of
October 7, 1697, which reads: "Ann Redman, a mulatto woman
born of Jane Redman, an English woman, was freed from slavery
and discharged from the service of Thomas Lloyd of Richmond
county."[56]

The application of the law of 1691 gave rise to problems that
were not anticipated by the lawmakers. Jefferson's reports give
the following case presented to the court in October, 1769:

> A christian white woman between the years 1732 and
> 1765, had a daughter, Betty Bugg, by a negro man. This
> daughter was by deed indentured, bound out by the
> church wardens to serve till thirty-one years of age.
> Before the expiration of her servitude, she was delivered
> of the defendant Bugg, who never was bound out by the
> church wardens, but was sold by her master the plaintiff.
> Being twenty-six years of age, and having cause of com-
> plaint against the plaintiff, as being ill provided with
> clothes and diet, he brought action in the court below
> to recover his liberty.[57]

[53] Charles G. Chamberlayne, *The Vestry Book and Register of Bristol
Parish, Virginia* (Richmond, 1898), p. 36.

[54] Ibid., pp. 2–63.

[55] Ibid.

[56] *William and Mary Quarterly Magazine of History and Biography,*
XVII (1909), 76.

[57] *Gwinn* v. *Bugg,* 1 Jefferson, *Virginia Reports,* p. 87 (1769).

A similar case is reported in the records of Augusta county, Virginia. This is the

> petition of John Anderson, as against Rev. John Craig, for detaining him as a slave. The deposition of Joel Barker, taken in Brunswick county shows that Anderson is the son of a free white woman and was bound out by the church wardens of the parish of Saint Andrews, in Brunswick, to serve until twenty-one years of age. He is now of age. The judgement of the court is that he be released.[58]

Violations of the law prohibiting the intermarriage of white women and Negro men are to be found in the colonial period in other states than Virginia.

Turner cites one case of this kind found in the records of Chester county in Pennsylvania. This case reported as follows:

> David Lewis constable of Haverford returned a negro man of his and a white woman for having a bastard childe—the negro said she inticed him and promised to marry him: she being examined, confessed the same: The court ordered that she shall receive twenty-one lashes on her beare backe—And the court ordered the negro never more to meddle with white women on paine of his life.[59]

In North Carolina, in 1725, John Cotton, a minister was indicted for marrying a mulatto man and a white woman.[60] When brought to trial this case was dismissed. In 1726, the Reverend John Blacknall was fined fifty pounds, according to law, for performing such a marriage.[61] Strange to relate, in this case, Blacknall himself, informed the court that he had performed this marriage, and so having played the part of the informer, he collected

---

[58] *Abstracts from the Records of Augusta County* (Washington, 1912), I, 107.

[59] Turner, op. cit., p. 30.

[60] Saunders, op. cit., II, 551, 504, 602.

[61] Ibid., II, 272.

one-half of the fifty pounds fine. Hawks explains this case. He
claims that the minister had already been paid fifty pounds and
that he was, therefore, making twenty-five pounds as a result of
his illegal conduct.[62] We are left to wonder who was willing or
able to pay the heavy fine. One more example of this kind is revealed when in 1727, we find, "a presentment against Elazabeth
Pucket for that she hath left her husband and hath for some
years cohabited with a negro man of Capt. Simon Jeffreys."[63]
This case was sent to a higher court, but we have no further record of it. In 1835 at the debates of the Constitutional Convention of North Carolina, it was asserted that almost all of the free
Negroes of that state before the Revolution were the mulatto
children of free white mothers.[64]

In Maryland it is found that two cases were presented to the
court that were very similar to cases already described. In the first
of these cases the record states that

> the petitioner is a mulatto, and the descendant of Irish
> Nell, who came into the province with Lord Baltimore,
> and intermarried with a negro slave, during the exist-
> ence of the act of 1665. After this act was repealed, Nell
> had children in consequence of this marriage, who
> were the ancestors of the petitioner.[65]

The courts were asked to determine whether these children were
entitled to freedom.

Evidence that white women were married to Negro men in
South Carolina is furnished by testimony presented to the courts
in cases recorded after the Revolution. Here, in several instances,
when the courts were asked to determine the race of the individual, the evidence showed that one of the defendant's ancestors, a

[62] Francis L. Hawks, *History of North Carolina* (Fayetteville, N.C.,
1857), II, 81.

[63] Saunders, op. cit., II, 126–27.

[64] *Proceedings and Debates of the Constitutional Convention of
North Carolina, 1835* (Raleigh, 1835), p. 351.

[65] *Boarman* v. *Boarman,* 1 Harris and McHenry, *Maryland Reports,*
p. 371 (1787); *Butler* v. *Craig,* 2 Harris and McHenry, ibid., p. 217
(1808).

white woman, had, at some remote date in the colonial period, been married to a Negro.[66]

The study of this subject shows that race mixture was caused by the union of the white man and the Negro woman and the union of the Negro man and the white woman, and also, that in the process of race mixture the Indian element plays an important part.[67] However, while the records of the courts furnish many examples of the union of the white woman and the Negro man, such unions do not, of course, account for the larger part of such race mixture. The greatest number of all the cases of the intermixture of the races were regarded as outside the province of the law and the courts, and the larger part of the mulatto population was, no doubt, due in colonial times and thereafter, to the exercise of passions by those who took no thought of marriage, law, or consent of clergy. The records of the time, letters, and memoirs give testimony to indiscriminate mingling of the races: the white, the Indian, and the Negro.[68] Perhaps Peter Fountaine was correct when he speaks of Colonial Virginia as swarming with mulattoes.[69] By no means all the Englishmen in colonial America were of the highest moral character; among their number were both gentlemen and vile rogues. I shall now attempt to show the reaction of both the governing gentlemen and the common man to the question of the intermixture of races.

Little evidence is to be found of legal marriage of the Negro in the aristocratic classes in the colonies. However, the will of John Fenwick, the Lord Proprietor of New Jersey, contains the following provision: "Item, I do except against Elizabeth Adams of having any ye leaste part of my estate, unless the Lord open her

[66] *State* v. *Haynes*, 2 Hill, *South Carolina Reports*, p. 278 (1829); *State* v. *Mayes*, Bailey, ibid., p. 275 (1829); *Johnson* v. *Been*, 1 Spears, ibid., p. 249 (1842).

[67] Reuter, op. cit., pp. 128, 129; Williams, op. cit., p. 121; Carter G. Woodson, "The Beginning of Miscegenation," *Journal of Negro History*, III (October, 1918), 335–53; Calhoun, op. cit., I, 323–30.

[68] John Brickell, *Natural History of North Carolina* (Dublin, 1737), p. 272; Hugh Jones, *The Present State of Virginia* (London, 1724), p. 27; Andrew Burnaby, *Travels through the Middle Settlements of North America* (London, 1798), p. 54.

[69] Maury, op. cit., p. 350.

eyes to see her abominable transgression against him, me her good father, by giving her true repentance, and forsaking ye Black ye hath been ye ruin of her, and becoming penetent of her sins; upon ye condition only I do will and require my executors to settle five hundred acres of land upon her."[70]

The above Elizabeth Adams was the granddaughter of John Fenwick. She took as her husband a Negro servant, and her grandfather shows his disgust at her action. This union resulted in the establishment in New Jersey of a settlement known as Gouldtown. The members of this community intermarried with the white settlers, and Gouldtown remains today a community of mulattoes, many of whom have acquired considerable property and have gained a degree of prominence.[71]

Another example is found in an aristocratic family in the state of New York. A son of this family begot a favorite slave with child. This is said to have created offense and scandal in the family, but the mulatto boy

> was carefully educated; and when he grew up, a farm
> was allotted to him, well stocked and fertile, but in the
> depths of the woods embraced, about two miles from
> the county seat. A destitute white woman who had wan-
> dered somehow from other colonies, was induced to
> marry him; and all branches of the family thought it in-
> cumbent upon them to pay a visit to Calk (for some
> unknown reason, they always called him).[72]

The colonial English aristocrat married with those of his own caste. Class prejudice made him disdain a marriage into the white servant class, and a person of the character and tradition of an aristocrat would not be expected to form a legal union with

[70] Francis B. Lee, *Archives of New Jersey* (Trenton, 1903), xxiii[1], 162.

[71] W. Stewart and T. T. Stewart, *Gouldtown* (Philadelphia, 1913); Robert G. Johnson, *An Historical Account of the First Settlement of Salem in New Jersey by John Fenwick* (Philadelphia, 1839), p. 35.

[72] Anne Grant, *Memoirs of an American Lady, with Sketches of the Manners and Customs in America as They Existed Previous to the Revolution* (London, 1808), pp. 22–26.

one of Negro blood. Nevertheless, some of the men of this class maintained permanent relations with Negro women to a more or less open extent.[73] Also, on the large plantations rumors often involved the planters' sons in affairs with Negro girls.[74] In case of illicit relations such as these, the man of high position sought to conceal his guilt, and accusation on these grounds was regarded as damaging to a man's character. In 1651 we find a suit brought before a Maryland court in which the complainant asks twenty thousand pounds sterling because he had been "defamed" and "disgraced" by the report that "he had got one of his Negroes with child." The court ordered the defendant in this case to appear in person at the next court and plead forgiveness or pay the complainant "fifteen thousand pounds of tobacco and cask."[75]

The planter class had no desire to be thought personally responsible for race mixture, and this class was in spirit responsible for the colonial legislative policy designed to prevent the evil. The system of life built up in the agricultural colonies resulted in planter control. Both social and governmental institutions were devices wrought by the planters. The system of Negro slavery may have been thrust upon them by England, but the problems arising from it were first of all the planters' problems, and on the governing class is the responsibility for the system of slave institutions worked out in the colonies.

The study of this question shows that the planter policy with regard to the intermixture of races, as it concerns the Negro, was as follows: to prohibit the marriage of the Negro and the white race but to tolerate illicit union of the Negro woman and the white man, provided always that the mulatto offspring should follow the condition of its mother. Possibly the planter had decided that under the existing system the prevention of intermixture was humanly impossible. Without doubt, he believed that more of evil would result from the mulatto reared by a white mother than from the mulatto reared by slave mothers, and if the mulatto child of the Negro mother were controlled by legislation

[73] Bruce, op. cit., p. 110.

[74] Philip V. Fithian, *Journal and Letters* (Princeton, 1900), pp. 244–45.

[75] Browne, op. cit., I, 114.

that watched over all his activities and kept him in the same status as his Negro kindred, dangers to planter society would be
averted.

A variety of causes operated to oppose the intermixture of
races. References are to be found to the natural race prejudices
of the Englishman, brought over with him from England.[76] In
the early days little distinction was made between the white indentured servant and the Negro slaves, and what is regarded as
race prejudice was, in these days, very closely akin to English
class prejudice. To the indentured servant and to the Negro slave
were assigned the same tasks, and many masters held both in
equal contempt.[77] White women servants were sometimes forced
by their masters to marry Negroes, and it is claimed that masters
were often milder in their treatment of Negro slaves since it was
always to their interest to prolong their lives, and that white servitude, being for a limited period, resulted in harsher treatment.[78] It is declared that the indentured servant was always run-
ning away to the open lands; he wanted freedom much more
than the slave who could not find himself on the frontier; moreover, the Negro was more tractable and docile. But, distinctions
soon began to be made by the master class.[79] The sentiment of
the lawmakers is shown in the wording of the laws, repeated
mention being made of "abominable mixture," "spurious issue,"
"disgrace of the nation," and "abusing himself to the dishonor of
God." The color of the skin in addition to the fact the early Negroes were heathen must help account for the feeling that is expressed in these words.[80] The letter of Peter Fountaine, as quoted
above points out that the union with the Indian was more to be

[76] James C. Ballagh, *History of Slavery in Virginia* (Baltimore, 1902),
pp. 72–73.

[77] Jeffrey R. Brackett, *The Negro in Maryland* (Baltimore, 1889), pp.
33–34; Reuter, op. cit., pp. 148–50; Turner, op. cit., p. 29.

[78] William Eddis, *Letters from America, Historical and Descriptive*
(London, 1782), p. 69.

[79] Jones, op. cit., p. 36; Robert Beverly, *History of Virginia, in Four
Parts* (London, 1722), pp. 235–36.

[80] Chandler, op. cit., xxv, 424; Burnaby, op. cit., p. 54; Jernegan,
"Slavery and the Beginnings of Industrialism in the Colonies," *American Historical Review*, xxv (January, 1920), 517.

desired because the offspring would not differ in color from that of the white man.[81] Also, the adoption of the law declaring that the conversion of the slave to Christianity would not liberate him shows the growth of the belief that the Negro was an abject being to be kept separate from the white race. The conversion of the Negro was opposed because of the belief that the equal association of the races in religious matters made the Negro dissatisfied and made him aspire to other forms of association.[82] The same forces that were opposed to conversion were opposed to intermarriage and for similar reasons. It would seem that colonial leaders, building on English class prejudice, had developed the spirit of those who today preach the doctrine of racial integrity.

Another cause for the adoption of the planter policy was the ever present fear of slave insurrection.[83] Free mulattoes who escaped to the frontier were harbored by the Indians and later participated in attacks on the settlers on the border.[84] The most stringent measures were adopted to punish the runaways and to secure their return.[85] Strong measures were adopted to prevent secret meetings of the slaves, at which free Negroes might be present, because of the belief that this might lead to Negro uprising.[86] The very harsh laws which controlled the free Negro show that the mulatto was feared as a danger to the peace of the colony and help explain the belief that the mulatto should be forced to accept a distinctly subordinate position in society.

Still another cause for the adoption of the planter policy would seem to be the preservation of the economic system established in the colonies. The economic system had proved to be entirely beneficial to the planters. Slave labor was a profitable institution, and, it was reasoned, it would be extremely unfortunate

[81] Maury, op. cit., p. 350.

[82] Jones, op. cit., pp. 70–71; Jernegan, "Slavery and the Beginnings of Industrialism in the Colonies," *American Historical Review,* xxv (January, 1920), 517.

[83] Maury, op. cit., p. 347; William P. Palmer (ed.), *Calendar of Virginia State Papers* (Richmond, 1875), 1, 130; Russell, op. cit., pp. 51–53, 55, 153.

[84] Palmer, op. cit.

[85] Hening, op. cit., IV, 126, 131, 132, 133.

[86] Ibid., p. 126.

for the planters if this source of labor should fail them. Nothing could be permitted to interfere with their labor supply. If indiscriminate intermarriage had been permitted and the mulatto offspring of free white parents set free, the supply of Negro slave labor might have been seriously affected and loss would have resulted for the planter.

It is also to be believed that the planter wished to develop an attitude of race superiority on the part of the poor white and the Negro groups through a fear that at some future time the poor white might lead the mulatto and the Negro in revolt against the established order. Reflecting this sentiment in part, even in the North Judge Horsmanden, who published a very complete account of the Negro plot at New York in 1741, claimed that the purpose which led him to publish this book was to warn the other colonies of the danger that he believed had been narrowly averted in the city of New York. This judge placed much emphasis on the evidence of the intermarriage of Negroes and the lower white element of the city, warning that disaster might be expected to come to other colonies if association between Negroes and the poor whites were permitted.[87]

After the colonial period much evidence will be found of the increasing fear of the mulatto leadership of the Negro.

In the seventeenth century the association of the indentured servant and the slave was very close.[88] They were often subjected to the same treatment and held by the master in the same esteem. Such associations led to many of the marriages that have been recorded. In those colonies where the numbers of the Negro slaves were comparatively few and when the master's only interest in his indentured servant was in the profits of his labor, many masters must have been little concerned to prevent the intermixture of the two races. Many instances of this lack of interest in race relations could, no doubt, be discovered throughout the entire colonial period. Thomas Branagan, writing from Philadelphia

[87] Daniel Horsmanden, *The New York Conspiracy, or a History of the Negro Plot, with a Journal of the Proceedings against the Conspirators at New York in the Years 1740–1741* (New York, 1810), pp. 116–20.

[88] Bruce, op. cit., II, 111–12; Ballagh, *Slavery in Virginia*, p. 73; McCormac, op. cit., p. 67; Reuter, op. cit., p. 130.

shortly after the Revolution complains of a condition which he seems possibly to exaggerate but which may have existed in certain of the colonies. According to Branagan's testimony:

Many respectable citizens who are reduced in temporalities; on their decease their poor orphans are bound out in gentlemen's homes, where the maid servants are generally white, the men servants are black, and the employers allow the blacks as many liberties as they think proper to take; and no distinction is made between the white girls and black men. . . . The poor reputable child is thrown by her unfeeling master and mistress in the road to ruin. Instead of protecting the white orphan (the brutal wretches) put her in the power of black people. Hence she loses all sense of propriety; being degraded she becomes an easy premature prey.[89]

This author contends also:

It is a stubborn fact that there are more bound and hired white girls in rich men's houses, deluded by black men than anywhere else. If I were to give an account of the instances which have come to my knowledge to authenticate and demonstrate the assertion, it would make my readers shudder, yes, it has frequently happened, that negroes have forcibly violated white girls, and certain white men have attempted to screen them from the penalty of the law demanded.[90]

Advertisements found in colonial newspapers often show the very close relations of the indentured white servants and the Negro slaves. The following are typical examples:

The Pennsylvania Gazette, June 26, 1740.
Runaway from the subscriber in Baltimore county, Marland, a negro man named Charles. . . . He is sup-

---

[89] Thomas Branagan, *Serious Remonstrances Addressed to the Citizens of the Northern States and Their Representatives* (Philadelphia, 1805) , p. 74.
[90] Ibid., p. 102.

posed to be in company with two servant men belonging
to John Muller, senr. One of them is a Scotchman.[91]

The American Weekly Mercury,
August 11, 1720.

Runaway in April last from Richard Tilgman, of
Queen Anne county in Maryland, a mulatto slave,
named Richard Molson, of middle stature, about forty
years old and has had the small pox, he is in company
with a white woman named Mary, who it is supposed
now goes for his wife; and a white man named Garrett
Choise, and Jane his wife, which said white people are
servants to some neighbors of Richard Tilgman.[92]

The Pennsylvania Gazette
June 1, 1746.

Runaway from the subscriber the second of last
month, at the town of Potomac, Frederick County, Maryland, a mulatto servant named Isaac Cromwell, runaway
at the same time, an English servant woman, named
Ann Greene.[93]

The indentured servant that had not lived long in the colonies
must have lacked much of "the natural race prejudice" that is at-
tributed to the governing aristocrat. Many of these servants were
of English birth and in their early years had not learned to hold
the attitude toward the Negro that had been developed among
the older settlers. When such persons found themselves often despised by the master class and apparently held in no higher regard than the Negro slave, there must have been strong forces
that developed class relations with the Negro. Benjamin Banneker, a Negro who for his scientific studies, won the praise of
distinguished revolutionary leaders, was born of such a union as
this.[94] Banneker was born in 1731,

[91] "Eighteenth-Century Slaves as Advertised by Their Masters," Journal of Negro History, I (April, 1916), 207.

[92] Ibid., p. 206.

[93] Ibid., p. 208.

[94] Henry E. Baker, "Benjamin Banneker, the Negro Mathematician,"
Journal of Negro History, III (April, 1918), 99–119.

his maternal grandmother, Molly Welsh, a native of
England, who came to Maryland—, with a ship load of
emigrants, and, to defray the expense of the voyage was
sold to a master with whom she served an apprenticeship of seven years. After her term of service had expired, she bought a small farm—, and purchased as
laborers, two Negro slaves, from a ship which lay in
Chesapeake Bay. They proved valuable servants. One of
them, said to have been the son of an African king, a
man of industry, integrity, fine disposition, and dignified
manners, she liberated from slavery and afterwards
married. His name was Banneker, which she adoped as
her surname, and afterwards was called Molly Benneker.
They had four children.[95]

While this case was a flagrant violation of the Maryland law, it
seems to be well authenticated.

Among the English convicts sent over to the American colonies
there were many immoral women. Many of these women held no
aversions to relations with the Negro.[96] The testimony taken in
New York at the trial of those accused in the "Negro Plot" reveals the following:

At Hugson's (the white keeper of a tavern) lodged one
Margaret Kerry, commonly called Peggy, or the New
Foundland Irish Beauty, a young woman of about one
or two and twenty years; she pretended to be married,
but no husband appeared; she was a person of infamous
character, a notorious prostitute, and also of the worst
sort, a prostitute to negroes. She here lodged and was
supported by Caesar (a Negro) before mentioned—.
With this Peggy, Caesar used frequently to sleep at
Hugson's with the knowledge and permission of the
family; Caesar bargained with and paid Hugson her
board; she came there a second time in the fall, not long
before Christmas, 1740, big with child by Caesar, as was

[95] Martha E. Tyson, "A Sketch of the Life of Benjamin Banneker,"
Maryland Historical Society Pamphlets (Baltimore, 1854), p. 4.
[96] Bruce, op. cit., II, 112.

supposed, and brought to bed there of a babe pertaking
of a dark complexion.[97]

The county records of York county, Virginia, show that women
of the same type were found in the Virginia colony.[98] The minutes of the Council of Virginia, May 11, 1699, contain "the petition of George Ivie and others for the repeal of the Act of the Assembly, Against English peoples marrying with Negroes, Indians
or Mulattoes."[99] This evidence would seem to indicate that an element of that colony was not in sympathy with the planter policy
on the question of race mixture.

The relations between the poor whites and Negroes remained
an interesting problem throughout the period of slavery. Despite
fierce antagonisms between them, which had their origin in economic causes, there continued to be sexual relations between
them as long as slavery endured.

There was much miscegenation in this period. It troubled the
colonial fathers who passed many acts pertaining to it. If we
agree that the acts were designed to prevent miscegenation, it
must be apparent that they failed of their purpose, for at the end
of the colonial period there were more than sixty thousand mulattoes in the English colonies.[100] Under the slave institutions
handed down from the colonial period, so far as the Negro man
and the white woman were concerned, the Negro man was to be
kept away from the white woman, but law and public sentiment
were insufficient to deny the white man the use of the Negro
woman.

[97] Horsmanden, op. cit., pp. 16–17.

[98] County Records, York County, Virginia, Vol. 1692–1694, pp. 12–13.

[99] Henry E. McIllwaine (ed.), *Legislative Journal of the Council of
Virginia* (Richmond, 1918).

[100] Reuter, op. cit., p. 112.

EIGHT

The Problem of
Racial Identity

THE INTERMIXTURE of races had become so extensive by the end of the colonial period that many mulattoes seem to have lost all the distinguishing physical features of the Negro.[1] There were now to be found many individuals classified as Negroes whom the observer would regard as whites or Indians. A traveler in 1788 reports, "I saw in this school [Philadelphia] a mulatto; one-eighth a negro; it is impossible to distinguish him from a white boy. His eye discovered an extraordinary vivacity; and this is a general characteristic of people of this origin."[2] In 1783 another observer reports that in Maryland,

> there were female slaves, who are now become white by
> their mixture. There are at this time many beautiful
> girls, many of whom are as fair as any living . . . and
> whose posterity must remain in the same degraded con-
> dition.[3]

With the passing of the years the number of such persons constantly increased and advertisements appear which contain such descriptions of runaway slaves, as, "he has straight hair and a complexion so nearly white that a stranger would suppose there

[1] Francois Jean Castellux, *Travels in North America in the Years 1780, 1781, and 1782* (London, 1787), II, 206.

[2] Jean P. B. De Warville, *New Travels in the United States of North America* (London, 1794), p. 221.

[3] John F. D. Smyth, *Tour in the United States of America* (London, 1784), II, 181.

was no negro blood in him,"[4] and, "a very bright mulatto, would be taken for a white boy if not closely examined; his hair is black and straight,"[5] or, "light sandy hair, blue eyes, ruddy complexion; he is so white as to easily pass for a white man."[6] Petitions presented to the legislature of Virginia often mention the bright complexion of Negro memorialists. Such quotations as the following are very frequent: "They are so nearly white that they would not be taken for mulattoes where they are not known."[7] Such persons, having more than one-half of white blood, though commonly called mulattoes might more properly be styled quadroons or octoroons. In the lower South where Indian blood was mixed with that of the Negro we find use made of the term "griffe."

There seems to have been no legal necessity for a definition of the term "mulatto," until after the Revolution. The states then began to define this word. The acts of the state legislatures may be considered as a part of the effort then being made by the independent American states, to transform the common law of England in accord with peculiar American institutions and social ideals. The action of the lawmakers may also be considered as recognition of the fact that, because of the wide extent of the intermixture of the races, the racial identity of many persons had become, and would continue to be, an important consideration in the American states.

In all the states there was much similarity in the racial laws. The Virginia law of 1785 declared that "every person, who has one-fourth or more of Negro blood shall be deemed a mulatto, and the word negro in any section of this or any other statute, shall be construed to mean mulatto as well as negro."[8] When

---

[4] Charles Elliot, *Sinfulness of Slavery in the United States* (Cincinnati, 1857), II, 65.

[5] Ibid.

[6] Ibid.

[7] Archives of Virginia, Legislative Papers, Petition 5818, Amherst, Dec. 4, 1811. Hereafter Archives of Virginia, Legislative Papers, will be omitted and the petition identified by number, county, and date (insomuch as this information is available).

[8] William W. Hening, *Statutes at Large of Virginia* (Richmond, 1823), XII, 184.

Kentucky became a state, the Virginia definition of the word was incorporated into her law.[9] The North Carolina law on this subject stipulated that "all persons descended from negro ancestors, though one ancestor of each generation may have been a white person, shall be deemed free negroes and persons of mixed blood."[10] The code of Tennessee contained a similar provision. Georgia defined the mulatto as "one in whose veins there is less than one-fourth of negro blood."[11] South Carolina left the term undefined.[12] Florida provided that "every person other than a negro, who shall have one-fourth part or more of negro blood, shall be deemed a mulatto."[13] Alabama declared that "the term mulatto or person of color within the meaning of this code, is a person of mixed blood, descending, on the part of the father or mother, from negro ancestors to the third generation inclusive, though one ancestor of each generation may have been a white person."[14] Mississippi enacted that "every person other than a negro, whose grandfather or grandmother is, or shall have been a negro, although all his progenitors, except that descended from the negro, shall have been white persons, who shall have one-fourth part or more of negro blood, shall in like manner be deemed a mulatto."[15]

It will be noted that in no case does the law provide that a person having less than an eighth of Negro blood shall be deemed a mulatto. It would appear that the lawmakers of the early national period feared that a declaration to the effect that the possession of any Negro ancestry, however remote, made a man a

[9] C. A. Wickliffe, C. Turner, and S. S. Nicholas, *Revised Statutes of Kentucky* (Frankfort, 1852), p. 627.

[10] B. T. Moore and W. Briggs, *Revised Code of North Carolina* (Boston, 1835), p. 580.

[11] H. R. Clark, T. R. R. Cobb, and D. Irvin, *Code of Georgia* (Atlanta, 1861), p. 481.

[12] *State* v. *Cantey*, 2 Hill, *South Carolina Reports*, p. 278 (1835).

[13] Lawrence A. Thompson, *Digest of the Statute Law of Florida* (Boston, 1842), p. 537; Act of Nov. 21, 1828.

[14] J. J. Ormond, A. P. Bagby, and G. Goldwaite, *Code of Alabama* (Montgomery, 1852), p. 58.

[15] T. J. T. Alden and J. A. Van Hoesen, *Digest of the Laws of Mississippi* (New York, 1839), p. 748; Act of Dec. 20, 1831.

mulatto might bring embarrassment on certain supposedly white citizens. No doubt, it was also believed that it would be exceedingly difficult, if not impossible, to enforce a more drastic law.

The attempt to apply the laws that had been enacted illustrates the difficulty, under the system as adopted, of determining who were white men and who were mulattoes or Indians or Negroes. Many cases are recorded in which the courts were asked to determine the race of the individual. Such cases were submitted to a jury which was expected to determine, on inspection, whether the person possessed more than the limited degree of Negro admixture. In 1806, a case of this kind appears in Virginia. In this instance the judges rendered an opinion that,

> where white persons are claimed as slaves, the *onus pro bandi* lies upon the claimant. It is said that the distinguishing characteristics of the different species of the human race are so visibly marked, that those species may be readily discriminated from each other by inspection; and that, in the case of a person visibly appearing to be of a slave race, it is incumbent upon him to make out his freedom.[16]

The case of a certain Nannie Pagee gives an interesting example of the difficulty of enforcement and of the mistakes that were possible under the Virginia law. The girl was bought in North Carolina as a Negro slave. There were doubts as to her race at the time of her purchase, but, "she was treated as a slave and compelled to marry, or rather to cohabit, with a negro, by whom she had several children."[17] This case became the subject of a long and tedious litigation, but in course of time the jury finally reported, "we find, therefore, that the plaintiffs are free persons and not slaves and we find for them one penny damages."[18]

In those cases in which the individual claimed that his dark

[16] *Hudgins* v. *Wright,* 1 Hening and Munford, *Virginia Reports,* p. 133 (1809).

[17] Edward S. Abdy, *Journal of a Residence and Tour in North America, from April 1833 to August 1834* (London, 1835), III, 9–10.

[18] *Hook* v. *Nannie Pagee,* 2 Munford, *Virginia Reports,* p. 79 (1814).

complexion was due to Indian rather than to Negro blood, the jury was asked to determine this matter, also, on inspection.[19]

In North Carolina also there are found recorded cases in which the courts were asked to determine the race of the individual. A case reported in 1802 recites that

> the plaintiff, when an infant, apparently about eight years old, was placed in a barn by some person unknown; that the defendant, then a girl of about twelve years of age found him there, conveyed him home, and has kept possession of him ever since; treating him with humanity, but claiming him as her slave. The plaintiff was of an olive colour, between black and yellow, had long hair, and a prominent nose.

In this instance, the individual, though obviously of a dark complexion, brought suit for freedom, and he won his suit, the court declaring "such persons may have descended from Indians in both lines; or at least in the paternal."[20] In 1828 the above decision was reaffirmed, although the plaintiff, this time, appeared to have been a mulatto rather than an Indian.[21] In 1842 a mulatto and a white woman were tried for fornication and adultery. These persons had been married and lived together as man and wife, but in this case the marriage was declared illegal, and the husband was declared to be a mulatto when it was proved to the satisfaction of the jury that one of his grandparents had been black.[22] In 1849 a free mulatto was accused of possessing firearms contrary to the law of North Carolina. This individual contended that the law did not apply to him because of the fact that he was of less than the prescribed degree of Negro blood. The following testimony was offered in this case:

> On behalf of the state, a witness deposed, that he formerly knew one Barncastle, who was a very old man, and died some years before the institution of the prose-

[19] *Gregory* v. *Baugh,* 4 Randolph, *Virginia Reports,* p. 611 (1827).

[20] *Gobu* v. *Gobu,* Taylor's *North Carolina Reports* (1709–1802), p. 164.

[21] *Scott* v. *Williams,* 12 *North Carolina Reports,* p. 376 (1828).

[22] *State* v. *Waters,* 3 Iredell, *North Carolina Reports,* p. 338 (1843).

cution; that the said Barncastle lived many years in the neighborhood of the defendant's father and his family, and that he the witness, heard Barncastle say, that he knew the paternal great-grandfather of the defendant, who was called Joseph Dempsey, alias Darby, and that he was a coal black negro. To the admission of this evidence the defendant objected; but the court received it. The defendant gave evidence that the mother of Joseph Dempsey, the great-grandmother, was a white woman, and that the said Joseph was a reddish copper colored man, with curly red hair and blue eyes; that the said Joseph's wife was a white woman, and that they had a son, named William; that the said William also married a white woman, and had issue by her a son, named Whitmel; and that the said Whitmel married a white woman, and that they are the parents of the defendant.[23]

In this case the court declared that the man was not a mulatto and that he therefore had the right to possess firearms and to exercise all the rights of other white citizens. The court, also, declared that it "could hardly undertake itself to construe the expression 'person of colour' so as to bring one within the statutes, creating felonies, or otherwise penal, merely because he derived from some remote ancestor a tinge of colour that was not white."

In a North Carolina decision rendered in 1859, we find interesting evidence of the apparent necessity for the use of "expert" testimony to determine racial classification. This is another case of the attempt to possess firearms. In this case the State called in an "expert" who deposed that

he was a planter, an owner and manager of slaves, and had been for more than twelve years, that he had paid much attention to and had had much observation of the effects of the intermixture of negro or African blood with the white or Indian races, and that from such attention and observation, he was well satisfied that he could distinguish between the descendants of a negro

[23] *State* v. *Dempsey,* 31 *North Carolina Reports,* p. 384 (1849); *State* v. *Jacobs,* 47 *North Carolina Reports,* p. 47 (1859).

and a white person, and the descendants of a negro and
an Indian; and further, that he could therefrom also say
whether a person was full African or negro, or had
more or less than half negro or African blood in him,
and whether the cross was white or Indian blood.

In the decision of the court, it is to be observed that in determining who were white, Negro, or Indian, North Carolina possessed
"experts" far superior to Lord Lyell or Agassiz. The court declared as follows:

The effect of the intermixture of the blood of the different races of people is surely a matter of science, and
may be learned by observation and study. Nor does it
require a distinguished comparative anatomist to detect
the admixture of the African or Indian with the pure
blood of the white race. Any person of ordinary intelligence, who for a sufficient length of time, will devote his
attention to the subject, will be able to discover, with
utmost unerring certainty, the adulteration of the
Caucasian with the Negro or Indian blood. . . . Mr.
Lyell, in common with tourists less eminent, but, on this
subject, not less misinformed, has somewhere stated that
the negroes in America are undergoing a manifest improvement in their physical type. He has no doubt, that
they will in time, show a development in skill and intel-
lect quite equal to the whites. This unscientific assertion
is disproved by the cranial measurements of Dr. Morton.
After admitting some physical improvement on account
of the increased comforts with which the negores are
here supplied, the authors add, one or two generations
of domestic culture effect all the improvements of which
the negro organism is susceptible. We possess thousands
of the second generation, and many more negro families
of the eighth or tenth generation, in the United States,
and (where unadulterated with white blood) they are
identical in physical and intellectual characteristics. No
one in this country pretends to distinguish the native son of a Negro from his great-grandchild (except
through occasional and ever apparent admixture of

white or Indian blood) while it requires the keen and experienced eye of such a comparative anatomist as Agassiz to detect structural peculiarities in a few African born slaves. The improvements among American born slaves noticed by Mr. Lyell, in his progress from the South to the North, are solely due to those ultra ecclesiastical amalgamations, which, in their illegitimate consequences, have deteriorated the white element in direct proportion that they are said to have improved the black. . . . We believe that it would often require an eye rendered keen, by observation and practice, to detect, with an approach to certainty, the existence of anything less than one-fourth of African blood in the subject. . . . He may . . . be a person who . . . has only a sixteenth of African blood in his veins. The ability to discover the infusion of so small a quantity of negro blood in one, claiming the privilege of a white man, must be a matter of science, and, therefore admitting the testimony of an expert, and we think that the witness, Pritchett, proved, in the present case, that he possessed the necessary qualifications, to testify as such.[24]

Having examined the evidence used in this study, I am not able to concur in the opinion of the learned judge.

In South Carolina also as shown by the records of the State courts, racial identity became an intricate problem. Here, again, are to be found individuals who had associated with, and were regarded as, white persons, but when unfortunate circumstances involved them in legal proceedings, they were challenged because of the tradition or suspicion that they had inherited the blood of the Negro and hence could not exercise the rights and privileges of white persons.

The following case shows how doubtful the racial origin of supposedly white persons might be:

. . . . the tax collector of St. Pauls issued his execution, which was about to be enforced, by Sheriff Rice, against the relators as free mulattoes. They applied for and ob-

[24] *State* v. *Jacobs,* 51 *North Carolina Reports,* p. 284 (1859).

tained a prohibition *nisi,* on the grounds that they
were free white men, but were ordered to declare in
prohibition. Two of the brothers, Thomas and John,
were in the court, and submitted themselves to the inspection of the jury. Their full brother, Henry, who
proved to be a darker man than either of them, was not
present; and his absence was accounted for in this way
he is the overseer of Colonel Perry, of St. Pauls, and
that he could not attend court. Sally Johnson the
mother was not at court, whether her presence was required by the respondents was not shown. Her sister of
the whole blood, Mrs. Patrick, was shown to the jury,
and from inspection, I should say was a quadroon. The
father of the relators, Benjamin Johnson [a white man]
proved the relators were his children by Sally Johnson.
She was the daughter of Lydia Tan by John Erick
Miller, a Dutchman [a white man] her second husband,
Lydia Tan's mother was a white woman; her husband,
Tan, was a colored man. According to this genealogy,
the relators could not have had more than one-eighth
of negro blood in their veins, possibly not so much as
one-sixteenth.[25]

The decision of the court was that these people should be classified as white persons. In 1850 we find a similar case. In this instance a witness was challenged as a free person of color. After
much testimony to the effect that the witness was, and was not, of
the prescribed degree of African blood, it was finally agreed that
she should be considered as a white person.[26]

The record in the two cases cited above shows that the persons
in question were of the poor white element of society, but the following case seems to offer evidence that Negro blood might be
found in the higher ranks of South Carolina society.

An important case was presented to the court, but
. . . on the trial two of the principal witnesses were ob-

[25] *Johnson* v. *Boon,* 1 Spears *South Carolina Reports,* p. 249 (1842).
[26] *State* v. *Belmont,* 4 Strobhart, *South Carolina Reports,* p. 445
(1850).

jected to, on the ground that they were persons of
color. An issue was made up, and the question was submitted to the jury. It appeared that the father of the
witnesses was a white man and the mother, a descendant
in the third generation of a half-breed who had a white
wife; their mother's father was the issue of this marriage, and he also married a white woman; so that the
witness had one-sixteenth part of African blood. The
maternal grandfather of the witness, although of dark
complexion, had been recognized as a white man, received into society, and exercised political privilege as
such; their mother was uniformly treated as a white
woman; and their relations of the same admixture have
married into respectable families, and one of them has
been a candidate for the state legislature. The witnesses
were ordinarily fair and exhibited none of the distinctive marks of the African race; they are respectable,
have always been received into society, and recognized
as white men—one of them a militia officer, and their
caste has never been questioned until now.[27]

The opinion rendered in this case by Justice Harper shows that
it was necessary to take a very broad interpretation of the term
mulatto. The opinion reads as follows:

We feel no disposition to depart from the rule laid
down in, The State vs. Hanna, 2 Bailey, 558. The
ground for that decision is, that neither of the several
decisions which speak of "negroes, mulattoes, and persons of color," nor the constitution of the state, which
restricts political privileges to free white men, give any
definition to those terms, nor is there any known techni-
cal meaning affixed to them. We must, of necessity, then,
suppose them to have been used in their ordinary and
popular signification, and to the ordinary and popular
signification we must resort for the interpretation of the
laws. From what possible source could a definition be
drawn that would make a person generally reputed to

[27] State v. Cantey, 2 Hill, South Carolina Reports, p. 278 (1857).

have been a free white person, a mulatto or person of color? Indeed, it would be an absurdity in terms to say, that such a one is, in the popular sense of the word a person of color. If we were to say that such a one is a person of color, on *any* mixture of negro blood, however slight or remote, we should be making instead of declaring a law, and making a very cruel and mischievous law. It is this which makes the question peculiarly proper for the jury. It belongs for them to settle questions of common usage and the meaning of popular terms, though their decisions may be matured into rules of law. The principal argument urged against this rule we have adopted is its want of precision. We can not say what admixture of negro blood will make a colored person, and by a jury, one may be found a colored person, while another of the same degree of blood may be declared a white man. In general it is very desirable that rules of law should be certain and precise. But it is not always practicable, nor is it practicable in this instance. Nor do I know that it is desirable. The condition of the individual is not to be determined solely by distinct and visible mixture of negro blood, but by reputation, by his reception into society, and his having commonly exercised the privileges of a white man. But his admission to these privileges, regulated by the public opinion of the community in which he lives, will very much depend on his character and conduct; and it may be well and proper, that a man of worth, honesty, industry, and respectability, should have the rank of a white man, while a vagabond of the same degree of blood should be confined to the inferior caste. It will be a stimulus to the good conduct of these persons, and security for their fidelity as citizens.[28]

The court, therefore, declared these persons to be members of the white race.[29]

[28] Ibid.

[29] In 1895 the South Carolina constitutional convention debated the question of racial identity. The following is a part of the record of the

In 1856 a Georgia court decreed that one Joseph Numez was to be a white man and not a mulatto, deprived of the rights of a free white man. In this instance, Joseph Numez was shown to have been the descendant of the early Spanish settlers of West Florida. But it was shown also that among his ancestors there were included both Indians and Negroes. Numez was a man of

---

debate: "Mr. Evans proposed to amend the section providing that the miscengenation law shall not apply to persons of mixed blood, whose status is that of white persons. Mr. George Tillman stated, that he was very feeble, but that he felt compelled to say something on this subject. For one, he had felt ashamed when the delegate from Beaufort had clapped his hands, and declared that the coons had a dog up a tree. He was further mortified to see that the gentleman from Newberry (Mr. Sligh) and the gentleman from Edgefield (Mr. Ben Tillman) goaded and taunted into putting into the constitution, that no person with any trace of negro blood should intermarry with a white person, and that for such marriage the legislature should provide punishment even beyond that of bastardizing children and adulterizing marriage. Mr. Tillman said the Mississippi law forbidding intermarriage between white people with those of more than one-eighth negro blood is the old South Carolina law. If the law is made as it now stands, respectable families in Aiken, Barnwell, Colleton, and Orangeburg will be denied the right to intermarry among people with whom they are now associated and identified. At least one hundred families would be affected to his knowledge. They had sent good soldiers to the confederate army, and are now landowners and taxpayers. He asserted as a scientific fact that there was not a full blooded Caucasian on the floor of the convention. Every member had in him a certain mixture of Mongolian, Arab, Indian, or other colored blood. The pure blooded white man has needed and received an infusion of darker blood, to give him readiness and purpose. It would be a cruel injustice, and source of endless litigation, of slander, horror, feud and bloodshed to undertake to annul or forbid marriage for a remote, perhaps obsolete trace of negro blood by the rule of evidence traditional notoriety was admissible in proving pedigree. The doors would be opened to scandal, malice, and greed; to statements on the witness stand, that the father or grandfather, or grandmother had said that A or B had negro blood in their veins. Any man who is half a man would be ready to blow up half the world with dynamite, to prevent or avenge attacks upon the honor of his mother or the legitimacy or purity of the blood of his father." (Theodore D. Jervey, *The Slave Trade, Slavery, and Color* [Columbia, S.C., 1925], p. 199).

great wealth. He had always associated with white men and was regarded as a white man by his associates. However, when he died it was found that his property had been willed to his natural children by a mulatto slave concubine. Those who wished to secure his property investigated his pedigree and discovered his remote Negro ancestry. They then possessed themselves of Numez's property and sold the mulatto children. The lower court supported them in their action, holding that since Numez was a mulatto, the will was void according to the laws of Georgia.[30]

In Alabama we find two instances in which the court directed that persons, supposedly white, should be classified as colored and be denied the privileges of white citizens. In 1859, Seaborn Heath resisted arrest by a certain William Chavis, constable of Autauga county. He claimed that the constable was a mulatto and hence disqualified for the functions of that office. Heath was able to show that the great-grandfather and the great-grandmother of the said Chavis were both mulattoes. The court sustained the contention of Heath, reversed the decision of the lower court that had considered Chavis a white man, and the former constable was now classified as a person of color.[31]

Social conditions under the early Spanish regime complicated racial problems in lower Alabama. In 1859 the supposedly white children of a certain "Clara" were offered as witnesses in a murder trial. Much evidence was offered concerning the ancestry of these "white children," but they were not permitted to testify; for they were finally declared to be mulattoes who, of course, were not able to bear testimony against a white man. In this instance the court accepted the evidence of a certain William Fisher,

> who was a gentleman about sixty years of age, and a
> Creole born in the city of Mobile, and who testified that
> Clara, her mother, and probably her grandmother, who
> was named Jean Seymour, were born at Twenty Mile
> Bluff on the Mobile river below the 31st degree of north
> latitude and had always lived there; that Anastasia the
> mother of Clara, was about his age, but he did not distinctly remember Clara's age; that Jean Seymour was a

[30] *Bryan* v. *Walten, Adm. of Joseph Numez,* 20 *Georgia Reports,* p. 480 (1856).

[31] *Heath* v. *Chavis,* 34 *Alabama Reports,* p. 250 (1859).

Griffe, dark in color, but not entirely black; that
Anastasia was the daughter of a white man, Simon
Andre by name, who always lived with Jean, as her husband; that they were called man and wife in Spanish
times before the change of flag, and had several children, who were all about the color and appearance of
Anastasia, that Jean never had any other husband than
the said Simon Andre and everybody recognized her children as his; that Simon Andre and Jean had both been
deceased for many years; that Anastasias only husband
was a white man, named Chastang, who was the father
of Clara; that Clara was recognized by everybody as
Chastang's child, and her children were by a white man;
that these colored women always were free and owned
slaves and other property; that they were treated as husbands and wives under the Spanish law.[32]

In this area there is much evidence of the mixture of the Indian,
Mexican, Negro with that of Spanish, French, and English.[33]

In the courts of Mississippi and Louisiana the state was asked
to determine the race of persons supposed to be mulattoes because of their dark complexion. Again, the courts of these states
held that such persons might be the descendants of Indians or
Mexicans, but the complicated mixture of racial blood in this
section of the United States made decisions as to pedigree more
difficult.[34]

In Tennessee we find legal problems similar to those described
in other states.[35] Mention may be made of many other cases of
pedigree not above described, which proved equally difficult for
the injuries and judges of the southern courts.[36] In northern

[32] *Dupree v. State,* 33 *Alabama Reports,* p. 380 (1859).

[33] *Ivey v. Hardy,* 2 *Alabama Reports,* p. 548 (1835); *Farrelly v.
Louisa,* 34 *Alabama Reports,* p. 284 (1859).

[34] *Raby v. Baptiste,* 27 *Mississippi Reports,* p. 731 (1854); *Heirn v.
Bridault,* 37 *Mississippi Reports,* p. 209 (1859); *Williamson v. Norton,*
7 *Louisiana Reports,* p. 393 (1852).

[35] *Vaughn v. Phebe,* 8 *Tennessee Reports,* p. 389 (1827).

[36] *Negro John v. Wood,* 1 Wheaton, p. 5 (1816); *Shorter v. Boswell,* 2
Harris and Johnson, *Maryland Reports,* p. 361 (1809); *State v. Hayes,*
1 Bailey, *South Carolina Reports,* p. 275 (1858); *Spriggs v. Negro*

states similar problems were presented to the courts on those occasions in which free Negroes attempted to enter the public
schools.[37]

The study of this subject leaves one with very serious doubts of
the absolute purity of the "Nordic" blood of the southern states.
The refusal of the lawmakers of any state to enact that any degree of Negro blood prevented the individual's being classed as a
white person may be interpreted as an admission that if such a
law were passed and applied it would prove "very cruel and mischievous." In certain sections, persons of dark complexion were
avoided because of the suspicion that they were of Negro ancestry.[38] The accompanying note seems to show that there were elements of the population that might have been led to believe rumors that prominent men were of Negro extraction.[39]

Mary, 3 Harris and Johnson, *Maryland Reports,* p. 395 (1815); *Johnson* v. *Basquere,* 1 Spears, *South Carolina Reports,* p. 307 (1860); Jacob
D. Wheeler, *A Practical Treatise on the Law of Slavery* (New York,
1837), pp. 4–22.

[37] *Bailey* v. *Fiske,* 34 *Maine Reports,* p. 77 (1852); *State* v. *Van
Waggener,* 1 Halstead, *New Jersey Reports,* p. 455 (1797); *Thomas
Lane* v. *Mathias W. Baker,* 12 *Ohio Reports,* p. 237 (1843); *Pirate, alias
Belt* v. *Dalby,* 1 Dallas, *Pennsylvania Reports,* p. 179 (1786): "Since the
act for the gradual abolition of slavery, a number of persons have
formed a society in Philadelphia, for the purpose of relieving those of
their fellow creatures, who were held in illegal slavery. This action is
owing to that institution.

"The plaintiff being the supposed issue of white and mulatto parents,
attended the defendant to Philadelphia in the autumn of 1784, and
presented so pure a complexion that the attention of the society was
excited."

[38] William Faux, *Memorable Days in America, Being a Journal of a
Tour to the United States* (London, 1823), p. 100; James S. Buckingham, *The Slave States of America* (London, 1842), I, 240.

[39] *Virginia Magazine of History,* XXIX (April, 1921), 191:

"Hermitage, Aug. 16, 1828.

"My dear Call

"On last evening I recd. yours by Major Clements. . . .

"The whole of the coalition is to caluminate me. Cart loads of coffin
handbills, forgeries, & pamphlets of the most base caluminies are
circulated by the franking privilege of Members of Congress, & Mr.
Clay. Even Mrs. J. is not spared, & my pious mother, nearly fifty years

The record of cases that were carried to the higher courts, as used in the above evidence, may be considered as proof that in many unknown instances acting on such precedents as these courts had established, individuals having less than one-fourth degree of the prescribed blood passed from the class of mulattoes into the ranks of the white race. The records of the Hustings Court of Petersburg, Virginia, afford an example in the case of a certain Sylvia Jeffers. In 1814, this woman was emancipated by the will of her deceased master, who was also the father of her children. In 1853, she and her children presented themselves before the court of the city and claimed to be entitled to the status of white persons. The court granted her petition, and legally these persons were no longer mulattoes. No doubt other examples of legal passing into the white race might be discovered.[40]

While it was possible to pass from the Negro into the white race according to the law, there was a much larger possibility that such "passing" went on to a much larger extent without thought of or resort to the courts or legal procedure. No one can ascertain the extent of this process, for those who attempted to pass out of the mulatto group had good and sufficient reasons to conceal the status of their ancestors and attempted to cut themselves off from all associates that knew their ancestral record. But the fact that light mulattoes, in many classes, attempted to gain the privileges of white men and throw off the restrictions of the mulatto is revealed in instances in which discovery was made of such action.

The records of the courts of Louisiana show that in 1852, a slave,

---

in her tomb, & who, from her cradle to her death, had not a speck upon her character, has been dragged forth by Hammond & held to public scorn, as a prostitute who intermarried with a Negro, and my eldest brother sold as a slave in Carolina. This Hammond does not publish in his vile press, but keeps the statements, purporting to be sworn to, a *forgery* & spreads it secretly.

"Yours truly,
"Andrew Jackson."

[40] Luther P. Jackson, "Slavery and Emancipation in Petersburg," Petersburg *Index-Appeal*, Jan. 1930; See Minute Book, Hustings Court, Petersburg (1851–53), p. 323.

being well dressed, and of genteel deportment, took a
cabin passage on the steamboat Western World, going
from New Orleans to the Western country, crowded
with passengers. His color was a shade lighter than that
of a new saddle, with a clear skin, his hair dark and
straight. He sat at the first table, in the cabin, near the
ladies. His appearance did not indicate African extraction, but that of a person born in the South and exposed
to the sun, a Mexican or a Spaniard. No person suspected his negro blood, until near Memphis, the steward
of the boat expressed his suspicion. An *eclair cissement*
was had, and the master of the boat took the responsibility of delivering him to the civil authorities at
Memphis as probably a runaway slave. He was brought
to New Orleans, and sold at auction. The auctioneer
and another think the discovery of his African blood
might have been easily made. All discoveries are easy
after they are made. The passengers on a crowded boat
did not make the discovery in traveling seven or eight
hundred miles with him, although he sat at the head of
the table—although, one of them says, he had the appearance of a modest unassuming gentleman; another
represents him as freely mingling with society. Even
after discovery, many thought the master to blame in
acting without more indications of color, or proof. We
think he boldly incurred risks, for the benefit of an unknown master. In this case the court held that masters
of Mississippi steamboats were not responsible for the
racial identity of their passengers.[41]

The *Semi-Weekly Mississippian* reports the case of George R.
Shaw, convicted by the court of Pittsburg, as a kidnaper.

The offense of which Shaw was found guilty was that
of kidnapping, though the proof and the charge of the
judge did not warrant the jury in finding such a verdict.
A very white negro belonging to Mr. George C. Ragland
of Tuscumbia, Ala. had run away from his master and

---

[41] *Williamson v. Norton, Louisiana,* p. 393 (1852).

settled in Pittsburg, as a white man, under the name of
George W. Ferris, where he married. Shaw also settled
in Pittsburg, and having known Ferris in Memphis,
Tenn. as "Wash" the slave of Mr. Ragland, informed the
latter where the slave was to be found. Wash, alias
Ferris, having gone to Missouri, in search of work, Shaw
followed him and had him arrested at Brunswick, Mo.,
and returned to his master, for which he received the
reward of $500.00 offered by Mr. Ragland for the re-
turn of the slave. Shaw returned to Pittsburg and was
there indicted upon a charge of kidnapping and convicted, as stated. It is to be hoped that a more honest
jury will be found at the next trial.[42]

An amusing report from Memphis shows how difficult it was to
distinguish the mulatto.

In the summer of 1838, the monotony of Memphis was
relieved by the sudden appearance of Monsieur Dukay,
an individual of foreign aspect, peculiarly French in his
accent and the color of his cuticle. He came in pursuit
of health; and to escape the heat and malaria of a
more Southern climate. Agreeable in conversation and
prepossessing in manner, he was not long in making
himself the center of a social circle. The ladies smiled
delightedly in his presence, and through the long summer months no party or fashionable assemblage was
complete without Monsieur Dukay. He sang charmingly
in French. But his greatest attraction was the possession
of two sugar plantations in Louisiana. Or the upper
plantation, he claimed an annual production of four
hundred hogsheads, and six hundred on the lower plantation. This was enough to sweeten his society, and give
a saccharine tinge to his general conversation. The
merchants, too, were happy to make his acquaintance.
He talked eloquently of finance. But all things have an
end, and it became necessary in the course of events for
Monsieur Dukay to depart, and on the event of this in-

[42] *Semi-Weekly Mississippian* (Jackson, Mississippi), January 11, 1859.

teresting occasion, he deplored with tearful eyes the necessity that compelled him to return to his plantations.
He was consoled, however, with the reflection that he
would shortly return. From a friend in the grocery line,
he purchased a bill of supplies for the upper plantation,
giving in payment a draft on his New Orleans merchant.
From a "dear old friend" he obtained, in similar manner, a fine riding horse, saddle and bridle; and from a
bosom friend and companion he reluctantly consented
to receive a diamond ring for his only sister. Months
passed away, and no tidings came of the elegant
Frenchman. The drafts were duly returned for non-ac-
ceptance. . . . But, during the ensuing winter, a gentleman with whom he had been intimate, happened in
New Orleans and found "Mon cher Dukay" manipu-
lating in the capacity of a quadroon barber.[43]

The following shows, again, how difficult it was for slavehood-
ers to distinguish persons of Negro ancestry. This is a case in
which the owner sought to recover damages from a white man for
enticing from his service a mulatto Negro woman. In this instance it appeared that the slave girl, "Harriet,"

was the daughter of a woman by the name of Rose, who
was possessed and claimed by Dennan, who resides in
Georgia. About two years before the occurrence which
forms the subject of this suit took place, the girl Harriet
made her appearance in Sevier county [Tennessee],
passing by the name of Irene Sanders, and assuming to
be free, and, as she was white, no one suspected that she
was a slave, or that she had any negro blood. The girl,
Harriet, was residing with the defendant, when the
plaintiff went to his house and claimed her as his slave.
The girl admitted she was a slave, and was taken by the
plaintiff into his possession, and they set out for Georgia.
Some of the neighbors of the defendant came to him
and wanted to know if there was no way of making the

[43] James D. Davis, *History of the City of Memphis* (Memphis, 1873),
pp. 123–24.

plaintiff prove that the girl was a slave. He suggested in reply that, as she admitted she was a slave, perhaps they had better let the matter rest. Afterward at their request, he drew up a blank process and gave it to them, and they arrested the plaintiff and brought him and the girl before two justices, who discharged the girl and committed the plaintiff to prison. After this the defendant was asked what was to be done with the girl; to which he replied, he supposed she might go where she pleased, which declaration was communicated to her. In a few days the girl left the community in company with a young man, by whom she was taken to Rhea county. Evidence was introduced by the defendant that Rose, the mother of Harriet, was reputed to have been free; that she came from Pennsylvania, and had been improperly reduced to bondage. . . . It was also shown that the girl was of fair complexion, with straight hair, high thin nose, with all the other indications of European descent, and that she had lived two years in the neighborhood without any person having the least suspicion that she had any African blood or was a slave.[44]

Lord Lyell relates an incident that also shows how easily race mixture might be undetected. He declares:

A recent occurrence in Louisville places in a strong light the unnatural relation in which the two races now stand to each other. One of the citizens, a respectable young tradesman, became attached to a young seamstress, who had been working in his mothers house, and married her, in the full belief that she was free and a white woman. He had lived with her some time when it was discovered that she was a negress and a slave, who had never been legally emancipated so that the marriage was void; yet a separation was thought so much a matter of course that I heard the young man's generosity commended because he had purchased her freedom

[44] *Miller* v. *Dennan,* 16 *Tennessee Reports,* p. 232 (1835).

after the discovery, and given her the means of setting
up as a dressmaker.[45]

The evidence seems to show that where the mulatto was not
known in many cases, the possession of a white skin was a pre-
sumption in favor of freedom. And there is evidence that public
opinion sometimes rebelled at the idea of holding white people
in slavery. *Niles Register* quotes from the *Emporium,* printed at
Louisville, Kentucky, as follows:

> A laudable indignation was universally manifested
> among our citizens, and even among the blacks, on
> Saturday last, by the exposure of a woman and two child-
> dren for sale at public auction at the front of our prin-
> cipal tavern. This woman and children were as white
> as any of our citizens, indeed we scarcely ever saw a
> child with a fairer or clearer complexion than the
> younger one. That they were not slaves we do not pre-
> tend to say; but there was something so revolting to the
> feelings, at the sight of this woman and children ex-
> posed to sale by their young master, it excited such an
> association of ideas in the minds of every one; it brought
> to the recollection so forcibly the morality of slavehold-
> ing states—that not a person was found to make an offer
> for them.
>
> The legal maxim of *par. seq. vent.* has made them
> slaves for life and the same maxim will make the off-
> spring of these children slaves. Who can think of this
> and not shudder? Can there not be, some limitation,
> some bounds fixed to the principle?
>
> We trust we shall not see a second attempt to sell
> them in this town.[46]

A similar case is reported from the Salt River *Journal,* a paper
published at Bowling Green, Missouri. The record is as follows:

[45] Sir Charles Lyell, *A Second Visit to the United States of America*
(New York, 1849), II, 215; *Niles Register,* Dec. 9, 1837, gives another
case of this description.
[46] *Niles Register,* June 9, 1821.

A case of a slave suing for his freedom was tried a few days since in Lincoln county, of which the following is a brief statement of particulars: A youth about ten years of age sued for his freedom on the ground that he was a free white person. Upon his trial before the jury, he was examined by the jury and by two learned physicians, all of whom concurred in the opinion that very little, if any, trace of negro blood could be discovered by any of the external appearances. All the physiological marks and distinctions which characterize African descent had disappeared.

His skin was white and fair, his hair soft, straight, fine, and white; his eyes blue, but rather disposed to the hazelnut color; nose prominent, the lips small and completely covering the teeth, the head round and well formed, forehead high and prominent, the ears large, the tibia of the leg straight, the feet hollow. Notwithstanding these evidences of his claim, he was proven to be the descendant of a mulatto woman, and that his progenitors on his mother's side had been and still were slaves; consequently he was found to be a slave.

From the feeling manifest by the community where the trial was held, we presume his freedom will be bought and his education provided for.[47]

The editor of *Niles Register* declares:

The case stated above is called a hard one. It is among the abominations that attend upon slavery—in which, in some cases, we fear that fathers have made a traffic in their own children, as slaves. We well remember a conversation with Mr. Calhoun, when secretary of war, in which he introduced this subject. He stated a case in which the feelings of a large assemblage had been much outraged by the exposure of a man, placed upon the stand for sale—whose appearance, he said, in all respects, gave him a better claim to the character of a white man than most persons, so acknowledged, could

[47] Ibid., Oct. 25, 1834.

show; and he thereupon suggested that some regulation ought to be made by which individuals so circumstanced should be declared to be freeman.[48]

Conditions and sentiment, as indicated above, helped to make the way easy for the mulatto who did not wish to remain in servitude or to live under the restrictions placed upon free Negroes to move and seek his fortune as a white man. In 1834 a free Negro fell into the hands of the law in Virginia. His is the story of a man so white, and hence so likely to make his escape that men would not risk enslaving him. The record of this case recites that

a mulatto called William Hayden was apprehended in the county of Prince William and committed to the jail of the said county, and advertised as the law in such cases directs, and was by order of the county court advertised for sale, and no person having claimed him, and he not having proved his freedom, he was offered at public auction for sale . . . when one Robert Lipscomb, being a bidder and making the highest bid became the purchaser of the said Hayden, as agent of a trader or dealer in slaves; and he, Lipscomb, informed your petitioner, that his principal would pay the purchase money in a few days. The said Hayden was returned to the jail to await the arrival of the trader, who in a short time came and being requested, refused to pay the amount which he had authorized the said Lipscomb to bid. Your petitioner afterwards sent the said Hayden to the town of Fredericksburg, and the city of Richmond, by one, Col. James Ferrell, of Prince William (who had a number of slaves to be offered for sale) to be sold if the amount could be obtained for him equal to the said Lipscomb's bid. The said Hayden was offered for sale to sundry persons in Fredericksburg by Ferrell and myself, he was also offered in Richmond by Ferrell, all of who refused to purchase him at any price, on account of his color. All alleging that he was too white. The said Ferrell returned him to your petitioner in the town of

[48] Ibid.

Brentsville, when he offered him for sale on a court
day, several traders were present, all of whom refused
to make any bid for him, all alleging that his color was
too light and that he could by reason thereof, too easily
escape from slavery and pass as a white man, and while
your petitioner was endeavouring to sell the said Hayden, he made his escape, and although your petitioner
has made every exertion to regain possession of him, he
had not been able.[49]

Economic and legal restrictions on free Negroes in slave and
free states would seem to, and did, operate to force many mulattoes of light complexion to desert their mulatto fellows and become white men, but this, by no means, was always the case.
Light mulattoes did not universally attempt to gain recognition
of white men. William Hayden, mentioned above, affords an example of this kind. He was seized and sold as a slave because he
had in Ohio and later in Virginia refused to associate with the
white race and let it be known to his associates that he was of
Negro blood. Of Hayden it is said,

that he was born free in the state of New York, was the
son of a white woman, and was educated in that state,
which was evident from his pronounciation. At the age
of fourteen he went to the state of Ohio where he continued about three years, when the increase of that
population with which he associated became so numerous as to induce the constituted authorities of that state
to enact severe laws in relation to the policy of the state,
which compelled all persons of his color, which were not
able to comply with the requisitions of the laws, to seek
asylum elsewhere, and that he was endeavouring to return to New York, the place of his nativity, and not having been acquainted with the Virginia laws, attempted
to pass through the said state without the evidence of
his freedom. . . . Your petitioners have a strong belief,
and so have others . . . that he the said Hayden was
born free, his knowledge of the state of New York, his

[49] Petition 10906, Prince William, Feb. 20, 1835.

acquaintance with the geography of New York, his acquaintance with the cities, towns, rivers, and the trade
of that state is calculated to convince any person that
he was born, raised, and educated, and migrated as he
the said Hayden represented to your petitioner.[50]

In the slave period, the governing classes did not desire to
admit persons of Negro or Indian blood to the ranks of white society. The laws (described in this chapter) were designed to preserve the racial purity of the white man's blood. These laws
failed to accomplish their object and in unknown numbers of
cases the blood of the proscribed races found its way into the
veins of many white families. Before the end of the slave period
there were, no doubt, many persons who could truthfully testify,
as did the "white" wife of a white citizen of Virginia, that, "she
did not know whether she was entirely white or not."[51] It is impossible to conceive of a legal system under which such an infusion of the dark man"s blood would have been impossible. Had
the state laws provided that any Indian or Negro blood made the
individual possessing such blood a person of color, there would
have been more delicate problems presented to the courts. In the
language of Chancellor Harper, such a law would have proved a
"very cruel and mischievous" law, and under the more drastic
law natural forces would still have defeated the purpose of the
lawmakers. But there were forces which served more effectively
than all laws and did more than any law to attain what the lawmakers desired. Had the existing laws been rigidly enforced and
every individual, slave or free, of less than one-fourth degree of
Negro blood been forced to accept the status of white citizens, it
is difficult to conceive of the resulting state of southern society.
According to such an interpretation of the law, hundreds of individuals who lived all their days as Negro slaves would then have
been forced to accept the status of white citizens. But, all the mulattoes did not wish to become white men, and the vast majority
of the "white Negroes" made no effort to desert the mulatto

[50] Ibid.
[51] Executive Papers, Archives of Virginia, Letters Received, Sept. 26,
1831.

group. A change of status might offer freedom, opportunity, and the end of persecution, but such persons were bound by the strong ties of friendship, relationship, affection, and family tradition to the despised and persecuted group, and in most cases they remained with those who loved them and they suffered with them. In this problem of racial identity, social forces proved stronger than economic inducements and far more effective in preserving racial integrity than legal acts.

NINE

The White Man &
His Negro Relations

HE MULATTO was in most cases, it seems certain, the descendant of the white man and the Negro woman. Sexual life in the slave period exhibited phenomena that would be characteristic of any community where subject women are controlled by men. As in the North, so also in the South men were neither entirely good nor entirely bad. As among human beings everywhere there were among the slaveholders many virtuous men and there were also many vile characters. Overseers and lesser whites on neighboring farms were of like character. It will also be remembered that there were always thoughtless and passionate young men about the plantations and it is evident that the adventures of these young men need not be considered as typical of men of maturer years or of the morality of the entire slave country. The Negro slave woman was an absolute dependent; dependent upon white men who dominated the little isolated world of the plantation. The black woman as other women subject or economically dependent upon controlling males made use of such powers as nature had given her for her personal aggrandizement. Was the white man or the black woman the aggressor? The answer is a matter of speculation, but in every case a problem of human relations and not a problem of white or black character.

Southern moral leaders recognized the temptations slavery offered to white youth. On this subject a Virginia minister wrote:

> Vice to a most shameful extent is proved by the rapid
> increase of mulattoes. How many have fallen before this

temptation! So many that it has almost ceased to be a
temptation to fall! Oh, how many parents may trace the
impiety, licentiousness, and shame of their prodigal sons
to temptations found in female slaves in their own or
neighbours households![1]

On this question Lord Lyell observed "to the dominant race one
of the most serious evils of slavery is its tendency to blight domestic happiness; and the anxiety of parents for their sons, and constant fear of licentious intercourse with slaves, is painfully
great."[2] The evidence points to many acts of youthful indiscre-
tion and the consequent regrets of maturer years. For example, a
slave woman writes, "She is the illigitimate daughter of the late
(_____) , who by his testement and last will as an act of justice
and attonement for an error of an unguarded moment, bequeathed to his innocent offspring the boon of freedom and a pecuniary legacy of $1,000."[3] No doubt there were many cases in
which the white boy "had followed the black girl to the spring
and had attempted an improper connection with the girl."[4] Records of such clandestine events as the above are seldom found in
the archives of a southern state. The records that the archives
preserve are rather the accounts of the acts of mature men. Such
documents refer to the efforts of old men to provide for their unfortunate children by legislative act or by will, or, as will be seen
in the following chapter, they relate to domestic difficulties
caused by the presence on the plantation of Negro mistresses and
their children. Also for obvious reasons I do not wish to include

---

[1] John D. Paxton, *Letters on Slavery, Addressed to the Cumberland
Congregation* (Lexington, Ky., 1833) , pp. 129–30; William G. Simms,
"Morals of Slavery," *The Pro-Slavery Arguments* (Philadelphia, 1852) ,
pp. 228–29.

[2] Sir Charles Lyell, *Second Visit to the United States* (New York,
1849) , 1, 271.

[3] Archives of Virginia, Legislative Papers, Petition, King William
County, Dec. 19, 1825. Hereafter Archives of Virginia, Legislative
Papers, will be omitted and the petition identified by number, county,
and date (insomuch as this information is available) .

[4] Petition 5018, Culpeper, Dec. 9, 1806.

in the body of this work the accounts of abolitionists regarding conditions in the prewar South.[5]

The petition of William Kendall affords an example of a master who sincerely regretted the past act for which he assumed responsibility. This case may be considered typical of many others. This petitioner

> respectfully sheweth, that . . . like many frail men, he
> hath fallen into a vice, that humanity and nature,
> added to moral principles, dictate the only alternative
> now left, viz. this zealous and devout petition. He is
> impelled with blushes and confusion to own and ac-
> knowledge the cause that brings him forward on this
> occasion. Your petitioner believes and acknowledges
> himself to be the father of the said mulatto boy by a
> woman at that time the property of himself, and as his
> parent he feels great solicitude for his future welfare
> and liberty. It is with great concern and uneasiness that
> he looks forward to the possibility of his being a slave
> to any person.[6]

De Tocqueville tells us:

> I happened to meet with an old man in the south of the
> Union who had lived in illicit intercourse with one of
> his own negroes and had had several children by her
> who were born the slaves of their father. He had indeed
> frequently thought of bequeathing to them at least their
> freedom, but years had elapsed without his being able
> to surmount the legal obstacles to their emancipation

[5] Robert Sutcliff, *Travels in Some Parts of North America in the Years 1804, 1805, 1806* (York, England, 1815), pp. 37–38; *American Slavery as It Is: The Testimony of a Thousand Witnesses* (New York, 1839), pp. 33, 51; Samuel A. Ferrell, *Ramble of Six Thousand Miles through the United States* (London, 1832), pp. 194–95; Baptist W. Noel, *Freedom and Slavery in the United States* (London, 1863), p. 86; Charles W. Jensen, *The Stranger in America* (London, 1807), pp. 383–84.

[6] Petition 6231, King George, Dec. 15, 1813.

and in the meanwhile his old age was come and he was
about to die. He pictured to himself his sons dragged
from market to market and passing from the authority
of a parent to the rod of a stranger until these horrid
anticipations worked his expiring imagination into a
phrenzy.[7]

It is not to be thought that the mulatto was always the
offspring of its owner. The deposition of Travers Daniel provides
an example of a white father who attempted to provide for his
child but in this instance the mother of the child was the property of another man.

> Travers Daniel . . . made oath that sometime in the
> year 1798 or 1799 William Simmons an old infirm
> white man applied to him to advance a sum of money
> for him to purchase a boy by the name of George Sim-
> mons, which he the said Simmons had begot on a
> woman slave belonging to Mr. Enoch Mason, and ex-
> pressed a particular desire that the said boy should be
> liberated and become a free man when he arrived at
> the age of 21 years, and he and his son the said boy
> would make him compensation by their services by the
> time the said boy became of age. To gratify the old
> man (who I understand had no other children and was
> not married) I applied to Mr. Mason to know if he
> would sell the boy. He appeared to be rather unwilling
> to part with him, but when he understood that he was
> to be liberated when he became of age he agreed to part
> with him.[8]

Where harsh laws applied to the mulatto, they were applied to
the children of white men. Fathers of such children would have
been inhuman had they not sought to lighten the burden of their
children. On examination of the wills of deceased slaveowners it

[7] Alexis de Tocqueville, *American Institutions and Their Influence*
(New York, 1855), p. 384.
[8] Petition 5481a, Stafford, Dec. 15, 1809.

frequently appears that the deceased master is the father of certain slaves and seeks to make provision for his children. The following document affords an example:

> I, Thomas Wright . . . give and bequeath to Sylvie,
> a woman of color, formerly my slave but since emanci-
> pated and with whom I have had children, the sole and
> exclusive enjoyment and use of the house or tenement
> on my plantation, in the said county where I now reside
> . . . also all the household furniture therein . . . also
> all the monies of which I die possessed; secondly I give
> and bequeath to my natural son, Robert Wright,
> by the said Sylvie who I have duly emancipated all that
> tract of land on which I now live with its apperten-
> ances, containing by estimation three hundred and sev-
> enty acres . . . also all my stock of every description
> and plantation utinsils.[9]

The will of Philip Henshaw declares:

> I give and bequeath to my daughter (for such I believe
> her to be) Floreal Floretta (a girl I bought of Robert
> Robb, she was born of a yellow woman whom I bought
> of the said Robert Robb) her freedom, I also bequeath
> to her one-half of my estate of every description what-
> soever, to her and her heirs forever. . . . It is my desire
> that my sister Sallie Gatewood, out of the estate have
> devised to Floreal Floretta, shall board her at some de-
> cent white woman's house, and have her educated.
> . . . In event of my Sister Sallie Gatewood complying
> with the foregoing request, I give her and her heirs
> forever one-half of my estate of every description what-
> soever, but should my sister pay no regard to and fail to
> proceed to comply with this request, then and in that
> case the moity hereby devised to her, I also bequeath to
> the said Floreal Floretta. I do not give anything to my

[9] Petition 6730, Campbell, Nov. 16, 1816; see also petition 9155.

brothers Edmund and John or my brothers children, knowing that they are well off.[10]

The will of John Stewart, of Petersburg, provided that Mary Vizzaneau, "my natural colored daughter" shall have all I have at the bank, amounting to $19,500, and the house and lot in that part of the town called Gillfield, in which I now reside."[11]

A petition to the legislature of the State of Virginia describes the legatees of a certain Craddock Vaughn in the following manner:

> Your petitioners, Elenor Vaughn, Margaret Vaughn, and
> Dicey Vaughn, respectfully represent and show unto
> your honorable body, that Craddock Vaughn, lately a
> resident of the county on Halifax, and state of Virginia
> made a last will and testament in writing which has
> been duly admitted to probate in the clerk's office of the
> county of Halifax by which he emancipated your peti-
> tioners and intends to give them the full and free enjoy-
> ment of all the rights and immunities of free persons of
> color. That the said testator in his lifetime raised them
> as his own children and paid them every regard which
> a paternal care for their interest seemed to require.
> That though they were by the laws of the land neces-
> sarily regarded as slaves (their mother being a slave)
> and now are taken by the laws to not be as free negroes
> —they are in fact and in truth much more than three-
> fourth white as far as blood is concerned and in color
> almost entirely so—that the said Elenor is their mother
> and Dicey was a favorite of their master—the rest
> being his children. Your petitioners further represent
> that the said Craddock Vaughn though in his lifetime a
> man of intemperate habits had by industry and unusual
> economy accumulated an estate of not less than seven
> or eight thousand dollars—all of which he bequeathed
> to his executors to be held and controlled for the just
> and exclusive benefit of your petitioners . . . that the

[10] Petition 8468, Essex, Dec. 15, 1825.
[11] Petition 6323, Buckingham, Oct. 18, 1814.

said estate consists of seven slaves, all of whom are
valuable and whose value will increase since all are
young, and several of them are children, of . . . acres
of land, very productive and finely located on the Dan
river, of a large stock, and such perishable property as
is usually attached to such a farm.[12]

It is to be noted that in many wills no intimation is made by
the white man of his paternal relation. In many cases it is only by
the study of accompanying documents that the paternity of many
mulattoes can be discovered. In the following case the "bosom
friend" is the mother of the testator's mulatto children:

I, Walter Robertson, late of Virginia, but now of New
Bern, North Carolina—do make this my last will and
testament, that is to say, First. . . . Second, it is my will
that my bosom friend, Ann Rose, for her long and faithful services, be immediately after my death put in possession of all my lands, slaves, household furniture,
plate, stocks of horses, cattle, and every king of real and
personal estate which may belong to me, which real and
personal estate I lend to the said Ann to enable her to
support herself and to maintain and educate my daughter Margaret by the said Ann, as also a child with which
she is now pregnant, provided the said child be born
within nine months from the date of these presents. It is
further my will that whenever peace shall be established
between Great Britain and America or a cessation of
hostilities take place so that an intercourse takes place
between the now contending powers, that then (if such
peace or cessation takes place within seven years) the
whole of my real and personal estate, including my
stock in trade with William Beattie and Samuel Call be
turned into money by my executors hereafter to be
named and the proceeds thereof to be divided between
the said Ann Rose, our daughter, Margaret, and the
child she is now supposed to be pregnant with or the
survivors of them, share and share alike and it is fur-

[12] Petition 17511, Halifax, Jan. 15, 1851.

ther my will that my executors shall furnish the said
Ann with money sufficient to pay her and her child or
children's passage and expenses to Glasgow, where the
aforesaid remittance shall be made. . . . It is my will
that if the said Ann forgetful of our long acquaintance
and unmindful of the good of her child or children,
should at any time within the said seven years aforesaid
form a connection with any man or marry so as to live
in carnal intimacy with him that then all and every part
of this will which respects the said Ann shall cease and
become void and she therefore shall be entitled to no
benefit or emolument from it whatever. [13]

This will makes no mention of the slave status of Ann Rose but
upon the death of the master and father, Ann, a mulatto, petitions the legislature of Virginia that she and her children shall
not be sent to Great Britain, but be permitted to remain in the
state, retaining the property left to them by Walter Robertson.

In the same county (Halifax) and at about the same time, a
Reverend James Fowles by will set free and gave lands to his
slaves Molly and John. Many years later when the individuals in
question petitioned to be permitted to remain in the state, it is
testified that their benefactor, the Reverend James Fowles, "was
confessedly, both their master and natural father."[14] The petition
of Lucy, Polly Rose, Ottey Rose, and Alexander Rose, shows that
they were emancipated by the will of James Haliburton, and they
certify that they are "the children of their master, who by his will
has made ample provision for their support."[15] The will of
Thomas Moody provides: "My house maid Laury, shall be put
under some persons that shall learn her the said Laury to weave
and sew and she shall be emancipated at the age of twenty-one
years." Here again the father fails to mention the relation of his
paternity, but the executor of his will states that "he firmly believes that the strongest of all human ties induced his testator

[13] Petition 1005, Halifax, Dec. 5, 1783.
[14] Petition 3127, Halifax, Nov. 4, 1793.
[15] Petition 13107, Nelson, Jan. 11, 1841.

first to purchase and then to give her freedom."[16] The will of a prominent planter makes the following provision for two of his slaves:

> I desire that Lucy, a mulatto girl daughter to Sophia may be set free—I lend to the said child one thousand dollars to be laid out in bank stock, and the profits therefrom to be paid annually to her by my executors for her support so long as she lives, and at her death I give the same to be divided among her children should she leave any lawfully begotten; should she die without issue as above I desire that the said money shall return to my estate—I also give to the said child, Lucy, one bed and furniture—I give to Sophia the mother of the said Lucy, her freedom and five pounds per year for her support to be paid to her by my executors during her natural life.
>
> I desire my executors to keep the mulatto girl Lucy before mentioned until she is twelve years of age before she is emancipated for the purpose of sending her to school.
>
> I also desire the woman Sophia not to be emancipated until the emancipation of her child, that she may have the liberty of living with her child, providing she comply with my request. Viz. to spin three pounds of yarn thread for each of my sisters each year, she to be under the particular direction of my executors until she is emancipated and to be supported by them with three barrels of corn, one hundred weight of pork, four pounds of coffee, and ten pounds of sugar per year.[17]

Here as in other cases the father appears to desire to conceal the relationship but a later petition asking that Lucy be permitted to remain in the State declares that "Lucy Ann is the illegitimate daughter of _____, Esq."[18] Other examples of emancipation by

[16] Petition 7247, New Kent, Dec. 18, 1818.
[17] Petition 7325a, King William, Dec. 28, 1818.
[18] Petition, King William, Dec. 19, 1825.

will of the master and father are to be found in the Virginia Archives.[19] Cases similar to the above are found in the other southern states.[20]

In the lower South, because of the liberal attitudes and traditions handed down from the Spanish and French colonists, there appears to have been more sympathy for the mulatto and consequently many interesting social situations are reported in this region. Here in the early slave period, much valuable property had been accumulated by the mulatto heirs of white fathers. But with the passing of time, as in Virginia, sentiment became more and more adverse to the free Negro; the slave code became more severe; and, finally, laws were enacted that prohibited the emancipation of Negro slaves. But the human attachments of fathers to their children could not be destroyed, and white fathers sought means to evade the law as it affected their own children. It is because of this situation in the lower South that interesting communities of free Negroes were established in southern Ohio and Indiana. Many white fathers took their Negro families to this region and emancipated them. Because of this paternal interest

[19] Petition 6110b, Dec. 14, 1812: "Your petitioner has been married to and has had several children of the said Nelson, who is a white man, has lately been enabled to purchase him, with the design to have him emancipated, but he refusing to accept freedom on conditions required by the existing provisions of the law, of departure from the state, and consequent eternal separation from his family; his said father has had the conveyance of him made to your petitioner and his children, in whom the whole right and property in the said Nelson now resides. Your petitioner under the influence of feelings most natural to a wife has the utmost unwillingness to hold her husband in servitude and she has moreover been advised that in event of her death he would be liable to, and must of necessity be sold, for the distribution of his value among his children, or worse, must remain in slavery to those children who would also be his own."

[20] *Cunningham's Heirs* v. *Executors of Thomas Cunningham,* Cameron and Norwood, *North Carolina Reports,* p. 353 (1801); *Ford* v. *Ford, 26 Tennessee Reports,* p. 92 (1846); *Laura Jane* v. *Hagen, Adms.,* 10 Humphrey, *Tennessee Reports,* p. 352 (1849); *Cooper* v. *Blakey,* 10 *Georgia Reports,* p. 263 (1851); *Thornton* v. *Chisholm,* 20 *Georgia Reports,* p. 263 (1856).

many intricate problems were presented to the courts of the slave states.

In 1863, John Hooper, a native of Alabama, died leaving a will which among other provisions declared:

It is my wish, that all my just debts be paid, and that my brother Zachariah L. Hooper, act as my executor—after administering on my estate or as soon as he can do so, It is my wish that he take Harriet, a yellow woman, and her six children (Namely Ellen, William, Mary Jane, Zachariah, Eliza Ann, and Joseph) to the state of Ohio, and free them there; settle them comfortable in the country, not in the city, and after settling Harriet and her six children as above named, my executor is requested to place in some solvent bank in Ohio the sum of ten thousand dollars, to be used in the following manner—That Harriet and her six children are to be supported from the interest of the ten thousand dollars; and the principal not to be used unless Harriet marries, and then she may draw her proportionate part.[21]

In this case it was decided that these people, who had been settled in Ohio, were to be regarded as free persons of color according to the laws of Alabama, but that they could not receive the property for the will had been administered before they left the state of Alabama, at which time they were still slaves and as slaves they could not possess property. The legacy therefore reverted to the white relations of the deceased.

In 1858 a similar case appears in the records of Alabama. In this instance the white relations attempted to recover the property of the deceased on the ground that the mulatto woman had used undue influence on her master, that the will was the result of his attachment for the woman and his children, and that the will was made "to spite his brothers and sisters, who would not associate with him on account of his adulterous intercourse with the negro woman."[22]

[21] *Hooper* v. *Hooper, 32 Alabama Reports,* p. 669 (1858).
[22] *Poole Heirs* v. *Poole Executors, 33 Alabama Reports,* p. 145 (1858); *Atwood Heirs* v. *Beck Adms., 21 Alabama Reports,* p. 590

Cases of the same description are to be found in the records of Mississippi. Here it is found that Elisha Brazelle

> left his residence in this state sometime in the year 1826, and took with him to the state of Ohio a negro woman and her son John Monroe Brazelle to be emancipated and brought them back to the state of Mississippi. During his stay in Ohio he executed a deed of emancipation of the said slaves and then returned with them to his residence in Jefferson county. In his will Elisha Brazelle recited the fact that he had executed a deed of emancipation declared his intention to ratify the said deed, and devised all his property to John Brazelle, whom the testator acknowledged to be his son.

In this instance the courts refused to permit the mulatto son to receive the legacy, the decision declaring that

> the statement of the case shows conclusively that the contract had its origin in an offence against morality, pernicious, and detestable as an example. But above all, it seemed to be planned and executed to evade the rigor of laws of this state.[23]

The following case is interesting in its details.

> In 1855 on the death of Jonathan Carter, a Mississippi planter, a settlement was made of his estate, and all of his slaves were sold for the benefit of his creditors. Among the slaves thus sold were included his two mulatto children. However, prior to his death Carter had attempted to provide for the two children as described in the following document. A certain friend of the deceased Carter, Barksdale, claimed Jane and William, by virtue of the purchase of them made by him from Jona-

---

(1852) ; *Ambercrombie's Heirs* v. *Ambercrombie Exc.,* 27 *Alabama Reports,* p. 489 (1855) .

[23] *Hinds et al.,* v. *Brazelle et al.,* Howard, *Mississippi Reports,* II, 837 (1838) .

than Carter in his life time. He relied upon a deed executed by himself and the said Carter, on the ninth of
February 1853, by which the said slaves, Jane and William, and some other property were conveyed to the
said Barksdale (the said Carter retaining possession and
control of them during his life) upon the condition
"that the said Barksdale, at the death of the said Carter,
to take charge of the yellow girl, nearly white named
Harriet, aged twelve years, born of a house woman
Fanny, belonging to the said Carter, and to keep the
said Harriet in his house as a free white person, and in
no way to be treated as a slave, but the said Harriet to
be fed from his table; to sleep in his house, and to be
clothed from his store, both fine and common; and the
said Harriet shall have the full benefit of her labor, and
also the full right, power, and privilege of making complaint to the guardian. . . . Now if the said Harriet
shall marry any free white man, at any time during the
life of the Barksdale and the said guardian shall con-
sult together, and if they deem it proper and right, they
shall give the said Harriet a portion of the said property, or so much as they may deem equitable and
just."[24]

The children were sold, but Barksdale seems to have done all he
could to carry out the wishes of his friend.

In 1858 the white relations of James Brown, a deceased Mississippi planter, attempted to secure the estate left by the deceased
to his two mulatto sons. Of these two boys it is reported that

during the time Francis and Jerome were at Brown's
house, Brown did not treat them as slaves; they ate at his
table, slept in the house, etc. Francis went when and
where he pleased, hunted, fished, exercised authority on
the place, as any young man would on his father's plantation, ordered the negroes to do what he considered
necessary. Francis is reported in Indiana, married and
doing well.

[24] *Barksdale* v. *Elam et al.*, 30 *Mississippi Reports*, p. 694 (1855).

In 1849 their father had carried them to Cincinnati, "with intent to evade the laws of this state with respect to emancipation of slaves" and afterwards returned with them to reside in the state of Mississippi. In this instance the courts held that the young men were still slaves and the property of the estate of the deceased father.[25]

In 1857 Nancy Wells brought suit as a citizen and resident of the state of Ohio against the executor of the will of Edward Wells, deceased. This is the case of a mulatto woman who had been left a small estate by her deceased white father. In 1846 her father had taken her to Ohio, where he emancipated her. She, however, came back to Jackson, Mississippi, where she married Samuel Watts, a free Negro barber of that place. The courts refused to grant her petition.[26]

In the state of Louisiana, racial relations differed from such relations in the states already studied in proportion as such relations were influenced by the Napoleonic code or by characteristic Spanish and French social attitudes. In the early years of this state's history there are to be found many contrasts, but these contrasts become less evident as more and more Anglo-Saxon settlers migrate into the state, and by 1860 there is much unity, as it concerned racial mixture, in all the slave states, Louisiana included. In colonial Louisiana in contrast to the southern states, the principle of the Roman law, that the son follows the condition of the father, was applied to the mulatto offspring of white fathers. A Louisiana judge informs us:

> Such was the law of Louisiana after it came under the
> dominion of Spain, and as there were at that time but
> few of the white women in the colony, and hardly any
> of equal condition with the officers of the government
> and of the troops stationed here, the inevitable conse-
> quence was that these gentlemen formed connections
> with women of color. This custom coming as it did from
> the ruling class soon spread through out the colony, and
> was persevered in long after there ceased to be any ex-

[25] *Shaw* v. *Brown,* 35 *Mississippi Reports,* p. 246 (1858).
[26] *Mitchell* v. *Wells,* 37 *Mississippi Reports,* p. 235 (1859).

cuse for its continuance. It was to remedy this state of
affairs, that the framers of the Code of 1808 first created
the incapacities of which the plaintiffs claim the benefit.[27]

Social conditions as they developed under the above regime will
be described at a later point in this study. But it will be found
that the fathers of Louisiana mulattoes manifest a very real attachment to their children and in very many cases such children
inherited, according to law, large and valuable estates. After 1808
we find laws enacted which placed on the mulattoes restrictions
which were to cause many of the problems that we are about to
consider. A decision of the Louisiana courts in 1832 declared that
the decisions of the courts of France were no longer binding as
they affect the mulatto offspring of white men and that it has
been found necessary to pass many restrictive acts to protect
white "heirs from the too great fondness of the natural parents of
such children."[28] An act of 1857 prohibited the emancipation of
mulatto children, and a decision handed down in that year declared, "an acknowledgment by the father of natural children, by
his own slave, besides being an offsense to morals, is a mere
nulity."[29]

After 1833 in the records of the Louisiana courts are to be
found more cases involving the status of the mulatto than in any
other state. The explanation of the large number of these cases is
to be found in the wide extent of the intermixture of races
among the French and Spanish population of the region, and in
the conflict of the French and Spanish racial attitudes with English attitudes and institutions. Anglo-American institutions finally triumphed over Spanish-French resistance, and Anglo-American ideals and prejudices were superimposed on Latin Louisiana,
but when the ancient customs and traditions conflicted with the
American slave code, there were many in Louisiana who sought
to evade and nullify the law. Hence, the records of the courts

[27] *Baldillo* v. *Tio,* 6 King, *Louisiana Reports,* p. 129 (1848).

[28] *Jung* v. *Doriscourts et al.,* 4 Miller, *Louisiana Reports,* p. 175
(1832).

[29] *Turner* v. *Smith et al.,* 12 Ogden, *Louisiana Reports,* p. 417
(1857).

preserve abundant evidence of the efforts of white fathers, in this state, to protect and provide for their mulatto offspring.

One of the first restrictions placed upon the mulattoes of Louisiana was a requirement that a white father must legally acknowledge his mulattoes to be his natural children in order that they might inherit his property. In 1840 the white relations of one Alexander Verdun attempted to gain possession of his estate on the ground that the children to whom his estate had been left were not legally acknowledged as his natural children.[30] In 1844 the white relations of Eugene Macarty attempted to show that the son to whom his estate had been left had not been acknowledged according to the law.[31] Another of the restrictions placed on the mulatto was that which limited the donation of more than one-fourth of the value of the deceased man's estate to persons of color. In 1843 when one Maurice Prevost bequeathed to Clarine and her daughter, Florestine Cecile, certain valuable property, his relations attempted to show that his will was void and illegal because "Clarine was his concubine, and could not receive a greater portion than that allowed by law, and because Florestine is the bastard daughter of the deceased, begotten by him from his said concubine."[32] Another case of this kind is reported in 1845. In this instance it is recited that,

> the deceased was possessed of a very large estate, composed of real and personal property, and of slaves, which were inventoried after his death amounting to a very large sum. That as the sisters of the late Sebastian Ripoll, otherwise known as Francisco Ballista, they are entitled to inherit from him each the undivided half of his entire succession; but that it appears, that the said Sebastian, in 1832, made a will, under the fictitious name of Francisco Ballista, by which he gave the bequeathed to a natural child, named Floresa Horina, the defendant the entire estate.[33]

[30] *Robinson* v. *Verdun,* 14 Curry, *Louisiana Reports,* p. 542 (1844).
[31] *Macarty* v. *Roach,* 7 Robinson, *Louisiana Reports,* p. 357 (1844).
[32] *Prevost* v. *Martell,* 10 Robinson, *Louisiana Reports,* p. 512 (1845).
[33] *Ripoll* v. *Morina,* 12 Robinson, *Louisiana Reports,* p. 552 (1845).

In this instance it was decided that the mulatto child could inherit but one-fourth of the property, according to the law. In the same year 1845, a certain L. B. Compton died leaving an estate valued at $184,640.35. He bequeathed to "my two children, Scipio and Loretta, who have been acknowledged by me" one-fourth of his estate. To them he made specific bequests of a plantation, five hundred forty-five acres in extent, with its improvements, many slaves, etc. The white relations of the deceased attempted to upset the will, but the court supported the claim of the mulatto children to one-fourth of the value of the property.[34] A decision of the courts of Louisiana in 1847 declared that "donations of moveables to a concubine are valied, but they may be reduced to one-tenth of all the property left by the testator."[35]

The following record of social conditions in Louisiana illustrates the efforts of a white father to secure the right of his colored children to his entire estate. Here, again, the state refused to permit the children to receive the entire estate. The record declares:

Macarty (the deceased) was a nobleman and an officer in the Spanish army. At the age of seventeen he dwelt with one of his uncles, also a Spanish officer, who lived with a woman of color. Augustin soon followed his example, and had in succession several liasons with women of that class, until in 1799, he took Celeste Perrault, with whom he lived nearly fifty years, she lived in his house, and her conduct was such as to enable her to retain his regard and affection to the last. Patrice was the issue of this connection; and the correspondence between him and his father clearly shows, that he and his mother were to Macarty all that a legitimate wife and son could have been. In the later part of his life he had no other society but that of Celeste, and no occupation save that of purchasing and sending goods to Patrice, who kept a shop in Pensacola. His letters to his rela-

[34] Compton v. Prescott, 12 Robinson, Louisiana Reports, p. 56 (1845); Franchon Morris v. Compton, 12 Robinson, Louisiana Reports, p. 76 (1845).

[35] Oliver v. Blaneq, 14 Louisiana Reports, p. 517 (1847).

tions show that he was completely estranged from
them, and show a strong desire on his part to convince
them that he was poor and that they had nothing to expect from him.

This old gentleman had attempted to give his property to his son
prior to his death and thus avoid the laws of inheritance. However, the state denied the wishes of the father.[36]

In 1855 there appears a similar case. In this instance William
Weeks gave to his mulatto son, David, $16,000 in donations of
$4,000 per year. The white relations of William Weeks objected
on the ground that the father sought to avoid the act providing
that a mulatto heir should not receive more than one-fourth of
the estate of a white father and the court sustained the objection
of the white litigants.[37]

When in 1857 Elisha Crocker died in the state of Louisiana, he
left a large estate and "by his will he appointed H. H. Crocker,
one of his natural children, his executor, and distributed his
property between his housekeeper, who is a colored woman and
was once his slave, and his children whom he had by her, and
who were legally acknowledged by him previously to his death."
This is the case of a native of New York who went to live in
Louisiana. He followed the example of many of his predecessors
and the relation described above was easily established. This man
was much attached to his Negro family, and several years before
his death he journeyed to New York and gave one-third of his
property to his white relations from whom he secured a release
from any claim that they might have to the remainder of his estate. His object was to give the remainder of his wealth to the
Negro woman and his children. After his death his New York relations again certified that "in consideration of the promises, and
from love and affection for the deceased, and from regard to the
children of the said deceased and of their mother Sofa . . . we
give up all claim to the estate of Elisha Crocker," but, in spite of
the efforts of the deceased and the liberality of the white rela-

[36] *Badillo et al.* v. *Tio,* 6 King, *Louisiana Reports,* p. 129 (1851) .
[37] *O'Hara* v. *Conrad,* 10 Randolph, *Louisiana Reports,* p. 638 (1855) .

tions the court decreed that the Negro heirs could receive but one-fourth of the estate, the remaining part to be distributed among the white relations of the said Elisha Crocker.[38]

Other examples of the desire of the parents to provide for mulatto children are to be found in the records of the Louisiana courts.[39]

In this state, also, as in the states of Alabama and Mississippi, it is to be found that many fathers and masters carried their Negro families to the state of Ohio and emancipated them there.[40] Problems similar to those already described resulted and might be cited for the state of Louisiana. From 1857 to 1860 other cases appear in which women and children have been promised their freedom and a share of their master's and father's property, and the will of the deceased provided for their care, but by this time emancipation was no longer possible and the condition of these women and children had been declared "offensive to morals." Therefore, in such cases, being valuable property and a part of the master's estate, these mothers and their children were ordered to be sold for the benefit of the legal heirs.[41]

The evidence used in this chapter leaves no reason to doubt that there were in the slave country men who recognized responsibilities and obligations imposed upon them by the errors and frailties of their humanity. There is reason to believe that in the case of these men the victims of their human passions were

[38] Reed v. Crocker, 12 Ogden, Louisiana Reports, p. 436 (1857).

[39] Cecile v. Lacoste, 8 Randolph, Louisiana Reports, p. 142 (1853); Bird v. Vail, 9 Randolph, Louisiana Reports, p. 176 (1854).

[40] Mary v. Brown, 5 King, Louisiana Reports, p. 269 (1850); Haynes v. Frone, 8 Randolph, Louisiana Reports, p. 25 (1855); Henrietta v. Barnes, 11 Randolph, Louisiana Reports, p. 453 (1856); Virginia and Celesie v. Himel, 10 Randolph, Louisiana Reports, p. 185 (1855); Hardesty v. Wormley, 10 Randolph, Louisiana Reports, p. 239 (1855); Barkley v. Sewell, 12 Ogden, Louisiana Reports, p. 263 (1857).

[41] Turner v. Smith, 12 Ogden, Louisiana Reports, p. 417 (1857); Collins v. Hallier, 12 Ogden, Louisiana Reports, p. 778 (1857); Delphine v. Guillet, 13 Ogden, Louisiana Reports, p. 13 (1858); Price v. Roy, 14 Ogden, Louisiana Reports, p. 697 (1859); Louisiana v. Baillio, 15 Ogden, Louisiana Reports, p. 555 (1860).

placed above the slave law and above slave institutions; they were the masters' children, and the masters were sorely troubled for their children.

The large number of mulattoes found among the free Negroes indicates that many planters freed their mulatto offspring rather than have them remain as slaves or, perhaps, be sold when the master or father died.[42] However, it is not to be supposed that all fathers recognized such obligations. Attention must be called to the large number of mulattoes found among the slaves and to whom all the statutes of the slave code applied. If certain fathers were kind to their mulatto children other fathers, being human, were not kind or thoughtful. The accidents of life under the system could bring misfortunes and the rigors of slavery did apply often to persons of a larger degree of white than of Negro blood. In certain cases mulatto children knew their fathers and the fathers knew their children but if in other cases fathers can be regarded as irresponsible, in every case, the responsibility for these evils must be placed upon human nature, existing in an unfortunate economic system.

[42] *Negro Population**

	SLAVE POPULATION	FREE NEGRO
Black	2,957,657	275,400
Mulatto	246,656	159,095

* *Compendium of the Seventh Census,* 1850, pp. 82–83.

TEN

The Status of
the White Woman in
the Slave States

I N THIS CHAPTER I must relate certain social conditions revealed by the records. It is my conviction that conditions as here described were not typical of all the men or all the women of the South.

In many cases the position of the white woman in the slave period was far from happy. Mrs. Madison is quoted as referring to the southern wife as "the chief slave of the master's harem."[1] Many wives must have been painfully conscious of the relations of their men folk as described in previous chapters. A Virginia woman writes on this subject:

This question demands the attention, not only of the religious population but of the statesmen and lawmakers. It is one great evil hanging over the Southern states, destroying the domestic peace and happiness of thousands. It is summed up in a single word—amalgamation. This and this only causes the vast extent of ignorance, degradation, and crime that lies like a black cloud over the South. And the practice is more general than even Southerners are willing to allow. Neither is it to be found only in the lower orders of the white population. It pervades the entire society. Its followers are to be found in all ranks, occupations and professions. The white mothers and daughters of the South have suffered under it for years—have seen their dearest affections

[1] Harriet Martineau, *Society in America* (London, 1837), II, 328.

trampled on—their hopes of domestic happiness destroyed and their future embittered even to agony by
those who should be all in all to them, as husbands, sons,
and brothers. I can not use too strong language in reference to this subject; for I know it will meet heartfelt response from every Southern woman.[2]

In many instances the marriage of the master broke his connections with slave mistresses, but often these relations with slave
women continued. At times embarrassments arose because of
swarms of mulatto children that sometimes maintained superior
privilege on the plantation of their fathers. The evidence about
to be given will make it clear that, in many cases, the planter's
wife lamented her unfortunate condition and that homes were
broken because of the white woman's jealousy or hatred for her
dusky rival.[3]

In Virginia in the slave period all divorces were granted by the
legislature of the state, not by the courts. Because of this procedure the evidence in these cases is today preserved in the archives
of the state. The petitions of many persons asking for divorce describe complications arising because of relations with persons of
color. It is therefore natural to find that in many cases of marital
infidelity the white wife names a slave woman as the cause of her
distress.

The wife of a citizen of Culpeper testified that when she, her
mother, and her husband were visiting at the home of a certain
friend, her husband "had followed a black servant girl to the
spring and had attempted an improper connection with the girl,
but the girl discharged a vessel of water on him and in the scuffle
made her escape." At a later date the said husband called at the
same plantation "in company with certain gentlemen to spend
the night, that when supper was ready the husband was not in his

[2] Frederick L. Olmsted, *The Cotton Kingdom* (New York, 1861), I,
307–08.
[3] Fanny A. Kemble, *A Journal of a Residence on a Georgia Plantation, in 1838–1839* (New York, 1863), p. 228; Charles Elliot, *The
Sinfulness of Slavery in the United States* (Cincinnati, 1857), II, 69,
152; Edward S. Abdy, *Journal of a Residence and Tour in North
America, from April 1833 to August 1834* (London, 1835), II, 93; James
Benwell, *An Englishman's Travels in America* (London, 1853), p. 95.

place, and in consequence of his former conduct the plantation owner suspected that all was not right; consequently he commenced a search and found him behind an outhouse in company with a negro girl." In this case the wife testified that she "saw him cohabiting with a negro girl belonging to her mother." A friend of the wife declared, "he frequently told me he had carnal knowledge of women after his marriage, both white and black."[4]

In 1814 the wife of an Augusta citizen testified, "The negro woman named Milly of whom the said husband became possessed by intermarrying with your petitioner, the said husband was criminally, unlawfully, and carnally intimate with, and kept her the said Milly, from the time your petitioner first married him until she was from necessity compelled to leave him." The witness testified that

> he the said _____, from his own confession not only
> in the presence of those affiants, but also in the presence
> of his said wife Ellen, had repeated carnal knowledge
> of the said negro woman Milly, and moreover acknowl-
> edged that he perpetrated that diabolical act against
> which every generous and virtuous principle of the hu-
> man soul revolts, he took her in his own wife's bed and
> there carried out his licentious designs, and those affi-
> ants further sayth, that the said negro woman Milly
> has since been delivered of a mulatto child.[5]

In 1817 another wife brought testimony that the witness "heard the said husband boast to his wife that in her absence he had taken one of his own negro woman into her bed and that he would do it again whenever it suited him."[6]

Still another unfortunate wife testifies that

> she is the daughter of Captain _____, of the county of
> Hanover, that having been raised in the bosom of an
> amiable family, under the immediate guardianship of

[4] Archives of Virginia, Legislative Papers, Petition 5018, Culpeper, Dec. 9, 1806. Hereafter Archives of Virginia, Legislative Papers, will be omitted and the petition identified by number, county, and date (insomuch as this information is available).

[5] Petition 6300c, Augusta, Oct. 12, 1814.

[6] Petition, Bedford, Dec. 16, 1817.

most affectionate parents, the years of her infancy had been as happy as they were innocent; that in the year 1809 she was addressed by _____, who, assuming the appearance of a gentleman, and obtaining the sanction of her parents to his visits, young and inexperienced as she was soon won her heart; and that yielding to those anticipations and feelings which constitute so much happiness of youth, she gave him her hand, and in the course of some years with the approbation of their parents they were married. Scarcely was the marriage ceremony performed, when her husband began to exhibit traits of character which she had never imagined belonged to him, and which too plainly manifested the fatal deception which he had practised upon her. Engaged in every wicked and vicious pursuit, he left your petitioner for months together, alone and unprotected. In order to give a color to his meditated neglect, he entered into the slave trade, purchasing negroes in Maryland and Virginia and conveying them to South Carolina and Georgia, for sale—in this odious traffic he would be absent from his house for months at a time, and would return only to disturb the solitude of your petitioner by bringing with him colored female slaves, *his kept mistresses*. These he would place under the same roof with your petitioner, and developing a character as degenerate in its principles as his practices were infamous, instead of restraining, he would actually promote, their insolence; and on one occasion when your petitioner was making a plain effort to preserve the decorum of her home and prevent it from becoming a sink of debauchery, he inflicted upon her the most cruel violence. The life of your petitioner was thus rendered a continued scene of violence and indescribable distress. Yet unwilling to disturb the repose of her aged parents, she suffered and was silent.

Additional evidence was offered to show that the husband kept "a woman of color in his house" and that this was a source of "great unhappiness to his wife."[7]

[7] Petition 7396, Hanover, Dec. 13, 1819.

In still another instance the wife declares that

> her husband abused and neglected her in a most inhu-
> man manner; in a manner to a woman raised as she had
> been by pious and moral parents and connected as she
> was to a respectable family, more distressing to her
> feelings that can be described. Your petitioner states
> that shortly after her marriage with her present husband
> she discovered that he had taken up with one of his fe-
> male slaves who acted as cook and waited about the
> house, that in less than three months after your peti-
> tioner's marriage, she made this discovery, and indeed so
> regardless was her husband of her feelings, that he would
> before her eyes and in the very room in which your pe-
> titioner slept go to bed to the said slave or cause the said
> slave to come in and go to bed to him. Your petitioner
> forbears to state the pain of such conduct. . . . During
> one year and eight months that they lived together as
> man and wife, her husband has for three months with-
> out interruption, night after night, slept with the said
> slave. Your petitioner states that without complaint, she
> submitted in silence to her husband's infidelity, and at-
> tempted to reclaim him by carresses and obedience, but
> in vain.[8]

The petition of this woman appears to have been refused, for the
same case is presented at the following meeting of the
legislature.[9]

The feeling and emotion expressed in the following document
will possibly justify quotation at length.

> Your petitioner is the wife of a certain _____, from
> whom she has been compelled by most cruel, unnatural
> and disgraceful conduct to separate herself and from
> whom she most humbly and earnestly entreats the rep-
> resentatives of her county grant her a divorce, for rea-
> sons she begs hereafter most respectfully to set forth:
> At an early age (being at the time scarcely twelve years
> old) she became acquainted with the man who is now

[8] Petition 7507, Henry, Dec. 7, 1820.
[9] Petition 7643, Henry, Dec. 7, 1821.

her husband. Young, inexperienced, ignorant of mankind starting into life with all those high wrought feelings and expectations too common to youth, and too seldom realized. Innocent and guileless herself, she believed others to be so, she too readily listened to all the tales of future happiness, recounted by those she believed to be her friends. To the warm profession of ardent and never ending love, from one whose object was self gratification, she too readily yielded; and became a wife, when she should still have considered herself a child. But is she not rather deserving of pity rather than censure for the act of rash precipitation and irremediable folly and imprudence. From every quarter she was assailed with the praises of him who was to be her husband. The most extravagant and glowing descriptions were every day given her, of the splendor and happiness that awaited her, whilst, a picture, the most captivating to the eye of a daughter was held up to the imagination, in which she was herself placed in a position to afford ease and comfort to her devoted mother, herself at the time the envy of all her female acquaintances. Fortune and friends were all in attendance upon her and she could but be the happiest of the happy. Fatal delusion! Is it to be wondered at that her youthful heart was led away by the darling prospect thus presented to her, and that she too readily yielded to the solicitations with which she was assailed? Or would it not have been most wonderful had she not yielded? She married, and for a while the fairest prospects bloomed before her, and flattering fancy placed her in Elysium. Too soon, alas, those visions fled, and your petitioner awoke, as from a delightful dream, to all the horrors of her unhappy state. Scarce had the first few weeks of her ill-fated marriage passed, when the mark of hypocrisy in which her vile and profligate husband had too successfully hidden his real character was thrown aside, and the ardent, tender lover became the cold, senseless, hard hearted tyrant. But had this been the only cause of complaint, she would have submitted without a single murmur to

her fate, in the fond hope that an affectionate, meek,
and dutiful wife would in time have conquered his in-
difference and restored her to love and happiness. But
the cup of misery was yet undrained; she had yet to
learn the dreadful, heart-rending truth that she possessed no place in his heart; that another had usurped
her empire over him, and that other (shameless truth)
his own slave. Was she to submit to all this? Or can any
one blame her for separating herself from the man who
would act thus basely and add the cruelest insult to the
grossest injury? Should she submit to have a mistress
kept, as it were, under her nose, and thus give countenance and sanction to his mean and disgraceful adultery?
Surely none can blame and every feeling heart must pity
her, whilst it applauds her for the separation—But although she left him still she was anxious for a recon-
ciliation and reunion; she was too well aware of the ill-
natured and malevolent world in which she lived, to
expect she could escape censure, and whilst her conscious
heart acquitted her of every intentional wrong, every effort
was made to induce him to return to a sense of duty and
again unite himself to his betrothed wife—But her efforts
have been unsuccessful, to every proposition to return and
live with him, on sole condition of his parting with his
mistress, the most unqualified refusal has been given, accompanied always with taunting and insulting language.
Till at last, as if to cap the climax of infamy he is on the
point of removing himself with his property, (his beloved
Miss among the rest) to the western country. Thus leaving
your petitioner a charge upon her mother to whose love
and comfort she lately flattered herself she should immediately contribute.

In additional testimony, it is declared that the husband in this
case refused to sell the slave girl, Betty, and that he publicly said
to his wife, "damn you, if that sticks by you, I will bring her by
here tomorrow in the gig by the side of me in style."[10]

[10] Petition 7546, Dinwiddie, Dec. 13, 1820.

In 1825 the wife of a citizen of the city of Petersburg petitioned for a divorce from her husband; she asserted that the husband "became habituated to the most open and shameless adultery—in his own house with the vilest blacks of the town" and that "he openly boasted of the number of his black wives."[11]

The young wife of an elderly "widower" of King William county, informs us that in her own home,

> a school of benignant instruction where kind providence
> had cast her lot, it became her misfortune to attract the
> notice of the said _____ then a widower. He had not often
> visited her father's house before these circumstances under
> which he solicited your petitioner's hand were well cal-
> culated to inspire her youthful heart. She beheld in the
> person of her suitor the son of a man whom her father had
> often mentioned in the bosom of his family, and with all
> the interest and affection of a brother . . . his name was
> sufficient to herald his claims. . . . Before the wedding
> took place it appears that the girl's brother had forced him
> to send the Negro woman away from the plantation. After
> the wedding it soon appeared that this man's chief inter-
> est had been the wealth he believed the marriage would
> bring to him.

The petition continues:

> He now averted to her peculiar situation, as being the evi-
> dence of her future destiny in becoming the mother of his
> children, and said if he had not supposed her father would
> give her a fortune, he would not have married; that he had
> two mulatto children who were more comely and hand-
> some than any she would ever have and that he would
> bring the mother and her children home—and not permit
> them to suffer any longer, and he spoke in strong terms of
> the satisfaction of the negro woman. . . . In a few more
> days this negro woman and two mulatto children were
> brought upon the plantation. They were received by her
> husband with much interest and shew of affection. He now

[11] Petition 807a, Dinwiddie, Dec. 15, 1823.

again acknowledged the children openly, and admitted
the eldest to every act of familiar intercourse of which its
age was capable. He would take it upon his knee, and instructed it to abuse your unhappy applicant and place her
under the most positive and threatening injunction not
to correct it—declaring his strong attachment for the
mother and stating that the two children were his and
that he meant to do more for them, upon principle, than
for his lawful children. This negro woman was placed in
an easy situation, made happy and cheerful in idleness and
the undisguised friendship of her master.[12]

In 1828 the wife of a citizen of Henrico county asked that she
be divorced from her husband because "he has deserted me, and
is now in the city of Richmond or its vicinity with a colored
woman in a state of open adultery."[13] A similar case is reported
in the city of Lynchburg. In this instance the husband "became
attached to a free woman of color and claimed her as his wife and
carried her away with him as his wife when he left Lynchburg
where he had enlisted as a soldier."[14] In still another instance the
wife protests that "the said Alfred indulged in the most shameful, sinful and degrading intercourse with other women, white
and black—that he frequently left the marriage bed to seek the
bed of a colored woman."[15]

In 1837 a petition for divorce states that the husband has

indulged in the most shameful, sinful, and degrading intercourse with other women; and particularly with a colored
negro woman named Grace, whom he hired of Captain
Sterling Lipscomb. That the said Edmund in October or
November last attempted to run off with the said negro
woman, but was detected and prevented by some gentlemen in the neighborhood—that he has squandered and
consumed the whole of the personal property which he derived by the marriage (having little himself at the time of

[12] Petition 8122, King William, Dec. 2, 1824.
[13] Petition 9080, Henrico, Dec. 4, 1828.
[14] Petition 10681, Amherst, Dec. 8, 1834.
[15] Petition 11312, King William, Dec. 9, 1836.

the marriage) in the most dissipated and vicious practices. That he suffered and even encouraged the said negro woman, Grace, to use not only the most insolent language, but even to inflict blows upon the said Elizabeth, his wife.[16]

A petition from Campbell county affirms that the derelict husband "has wholly abandoned his said wife and notoriously lived in habits of illicit intercourse with lewd black women and had children by them."[17]

The mother of four children declares concerning her husband, then serving a sentence for horse stealing,

> that sometime in the year of our Lord 1839, he withdrew his affections from her and took up with a female colored slave in the neighborhood by the name of Cynthia belonging to the estate of Robert Hoffman, decd.—that he carried on an illicit intercourse with the said woman Cynthia for a considerable time, until he at length determined to carry her off altogether, and to facilitate his purpose, he stole a horse from the said Robert Hoffman to carry the woman and her baggage. On the way, however, having become scarce of funds, he sold the horse and travelled on foot as far as Wheeling in Virginia, on his way, as it is supposed, to some free state where being overtaken by his pursuers he made his escape and left the woman behind him.[18]

The man in this case was captured and sentenced to three years for stealing the girl and to four years for the theft of the horse.

The wife of a citizen of Henry county asserts that her husband married her for her "large Estate of land and negroes," but in her petition for divorce she claims that shortly after her marriage the husband "formed a meretricious connection with one not of his own color, and had not scrupled under the cover of night to introduce her into the chamber occupied by your petitioner . . . he then lived in open adultery with the said woman of color." Testimony in support of this petition explains that

[16] Petition 11713, King William, March 5, 1837.
[17] Petition 13237, Campbell, Dec. 7, 1841.
[18] Petition 13726, Culpeper, Jan. 18, 1843.

the defendant often displayed a strong dislike and aversion to the company of the petitioner and frequently used insulting, indecent, and abusive language toward her. During the same time he appeared to be strongly attached to a servant girl of the family with whom he habitually had illicit criminal intercourse. He frequently slept with her, the said negro servant girl—sometimes on a pallet in his wife's room and other times in an adjoining chamber. He often embraced and kissed her in my [the witness's] presence and invited her to a seat at the table at dinner with himself and family and appeared to be passionately attached to her. This course of conduct did not, of course, escape the observation of his wife, who ofttimes in my presence feelingly and earnestly remonstrated against it. But he generally turned a deaf ear to her entreaties—sometimes flew into a rage and passion and did not scruple to declare that the said negro servant girl was as good and as worthy as the said petitioner. I heard him on one occasion seriously threaten the petitioner, if she laid her hands in an angry manner on the said servant; and generally to her remonstrances he told her if she did not like his course, to leave his house and take herself to some place she liked better.

Another visitor at this plantation declared:

On the next morning when Mrs. _____ and myself had finished breakfast, he directed the said servant girl to seat herself at the table from which I had just risen—to which Mrs. N. objected, saying to the girl, if she seated herself at that table, that she (Mrs. N.) would have her severely punished. To this Mr. N. declared that in that event he would visit her (Mrs. N.) with a like punishment. Mrs. N. then burst into tears and asked if it was not too much for her to stand.[19]

In 1848 an accused husband, said to have been guilty of infidelity with one of his negro slave women, declared in his defense

[19] Petition 16315, Henry, Dec. 20, 1848.

that "he sold one negro girl, a short time before his wife left him, because he had been informed that this girl had been the cause of the jealousy in his wife."[20] In 1851 the wife of a citizen of Hanover declared that "her husband made frequent declarations of love to a negro woman living in her house—, and said he loved her better than he did his wife—and committed adultery with her."[21]

The unfortunate situation of the wife in the following instance gives another example of the sad conditions often found in the slave country. This wife recited that,

> about fifteen years ago, she became wife of _____ of
> the county of Goochland; that they lived together from the
> time of their marriage until about two years ago, when
> the said _____ abandoned her and her five children; took
> up with a free negro woman living in the neighborhood,
> and with her left the county and state and since that time
> has, as she is informed, resided in the state of Ohio. Your
> petitioner represents that her conduct, during the time
> they lived together was that of an affectionate and dutiful
> wife, and that the extraordinary conduct of her said hus-
> band has not been brought about by any neglect on her
> part.[22]

The evidence here submitted indicates that in many cases the lust of the white master for the black bond woman destroyed the peace and happiness of the slaveholder's home, but the student is left to question how many white women saw the conduct of their derelict husbands and suffered in silence. In a day when divorces were few and when religion, custom, and law made divorces hard to procure, there must have been many women who calmly or sullenly submitted and accepted the position of the "chief slave of the husband's harem."

The conditions described in this chapter were not peculiar to the state of Virginia. In the other southern states the records

[20] Petition 16131, Halifax, March 1, 1848.
[21] Petition 17611, Hanover, Feb. 2, 1851.
[22] Petition 16952, Goochland, Jan. 15, 1850.

show that white wives attempted to divorce their husbands for adultery with slave women.[23]

Home life on the plantations could not be ideal where jealousies and strife between white and mulatto women were possible. Other examples are to be found which indicate problems resulting from sexual relations in the slave states. In 1820 the courts of Louisiana ordered a father to contribute to the support of his children.[24] In this instance the children in question had returned from a boarding school and discovered that their father had taken a mulatto woman as his concubine. The children refused to live in the residence of the woman and the father refused to contribute to their support until they agreed to occupy his residence. In 1834 a Virginia planter died and by will devised that a certain mulatto woman slave should be emancipated. The white wife and children of the deceased opposed the generous act of the master and attempted to sell the slave woman. In this instance the son of the deceased testified: "I, of my own knowledge, knew that my mother had to give up her bed to Lucy, the negro woman let free by my father's will, in the lifetime of my father for twelve or fifteen years." A witness in this case testified that, "Lucy, after the death of _____, who let Lucy free, said she was free and would not serve as she had formerly done and demanded her support, and that Aunt Priscilla _____*___, had to strip her and whip her, before she would submit to do her business."[25] In 1857, a Mississippi planter owned a mulatto woman and her daughter who were accused of poisoning the white wife and infant child of the planter. In this instance the evidence shows that the planter was at the same time the father of the daughter of the slave woman's child, that he had had sexual intercourse with the slave woman on the day before the murder of the woman and child, and that on the occasion of the death of a former white wife of this planter, the slave woman had been suspected of poisoning her mistress and had been whipped and kept tied up for

[23] *Mosser* v. *Mosser*, 29 *Alabama Reports*, p. 313 (1852); *Ledoux* v. *Her Husband*, 10 Randolph, *Louisiana Reports*, p. 663 (1855); *Adams* v. *Hurst*, 9 Curry, *Louisiana Reports*, p. 243 (1835).

[24] *Heno* v. *Heno*, 7 Martin, *Louisiana Reports*, p. 543 (1820).

[25] Petition 10590, Lunenburg, Feb. 6, 1834.

several days while the planter debated turning her over to the officers of the law.[26] In 1859 the white family of another Mississippi planter attempted to prevent the mulatto concubine of the deceased master from receiving the estate that had been willed to her. In this case it was shown that the white family had deserted him because he had persisted in living with the mulatto woman.[27] In a similar instance, it was shown that an Alabama planter had given his property to his Negro children "to spite his brothers and sisters, who would not associate with him, on account of his adulterous intercourse with a negro woman."[28]

So much has been written concerning the virtue, probity, and chivalry of the southern white man that it need not be repeated that the records used in this study are not typical of every southern white man. However, racial relations are a human problem, and the man of the South being human and unfortunately tied down by an evil economic system, reacted in a human way to his Negro property.

It is to be noted that the white woman also reacted in a human way. The records of Virginia divorces give interesting evidence of jealousies, hatreds, and suspicions that were both natural and human, but these same records of divorce cases make it plain that the white woman in the slave period, in many cases, succumbed to the same human weaknesses, lusts, and temptations that white men seemed too human to overcome.

The following petition is typical of others that are to follow. In this case a citizen of Fluvanna county asks the legislature to grant him a divorce from his wife, Elizabeth. He declares that,

> in the month of March, 1801, he intermarried with a certain Elizabeth _____, a woman descended from honest and industrious parents, and of unspotted character so far as your petitioner heard, or had any reason to believe. Your petitioner lived with the said Elizabeth, with all the affection and tenderness that could possibly exist between husband and wife, for about four months, when to the great astonishment and inexpressible mortification of your

[26] John S. Morris, *Mississippi Cases* (New Orleans, 1870), II, 1448.
[27] *Heirn* v. *Bridault*, 37 *Mississippi Reports*, p. 209 (1859).
[28] *Pool* v. *Pool*, 35 Shephard, *Alabama Reports*, p. 12 (1860).

petitioner, the said Elizabeth was delivered of a mulatto child, and is now so bold as to say it was begotten by a negro man slave in the neighborhood.[29]

In 1803 a citizen of Norfolk applied for a divorce, stating that,

in the year 1802 from the most affectionate, pure, and honorable motives and from an exalted opinion he had formed of the chastity and virtue of Lydia _____, daughter of William _____, of the said county, he paid his addresses to her, and on the 17th day of September in the same year the rights of matrimony were celebrated between them,—that from that time until the 11th day of May in the year of 1802 they lived together as man and wife. That on the 11th day of May, while your petitioner was absent from home on business, his wife was delivered of a child, which on your petitioner's return and to his inexpressible grief and astonishment proved to be a mulatto, and which she shortly afterwards confessed was the child of a negro slave. . . . Your petitioner further begs leave to state that from the time of the above mentioned distressing event his affections have been totally alienated from the said Lydia, and he has resolved never to cohabit with or acknowledge her as his lawful wife.[30]

A citizen of Accomac county declares that,

about twelve years ago he intermarried with a certain _____ Tabitha _____, of the county aforesaid; that for a number of years he lived in peace and harmony with his said wife, and apparently possessed her affections, without any suspicions on his part of a defect of fidelity on her part; that during this period he had three children by his said wife, two of whom are now living, the other departed this life within the last two or three months past. Under such circumstances your petitioner, who is a plain labouring man, seeking his sustenance by honest industry, had flattered himself with such portion of domestic happiness as

[29] Petition 4472, Fluvanna, Dec. 13, 1802.
[30] Petition 4594, Norfolk, Dec. 7, 1803.

might be reasonably expected in his condition of life; but about the close of the year 1803, his prospects in this respect were darkened by an occurrence—which he feels himself constrained with infinite regret to recount. His said wife being pregnant was at that time delivered of a child, which was obviously the issue of an illicit intercourse with a black man. It is vain for your petitioner to describe his distress on that occasion or the shame and confusion of a woman whom he had cherished with the kindness due to the relation in which she stood to him.[31]

A similar case is found in 1806. In this instance the petitioners declare: "They have understood that a negro the property of the grandfather of the said Henrietta was the father of the said child."[32]

A petition from Loudoun county tells of the marital difficulties of a certain citizen residing in that locality. This husband declares:

Your petitioner (just entering the twenty-first year of his age) and a certain Elizabeth _____, daughter of Charles, of Fairfax county were married. . . . The said Elizabeth being then, as your petitioner believed, of fair character and unsullied reputation. That your petitioner and the said Elizabeth continued to live together in the strictest love, friendship, and happiness, about three years after their marriage. But that at length your petitioner discovered, with most heartfelt grief and sorrow, that his said wife Elizabeth was of a lewd, incontinent, profligate disposition and practice. But being so much attached to her person, having from his first acquaintance with her cherished the most ardent, tender affection, love and regard for her and the respect which the most upright and virtuous woman ought to expect, admonished her repeatedly of the wickedness of such a course, and of the infamy and disgrace which must result from it, and that if persisted in a separation would take place. But alas! All this produced a contrary effect

[31] Petition 4888, Accomac, Dec. 13, 1805.
[32] Petition 5021, King William, Dec. 9, 1806.

and your petitioner having at two different times detected
her and the partner of her crime (a certain James Watts,
a man of colour) in bed together. He resolved to leave
her. That your petitioner accordingly set out for the Western Country, determined never more to have any connection with a woman who so basely disgraced herself and
dishonored her husband, whose misfortune it was to have
been attached to her and merited better treatment from
her.[33]

Another husband complains that,

his wife Nancy, was delivered of a mulatto child, which he
considers such a horrid violation of the marriage bed, that
he is induced to pray your honorable body to pass a law
divorcing him from his wife. He forbears making further
observations upon his case, as he is convinced it must be
obvious to any person the disagreeable situation in which
he at present stands, and must remain without your interposition.[34]

Still another husband testified that in 1810 his wife "Elizabeth
was delivered of two mulatto children,"[35] because of which he
felt that the state might declare his marriage dissolved.

In still another case the unfortunate husband declares that his
wife,

was delivered of a female child which your petitioner did
not at first at all doubt to be his, notwithstanding its darkness of color, and its unusual appearance. It was in a little
time, however, discovered to your petitioner as well as to
those who saw it, that it could not be the offspring of your
petitioner or of any other white man. . . . The said Peggy,
the wife of your petitioner, does not hesitate to acknowledge, that the father of the said child is a negro,
all of which facts are notorious in the neighborhood. Your
petitioner, therefore, finding his wife so abandoned to ev-

[33] Petition 5321, Loudoun, Dec. 22, 1808.
[34] Petition 5424, Patrick, Dec. 11, 1809.
[35] Petition 6014, Boutetout, Dec. 2, 1812.

ery principle of virtue and chastity, which ought to govern the conduct of a woman and a wife, finds it impossible to continue with her on those terms of harmony and affection which ought to subsist between those united by such intimate ties.[36]

The experience of another white husband is related as follows: "But your petitioner not being willing to lend too favorable an ear to reports prevalent in the neighborhood, determined to see for himself; and it is now with painful recollection that he states, that on his return home, at a late hour of the night, on entering his house he found the said Elizabeth, undressed, and in bed with a certain Aldrige Evans, a man of color."[37]
In still another instance it is stated that

his wife was delivered of a mulatto child, and that soon after the birth of the said child she acknowledged that a negro fellow in the neighborhood was the father of the child. She has since left your petitioner and has removed with her mother to the state of Ohio.[38]

In 1825 the patrollers in Louisa county went over the countryside to search the Negro cabins for stolen leather. They report "that the wife of _____ was taken out of one of John Richardson's negro houses, in November last, after midnight—she got away." In this case other witnesses testified of the same woman and slave that "they went to the house of the said Dorothea, about the first day of this month of November last, a little after daybreak and found a mulatto man named Edmund, the property of John Richardson, in bed with Dorothea." The owner of this slave testified that when she heard that his slave was about to forsake her it caused her much discontent. The husband of this woman is said to have been old and infirm, and the slave is said to have been "so bright in color, a stranger would take him for a white man." A witness declared that "the white slave and Lewis _____'s wife lived together, almost as man and wife" and

[36] Petition 6364, Northampton, Nov. 2, 1814.
[37] Petition 5370, Amherst, Dec. 6, 1809.
[38] Petition 6729, Fauquier. Nov. 16, 1816.

another witness declared, "I believe the only cause of
Lewis _____'s wife quitting him and taking up with this slave
was that the slave was much younger and a more likely man
than _____. There being a great difference in the age of
Lewis _____ and his wife." The divorce petition of the husband
in this case states that,

> in spite of the remonstrances and persuasions of your pe-
> titioner, she has lived for the last six or seven years and
> still continues to live in open adultery with a negro man, a
> slave, the property of one of your petitioner's neighbors.
> That the said slave is known by your petitioner and many
> respectable persons to be upon such terms of intimacy
> with her that there is no room to doubt that an illicit in-
> tercourse is regularly kept up between them. That your
> petitioner believes and such is the belief of all living in the
> neighborhood, as your petitioner will shew that the said
> negro man has had by her two children, one of whom is
> now alive, and is living evidence of her guilty and dishon-
> orable course of conduct. . . . Your petitioner further
> states that he has never either before or after his wife left
> his house and his bed, treated her with cruelty or inhu-
> manity, but has permitted her to remain peaceably in a
> house upon his own lands.[39]

In 1835 a citizen of Norfolk testified that his wife had left him,
and, "that since the said Caroline has made her elopement, she
has repeatedly associated with negroes, and from information
which your complainant has received, there can be no doubt she
has had carnal intercourse with black men or negroes."[40]

In 1838 a native of Orange county reports that,

> in the month of April 1829, he intermarried with a young
> lady by the name of Nancy _____ of respectable parentage
> and occupying a respectable standing in society. He flat-
> tered himself with the hope of adding to her, and to his
> own happiness for life. They lived together for six or seven

[39] Petitions 8218, Louisa, Dec. 16, 1824; 8305, Louisa, Jan. 20, 1825.
[40] Petition 10943, Norfolk, Dec. 9, 1835.

months, when the said Nancy, to your petitioner's shame
and mortification was delivered of a mulatto child. . . .
Since that time the said Nancy has had two other children,
both colored.[41]

In still another instance the husband regretfully explains that,
"his wife has frequently had criminal intercourse with slaves and
persons of color, by whom or one of whom she has had one or
more children of color; she has, moreover, urged no doubt by a
sense of shame and a consciousness of her guilt, separated from
your petitioner and voluntarily removed up to the state of North
Carolina."[42]

A citizen of Fairfax county explains that,

in 1827 he lawfully intermarried with one Rebecca _____,
who in about three weeks thereafter, without the least
cause known to your petitioner, eloped from his bed and
board, and has never since returned; and that during all
that time she has lived in open adultery with a free man
of color, named Wilfred Mortimer. That since her elopement, she has had a bastard child.[43]

In 1833 a similar petition was presented by a citizen of Charles
City county.[44] In 1840 a citizen of Nansemond county certified
that "his wife has been delivered of a colored child, begotten by a
negro long since she married the said _____. She has recently
been engaged in illicit intercourse with a negro man at my own
house and on my own bed."[45] Another husband reports that, "his
wife was delivered of a child about eighteen months ago, the
child is a mulatto, living now as a pauper in the house of a free
negro, by order of the overseers of the poor of Nansemond
county; that she lived with her husband at the time of the deliv-
ery, and she had three children by her lawful husband."[46] In another instance it is reported that, "on two separate occasions,
since her intermarriage with the said Thomas, the said Mary has

[41] Petition 11955, Orange, Jan. 29, 1838.
[42] Petition 8683, Nansemond, Dec. 8, 1826.
[43] Petition 9781, Fairfax, Dec. 8, 1831.
[44] Petition 1403, James City, Dec. 10, 1833.
[45] Petition 13042, Nansemond, Dec. 14, 1840.
[46] Petition 13025, Nansemond, Dec. 14, 1840.

been delivered and become the mother of black children, who could not be other than the fruits of adulterous intercourse with a negro."[47] The records show in still another case, that "Mary Jane _____, the wife of Jacob _____, about twelve or fourteen years ago gave birth to a mulatto child, that some time before the birth of the said child she was caught in the act of adultery with a colored man."[48] In another case it is recorded that, "Elizabeth _____ had a mulatto, and the last time that I saw the said Elizabeth, my wife, she and the said mulatto child were in the state of Ohio."[49]

The white woman that followed the example of the white man and helped to bring mulatto children into the world had to fear the consequences of her conduct. There was, for her, always fear of the embarrassing responsibility of the white mother of the mulatto—a responsibility that, too often, was nonexistent in the case of a guilty white man. Natural fears of the physical consequences, together with the forces of law and public opinion, must have served to limit the number of mulattoes born of white mothers; however, cases of divorce granted for reasons of this kind are to be found in other states than Virginia.[50]

Only married women were involved in the documents used above, but from another source evidence is found that makes it clear that unmarried white women were concerned in similar relations with Negro men. It is a common belief that the crime of rape committed by Negro men against white women was nonexistent before the Civil War; that southern social ideals and the system of slave control made such a thing impossible. However, this was not the case. A table is given in the note below which indicates the number of such alleged crimes committed in Virginia between the years 1789 and 1833.[51] This table is based upon the

---

[47] Petition 13079, Frederick, Jan. 9, 1841.

[48] Petitions 13261, Preston, Dec. 9, 1841; 15686, Dec. 14, 1847.

[49] Petition 16648, Allegheny, March 5, 1849.

[50] *Scroggins* v. *Scroggins,* 14 Devereux, *North Carolina Reports,* p. 535 (1829); *Barden* v. *Barden,* 14 Devereux, *North Carolina Reports,* p. 548 (1829).

[51] *Virginia Negroes Condemned for Rape, 1789 to 1833.*

1789 May 30, Powhatan	Jim
1792 August 12, Spotsylvania	Fern

record of such crimes as reported to the governors of Virginia. In each case the Negro had been condemned and the evidence submitted to the governor for his examination before the sentence of death could be put into execution. It is no doubt true that in most of these cases the slave was guilty as charged, but the student who reads the evidence as submitted to the governor is astonished at the number of cases in which white citizens of the communities in which these events transpired testify for the Negro and against the white woman and declare that the case is not a matter of rape, for the woman encouraged and consented to the act of the Negro. In twenty-seven of the sixty cases the justices that imposed sentence upon the slave recommended him to the mercy of the governor, stating that they had doubts that the man was guilty or citizens of the community sent petitions for

1796	October 22, Fredericksburg	Hamilton
1797	April 26, Frederick	Norman
1799	August 3, Northampton	Abraham
1801	June 20, Prince George	Grenock
	November 6, Richmond (county)	Isaac Venice
1803	May 9, King and Queen	Carter
1804	March 4, Fairfax	Luke
	August 6, Nansemond	Jesse
	June 8, Augusta	John
	August 14, Nansemond	Tom
1805	February 4, Boutetout	Archy
	April 10, Henrico	Billy
	September 20, Chesterfield	Cyrus
1807	June 4, Henry	Jerry
1808	April 18, Amherst	David
	September, Fluvanna	Spencer
	October, Hanover	Ben
1810	August 7, King William	Ben
	November 3, Greenville	Dick
1811	March 25, Fauquier	Stephen
1812	September 1, Nansemond	Isaac
	October 21, Powhatan	George
	October 2, Rockingham	David
1814	May 27, Bedford	Isaac
	June 2, Fairfax	Isaac
	September 28, Berkley	Sam

the man's pardon and presented evidence not admitted on the occasion of the trial. The petitions that follow may be considered as typical:

To the honorable the Governor and Council of the Commonwealth of Virginia—

Your petitioners with all due deference state that at a court of Oyer and Terminer, held for King and Queen County, on Monday the 9th of May, 1803, for the trial of Carter a negro man slave belonging to William Boyd,

1817 October, Shenandoah	John Holloman
1818 August 5, Orange	Jack
1819 June 26, Cumberland	Dennis
July 12, Campbell	Reuben
June 19, Norfolk	Ned
1823 June 4, Orange	Alexander
June 9, Campbell	Charles
August 11, Chesterfield	Spencer
November 3, Henrico	Thomas
1824 September 23, Culpeper	Lawrence
1825 May 8, Monongalia	Moses
1826 August 26, Montgomery	James
1827 March 21, Northampton	Arthur
June 15, Southampton	Henry Hunt
June 15, Halifax	Buck
December 11, Loudoun	Ben
1828 May 2, Cumberland	Sam
July 22, Louisa	Jeffry
1829 May 28, Patrick	Gabriel
June 20, Wythe	Gabriel
September 29, Shenandoah	Joseph
1830 May 3, Franklin	Henry
May 30, Henry	Patrick
1831 May 21, Loudoun	Dick
September 26, Westmoreland	Dick
June 10, Caroline	Abram
1832 May 14, Stafford	William
July 9, Henry	George
August 23, Prince Edward	John
1833 April 27, Frederick	Ben
October 18, Frederick	Tasso

charged for a rape on the body of Catherine Brinal, of
which said court your subscribers were sitting as members,
it appeared by the testimony of the said Catherine, that
Carter did commit the said offense—from the whole of the
evidence your subscribers felt themselves bound by law
to pass sentence of death upon the said Carter. Yet for
reasons, hereinafter mentioned the court aforesaid are of
the opinion that the said Carter is a proper object of
mercy—to wit—From the testimony of Philip Sears and
Kaufman Watts it appeared that the said Catherine Brinal
was a woman of the worst fame, that her character was
that of the most abandoned in as much as she (being a
white woman) has three mulatto children, which by her
own confession were begotten by different negro men; that
the said Catherine has no visible means of support; that
from report she had permitted the said Carter to have
peaceable sexual intercourse with her, before the time of
his forcing her. Your petitioners farther state that the said
Carter, by the testimony of William and Robert Boyer,
was a negro of tolerable good character, not inclined to be
riotous but rather of a peaceable disposition.[52]

A petition in behalf of the slave, Jerry, informs the governor
that,

he was condemned on a charge of having ravished a
woman named Sands. I am of the opinion, and several
others amongst whom were some of the members of the
court that sat upon his trial, that he should be transported
rather than executed. The woman I learn from a variety
of sources is under a very infamous character. She has lived
as a concubine for some time past with a man named
Vaughn, in whose house this negro I am informed was as
intimate as any white man. The woman appears large and
strong enough to have made considerable resistance if she

[52] Executive Papers, May 9, 1803.
(Executive Papers, Archives of Virginia, Letters Received. Hereafter
Archives of Virginia, Letters Received, will be omitted and the docu-
ment will be identified by the date.)

had been disposed, yet there was by her own confession no mark of violence upon any part of her.[53]

Sixty-two citizens of the county of Hanover petitioned the executive in behalf of a slave called Peter, who had been accused by a certain Patsy Hooker. Concerning this woman the petitioners declared that, "the said Patsy Hooker, from the best information they can get upon the subject, is a common strumpet, and she was the only witness introduced on the part of the Commonwealth in the prosecution of the said slave."[54]

In 1813 the slave David was condemned for a rape committed in Rockingham county. The following document accompanied a petition sent to the governor in his behalf:

I, John Lightner, do certify that an improper intimacy has subsisted upwards of three years past between Dolly Getts, daughter of Philip Getts, and David, a negro slave, of the said Zachary Shackelford. That I have been informed by the said Getts and his daughter that the said boy David first began his visits to the house of the said Getts on the invitation of him the said Getts; that the said Dolly and David were permitted to bed together frequently in the house of the said Philip with his knowledge. That the said Dolly has admitted to me that his improper conduct arose from her persuasions, that she frequently made use of great importunities to the said David for the purpose of prevailing on him to run off with her which he for some time refused to accede to. I have caught the said Dolly and David together, while he the said David was lying out, as often as three times, to wit, once about the 20th of May, last, between midnight and day, about nine miles from their respective house; once a short time after that near the same place when they were lying together in the lap of a tree, I have heard the said Dolly acknowledge that when they were lying out together she procured provisions and carried them to David. The first time I took Dolly and David together their clothes were tied up together in a

[53] Executive Papers, May 27, 1807.
[54] Executive Papers, Oct., 1808.

bundle and put in a coat of hers; at which time she earnestly solicited David to go to her father and tell him they were married and perhaps they might be permitted to remain together. David refused and charged her with having brought him into his then unpleasant situation; she confessed the charge.[55]

The record in the case of Tasco Thompson, a condemned free Negro, includes the following document.

The executive of Virginia, having requested to be informed of the reasons which induced the jury who passed upon the case of Tasco Thompson, now under sentence of death for an attempt to commit a rape upon the body of Mary Jane Stevens, to recommend the said Tasco Thompson to mercy. I, the undersigned, Sam. H. Davis, foreman of the jury, in compliance with the request, give the following verified by oath.

1st. The exceedingly disreputable character of the family of the said Stevens. It consisted of the mother and herself, with a younger sister, a small girl. It was notorious that the mother had long entertained negroes, and that all her associations, with one or two exceptions were with blacks. All the evidence went to shew that she visited no white families save the one or two referred to, who were upon her own level. In a word she was below the level of the ordinary grade of free negroes.

2nd. Although the evidence of Mary Jane Stevens was direct, and apparently artless, and sustained by a girl of about eleven years old, who was present at the attempted rape, yet it was clearly proved that long settled malice had existed against the prisoner in the bosom of another witness (the mother of the girl of eleven years) who was looked upon as one of the getters up of the prosecution and who was proved to have declared before the offense that she would have the prisoner hung if it took her seven years.

3d. . . . There is no doubt that he repaired to the house

[55] Executive Papers, Oct. 2, 1813.

of Mrs. Stevens in the belief that she would cheerfully submit to his embraces, as she doubtless had often done before,
but finding her absent he probably supposed his embraces
would be equally agreeable to her daughter, and in making the attempt the jury considered the offence as differing
only *in name* from a similar attempt made upon one of his
color. They also considered that the law was made to preserve the distinction which should exist between our two
kinds of population, and to protect the whites in the possession of their superiority; but here the whites had
yielded their claims to the protection of the law by their
voluntary associations with those whom the law distin-
guishes as their inferiors.

4th. As a prosecution would not have a claim in the case
if the female concerned had been a colored girl, so the jury
thought it hard to convict the prisoner for an offence not
greater in enormity than had the prosecutrix been colored;
but her maker had given her a white skin, and they had no
discretion. They could only convict him capitally and urge
the recommendation which they did.[56]

A similar situation is described in the case of Henry Hunt, a
free negro of Southampton county. In this case Hunt had been
convicted for a rape committed upon a certain Sydney Jordan.
Investigators found that Sydney Jordan "acknowledged that she
had been delivered on Friday before of a child, of which one
Nicholas Vick another free negro was the father, that she had frequent criminal intercourse with the said Nicholas Vick and also
with Henry Hunt; and that on the night laid in the indictment
against the said Hunt, she did have criminal connection with the
said Vick."[57]
It is not possible to determine the extent of such practices as
have been described in this chapter. The writings of travelers and
visitors to the southern states give the student the impression that
such cases were few. Olmsted reports that he heard of but one
case in which a white woman had given birth to a mulatto

[56] Executive Papers, Oct. 18, 1833.
[57] Executive Papers, June 15, 1827.

child.[58] An Englishman reports that, "although many white men have a wonderful inclination for black women, I could never learn of but one instance where a white woman was captivated by a negro, and this was said to have been in Virginia; a planter's daughter having fallen in love with one of her father's slaves, had actually seduced him; the result of this amour was the sudden mysterious disappearance of the young lady."[59] A visitor declares that a rumor got abroad, at Talboton, Georgia, that a young white woman had given birth to a mulatto child. The visitor found the community in great commotion because of this scandal. "Such an offence was considered so great, that, in the words of those who spoke of it, all the waters of Georgia would be insufficient to wash it out."[60] However, there is evidence that the birth of a mulatto to a white woman was not an uncommon affair.[61] A former Kentucky minister reports: "Were it necessary, I could refer you to several instances of slaves, actually seducing the daughters of their masters. Such seductions sometimes happened

[58] Frederick L. Olmsted, *A Journey in the Seaboard Slave States* (New York, 1859), II, 297.

[59] Peter Neilson, *Recollections of a Six Years Residence in the United States of America* (Glasgow, 1830), p. 297.

[60] James S. Buckingham, *The Slave States of America* (London, 1842), I, 240.

[61] "A Friend to Humanity," Richmond *Enquirer,* Feb. 24, 1859: "But, gentlemen are mistaken if they believe Virginia will ever be rid of free Negroes. Those who advocate it, see not what are to be the consequences. As long as there are Negro slaves in Virginia, and bad white women, we shall have a mulatto population free. If every free Negro in Virginia, were sent away today, they would in a hundred years, beget a large number or rather a large number of persons of mixed blood, having at least one-fourth Negro blood, so that if you could by magic, get clear tomorrow of every free Negro in Virginia and repeal every statute in relation to them, you would yet have to retain this well dressed 17th Section.

"Suppose you repeal the 17th Section of the Code (Chapter 107, page 468, Code of Virginia). What is to become of these black children of white women? Are they to be registered as free Negroes? If so, the legislature ought to pass a law saying how the courts are to ascertain the facts. Surely white women, whilst the wives of white men, have had children by them as free Negroes and Mulattoes."

in the most respectable families."[62] A resident of North Carolina writes:

> Hardly a neighborhood was free from low white women who married or cohabited with free negroes. Well can I remember, the many times when, with the inconsiderable curiosity of a child, I hurriedly climbed the front gate to get a good look at a shriveled old woman trudging down the lane, who, when young, I was told, had had her free negro lover bled and drank some of his blood, so that she might swear she had negro blood in her, and thus marry him without penalty. Since I became a man, I have heard it corroborated by those who knew, and I still see children of this tragic marriage, now grown old men.[63]

An examination of the United States census returns for 1830 seems to indicate that there were many more of these cases than is usually suspected.[64] In repeated instances and in all of the states, it is found that if we add the number of slaves and free persons of color as enumerated for many of the free Negro families, the sum falls one person short of the total number of persons included in the family. The explanation seems to be that the additional female was the white wife of the free Negro head of the family. This conclusion is supported by the census record as given for the county of Nansemond, in Virginia, 1830. In this case the enumerator was more zealous than in any of the other districts and in addition to the information required of him, added the notation "and white wife" after the name of the free Negro head of the family. The following persons are listed as heads of families in this Virginia county:

Jacob of Rega, and white wife
Syphe of Matthews, and white wife
Jacob Branch, and white wife
Ely of Copeland, and white wife

---

[62] John Rankin, *Letters of Slavery* (Newburyport, 1836), p. 69; Abdy, op. cit., III, 27.

[63] David Dodge, "The Free Negroes of North Carolina," *Atlantic Monthly*, LVII (January, 1886), 95.

[64] Manuscript Returns, United States Census, 1830.

Tom of Copeland, and white wife
Will of Butler, and white wife
Davy of Sawyer, and white wife
Stephen of Newby, and white wife
Amarian Reed, and white wife.

Evidence of a similar kind is found in an enumeration of free Negroes and mulattoes made by the State of Virginia in 1844. In this instance the census taker for one of the districts of Southampton added the notation, "white mother," after the names of certain mulatto children living in that county. The following is his record:

Eva Chitty, white mother
John Drake, white mother
Spencer Drake and Thomas Drake, white mother
Jane Gray, white mother
Alex., Bob., Samuel, and Gideon Scholar, white mother.[65]

In the correspondence of the governors of Virginia there are to be found many references to the relations of white women and the Negro. A letter from Northumberland county informs the governor that, "in the course of the present term, three men . . . have been tried upon indictments for stealing a free mulatto boy, about 12 or 14 years of age, named Jack Cox of Knox, from his mother Nina Cox, a white woman, residing in this county."[66] In 1826 a letter sent to the governor in behalf of a convicted free Negro informs the governor that "he [the convicted man] is the son of a white woman."[67] In 1825 a Negro slave escaped from his master and went into hiding in Dismal Swamp. A white woman went into hiding with him. Concerning this affair the governor is informed: "Some two or three years ago a certain Jeremiah Delk, a respectable citizen of Isle of Wight county, owned a negro man slave, who had taken up, and cohabited with a base white woman of Southampton county, by the name of Catherine Britt, who lived near here."[68]

[65] Archives of Virginia, Auditor, No. 161.
[66] Executive Papers, April 4, 1798.
[67] Executive Papers, May 1, 1826.
[68] Executive Papers, April 6, 1825.

In 1826 a white woman of King George county, Virginia, was tried for the theft of a Negro and a horse and at the same time the Negro said to have been stolen, was tried for his share in the stealing of the horse. A letter to the governor informs him that they were captured in what is today the state of West Virginia and that,

the woman traveled from this county to the county of Hampshire incognito and in disguise, for she was dressed in man's clothes when they were captured. Is it not probable, is it not almost certain that she persuaded him off and that she was the whole and sole cause of his stealing his master's horse?[69]

A letter from the town of Suffolk informs the governor of a similar attempt of a white woman to carry a Negro slave out of the country. The letter reads as follows:

Sir: A negro slave called Ben has lately been apprehended and brought before me. It appears that he has come into the state contrary to the act of the Assembly concerning slaves, free negroes and mulattoes. A white woman who was with the fellow late at night claims him as her property. She declares that it was her design to emancipate and fix him here, that she then intended to return herself to North Carolina, from whence she came. It is the opinion of those who apprehend them that improper connection exists between them.[70]

The white man is most responsible for the creation of the mulatto population of the slave days. However, the human passions which motivated the man were also the passions of the woman of the South, and the white woman has a share of the responsibility for the existence of the mulatto.

On the occasion of the examination of the guilty wife of a citizen of Powhatan county, in Virginia, this woman declared "that she had not been the first nor would she be the last guilty of such conduct, and that she saw no more harm in a white woman's hav-

[69] Executive Papers, June 10, 1826.
[70] Executive Papers, July 13, 1801.

ing been the mother of a black child than in a white man's having one, though the latter was more frequent."[71]

In concluding this chapter, may I repeat my sincere conviction
that conditions described above were not typical of the men or
the women of Virginia or the South.

[71] Petition 6428, Powhatan, Dec. 6, 1815.

ELEVEN

Indian Relations

I N THE SLAVE PERIOD the relations of the Indian to the white man and to the Negro and the interrelations of the three races add to the complexity of this study.[1] There was much intermixture of the blood of these three races, and there were perplexing problems resulting from the difficulty in distinguishing the racial identity of these races. In many instances the slave code was applied to men who were in reality Indians, though styled Negroes, and in many cases we find the conflict of the law of the land with the influences of human nature.

After the colonial period it is found that there were some efforts made to promote the intermarriage of the Indian and the white man. Such efforts were probably the result of the experience and influence of agents and traders who had lived upon the frontier. Sir William Johnson is a distinguished example of such an agent. He had an Indian wife and children born of this marriage. He was very faithful to his Indian wife, and it is said that his great influence over the Six Nations was in part due to this marriage relation.[2] He advised other men to follow his example. The constant danger of Indian attacks upon the people of the frontier was probably the cause of the presentation in 1784 of a

---

[1] Kenneth W. Porter, "Relation between Indians and Negroes within the Present Limits of the United States," *Journal of Negro History,* XVII (July, 1932) , 287–367.

[2] Ann Maury, *Memoirs of a Huguenot Family* (New York, 1872) , p. 360; James Grahame, *History of the United States of America, from the Plantation of the British Colonies till Their Assumption of National Independence* (Boston, 1845) , IV, 151; James S. Buckingham, *The Slave States of America* (London, 1842) , I, 77–78.

bill to the Virginia legislature providing that "every white man who married an Indian woman should be paid ten pounds, and five for each child born of such a marriage; and that if any white woman married an Indian she should be entitled to ten pounds with which the county court should buy them live stock; that once each year the Indian husband to this woman should be entitled to three pounds with which the county court should buy clothes for him; that every child born to the Indian man and white woman should be educated by the state between the ages of ten and twenty-one years."[3] Patrick Henry was the author of this bill and it had the full support of John Marshall. The bill passed the house on its first and second reading, but it finally failed to pass, possibly because Patrick Henry, its sponsor, had been called away from the house to assume more important duties. It appears also that in 1824 William H. Crawford advocated a similar bill before the Congress of the United States. In this case, again, the policy did not prove to be a popular one and the bill failed to pass.[4]

As a rule the white man disdained legal marriage with the Indian.[5] This attitude toward legal marriage was, in the case of the Indian, as in the case of the Negro, followed by much licentious intermixture of the Indian and the white race. In this respect the observer would seem to be correct in his conclusion that "there is a degree of repulsion between the Anglo-Americans and the Indians which prevents their intermixing."[6] There is abundant evidence of much promiscuous intermixture of the two races in all

[3] Albert Beveridge, *Life of John Marshall* (New York, 1919), I, 239–41.

[4] *Strictures Addressed to James Madison on the Celebrated Report of William H. Crawford Recommending the Intermarriage of Americans with the Indian Tribes* (Philadelphia, 1824).

[5] Almon W. Lauber, *Indian Slavery in Colonial Times, within the Present Limits of the United States,* (New York, 1913), pp. 207–08; John Oldmixon, *The British Empire in America, Containing the History of the Discovery, Settlement, Progress and Present State of All the British Colonies on the Continent and Islands of America* (London, 1708), p. 252.

[6] James Stewart, *Three Years in North America* (Edinburgh, 1833), II, 201.

the territory east of the mountains. Such relations were no doubt frowned upon or ignored as in the case of similar relations between white men and slaves, but on the frontier, uncontrolled by the opinions or prejudices of his fellows, the white man mingled his blood freely with that of the Indian. It is recorded that "it is the custom when a white man enters an Indian village or nation, with the intention of residing there for some time, if only a few months, for him to have a wigwam, or hut, erected in which he lives with some young squaw, whom he either courts to his embraces, or receives from her parents as his wife and servant, during the time of his stay with them."[7] White men were sometimes adopted into the tribes, and there are reports of cases on the frontier in which white children, kidnapped when very young, were reared by the Indians. When they became of age they married with the Indians.[8] No inducements are said to have been able to bring such persons back to their own people.[9] Descendants of mixed unions were sometimes the leaders of depredations on the frontier.[10] Soldiers on the frontier are reported as having Indian wives.[11] Examples are to be found in which the Indian squaw of some trader disclosed the plans of the tribe on the occasion of plotted attack upon the white settlers.[12] Missionaries complained bitterly because of the relations of white men with the Indian women. In 1801 a missionary to the Chickasaw tribe complained that,

> he undertook to admonish an Indian of considerable influence on taking a second wife while his first wife was liv-

[7] John F. D. Smyth, *Tour in the United States of America* (London, 1784), I, 191.

[8] Ibid.

[9] Michel de Crevecoeur, *Letters from an American Farmer* (London, 1783), p. 294.

[10] Maury, op. cit., p. 360.

[11] Henry Timberlake, *Memoirs of Lieutenant Henry Timberlake* (London, 1765), p. 65; John Carr, *Early Times in Middle Tennessee* (Nashville, 1857), p. 266.

[12] Executive Papers, Archives of Virginia, Letters Received, June, 1781. Hereafter Archives of Virginia, Letters Received, will be omitted and the document identified by the date.

ing with him. He replied, "There is a A. B. 'meaning a white man,' he has five wives, and may I not have two?"[13]

Another missionary writes from Indiana in 1818: "I can with truth, inform you that there are among the Indians, white men who have a dozen wives."[14] In 1824 still another missionary informed John C. Calhoun, then the secretary of war: "All they know of us in relation to morals has been learned from those that have been among them, and painful to relate from this source they have learned nothing but the most libidinous and abandoned licentiousness."[15] White men living among the Indian tribes and the offspring of such men and the Indian women exercised a powerful influence over the Indian, and this influence must be given special consideration in the study of racial attitudes in the southwestern territory.[16]

In all the seaboard states there was much mingling of the blood of the Indian and the Negro.[17] In these states the white man enslaved the Indian and debased the Indian woman as he did the Negro woman. Legal marriages with the Indians became as unthinkable for the average white man as were legal marriages with the Negro, and the slave code made possible a race of mulattoes, mestizos, and griffes while both law and custom forbade and frowned upon legal marriage of the white man and the other two races. However, neither law nor social barriers forbade the intermixture of the Indian and the Negro; both shared the antipathies of the white man and when held as slaves their treatment differed in no essential degree.[18] Hence, conditions of life, slave

[13] James Hall, *A Brief History of the Mississippi Territory* (Salisbury, N.C., 1800), p. 5.

[14] Jedidiah Morse, *Report to the Commissioner of Indian Affairs*, 1820 (New Haven, 1829).

[15] Office of Indian Affairs, Osage Tribe (Letters Received), Jan. 25, 1824.

[16] Ibid.

[17] Lauber, op. cit., p. 252; Hugh Jones, *Present State of Virginia* (London, 1724), p. 37; George Chamberlain, "African and American," *Science*, xvii (February, 1891), 85–90.

[18] John H. Russell, *The Free Negro in Virginia* (Baltimore, 1913), pp. 127–28.

and free, often led to the union of the Negro and the Indian. The end of Indian slavery came with the final absorption of the blood of the Indian by the more numerous Negro slave. But the blood of the Indian did not become extinct in the slave States, for it continued to flow in the veins of the Negro.[19]

Proof of the early sympathies and unity developed among Indians and Negroes is to be seen in the fact that in certain Indian massacres the Indians murdered every white man but spared every Negro, and in the concerted action of Indians and Negroes in time of insurrection. But, the most convincing proof of the unity of the two races is to be found in the mixed racial elements in the remnants of the Indian tribes of the original states.

The best published account of the remnants of such Indians is a description of "The Relations of Indians and Negroes in Massachusetts," the work of Carter G. Woodson.[20] A report to the secretary of war, 1822, says of the Massachusetts Indians: "Very few of them are of unmixed blood, the number of pure Indians is very small, say fifty or sixty, and is rapidly decreasing. The mixture of blood arises far more frequently from connection with Negroes than with white."[21] Two very carefully prepared reports concerning these Indians were made to the legislature of Massachusetts. In 1847 the first of these reports recites that,

the whole number of the Indians, and people of color connected with them, not excluding the Natick, is 847. There are about six or eight Indians of pure blood, in the state. . . . All the rest are of mixed blood, mostly of Indian and Negro.[22]

The final report made in 1861 shows that the people of mixed blood had increased.[23]

[19] Lauber, op. cit., p. 250; James Franklin, *Philosophical and Political History of the Thirteen United States* (London, 1784), p. 20.

[20] *Journal of Negro History,* v (January, 1920), 45–57.

[21] Morse, op. cit., pp. 24–25.

[22] "Report of the Commissioners Relating to Indian Affairs in the State of Massachusetts," House Report, No. 46, 1849.

[23] Senate Report (Massachusetts), No. 96, 1861.

Conditions in Massachusetts are found to be duplicated in the other eastern states. A report to the secretary of war from Rhode Island, 1822, says of the Narragansetts: "There are about 429; of these twenty-two are denominated Negroes; the rest are of Indian extraction but are nearly all, if not all, of mixed blood and color, in various degrees and shades."[24]

At Southampton and at Montauk Point, New York, there were located tribes that were related to the Indians of Massachusetts. A report to the legislature of New York says of these people: "Their social condition is not enviable; during the time the negroes were held as slaves in this state, these Indians largely intermarried with and their descendants have more of the negro than of the Indian in their veins; in fact they are Indian only in name."[25] A decision of the supreme court of the state in 1910 declared that,

> for nearly two hundred years the Indians and their descendants lived on Indian field [Montauk]. . . . During this long period the number of Indians became greatly reduced. Their blood became so mixed that in many of them Indian traits were obliterated.[26]

Of the New Jersey Indians it is said that

> throughout the colonial history of New Jersey there were few marriages of the white men and Indian women, and those contracted were looked upon in the light of miscegenations. For this reason unions between Indians and negroes were so commonly frequent, indeed, as to have left permanent impress upon many families of Negroes of the present day.[27]

[24] Morse, op. cit.

[25] *Report of a Special Committee to Investigate the Indian Problem of the State of New York* (New York, 1889), No. 51, 1889.

[26] *Pharoah* v. *Benson, 69 New York Reports,* p. 54 (1910); James T. Adams, *History of the Town of Southampton* (Bridgehampton, 1912), p. 44.

[27] Robert B. Lee, *New Jersey as a Colony and as a State* (Trenton, 1903), I, 65–66.

Advertisements in colonial newspapers often give evidence of the mixture of the two races in the state of New Jersey.[28]

In Virginia there are records of the following tribes: the Pamunky, Nattaway, Gingaskin, and Mattopony. The Pamunky, located in King William county, are the largest of these groups. In 1800 Thomas Jefferson describes the Pamunky as "tolerably free from mixture with other colors."[29] But in 1854 Father William, a priest of the Catholic church, describes these people in the following manner: "Few of them deserve the name of Indians, so mingled are they with other nations by intermarriage. Some are partly African, others European, or rather, I should say Virginian." The settlement, says he, "is inhabited by the most curious intermixture of every color and class of people."[30] According to the Bureau of American Ethnology, in 1894:

No member of the Pamunky tribe is of full blood. While the copper colored skin and straight coarse hair of the aboriginal American shows decidedly in some individuals, there are others whose Indian origin would not be detected by the ordinary observer. There has been considerable intermixture of white blood in the tribe, not a little of that of the Negro.[31]

[28] *New Jersey Gazette,* April 15, 1778: "Was stolen from her mother, a negro girl, about 9 or 10 years of age, named Dianah, her mother's name is Cash, was married to an Indian named Lewis Wollis, near six feet high, about thirty-five years of age. They have a male child with them, between three and four years of age. Any person who takes up the said negroes and Indian and secures them shall have the above reward and reasonable charges."

[29] Thomas Jefferson, *Notes on Virginia* (Trenton, 1803).

[30] Father William, *Recollections of Rambles at the South* (New York, 1854), pp. 122-30.

[31] John G. Pollard, "Pamunky Indians of Virginia," *Bull., 17, 1894, Bureau of American Ethnology* (Washington, 1894), p. 10; Pennsylvania *Journal,* Oct. 1, 1747: "Runaway on the 20th of September last, from Silas Pavin, at Cohansie, in New Jersey, a very lusty negro fellow named Sampson, aged about 53 years, and had some Indian blood in him. He is hip short and goes lame. He had with him a boy about 12 or 13 years of age named Sam, was born of an Indian woman, and looks like an Indian only his hair. They are both well clothed, only the boy is

In 1843 an effort was made by the white inhabitants of King William county to dispossess the Pamunkies of their lands. The reasons given in their petition to the legislature of Virginia emphasize their belief that these Indians had now become Negroes and hence had no claims to the rights of Indians. The petition recites:

> There are two parcels or tracts of land situated within this county, on which a number of persons are now living, all of whom, by the laws of Virginia would be deemed and taken to be free mulattoes, in any court of justice; as it is believed they all have one-fourth or more of negro blood; and as proof of this they rely on the generally admitted fact that not one individual can be found among them whose grandfathers or grandmothers one or more is of negro blood, which proportion of negro blood constitutes a free mulatto. . . . Your petitioners do not question the justice and propriety of the law of the colonial legislature; it was a benevolent act and for those who had some claim on the consideration of the public officials of the colony. But time and circumstance have wholly changed the nature of the question and completely unhinged the designs of those who enacted the provisions of the law. The object of the colonial assembly was to protect a few harmless and tributary Indians, but the law which was passed to secure the Indians from intrusion on the part of the same white inhabitants has unwittingly imposed on the posterity of the same white inhabitants a great grievance, in the presence of two unincorporated bodies of free mulattoes in the midst of a large slave holding community. A greater grievance of such a character can not be well conceived, when it is known that a large number of free negroes and

---

barefooted. . . . They both talk Indian very well, and it is likely they have dressed themselves in the Indian dress, and gone to Carolina"; *American Weekly Mercury*, Oct. 24, 1734: "Runaway the 26th of June, last, from Samuel Leonard, of Perth Amboy, in New Jersey, a thick short fellow, having but one eye. His name is Wan. He is half Indian and half negro; He had on when he went away a blue coat. He plays the fiddle, and speaks good English and his country Indian."

mulattoes are now enjoying under a law enacted for
a praiseworthy purpose peculiar and exclusive privileges,
such as entire exemption from payment of taxes, holding
land without liability for debt, and the land so held properly speaking public land belonging to the Commonwealth. . . . The claim of the Indians no longer exists. . .
his blood has so largely mingled with that of the negro
race as to have obliterated all the striking features of Indian extraction. Your petitioners express the general voice
of the free white inhabitants of the county and as slave
holders they protest against this dangerous and anoma-
lous condition, for it has assumed all the feature of legally
established body of free negroes, the general resort of free
negroes from all parts of the country . . . the harbour for
runaway slaves. . . . Your petitioners further represent to
the General Assembly that, serious apprehensions are felt
by the white inhabitants from the increase of these free
mulattoes and their present combination in places access-
ible by a bold and early navigation to every vessel that
enters the river. They could be easily converted into an
instrument of deadly annoyance to the white inhabitants
by northern fanaticism. This is a more than possible event
and must be considered in the light which its nature and
importance suggest.[32]

A counterpetition was presented to this session of legislature by
the members of the Pamunky tribe. In it the members of the
tribe do not deny that there was a Negro element among them
but they assert that all of the tribe are persons of more than one-
half Indian blood.[33]

Typical of the conditions among the Pamunkies is the case of a
certain John Dungee and Lucy Ann, his wife. This Pamunky Indian and his mulatto wife tell of their difficulties in the following
petition to the state legislature:

[32] Archives of Virginia, Legislative Papers, Petition 13733, King William, Jan. 20, 1843. Hereafter Archives of Virginia, Legislative Papers,
will be omitted and the petition identified by number, county, and date
(insomuch as this information is available).

[33] Petition 13734, King William, Jan. 24, 1843.

Your petitioner and his wife Lucy Ann, who are free persons of color living in King William county ask permission most respectfully to present to the senate and house of representatives of Virginia that your petitioner John Dungee (who is descended from the aborigines of this dominion) was born free and 'tis his birthright to reside therein. That having many relations and connections in the section of the county in which he was raised, all his feelings and attachments have bound him to Virginia and he has never for a moment entertained the idea of leaving the land of his forbears. . . . Your petitoner Lucy Ann is the illegitimate daughter of the late _____, a highly respectable and wealthy citizen, who by his last will and testament, as an act of justice and atonement for an error of an unguarded moment bequeathed to his innocent offspring the boon of freedom and a pecuniary legacy of $1,000.00. . . . During the last year your petitioners urged by the strongest and purest attachment to each other were lawfully united to each other in matrimony and fondly flattered themselves that they had the prospect of passing through life with a portion of happiness that is decreed to but few. Only a few months had passed away, however, before your petitioners were aroused from their halycon state by being informed that by the laws of the land it was necessary that your petitioner Lucy Ann should remove from the Commonwealth or be sold into slavery. The intelligent and humane can at once imagine how appalling the information was to your petitioners, how frightful the consequences of a rigid and unbending application of the law, how totally destructive of the right, the interest and happiness of your petitioners. An enumeration of the disastrous effects of the enforcement of the law in this case is almost unnecessary to your enlightened body, but they will briefly state, that if they are compelled to leave this land, your petitioner, John, in a moment loses the labour of a lifetime spent in acquiring an accurate knowledge of the Chesapeake Bay and of the rivers which disembark themselves therein, by which knowledge he is rendered useful to himself and others, and the legacy bequeathed to Lucy

Ann will be lost or of little value to them. They will be
torn from their parents, relatives and friends and driven
in a state of destitution to migrate to a foreign land.[34]

Citizens of the county gave John Dungee, the Indian husband
of the mulatto Lucy Ann, the following testimonial:

Captain Dungee is a free born native of Virginia, was
raised in the calling of a sailor, and has for many years
been commander of a vessel constantly employed in the
navigation of the Chesapeake Bay and the rivers of Virginia. He never failed to give satisfaction and to secure
to himself the unbounded confidence of his employers and
those who committed their possessions to his care.[35]

Another Virginia Indian group are the Nottoways. Of these it
is reported, in 1818, that,

their number is about thirty, there are about six men who
inherit, though not more than about two are true blood,
about the same number of women are blood, the rest are
children. Their husbands and wives are chiefly free negroes.[36]

In 1808 an enumeration was made of the members of this tribe.
The following are examples of family and racial relations found
at the time of the enumeration.

John Turner, his employment is tillage, when he works,
his employment is at present unknown, as he has left his
farm in the possession of a mulatto woman who has been
kept by him as his wife. . . .
Littleton Scholar; no Indian but himself in his family,
his wife being a white woman.[37]

The trustees of this tribe were accused of reducing the children
of the Nottoways to slavery. The governor wrote to the trustees
advising that such practices were forbidden.

[34] Petition, King William, Dec. 19, 1825.
[35] Ibid.
[36] Petition, Southampton, Dec. 16, 1818.
[37] Executive Papers, July 18, 1808.

The Gingaskins, located in Northampton county on the eastern shore of Virginia, are the remnant of another Indian tribe.
Repeated efforts were made by the people of this county to take
over the land of the Gingaskins on the ground that they had become Negroes and the Indians were extinct. The first document
in this case appears in 1784. At that time it is said that "the land
is at present an asylum for free negroes and other disorderly persons who built huts thereon and pillage and destroy the timber
without constraint to the great inconvenience of the honest inhabitants of the vicinity, who have ever considered it a den of
thieves and a nuisance to the neighborhood."[38] The legislature
refused the first request of the petitioners, and a second effort to
take the lands of the tribe was made in 1787. This time it is said:
"They have at length become nearly extinct, there being at this
time not more than three or four genuine Indians at most . . .
the place is a harbour and convenient asylum for an idle set of
free negroes."[39] A final and successful effort to gain possession of
the lands of the tribe was made in 1812. In the petition of this
year, it is said:

> The place is now inhabited by as many black men as In-
> dians . . . the Indian women have many of them married
> black men, and a majority of the inhabitants are black or
> have black blood in them. . . . It is generally believed that
> since the introduction of so many free negroes and mu-
> lattoes into the town, that it has become the place of resort
> for the most vicious part of the black population.[40]

The petitioners, also, declare that an insurrectionary plot was
discovered in this community. The legislature decided to take
away the tribal rights of this tribe and to allot the land in small
plots to the heads of families. Citizens of the county predicted
that through failure to keep contracts these lands would soon get
into possession of the white inhabitants; however, according to
the clerk of Northampton county, in 1828, the descendants of the

[38] Petition 1230, Northampton, Nov. 26, 1784.
[39] Petition 1675, Northampton, Oct. 10, 1787.
[40] Petition 6001a, Northampton, Nov. 22, 1812.

Gingaskins were respectable Negro landowners in that community.

The Mattoponies, another Virginia Indian group, seem to have become extinct at an early date. In 1811 Thomas Jefferson said of these people that, "there remains of the Mattoponies three or four men only and they have more Negro than Indian blood."[41]

In other states there are to be found groups whose racial identity is disputed, such as the Croatans, of North Carolina, the Moors, of Delaware, the Meguleons, of Tennessee.[42] In their several localities these people are supposed to be of mixed Negro and Indian origin. In Ohio in 1843, a group of persons were excluded from the public schools because they were declared to be mixed Negroes and Indians. In Maine also we find opposition to the admission of such persons to the public schools.[43] In all the southern states there are found to be records of cases sent to the courts of appeals in which the litigants attempt to show that they are descendants of Indians and not of Negroes and hence that they do not fall subject to the slave code.[44] These cases add interest to the study of pedigree, but they must be considered as additional evidence of the extensive mixture of racial blood in the slave states. To the visitor in the South the physical characteristics of many Negro slaves bore witness to their Indian origin.

In the state of South Carolina early Negro-Indian history was much influenced by conditions that resulted from the occupation of the territory to the south by the Spanish. From early times the Spanish and their Indian allies in Florida stole South Carolina slaves and harbored runaways from the South Carolina planta-

[41] Jefferson, op. cit.

[42] Samuel W. Burnell, "Notes on the Meguleons," *American Anthropologist*, II (1889), 347–49; James Fisher, "The So-Called Moors of Delaware," Milford *Herald*, June 15, 1805; "Croatans," Sen. Doc. no. 677, 63d Cong., 3d sess.; *Handbook of American Indians*, Part I, p. 365; John R. Swanton, *Indians of the Lower Mississippi Valley* (Washington, 1911), p. 291; Minnie Moore-Wilson, *The Seminoles of Florida* (New York, 1911), p. 14.

[43] *Lane* v. *Baker*, 12 *Ohio Reports*, p. 237 (1843).

[44] *Bailey* v. *Fiske*, 34 *Maine Reports*, p. 77 (1852).

tions.[45] This situation seems to have led the people of the state to devise racial policies that are not found in other states. Here an effort was made to keep the Indian, the mulatto, and the Negro in distinct castes to create a feeling of superiority on the part of the Indian toward the free mulatto, and on the part of the free mulatto toward the slave. South Carolina Indians were used against the Spanish and Indians of Florida and were used to track and capture runaway slaves. For such work they were liberally rewarded, and in these early years antipathies and prejudices developed between the Indians and the Negroes such as are not discovered in other original States.[46] There is evidence that the Catabaw Indians of South Carolina maintained their racial purity in a higher degree than was true in the case of most of the tribes that came into contact with the Negro; however, in this state, as in the other states, the forces of nature and human passions combined to effect the mingling of the blood of the two races, and the courts of the state were called upon to settle the status of persons of Indian-Negro ancestry.[47]

Possibly South Carolina Indian policy, to a certain extent, affected Indian relations in the entire southwest territory. To the student it appears that on the southwestern frontier the racial situation was more complicated than in any other section. Here there appear among the Indian tribes conflicting attitudes toward the Negro. Among others there were relations of brotherhood and affection. Racial prejudices are especially evident among the Chickasaws and Cherokees among which tribes the attitude of the Indian toward the Negro resembled that of the slaveholder toward the slave. The entire southwestern territory

[45] Andrew D. Chandler (ed.), *Colonial Records of Georgia* (Atlanta, 1902), III, 377, 396; XII, 146; XXII, Part I, 137, 142; Part II, 232–34; *Collections of the Georgia Historical Society* (Atlanta, 1902), p. 168; Caroline Bevard, *History of Florida* (Tallahassee, 1900), I, 42–43.

[46] *A South Carolinian, a Refutation of the Calumnies Circulated against the Southern and Western States, Respecting the Existence of Slavery among Them, to Which Is Added a Minute and Particular Account of the Actual Condition of Their Negro Population* (Charleston, S.C., 1822), pp. 84–85.

[47] *Miller* v. *Dawson*, 4 Dudley, *South Carolina Reports*, p. 174 (1838).

was very much infested by settlers from the slaveholding states. Many of these white settlers intermarried with the Indians and became leading men in the tribes. David Reese, an Indian agent among the Cherokees, in 1832 wrote to the bureau of Indian Affairs:

> Among the Cherokees, as in all communities, there are different grades or ranks or society. . . . The first is composed mainly of the offspring of intermarriages between the whites and the Cherokees. . . . In this class may be included a few full blooded Indians.[48]

The white settlers who came into the Indian country brought with them the antipathies of the slave South, and from them the tribes learned to regard the Negro as he was regarded in the slave country.

It is also true that much of what we know of the Cherokees and Chickasaws comes to us from these white settlers or their halfbreed children and may not represent the attitudes of the true Indian. Governor Lumpkin of Georgia in a message to the legislature of that state describes the extent to which the settlers had gained influence in these tribes. He declares that,

> a class of individuals chiefly of white or mixed blood, and who claim the rights of natives within the limits of Georgia, are persons, who, under the treaties of 1817 and 1819 took valuable fee simple reservations of the best land then ceded. . . . Moreover these very individuals, by their superior intelligence and advantages of education, now have had once abandoned to their fate—so far as to rule, govern, and influence them in all matters relating to their most important interests.[49]

These men were slaveholders and carried slaves into the Indian territory, and from them the Cherokee became a holder of Negro slaves. A letter to the secretary of war written by David Brown, a Cherokee, contains the following quotation:

[48] Office of Indian Affairs (hereafter cited as O.I.A.), Cherokee of the East File (Letters Received), March 10, 1832.

[49] *Journal of the House of Representatives of the State of Georgia* (Atlanta, 1833), p. 16.

The census of this division of the Cherokees—has been
taken within the current year, and the returns have been
made thus—Native citizens, 13,563, white men married in
the nation 147; white women 73; African slaves 1,277. . . .
White men in the nation enjoy all the immunities and
privileges of the Cherokee people. . . . In the computation
for the present year you will perceive that there are some
Africans among us. They have from time to time
been brought in and sold by white men; they are, however,
generally well treated and they much prefer living in the
nation, to a residence in the United States. There is hardly
any intermixture of the Cherokee and African blood.[50]

The following letter seems to indicate that the Cherokee objected
to the racial attitude of certain neighboring tribes toward the
Negro.

Sir: We deem it our duty to represent to you that there
has been for a long time past under the protection of the
United States government or its accredited agent a large
number of negroes claimed by the Seminoles located and
living in our immediate and proper country. We speak sincerely when we say that we express not only our convictions but the wishes of all classes of the Cherokee people
that this state of affairs is objected to and that some other
disposition should be made of the said negroes. If slaves it
seems to us that they should be returned to their owners,
if not we do most earnestly protest against their longer
continuance in our country, as so large a number of that
description of persons is a nuisance to themselves and to
the people we represent. We do, therefore, respectfully ask
that for their own safety as well as for that of the rights of
the Cherokee they may be removed without necessary delay
beyond our limits.[51]

The racial attitudes manifest in the above documents may not be
regarded properly as indicative of antipathies existing between

[50] o.i.a., Letter Book, No. 2 (Letters Sent) , p. 303.
[51] o.i.a., Cherokee File (Letters Received) , July 17, 1848.

the Indian and the Negro; they must rather be considered as the attitude of a "Southern-White-Slaveholding-Indian" toward a people that he hoped to enslave.

However, all the tribes of the southwest did not exhibit antipathies toward the mixture of their blood with that of the Negro. Indians living more nearly in the tribal state and less influenced by the opinions and civilization of the white man welcomed the Negro into the tribes and united freely with him. The Creeks are an example of such Indian relations. The first census of the Creek nation is the Abbott-Parsons census of 1832. The letters of these census enumerators describe conditions existing in the tribe. On September 7, 1832, Parsons wrote to the secretary of war:

> Sir: We the commissioners engaged in taking the census of the Creek Indians, meeting with some difficulty in the construction of a part of the instructions . . . beg leave to respectfully propose the following questions. . . . 3d. If an Indian have living with him as his wife a negro slave, the property either of himself or of another, is he to be considered as the head of a family in the sense contemplated in the instructions transmitted to us and to be enrolled as entitled to a reservation? 4th. Is one of mixed blood of Indian and Negro, free, keeping a separate house and having a negro slave for a wife, to be ranked and enrolled in like manner as the Indian is?[52]

On October 16, 1832, Parsons again wrote to Secretary Cass:

> I beg leave to propound a few enquiries in addition to some already made. There is a number of free black families that seem to be in every way identified with these people and the only difference is color. I have taken their number in all cases, but am I to take them as heads of families for reservations or not?[53]

In turn the commissioner issued the following instructions to his agents:

[52] O.I.A., Creek File (Letters Received), Sept. 7, 1832.
[53] Ibid., Oct. 16, 1832.

. . . an Indian, whether of full or half blood, who has a
female slave living with him as his wife, is the head of a
family and entitled to a reservation.[54]

Also . . . free blacks who have been admitted as members of the Creek nation, and are regarded as such by the
tribe, if they have families are entitled to reservations of
land under the second section of the Creek treaty.[55]

There is much evidence of the intermixture of the Negro and the
Creek Indian.

The Seminoles are another Indian tribe whose blood mingled
freely with that of the Negro. In this instance common hatred of
the slaveholders of the lower South developed the unity of the
black and the red man. Indeed, there is reason to believe that the
Seminole wars were not so much Indian wars as Negro wars.[56] In
many cases the instigators of the wars were Negroes and the strat-
egy the work of Negro leaders. General Jessup reported to the
secretary of war, June 16, 1837: "I have ascertained that at the
battle of Wahoo, a negro, the property of a Florida planter, was
one of the most distinguished leaders, and I have learned that the
depredations on the plantations east of St. Johns, were perpetrated by Plantation negroes, headed by an Indian Negro, John
Caesar, since killed."[57] Florida from the Spanish days until 1849
was a refuge for escaped slaves. One of the causes of the Seminole
wars was the intermixture of the blood of the Negro and the Indian. Children born of escaped Negro slave women and Indian
men were claimed by the planters as their property. In the Congress of the United States the Seminoles were defended on the
grounds that they, the Indian fathers of Negro-Indian children,
were fighting to protect their children from the slave catchers

[54] Ibid., Oct. 10, 1832.

[55] Ibid.

[56] O.I.A., Florida File (Letters Received), Jan. 1, 1834; Aug. 27, 1838;
Florida Emigration File, Nov. 27, 1838; John T. Sprague, *Origin,
Progress, and Conclusion of the Florida War* (New York, 1850), pp. 52,
81, 100; Samuel A. Drake, *Aboriginal Races of America* (New York,
1889), pp. 417, 433, 462, 479.

[57] O.I.A., Seminole Emigration File (Letters Received), June 16, 1837.

who were carrying them away to the cotton and sugar fields of the South.[58] Of this war, Harriet Martineau says,

> According to the law of the slave states, the children follow the condition of the mother. It will be seen at a glance, what consequences follow from this, how it operates as a premium on licentiousness among white men and also what effect it must have had upon the Indians with whom the slave woman had taken refuge. The Seminole war arose out of this law. The escaped slaves had intermarried with the Indians. The masters claimed the children. The Seminole fathers would not give them up. Force was used to tear the children from the parents and the Indians began their desperate but very natural work of extermination.[59]

From very early times the children born of the Negro woman who had lived among the Indians had been a cause of difficulty with the Indian tribes.[60] Negro runaways found refuge among the Indians on the frontier. Many treaties called for the return of these fugitives, but the Indians concealed the fugitives and passed them on into the interior of the country, where they were assimilated among the Indians.

[58] *Congressional Globe,* 26th Cong., 2d sess., pp. 346–52.

[59] William G. Simms, "The Morals of Slavery," *The Proslavery Arguments* (Philadelphia, 1822) , pp. 237–38.

[60] Theodorick Bland, *The Bland Papers* (Petersburg, Va., 1840) , p. 25:

"Shawneetown, June 15, 1775.

"Brothers The Big Knife:

"I was with you a few days ago, and you desired to know what my people had concluded on, now we have concluded to inform you, that your younger brothers, the Swanee, is always willing to comply with any reasonable request that Big-Knife shall ask. You desire me to send you the Negro wench and children, but I have only sent you the wench, as my people will not give up the children, as they say they are their own flesh and blood, and can't think of parting with them, therefore hopes you won't ask for them no more, as we are brothers and good friends.

.   .   .   .

"Signed, Cornstalk."

The friends of the Seminole and the Indian seem to be correct in their claim that the Seminole war was largely caused by the blood relationship of the two races and their efforts to protect the children born among them.[61] A letter sent from Cattahoochee, Florida, and signed by E-Con-Chatte-Micco, John Waller, and twelve subchiefs, demands that the agents of the government of the United States go "into Georgia, near Columbus, and bring Sarah Factor, a coloured woman, and her three children back to us; who were stolen away two years ago—Grant us this request and all will be well."[62] The story of Sarah Factor is told in another document which reads as follows:

> Florida, Jackson County
> July 15, 1828
>
> Dear Sir:
>
> There is another matter which I wish to lay before, there is an old Indian by the name of Tom Factor, who took a negro woman who belonged to him for his wife. I am well convinced that she did as I could be of any fact. From the various certificates to the said facts, the case is this. The last visit that General Thompson made to the Appalachacola Indians, he appointed me as one of the agents to try and protect this old Indian's property for him, which I did as long as I could. There was a gentleman came down from the neighborhood of Columbus by name of Ezekiel Robertson and claimed the negroes that Factor had in his possession. I told him that I was willing to compare titles and that if his right was thought to be better than the Indians, I would give the negroes to them without putting him to any trouble about them. He readily consented to the proposition. The day was appointed for the right to be investigated. I met with my papers and other proof I deemed necessary. At a late hour

---

[61] John R. Brodhead, *Documents Relating to the Colonial History of the State of New York* (Albany, 1858–1887), v, 964–68; vi, 546; Joshua R. Giddings, *The Exiles of Florida* (Columbus, 1858), p. 78; Marion G. McDougal, *Fugitive Slaves, 1619–1865* (Boston, 1891), pp. 7–8; Moore-Wilson, op. cit., p. 14; Russell, op. cit., p. 128.

[62] o.i.a., Florida File (Letters Received), March 24, 1838.

in the day, he came and stated that they could not procure
his papers, that he had left them with Isaac Brown and he
had gone down the river and the probability was that he
had them with him. Though late we heard the boat coming up the river, and there could then be no excuse about
his getting his papers for Brown had returned. His reply
was then that he would sue me for the negroes as
that would put a final end to any further disputes about
titles. I told him that I was perfectly willing to do that;
but he took care not to do it and lay about Lick a Wolf
and when he thought that he was forgotten, gathered
a company of about 15 or 20 men of his own choosing and
took the negroes out of the possession of the said Factor by
force of arms and carried them off. The old woman and her
son Billy have made their escape from him and another
got back to the territory again. There is yet behind this old
Indian's only daughter and two or three children in possession of Robertson, using of them as slaves, who has no
more right to them than you have. . . . The Indians taken
by Robertson is some seventy-five or 80 miles up the river
in Stewart County Georgia.

Daniel Boyd.[63]

Many documents substantiate the above record.[64] The records
of the Indian office contain voluminous accounts of the efforts of
the white men of the slave states to carry off the negroes living
among the Indians. The records of the Seminoles and the Creeks
bear witness to the loyalty with which the Indians protected the
Negro fugitive. The united action of the two races was, in many
cases, the result of kindred blood. In 1835, General Wiley
Thompson, commanding the American forces in Florida, said of
the Florida Indian-Negroes: "They are descended from the Seminoles, and are connected by consanguinity."[65] In 1837, General
Jessup wrote to the secretary of war: "The two races are rapidly
approximating."[66] When the Seminoles were finally sent beyond

[63] Ibid., July 15, 1838.
[64] Ibid., April 22, 1837; May 14, 1837; April 20, 1837; Nov. 20, 1838.
[65] Ibid., Jan., 1835.
[66] O.I.A., Seminole File (Letters Received), June 16, 1837.

the Mississippi, they left behind many of their Negro relations, many of whom had been forced into slavery or forced to hide away in the Everglades.

The Creeks and the Seminoles were not the only tribes of the southwest that intermarried with the Negroes. The claim has been advanced that the Choctaws did not intermarry with Negroes, but a census of the Choctaw tribe in 1834 shows that this claim is not justified. In this census such persons as the following are identified:

> Jacob Daniel, has a half Indian and half Negro for a wife, seven persons are in the family.
> William Lightfoot, a mulatto, half Indian and Half Negro, five persons are in his family.
> James Blue, a Negro Indian man, had an Indian wife, there are three persons in his family.
> Jim Tom, half breed Negro, has an Indian wife, four persons are in his family.[67]

The study of the Indians seems to show that in many cases they intermarried freely with the Negro, but the records of the tribes can by no means be taken as indicative of the extent of the intermixture of these races. Marriage among the tribes was not a matter of legal record.[68] Under such conditions it was difficult to say whether the slave woman was the wife or the concubine of the Indian. A letter from Talladaga county, 1833, recites that "some of the Indians have several wives, who sometimes live in different towns, and at considerable distance from each other, they are allowed by the Indian to own property, not subject to their husband and from the facility with which they can at any time dis-

[67] *American State Papers, Public Lands* (Washington, 1834–35), VII, 39; Annie H. Abel, *The American Indian as a Slaveholder and Secessionist* (Cleveland, 1915), I, 20. (Miss Abel feels that there was little intermixture of the Choctaw and the Negro.)

[68] William Bartram, *Observations on the Creek and Cherokee Indians* (Philadelphia, 1789), p. 65; John Lawson, *History of Carolina* (London, 1709), pp. 157–89; Achille Murat, *A Moral and Political Sketch of the United States of North America* (London, 1833), pp. 47–48; John H. Logan, *History of the Upper Country of South Carolina* (Columbia, 1859), Chap. XI; Swanton, op. cit., pp. 24–99.

solve their marriage contracts it will be extremely difficult to determine who among them is entitled to reservations."[69] An Alabama court declared that, "among the Indians marriage must generally be considered as taking place in a state of nature."[70] Another Alabama decision held that "it was proved that under the laws and customs of the Creeks, a man was allowed to take a wife, and abandon her at pleasure, and that this worked an absolute disolution of the marriage state, and that the parties were not allowed to marry again until after the succeeding green corn dance."[71] In Tennessee the courts declared that "Gideon Morgan and Margaret Morgan, alias Servier, were married according to the usages of the Cherokees which were within the limits of the state of Tennessee, in 1813; that all that was necessary by their usages was a public agreement to live together as man and wife."[72] Much additional evidence can be produced to show the ease with which the Indian contracted and dissolved marriage. Under conditions such as these many Negro women who would be regarded by the white man as slaves among the Indians were in every sense the wives of the red man. A report of the commissioner of Indian affairs for 1866 declares that,

> there is a large number of young free women who have
> from one to eight children, born while they were slaves,
> and who never had husbands. Many of these children are
> of mixed blood, and, within time may make valuable citizens.[73]

When the Indians of the southwest were sent to the territory beyond the Mississippi, remnants of the tribes evaded the orders of the government and refused to move. These people were then in a situation similar to that of the remnant of the tribes in the eastern states. In time, they, like their kinsmen of the east, were

[69] O.I.A., Creek File (Letters Received), May 13, 1833.

[70] *Wall* v. *Williams*, 11 *Alabama Reports*, p. 826 (1847).

[71] *Wells* v. *Wells*, 13 *Alabama Reports*, p. 793 (1848).

[72] *Morgan* v. *McGhee*, 5 Humphrey, *Tennessee Reports*, p. 42 (1844); John L. McKinnon, *History of Walton County* (Atlanta, 1911), pp. 62–66; 96–97; Abel, op. cit., III, 253.

[73] *Report of the Commissioner of Indian Affairs* (Washington, 1866), p. 286.

absorbed in the more numerous Negro population. In 1859 a petition to the commissioner of Indian affairs from the state of Mississippi declares that, "we the undersigned petitioners would respectfully represent, that there is a small tribe of Chactaw
Indians scattered through our midst in the state of Mississippi, in
Neshobal, Scott, Gasper, Newton, and Leake counties, and we represent that owing to the depredations of the said tribe, and the
amalgamation of the Indians and blacks, it is the desire of the
said subscribers, as well as the wish of many of the most intelligent of the tribe that they be removed from the said Quarters."[74]

The evidence used in this study of the Indian seems to show
that there was much intermixture of the blood of the Indian and
the Negro. As a slave in the eastern states the Indian became the
companion and associate of the Negro slave. The white man's
law and the customs of the country made no distinction between
the Indian and the Negro. Those Indians that did not migrate
beyond the mountains finally became absorbed among the Negroes. Before the end of the slave period those who governed the
slave country and applied the slave code seldom thought of any
of their servants as Indians—for the master, all the servile class
were now Negro slaves.

On the frontier, in most cases, the Indian welcomed the Negro
into the tribe, and many children were born of Indian and Negro
parents. Where there appears to be evidence that the Indian disdained the Negro, the antipathies seem to be the result of artifi-
cial influences of the white slaveholder over the Indian or of the
tribe by men of mixed white and Indian blood.

There is no reason to believe that natural race prejudices
prompted the Indian to refuse to unite by marriage with the
Negro.

The mixed race in America today is the result of the union of
the Indian, the Negro, and the white man.

[74] O.I.A., Choctaw File, March 1, 1859; Abel, op. cit., 1, 20; Andrew W.
Loomis, *Scenes in the Indian Country* (Philadelphia, 1859), p. 200.

TWELVE

Mulatto Life
in the Slave Period

ACCORDING TO the slave code the mulatto held no other status in the southern society than the mass of the Negro population. The vast majority of these people, as slaves, lived as other slaves lived, and as free men, their status did not differ from that of other free men as described in a previous chapter. However, there were agencies that tended to force many of the mulattoes into a caste apart from the mass of the Negro population. When relations of affection existed between the white father and his mulatto children, such fathers were often inclined to consider their offspring not as Negroes but as persons of their blood, and there is evidence that such parents taught their children to consider themselves as better or superior to the members of the servile race. The story of the efforts of a certain citizen of Memphis to secure recognition for his mulatto children in the white society of that city affords an example of the unavailing efforts of the white father. In this instance it is said that,

Colonel Thomas H. Benton, who afterwards distinguished himself as United States senator from Missouri, and who commanded a regiment under Jackson at New Orleans, brought with him on his return a beautiful French quadroon girl, with whom he lived some two or three years, when in view, perhaps, of his future greatness, he concluded to turn her adrift and get married. He did so, but not without providing liberally for her, giving her property and money, which was placed in Winchester's hands for safe keeping. This brought those two attractive persons together and the consequence was a great error; but Winchester could not think of remedying it in the way Benton had done. He concluded to pursue the opposite course, and therefore took "Mary" to Louisiana, where the law permitted the intermarriage of the races and there formally married her. If Winchester thought that this act would modify the asperity of popular feeling against him he was greatly mistaken, for it increased in virulence ten-fold. White men living with colored women was, I am sorry to say, quite common at the time. My old friend Squire Rawlings was not faultless, and it never set him back in the least with the very set who were most bitter against Winchester; but there was a difference—Rawling's housekeeper was slave born and remained so, while Winchester's was born free, well raised and accomplished. Besides Rawlings did not marry. Poor Mary tried, by acts of charity, liberal donations to religious pursuits, exemplary and unobtrusive conduct, and all other conceivable means, to allay the intense hatred, but it only had the effect to increase, if possible, its vindictiveness. Winchester found himself shunned and avoided by men indebted to him for various favours. . . . When a regulating company was organized, it was all a few of us could do to prevent them from notifying Winchester, among others, to leave. But his greatest source of trouble, no doubt, was for the future of his children. I never knew any of them, except Owen, his oldest son, who was certainly the sprightliest boy I ever saw. At the age of ten years, being very much attached to me, he would frequently come, sit, and read the newspaper and make his comments in a manner that would have been creditable to a man of mature years. At twelve he was acknowledged to be the most expert weighter and marker on the bluff, and was with all very handsome and witty, and seemed to have fully inherited all the remarkable talents of his father. Incurable and irremediable prejudices against these children existed north and south. There was a slight copper tinge that embrowned the brow of the fairest, and this was socially fatal. Can it be wondered, then, that the unhappy father rushed into intemperance to drown the horrid thought, or perhaps hope that by association of the most degraded, to familiarize himself and children with that condition in life which seemed inevitably destined for them.[1]

The prejudices so evident in Memphis were no doubt equally or more evident in other sections of the South, and if the father wished to secure recognition among white persons for those who had won his affection, he had to establish them in localities where their genealogy was not known. An example of a case of this kind is found in the record of a citizen of Louisiana who moved with his mistress and family to Pas Christian, Mississippi, and established a new home there. In this case the mulatto status of the family was not discovered until the death of the father, at which time an effort was made to settle his estate.[2] An example might also be given of the provision of a dowry for a mulatto daughter if she should marry a white man.[3]

Whatever may have been the wishes of the fathers in such cases as these, public sentiment in the upper classes of the white South prohibited social or legal recognition of the mulatto if the Negro ancestry of such persons were known, but there is much evidence that on the plantations and in the households, where the authority of the father was undisputed, he often placed his mulatto sons over other slaves and gave to these sons all authority that other young men would be expected to exercise in the management of their father's property; for his mulatto daughter the father often demanded the respect and obedience that would be expected for the young white daughter of the house. Many examples describing relations such as these are to be found in other sections of this study. It is my belief that the following quotation from the petition in behalf of a mulatto woman who wished to gain permission to remain in the state of Virginia may be regarded as typical of the situation of many persons of color:

[1] James D. Davis, *History of the City of Memphis* (Memphis, 1873), pp. 73–76.

[2] *Heirn v. Bridault, 37 Mississippi Reports,* p. 209 (1859).

[3] *Barksdale v. Elam, 30 Mississippi Reports,* p. 694 (1855).

. . . always the confidant, the intimate, the nurse, and
friend of her master and mistress and their children; never
maintaining the relations to them and theirs of a menial.
She is a half-blood, her father a white man, and never was
the associate and companion of Negro slaves, except in the
superintendence of them in the place of her mistress whom
she relieved.[4]

The mulatto who lived a long life with associations such as these
or who had descended from parents so closely attached to white
kindred must have developed attitudes that made life difficult
when death broke the ties which had bound them to their protectors. Some of these people, possessing so much more of white
than of Negro blood and with traditions that separated them
from the Negro, could not think of themselves as a part of the
Negro race. With their inheritance and in their peculiar environment, they developed caste attitudes that were very strong and
that seem to explain some of the seeming contradictions in Negro
life. The petition of the Warton family of Stafford, Virginia,
gives us a description of the social attitudes of such a group of
mulattoes. In behalf of these mulattoes fifty citizens of Stafford
county make the following petition to the legislature of Virginia:

The undersigned citizens of Stafford county respectfully
represent, that some years past William Warton, Samuel
Warton, Barney Warton, Nancy Warton and Lewis Warton who now reside in the county of Stafford were nomi-
nally the slaves of John Cooke, senior, decd. But they are
all white persons in complexion and in fact; and although
they are remotely descended on one side from a colored
person, more than three-fourths of their blood is derived
from white ancestors. For several years past the parties
above named have been entirely free from the control of

[4] Archives of Virginia, Legislative Papers, Petition 11733, Accomac,
Jan. 2, 1833. Hereafter Archives of Virginia, Legislative Papers, will be
omitted and the petition identified by number, county, and date
(insomuch as this information is available).

the said John Cooke and of all other persons, having paid
a full consideration for their freedom and have continued
to live as free persons in the acquisition of property and
otherwise without interruption—until the last term of
the county court of Stafford county where they were presented for remaining in the state as free persons contrary
to law. The undersigned respectfully represent that the
parties above named are persons of excellent character,
some of them pursuing trades, and all of them useful and
industrious. They have no associations with persons
of colour, some of them have intermarried with white
persons and their partialities are decidedly for the whites—
one of them rendered important service to the county
by discovering and causing the apprehension of a man
of the city of Washington who had decoyed and stolen
off several of our slaves; and another of them rendered a
similar service by discovering and causing the apprehension of several slaves who had taken refuge in the city of
New York. These acts together with their general deportment and associations show that no evil would result to
the Commonwealth if they shall be permitted to remain
where they are. Their removal would also be productive
of serious distress and inconvenience to themselves and
to those citizens of the county with whom they have connections. Your petitioners are aware of the wisdom of the
law which requires emancipated slaves to leave the Commonwealth and they are anxious to see that law inforced,
but they are convinced that the cases herein presented to
the General Assembly are not within the policy and meaning of that law. These persons are neither free negroes
nor mulattoes; they are white persons and as such are subject to none of those laws which relate to *free negroes and
mulattoes*. If they had been emancipated before the act
of 1806, and become citizens of another state as white
persons (which they can unquestionably do) will they
not have the right to return immediately to this state and
become citizens thereof? There is no law prohibiting them;
there is a law prohibiting free negroes and mulattoes but

they are neither free negroes nor mulattoes, but free white persons.[5]

Problems of racial relations are exceedingly complex, but there can be no more intricate problem than that of the relation of the mulatto to the two races whose blood, in varying proportions, united in his veins. It is to be noted that the slaveholders were themselves interested in this problem, and that they did not agree in their opinions as to the attitude of the mulatto. A certain Judge John Scott writes to a friend at Warrenton, Virginia, January 9, 1835: "I believe the white negroes (if you will allow the term) which you have at Warrenton, are a great deal worse than the black bond or free."[6] The rigid laws that governed free Negroes and the efforts to drive all free Negroes out of the slave states were enacted by men who knew that a large proportion of the free Negroes were mulattoes and believed that the South had more to fear from the free Negro because so many of them were of white blood. There seemed to be a constant anxiety lest leaders should arise among them who would instill the Negro slaves with a desire for freedom.[7] Miss Martineau informs us that,

> a gentleman of highest character, a southern planter, observed, in conversation with a friend, that little was known, out of bounds, of the reasons for the new laws by which emancipation was made so difficult as it is. He said that the very general connection of white gentlemen with their female slaves, introduced a mulatto race whose numbers would become dangerous, if the affections of the white parents were permitted to render them free.[8]

A volume published in 1833 by a former Virginia minister gives very definite expressions to this fear. This author writes as follows:

[5] Petition 10243, Stafford, Jan. 14, 1833.
[6] Petition 10834, Fauquier, Jan. 9, 1835.
[7] James S. Buckingham, *The Slave States of America* (London, 1842), I, 337.
[8] Harriet Martineau, *Society in America* (London, 1837), II, 328.

There is, I think, to a considerable extent, a preference given to mulattoes as house servants. They are the neatest, the best looking, and for the most part, the most intelligent and active. Other equally natural reasons might be imagined as having an influence. But what I have in view chiefly is the fact that while their complexion proves their relation to the white, and while most can conjecture the particular individual to whom they are related, there is no reason to doubt but that the mulattoes themselves mostly know from their mothers, and especially when the individual is considered wealthy and respectable. To find themselves neglected and despised, perhaps sold or left in bondage by those most nearly related to them, must be bitter and galling, and may be expected to beget deep hatred of the white by whom it is commonly practiced. There is no doubt that such a thing as family traits of character, as to talents, mind, disposition, etc., are inherited. Its character may not have been so clearly marked as some have supposed; but it is in the face of all observation, wholly to deny it. That the high notions of liberty, the ardent feeling, and proud unbending spirit of the South should be imparted with their blood to the mixed race so numerous among them, is what must be expected. Many mulattoes know that the best blood of the South runs in their veins, they feel its proud, impatient and spirit-stirring pulsations; and see themselves cast off and oppressed by those that gave them being. Such a state of things must produce characters fit for treason, strategem, and spoil. . . . What are we to expect from a people thus treated should they gain the ascendency? What would be the condition of white females that might come under their power? If those do pass over the South that we have so much reason to fear, the event will probably show that in families of some of those who have been the greatest supporters of the slave system, and most devoted to its gains, and opposed to all attempts to do it away will have been raised and prepared the avengers of their people. Such masters often have favorite servants, sometimes mulattoes, who enjoy great advantages for gaining information, and who possess enlarged views of their own people and the world.[9]

Mrs. Kemble observed that "while the slave owners of the southern states insist vehemently upon the mental and physical inferiority of the blacks, they are benevolently doing their best, in one way at least, to raise and improve the degraded race; and the bastard population, which forms so ominous an element in the social safety of our cities certainly exhibit in their forms and features the benefit they derive from their white progenitors."[10]

While the fears of the white population lest the free Negro might endanger slave society can be regarded as evidence that the mulattoes were considered as hostile in attitude toward the white race, it is also true that certain leaders in insurrectionary movements were mulattoes. However, all the slaveholders did not regard the mulatto as dangerous to the slave system. The South Carolinians seem to have held very decided views on this subject. After the Denmark Vesey insurrection in that state, by order of the legislature of the state, a report was made which includes "a minute and particular account of the actual condition of their population." It is the conclusion of these gentlemen that the mulatto, if properly treated, rather than being a danger, might serve as a defense from future attempts at insurrection. This report declares that strong measures are needed to preserve the slave system, but concerning the free mulattoes it is said:

> There are many enlightened and intelligent men who are
> of the opinion that the same measures should be adopted
> in relation to our "Free Mulattoes"—and that they are a
> serious affliction, both to the morals and the security of the
> state as are the free blacks themselves. We are, however, of
> an opinion directly the reverse, and are decidedly opposed
> to any system of legislation that would end in banishing
> *them*. They are, in our estimation (but perhaps we have
> viewed the subject in an improper light) a barrier between

[9] John D. Paxton, *Letters on Slavery, Addressed to the Cumberland Congregation* (Lexington, Ky., 1833), pp. 34, 189–91.

[10] Fanny A. Kemble, *A Journal of a Residence on a Georgia Plantation, in 1838–1839* (New York, 1863), p. 14.

our own color and that of the black—and, in cases of insurrection, are more likely to enlist themselves under the
banners of the whites. Most of them are industrious, sober,
hardworking mechanics, who have large families and
considerable property; and so far as we are acquainted with
their temper, and disposition of their feelings, abhor the
idea of association with the blacks in any enterprise that
may have for its object the revolution of their condition.
It must be recollected also, that the greater part of them
own slaves, and are, therefore so far interested in this
species of property as to keep them on the watch, and
induce them to disclose any plans that may be injurious to
our peace—experience justifies this conclusion. The important discoveries, in most cases of insurrection, particularly
in the last, have been made through the immediate instrumentality and advice of this class. Would it be generous
then to drive them from the comforts of their present
situation, and exile them from our shores, when we at
the same time acknowledge the value of the services they
have performed? We think not—but it is for wiser and
better heads to determine. We feel satisfied that whatever
will be done in this respect will be dictated by sound and
wholesome judgment. It is politic and sound, at the same
time, to preserve a system of discipline in relation to them
as will effectually mark the "distinctive condition in society,
and regulate their *degree,* when placed in opposition to
our own. If this principle of prudent legislation be once
lost sight of, the barriers between us must necessarily become nothing more than a rope of sand.[11]

The South Carolina report appears to have influenced legislation in Virginia following the insurrection of Nat Turner. It is
possible that the slaveholders' knowledge of the free mulatto may

---

[11] *A South Carolinian, a Refutation of the Calumnies Circulated
against the Southern and Western States, Respecting the Existence of
Slavery among Them, to Which Is Added a Minute and Particular
Account of the Actual Condition of Their Negro Population* (Charleston, 1822), pp. 84–85.

have helped to defeat the aims of those who wished to drive the free Negroes out of the South. It would seem that in many cases the desire of the white man to separate the mulatto from the blacks must have united with other natural causes to make many mulattoes hold themselves apart from and to consider themselves superior to the masses of Negroes held in bondage. Such a conclusion is supported by traditional attitudes as reported to have existed between the slaves and the free Negroes.

It would be a mistake to conclude that all the free mulattoes considered themselves as better than the mass of the Negro population. As with all other human beings, all the mulattoes were not alike and did not react alike to their environment. While there were powerful forces that among many of these people made for attachment to the white race, in many other cases there were equally powerful forces that made for hatred of the white man and bound them by the strongest of ties to their black brethren. Moreover, it is to be remembered that all the mulattoes were not free. The majority of them were slaves, and for the mulatto held in bondage there were always possible, except in exceptional cases, all the misfortunes and all the accidents that characterized the system. Where wrongs were suffered by these people there could be no love for the white man. Common experiences drove them into unity with their fellow bondmen and made them forget that they differed in color from their fellows.

So much has been said in this work about the virtues of the white men who befriended their Negro relations that I may have given a false picture of the condition of the mulatto. As with all slaves, it was the lot of many of the mulattoes to fall into the hands of men who made the position of the slave woman horrible and the slave system a greater crime. Many mulatto children were born of white fathers whose sole interest was in the value of their labor and the money value of their bodies, and in many other cases the fathers of these children did not have even a financial interest in their children. Many mulatto children, born of promiscuous and irresponsible intercourse, could expect no favors because of the accident of their color. Southern writers give us a picture of the unfortunate life of many a mulatto slave woman. The Reverend Mr. Paxton tells us that,

female slaves can be compelled to unclean living. The
direct power of the owner or manager to enforce his wishes,
by hard usage, and punishment in various forms, and
the want of the means of defense on the part of the slave,
even to the giving of evidence against a white man, places
the purity of the female, and the comfort and happiness
of both the male and female, as connected with purity and
mutual confidence, in the power of those over them. While
their marriages are not protected, while separations are
so often made, by sales and transfers and removals, while
so little protection has been given to female purity . . .
nothing has been done to give them a sense of character;
nothing to purify and elevate their feelings, nothing to
give them well grounded moral and religious sentiment.
They have been subjected to harsh and debased treatment, placed under the rule of the lowest and most unfeeling and debased part of the whites. The marriage and
family relations have been wholly unprotected—have been
disregarded at pleasure. They have seen their females
almost universally subjected to pollution, and believe
that in a multitude of instances, violence and unfair means
have been used to accomplish it.[12]

The author of the above may be regarded as having the best authority for his assertions, for he had lived in Virginia for forty-
five years, had himself owned slaves, and as a minister and
teacher had lived in many sections of the South.

Many conditions tended to make the slave woman encourage
the advances of the white man.[13] A North Carolina judge declares that "it is well-known that persons of this description [a
slave woman] have a strong bias in their minds to induce declarations from them, and, if possible, the impression on others, that
their illegitimate child, is the issue of a white man; if not to grat-
ify personal vanity in themselves, for the reason that it removes

[12] Paxton, op. cit., pp. 189–91, 197.
[13] William G. Simms, "The Morals of Slavery," *Pro-Slavery Arguments* (Philadelphia, 1852), pp. 228–29; Sir Charles Lyell, *Second
Visit to the United States* (New York, 1849), I, 271–72.

the offspring one degree from the humble caste in which it is placed by law, whereby it is excluded from the elective franchise and from competency as a witness between white persons and prohibited from intermarrying with them."[14]

Mrs. Kemble related an interview on this subject with a slave woman who had lately born a child to her overseer. The following is her account:

> Ah! but don't you know—did nobody ever tell you or
> teach you that it is a sin to live with men who are not your
> husbands? Alas! . . . what could the poor creature answer
> but what she did, seizing me at the same time vehemently
> by the wrist; Oh yes, missis, we know—we know all about
> dat well enough; but we do anything to get our poor flesh
> some rest from de whip; when he made me follow him
> into de bush, what use to tell him no? He have strength
> to make me.[15]

The advocates of the slave system found it difficult to defend slavery on moral grounds. On this issue William Gilmore Simms in his defense of the system admits the truth of Harriet Martineau's accusations while he denounces every other criticism of the South. Concerning this subject Simms writes:

> There is one painful chapter in the two volumes (*Society
> in America*) under the head of "The Morals of Slavery"—
> It is painful, because it is full of truth. It is devoted to the
> abuses, among slaveholders, of the institution of slavery
> and it gives a collection of statements which are, no doubt,
> in too many cases founded upon fact, of illicit and foul
> conduct of some among us, who make their slaves the
> victims and the instruments, alike of the most licentious
> passions. . . . We do not quarrel with Miss Martineau for
> this chapter.[16]

---

[14] *State* v. *Waters,* 3 Iredell, *North Carolina Reports,* p. 341 (1843).
[15] Kemble, op. cit., p. 228.
[16] Simms, op. cit., p. 228.

Without doubt there were many owners of slaves who instructed their people in morality and who protected their virtue, but the temptations that surrounded the slave woman must have been overwhelming.[17] The evidence tends to make it clear that among the people of the slave country there were many men who could not or who would not feel the prompting of a guilty conscience and attempt to alleviate the conditions of their innocent offspring. Such offspring could have no attachment for the authors of their being. They and their offspring lived as all other slaves lived in the southland.

The unfortunate relations existing between the white man and the Negro woman were productive of problems similar to those which were found to have developed for the same reason in the white man's home.

In 1801 a white man named Joseph Gooding was murdered by a slave named Ben. The record of this case shows that,

> by permission of the court, Ben, the slave, attempted to justify himself by stating that four or five years ago, he had with the consent of Mr. and Mrs. Bass taken for a wife a favorite house wench belonging to them—that he continued to live with her for two or three years when without having done anything to give offence he was ordered by Bass to discontinue coming to his plantation—that if he should be found there again he would punish him very severely— that he accordingly desisted from making any further visits to his wife—that affairs remained in this situation, but for a short time before he heard that Joe Gooding, a white man, was very much in favor with Mr. and Mrs. Bass and had taken up with his wife—this continued to be the case for about two years when it was reported to him in the neighborhood that Bass and Joe Gooding had had a falling out—that supposing this to be a favorite opportunity to be again taken into favor, he determined to apply to Bass the first opportunity that offered for permission

[17] Martineau, op. cit., II, 320; Kemble, op. cit., p. 199; Philo Tower, *Slavery Unmasked* (Rochester, 1856), p. 54; Charles Elliot, *Sinfulness of Slavery in the United States* (Cincinnati, 1857), II, 66.

again to come to see his wife—That he spoke to Mr. Bass
in private and endeavoured to prevail on him to permit
him to come to see his wife. Bass signified that he had no
objection provided that he could fall upon some plan to
put Joe out of the way and intimated to him that as Joe
had taken his wife from him, he would be justifiable in
putting him to death, especially as it could be so easily
done without a discovery, by poison. That many conversations passed between him and Bass upon this subject before
he consented to act as Bass advised. . . . That he at last
consented to act as aforesaid, and procured a dose of poison
from a negro doctor in that neighborhood which he secretly
put into a plate of victuals that he expected Joe Gooding
would eat but unfortunately it was eaten by his wife.
Having failed in the attempt at poisoning Joe and having
poisoned the last person in the world he wished to injure,
he determined on taking the first opportunity that offered
of stealing his master's gun out of the house where it
generally stood loaded and to go in pursuit of Joe Gooding
and shoot him, which he did.[18]

In 1820 the records of North Carolina show that a slave called
Daniel was murdered by a white man. The slave had had a free
mulatto wife living in the city of Raleigh. This slave was shot by
the white man when he, the slave, objected to the effort of the
white man to take his wife from him.[19]

In 1859 a Negro slave murdered his overseer. In this instance
the Negro prisoner

introduced as a witness in his own behalf a slave woman,
named Charlotte, who stated that she was the wife of the
prisoner. . . . The prisoners counsel then proposed to
prove that about nine or ten o'clock in the morning of the
day in which the killing took place, that Coleman, the overseer, had forced her, the witness, to submit to sexual

[18] Executive Papers, Archives of Virginia, Letters Received, Jan. 12,
1801. Hereafter Archives of Virginia, Letters Received, will be omitted
and the document identified by the date.

[19] State v. Tacket, 8 North Carolina Reports, p. 210 (1820).

intercourse with him; and that she had communicated that fact to the prisoner before the killing took place.

The court sustained objections to this testimony by a slave against a white person, and, the court declared that

> adultery with a slave wife is no defense to a charge of murder. A slave charged with the murder of his overseer can not introduce as evidence in his defense, the fact that the deceased, a few hours, before the killing had forced the prisoners wife to sexual intercourse with him.[20]

The following is a report of a portion of the evidence taken in the case of the slaves Peggy and Patrick, who were condemned to be hanged for the murder of their master. The story relates the experience of a slave girl and her slave lover and the unfortunate cause leading to their act of violence. To the credit of certain respectable citizens of New Kent county, Virginia, it may be added that they petitioned the governor that the sentence imposed on these slaves be changed from death to transportation. Witnesses for the slaves testified that,

> the deceased to whom Peggy belonged, had had a disagreement with Peggy, and generally kept her confined, by keeping her chained to a block, and locked up in his meat house; that he believed the reason why the deceased had treated Peggy in this way was because Peggy would not consent to intercourse with him, and that he had heard the deceased say that if Peggy did not agree to his request in that way, he would beat her almost to death, that he would barely leave the life in her, and would send her to New Orleans. The witness said that Peggy said the reason she would not yield to his request was because the deceased was her father, and she could not do a thing of that sort with her father. The witness heard the deceased say to Peggy that if she did not consent, he would make him, the witness, and Patrick hold her, to enable him to effect his object.[21]

---

[20] *Alfred, a slave* v. *State of Mississippi,* 37 *Mississippi Reports,* p. 296 (1859).

[21] Executive Papers, Sept. 10, 1830.

The evidence in this case is supported by the testimony of many witnesses, including white men living in the neighborhood. Peggy and her Negro lover, Patrick, murdered their master and attempted to destroy the body by burning the plantation house.

The petition of certain citizens of Virginia in behalf of a slave woman found guilty of infanticide reveals the fact that in this case the father of the child was a respectable white married man, and the woman, who confessed that she had murdered her own child, declared that she never would have done so, had the child been "of her own color."[22]

In other sections of this study, repeated reference has been made to the close association of the Negro and the poor white element of the population. The author is convinced that in many instances the only associates of many poor whites were the mulattoes. In southern society the lot of the poor white man was hard. In many cases the mulatto was his superior in possession of wealth and property and the poor white man found it to his profit to possess the friendship of the mulatto. There are instances in which white men brought suit to secure the property of the deceased woman of color with whom they had lived.[23] In other cases many of those classified as white were in fact persons of remote Negro extraction. Numerous slander cases in which the litigant objected to being called a mulatto seem to indicate local suspicions that certain supposedly white persons were not always of pure white blood.[24] It is also true that the criminal records of the southern states often show that the poor white and the mulatto were partners in crime. Adverse social distinctions and economic pressure drew these people together.

By far the larger proportion of the mulattoes were city dwell-

[22] Executive Papers, July 26, 1822.

[23] *Minvielle* v. *Barjac,* 15 Ogden, *Louisiana Reports,* p. 342 (1860); *Dreux* v. *Condreau,* Manning, *Unreported Cases Heard by the Superior Court of Louisiana,* p. 217 (1877).

[24] *Watts* v. *Greenlee,* 2 Devereux, *North Carolina Reports,* p. 115 (1829); *Eden* v. *Legree,* 1 Bays, *South Carolina Reports,* p. 171 (1791); *King* v. *Wood,* 1 Nott and McCord, *South Carolina Reports,* p. 208 (1818); *Smith* v. *Hamilton,* 10 Richardson, *South Carolina Reports,* p. 46 (1856).

ers.[25] In all the southern cities there were to be found groups whose color varied from the very dark shades of the mulatto to the condition where there was no perceptible variation from the color of the white race. The largest group and those most often described were those of the city of New Orleans. French and Spanish traditions left their influence on these people, but in many respects they were typical of other groups to be found in other southern cities.

Concerning the mulattoes of Louisiana a traveler in 1804 reports:

> All the men of color of free negroes make their sons learn
> a trade, and give special education to their daughters, whom
> they rarely marry off. When the girls attain the age of
> thirteen or fourteen, their mothers usually place them with
> white men, who have generally much more regard for
> them than they do for their legitimate wives. However, the
> white women show the greatest contempt and aversion for
> that type of woman. Those women inspire such lust
> through their bearing and their dress, that many well-
> to-do persons are ruined in pleasing them. It is worth
> noting that when these women perceive that the men
> with whom they live have nothing more, they desert
> and abandon them, and take up with another white man.[26]

Another author declares of the mulattoes of early New Orleans:

[25] Percentage of mulattoes in the total Negro population, 1850 and 1860, Census Bull., No. 8, 1904:

	1850	1860		1850	1860
Richmond City	20.5	21.4	Savannah	18.1	23.0
Rest of State	15.0	16.9	Rest of State	6.0	8.2
Charleston	16.8	25.2	Mobile	25.0	26.6
Rest of State	—	—	Rest of State	0.3	8.0
New Orleans	46.1	48.9			
Rest of State	9.3	11.0			

[26] James A. Robertson, *Louisiana under the Rule of Spain, France, and the United States* (Cleveland, 1911), I, 85.

He who was to strike one of these persons, although she has run away from him, would be severely punished. Also, twenty white could be counted in the prisons of New Orleans against one man of color. The wives and daughters of the latter are much sought after by the white men, and white women at times esteem well built men of color.[27]

Still another author declares that,

as in all the colonies [in Louisiana] their taste for women extends more particularly to those of color, who they prefer to white women, because these women demand fewer of those annoying attentions which contradict their tastes for independence. A great number, accordingly, prefer to live in concubinage rather than to marry. They find in that the double advantage of being served with the most exactness, and in the case of discontent or unfaithfulness, of changing their housekeeper (this is the honorable name given to that sort of woman.) [28]

As the years went by travelers continued to delight to describe the beauty and accomplishment of the quadroons of Louisiana. Mrs. Trollope speaks of

quadroon girls, the acknowledged daughters of wealthy American or Creole fathers, educated with all the style and accomplishments which money can procure at New Orleans, and with all the decorum which care and affection can give; exquisitely beautiful, graceful, gentle, and amiable. . . . They can not marry, that is to say, no ceremony can render any union with them legal or binding yet such is the powerful effect of their peculiar grace, beauty, and sweetness of manner, that unfortunately they perpetually become the objects of choice and affection.[29]

Lord Lyell says of the quadroon women of New Orleans,

[27] Robertson, op. cit., I, 71.

[28] Ibid., p. 204.

[29] Frances Trollope, *Domestic Manners of the Americans* (London, 1832), I, 15.

When they are rich, they hold a very peculiar and equivo-
cal position in society. As children they have often been
sent to Paris for their education, and being as capable of
improvement as any whites, return with refined manners,
and not infrequently with more cultivated minds than the
majority of those from whose society they have been shut
out.[30]

Another observer says of the quadroon girls: "The fourth removed or quadroons, furnish some of the most beautiful women
that can be seen . . . with lovely countenances, full dark eyes,
lips of coral, and teeth of pearl, long raven locks of soft and
glossy hair, sylphlike figures, beautifully rounded limbs, and ex-
quisite gait and manner, that might furnish models for a Venus
or a Hebe to the chisel of a sculptor."[31] The fate of the mulatto
girl that was not free was very hard. High prices were paid for
these for purposes of prostitution. Slave brokers made a business
of supplying young men with "sleeping companions."[32]

The economic aspects of life among the free mulattoes have
been described in a former chapter. At the conclusion of the
Civil War many of these men played an important part in the reconstruction. Concerning these men in Louisiana, a former reconstruction governor of that state reports:

There were a number of free men of color who were descendants of the original French, Spanish, and Canadian
emigrants who had cohabited with their slave women,
some of whom, at least, had been educated in France and
Spain, and who at the death of their white fathers inherited
a part, if not all, of their fathers' estates. This element was
important on the arrival of General Claiborne in 1803;
so much so that their recognition by him and his organization of them into the Territorial Militia was the cause of
serious criticism and controversy by the ancient Louisi-
anans. . . . This element of the colored population had

[30] Op. cit., II, 94–95.
[31] Buckingham, op. cit., I, 358.
[32] Tower, op. cit., pp. 315–18; Frederick L. Olmsted, *The Cotton
Kingdom* (New York, 1861), I, 306–07.

increased in numbers, wealth, intelligence and importance by 1867. Many of them were owners of slaves, and some of them were actually in the Confederate Army, but not registered as Negroes.[33]

The governor continues:

On November 23, 1861, the Confederate Grand parade took place in New Orleans—One feature of this review was a regiment of free men of color, 1,400 in number. The Picayune speaks as follows of another review on February 9, 1862: We must pay deserved tribute to the company of free men of color, all well dressed, well drilled, and comfortably uniformed. Most of these companies have provided themselves with arms unaided by the administration. They were planters, merchants, brokers, and mechanics of various trades. They paid taxes on over $15,000,000 of property in New Orleans alone.[34]

The description of the free mulattoes of Louisiana might be continued at length.[35]

The free mulatto found himself in a peculiar and intricate environment. His happiness and success depended upon his ability to adjust himself to his environment. Had he failed to adjust himself to the intricate social system that surrounded him he would have been driven from the slave country. The fact that so many of these people prospered in spite of the complications of their lives must be regarded as proof of their individual worth.

According to the United States census for 1860 there were at that time 4,441,800 Negroes in the United States, of which number 588,363 were classified as mulattoes. However, it was impossible to make a correct estimate of the mulatto population. The census returns are based on the inspection of the individual, and the study of inspection as a method of determining race, made in

[33] Henry C. Warmoth, *War, Politics, and Reconstruction* (New York, 1930), p. 56.

[34] Ibid., pp. 56–57.

[35] Alice Dunbar-Nelson, "People of Color in Louisiana," *Journal of Negro History,* I (October, 1916), 361–77; II (January, 1917), 51–79.

another section of this work, leads me to believe that the number of the mulatto population should have been much larger than the census indicates.[36]

The responsibility for the existence of this large mulatto group rests with the white man. Comparatively few of the mulattoes were born of white mothers. The Negro woman possessed no legal or social responsibilities and can not be held accountable for the lack of morality which the existence of the mulatto demonstrates. As found in other portions of this study, it may be repeated that all the slave masters were not immoral, and that there were many excellent men at the South who sought to abolish the institution of slavery and that much of their objection to the system was based on moral grounds. However, slavery could not be defended on moral grounds and with so much of evil demonstrated by the ever-present mulatto, it is to be wondered why the abolition of slavery did not move forward far more rapidly. With so much of moral right on their side and with such convincing arguments in their favor, it is hard to understand why the antislavery men met with effective resistance. Primarily, the responsibility for the persistence of the immoralities that have been portrayed must be placed upon those men who are remembered as the statesmen of the old South, and it is to be regretted that so many men of demonstrated talent and perhaps of personal probity cannot be found on the side of the forces of morality and virtue. These men knew that slavery was a great moral wrong, but they were not great enough to resist the profits that the slave system offered to the ambitious politician. It is probably an injustice to the people of the old slave country that the glory bestowed so lavishly on the proslavery politicians is not more often shared by less famous or forgotten men, who though they lived among slaveowners, denounced the slave system and its immoralities.

The study of miscegenation gives added support to the claim that laws are futile unless supported by sound public opinion. The law did little to prevent miscegenation, and this subject must be considered as a question of human, not of legal, relations. Possibly it would be more correct to style them animal

[36] *Bureau of the Census,* "Negroes in the United States," Bulletin No. 8, 1904, p. 327.

rather than human relations. In these pages there are recorded the conduct of black, red, and white men and women who exhibited themselves as human beings; many of them exhibited more of animal than of human traits. In the record there is nothing to support the claim of either race to peculiar moral superiority, for depravity, human lust, and animal passions are to be found alike among all the races and all have cause for shame. In the light of such evidence the white man has less right to claim moral superiority; for the white man had power, whereas the Negro and the Indian were powerless. Having power and freedom the white man gave to the world an exhibition of the exercise of animal passions which must always embarrass his descendants and make it exceedingly difficult for those who wish to demonstrate the peculiar moral superiority of the Caucasian.

The history I have related is not exclusively the history of the Negro. This history is the story of black and white Americans who shared in the making of the record. In every case the story could not have been told if I had excluded either the black or the white man. Possibly the mulatto is a sign of the interrelation of the races and an evidence of the union of white and black men in the making of our history.

Appendix
Bibliography
& Index

Appendix

NUMBER I

Slaves Condemned to Death for Murder of Masters and Overseers

1. *Commonwealth* v. *Robin,* Chesterfield, November 16, 1786
2. *Commonwealth* v. *Robin,* Brunswick, November 12, 1789
3. *Commonwealth* v. *Billy,* Charles City, November 28, 1792
4. *Commonwealth* v. *Nell and Daphe,* James City, June 1, 1793
5. *Commonwealth* v. *Will,* Chesterfield, January 16, 1797
6. *Commonwealth* v. *Auck,* Chesterfield, July 31, 1797
7. *Commonwealth* v. *Sam,* King and Queen, March 20, 1797
8. *Commonwealth* v. *Nat, George, and Jack,* Mecklenburg, November 20, 1799
9. *Commonwealth* v. *Isaac, Hatter Isaac, Sam and Jerry,* Southampton, November 20, 1799
10. *Commonwealth* v. *Ben,* Chesterfield, January 12, 1801
11. *Commonwealth* v. *Lewey,* Gloucester, September 19, 1801
12. *Commonwealth* v. *Jack,* Kanawha, December 7, 1801
13. *Commonwealth* v. *Patrick,* Caroline, February 9, 1802
14. *Commonwealth* v. *Hercules,* Southampton, February 11, 1802
15. *Commonwealth* v. *Dick,* Kanawha, March 10, 1802
16. *Commonwealth* v. *Dick,* Southampton, July 20, 1802
17. *Commonwealth* v. *Dick,* Goochland, November 15, 1802
18. *Commonwealth* v. *Sarah,* Albemarle, June 12, 1803

19. *Commonwealth* v. *Abraham,* Chesterfield, October 7, 1803
20. *Commonwealth* v. *Isaac et al.,* Kanawha, November 9, 1803
21. *Commonwealth* v. *Jack,* Bedford, March 30, 1804
22. *Commonwealth* v. *Daniel,* Lancaster, May 14, 1804
23. *Commonwealth* v. *Moses,* James City, October 14, 1804
24. *Commonwealth* v. *Sall and Creasy,* Chesterfield, April 14, 1806
25. *Commonwealth* v. *James,* Campbell, January 14, 1808
26. *Commonwealth* v. *Ben,* Charles City, March 17, 1808
27. *Commonwealth* v. *Flora,* Frederick, September 5, 1808
28. *Commonwealth* v. *Frank et al.,* Mathews, June 15, 1809
29. *Commonwealth* v. *Sam,* Montgomery, September 2, 1809
30. *Commonwealth* v. *Will,* Prince Edward, October 15, 1810
31. *Commonwealth* v. *Bob Toogood et al.,* Boutetout, December 29, 1810
32. *Commonwealth* v. *Abraham,* Bedford, February 8, 1812
33. *Commonwealth* v. *Ben,* Chesterfield, November 9, 1812
34. *Commonwealth* v. *Tom,* Powhatan, September 21, 1814
35. *Commonwealth* v. *Caesar,* Norfolk, June 1, 1815
36. *Commonwealth* v. *Caty,* Brunswick, December 23, 1817
37. *Commonwealth* v. *George et al.,* Goochland, April 22, 1818
38. *Commonwealth* v. *London,* Frederick, May 25, 1818
39. *Commonwealth* v. *Mingo,* Princess Anne, January 4, 1819
40. *Commonwealth* v. *Harry,* Boutetout, February 3, 1819
41. *Commonwealth* v. *Bob,* Sussex, July 12, 1820
42. *Commonwealth* v. *Jordan,* Henrico, February 16, 1820
43. *Commonwealth* v. *Ellis,* Tyler, September 20, 1820
44. *Commonwealth* v. *Armstead,* April 27, 1821
45. *Commonwealth* v. *Pat,* Charlotte, September 2, 1821
46. *Commonwealth* v. *Abel,* Southampton, June 28, 1821
47. *Commonwealth* v. *Patrick,* Louisa, June 30, 1821
48. *Commonwealth* v. *Peter,* Hampshire, November 18, 1822
49. *Commonwealth* v. *Rob,* Norfolk, June 24, 1823
50. *Commonwealth* v. *Anthony,* Henry, December 18, 1823
51. *Commonwealth* v. *Tom,* Greenbrier, January 20, 1823
52. *Commonwealth* v. *Billy Liggons,* Monroe, February 7, 1824
53. *Commonwealth* v. *Thornton,* Hanover, February 25, 1824
54. *Commonwealth* v. *Ben,* Frederick, March 2, 1824
55. *Commonwealth* v. *Reuben,* Orange, November 24, 1824

56. *Commonwealth* v. *Jenny Clarkson*, Amherst, September 20, 1824
57. *Commonwealth* v. *Johnson and Jim*, King William, March 3, 1825
58. *Commonwealth* v. *Moses*, Southampton, April 6, 1825
59. *Commonwealth* v. *Nathan*, Louisa, July 11, 1825
60. *Commonwealth* v. *Jim*, Cumberland, July 25, 1825
61. *Commonwealth* v. *Harry*, Bedford, November 29, 1825
62. *Commonwealth* v. *Tom*, Prince Edward, September 26, 1826
63. *Commonwealth* v. *David*, Brunswick, September 28, 1826
64. *Commonwealth* v. *Tom et al.*, Lunenburg, March 20, 1827
65. *Commonwealth* v. *Louis*, Cumberland, January 19, 1827
66. *Commonwealth* v. *Allen*, Washington, October 19, 1827
67. *Commonwealth* v. *Charles*, Amelia, September 5, 1828
68. *Commonwealth* v. *Horace*, Caroline, February 8, 1829
69. *Commonwealth* v. *Sandy and Daniel*, Hanover, February 23, 1829
70. *Commonwealth* v. *Parker*, Princess Anne, September 29, 1829
71. *Commonwealth* v. *Daniel*, Richmond (city), May 29, 1830
72. *Commonwealth* v. _____, Prince George
73. *Commonwealth* v. *Dan and Henry*, Page, November 18, 1831
74. *Commonwealth* v. *Reuben*, Chesterfield, March 24, 1832
75. *Commonwealth* v. *John*, Richmond, March 27, 1832
76. *Commonwealth* v. *Tom and George*, Chesterfield, February 7, 1832
77. *Commonwealth* v. *Humphrey*, Richmond (city), December 24, 1832
78. *Commonwealth* v. *Edmund*, Buckingham, January 14, 1833
79. *Commonwealth* v. *John*, King and Queen, May 6, 1833
80. *Commonwealth* v. *Mary*, Southampton, May 20, 1833
81. *Commonwealth* v. *Lee*, Albemarle, September 29, 1833
82. Petition 14462, Rockbridge, February 8, 1845

Slaves Condemned to Death for Poisoning

1. *Commonwealth* v. *Judah*, Brunswick, June 3, 1772
2. *Commonwealth* v. *Francis*, King and Queen, June 9, 1782
3. *Commonwealth* v. *Peter*, Louisa, August 11, 1783

4. *Commonwealth* v. *Will,* Chesterfield, November 15, 1784
5. *Commonwealth* v. *Kate,* Frederick, June, 1786
6. *Commonwealth* v. *Roger,* Pittsylvania, May 9, 1787
7. *Commonwealth* v. *Joe,* Nottoway, March 19, 1790
8. *Commonwealth* v. *Harry,* Henrico, December 6, 1792
9. *Commonwealth* v. *Moses and Nomrod,* Isle of Wight, July 7, 1797
10. *Commonwealth* v. *Punch,* Prince Edward, July 7, 1802
11. *Commonwealth* v. *Bob,* Lunenburg, February 1, 1802
12. *Commonwealth* v. *Dick,* Mecklenburg, March 18, 1802
13. *Commonwealth* v. *George,* Princess Anne, September 3, 1803
14. Petition 4762, December 10, 1804
15. *Commonwealth* v. *Fanny,* Charlotte, April 29, 1805
16. *Commonwealth* v. *Solomon,* Bedford, August 2, 1805
17. *Commonwealth* v. *Toma and Amy,* Pittsylvania, January 20, 1806
18. *Commonwealth* v. *Billy,* Nottoway, May, 1807
19. *Commonwealth* v. *Tom,* Albemarle, December 7, 1807
20. *Commonwealth* v. *Barnett,* Louisa, May 13, 1810
21. *Commonwealth* v. *Delphy,* Louisa, June 10, 1816
22. *Commonwealth* v. *Daniel et al.,* Cumberland, December 23, 1816
23. *Commonwealth* v. *Eppy,* Frederick, November 3, 1818
24. *Commonwealth* v. *Moses,* Culpeper, December 17, 1819
25. *Commonwealth* v. *Ned and Violet,* King William, May 8, 1820
26. *Commonwealth* v. *Hannah,* Fairfax, December 17, 1821
27. *Commonwealth* v. *Maria,* Amelia, December 2, 1823
28. *Commonwealth* v. *Maria,* Albemarle, March 27, 1827
29. *Commonwealth* v. *Jerry and Sampson,* Caroline, September 3, 1827
30. *Commonwealth* v. *Billy,* Hanover, September 27, 1827
31. *Commonwealth* v. *Alexander,* Bedford, September 4, 1828
32. *Commonwealth* v. *Susan and Kisiah,* Henrico, January 13, 1829
33. *Commonwealth* v. *Frederick,* Stafford, January 26, 1829
34. *Commonwealth* v. *Peggy,* King and Queen, March 29, 1829
35. *Commonwealth* v. *Anne,* Amelia, June 5, 1829
36. *Commonwealth* v. *Renah,* Princess Anne, August 20, 1832

Slaves Condemned to Death for Arson

1. *Commonwealth* v. *John,* Spotsylvania, July 1, 1789
2. ———— v. ————, June 6, 1791
3. *Commonwealth* v. *Winney,* Frederick, May 6, 1806
4. *Commonwealth* v. *Momouth,* King and Queen, June 11, 1808
5. *Commonwealth* v. *Sarah,* King George, June 11, 1808
6. *Commonwealth* v. *Barney,* Washington, May 29, 1809
7. *Commonwealth* v. *Charlotte,* Culpeper, June 20, 1810
8. *Commonwealth* v. *Fanny,* Culpeper, March 12, 1811
9. *Commonwealth* v. *Jim,* Buckingham, December 4, 1811
10. *Commonwealth* v. *Winney,* Greenbrier, December 23, 1818
11. *Commonwealth* v. *Pat,* Charlotte, March 31, 1820
12. *Commonwealth* v. *George,* Culpeper, April 5, 1830
13. ———— v. ————, Prince George, November 1, 1831
14. *Commonwealth* v. *Tom,* Rockingham, December 12, 1831
15. *Commonwealth* v. *Sam,* Greenbrier, October 1, 1832
16. *Commonwealth* v. *Tulip,* Fauquier, February 25, 1833
17. *Commonwealth* v. *Kike,* Amelia

NUMBER II

The Last Will and Testament of Lewis Turner

"In the name of God, amen: I, Lewis Turner, a free black man of the county of Sussex and state of Virginia, do hereby constitute make and ordain this my last will and testament revoking and disannulling all former wills and heretofore made. Imprimis, I direct that my body be buried in a decent and Christian manner and as soon afterward as conveniently can be, I direct that all my just debts be paid. Item: It is my will and desire that the woman Aggai which I purchased of Henry Chappell and which I have had for my beloved wife for many years, should be free and clear from control of any person as a slave. . . . I do therefore hereby direct my executor herein named to petition the Honourable Legislature of this State for leave for my said wife Aggai . . . to remain in this State as other free persons of colour do during her natural life or widowhood, and provided such leave is granted, which I pray Almighty God it may be, I do hereby emancipate the said woman Aggai, my wife as aforesaid and do lend to her during her natural life or widowhood the land and plantation whereon I now live, with all the improvements thereon also that tract or parcel of land which I purchased of Littleberry Turner, also all rents or profits that arises from that tract or parcel of land which I purchased from Reuben Watkins except that part thereof which I have agreed to sell to Harrison Jenkins a free Negro, and also that part thereof which I shall hereafter dispose of—also all my stock of horses, hogs, sheep, and cows, except one, my work steers, fowls of every description, all my household and kitchen furniture, all my tools, carts, plows, and farming utensils, all my crop of every description that may have been made or may be growing at my death, also all meats and liquors that may be on hand, also the services of the boy James Wright (a negro boy that will be free when he arrives to twenty-one years of age) until he arrives to lawful age, which said boy I had of his family, all of the above mentioned property to my said wife Aggai, during her life or widowhood, and no longer.

"Item; _____
"Item; _____
"Item; _____
"Item; _____
"Item; _____
"Item; _____
"Item; _____
"Item; _____

"His
"Lewis Turner
"Mark"[1]

NUMBER III

"The petition of Sarah Greene humbly sheweth. That your petitioner though born in slavery has never felt the hardships of

[1] Petition 7180, Sussex, December 10, 1818.

that miserable state. It having been her lot to fall into the hands of one of the best of masters, the Reverend Charles Greene, late of Fairfax, deceased.

"That having had the good fortune to recommend herself to the favour of her said master by many years of faithful service, he had determined to reward your petitions with liberty to herself and children. Your petitioner is informed that the laws of the country at that time would not admit of her master liberating her by will, and death prevented him from putting in execution (by legal means) his benevolent intentions toward your petitioner and her two children, but that in his last illness he exacted a promise from his lady that she would fulfill those intentions after his death. Your petitioner begs leave to show further to your honourable body that her said master left his whole fortune in this county to his widow Mrs. Sarah Greene who in the year 1767 intermarried with Dr. William Savage lately deceased; that previous to the said marriage Doctor Savage executed a bond to George Washington and Baron Fairfax Esquires, obliging himself to pay a certain sum annually for the use of Mrs. Savage during her life. That when the bond was prepared and before its execution Mrs. Greene insisted that a clause should be inserted enabling her to set free your petitioner and her children; that Doctor Savage agreed that your petitioner and her children should be set free but to save the trouble of drawing the bond over again promised that he would after the marriage execute an instrument of writing empowering and enabling his said wife to emancipate your petitioner and her two children, and called upon witnesses to take notice of the said promise and your petitioner had been informed that he actually executed an instrument of writing for that purpose. Some unhappy differences having arisen between Doctor Savage and his lady, he carried her to Ireland about the year 1769 and left her, he returning to Virginia. After this time your petitioner and her children were suffered to enjoy their liberty for many years. When a Mr. Rice, said to be a relative of Doctor Savage, took by force from your petitioner her two children and carried them to Carolina and has lately attempted to carry off your petitioner and her two other children since born, and still threatens to take the first opportunity of forcing them into slavery, which your petitioner fears he will do unless your honourable house will be pleased to interpose in her favour, and as it was the intention of their master to give them their freedom, and as Doctor Savage assented to his lady's having that power, it is presumable that Mrs. Savage (who your petitioner is informed, died in obscurity and great poverty in Ireland, without having any relations) did direct them to be set free by will."[1]

NUMBER IV

"Fredericktown
"March 12, 1802

"Sir:

"Tho I have not been acquainted long enough with you to expect that an application in behalf of injured innocence could acquire an additional weight by being presented by me, I know too well your benevolent disposition to hesitate a moment to solicit your executive interference in a case where both justice and humanity claim it. The circumstances of the business which I take the liberty to lay before you have been related to me by several gentlemen of respectability and integrity and particularly by Gen. Carberry who I expect will write to you also on the subject. Being a stranger to you and knowing I had the happiness to be acquainted with you in my last visit to Richmond, he desired me to join him in soliciting your protection in behalf of an innocent and much injured black man who may perhaps lose his life on a scaffold in a few weeks, unless by granting him a reprieve or postponing his trial you give him an opportunity to prove his innocence.

"The name of this poor Negro man is Jack Neale, alias Jack Warren, born and bred in St. Mary's County in the State of Maryland. He was carried to the jail of Kanawa county in the State of Virginia to be tried for murder committed, I think, on the Ohio. He was tried and having no means to prove his innocence was condemned; but on account of an error committed by

[1] Petition 1284, Fairfax, December 3, 1784.

the Court in the forms prescribed by law, the execution did not take place. The same Court was called again to give new judgment but a letter from Gen. Carberry having been read at the bar, they would not take up the business and put off the trial until the last day of April. But such is the distance and the difficulty of correspondence between that part of the country and this, that it will be impossible to procure the necessary evidence to clear the unhappy man and it was only a few days ago that Gen. Carberry was informed that Jack was yet alive and that something could yet be done for him. The circumstances of this extraordinary business are as follows: It appears that Jack, who formerly belonged to Mr. Jeremiah Neale of St. Mary's County, was sold by him to Mr. Lyles near Piscataway with whom he remained several years as blacksmith. About two years ago he instituted a suit vs. Mr. Lyles of his freedom in upper Marlborough and compromised for four years service. It was generally reported that the fellow had already paid two hundred dollars towards his freedom to his master and would have paid the whole had not people abused of his being a black man to keep him out of his money. But whether that money was in addition to the four years service or only as a satisfaction for the said four years I could not assertain. But certain it is that at the time the poor fellow expressed to Gen. Carberry some uneasiness that the said Lyles would sell him, which he did shortly afterwards to a man going to New Spain, notwithstanding the agreement he had made and the money he had already received. The idea of being torn thus from his wife and children and from his native country drove the poor fellow to despair. He informed the man of his situation with his master and declared to him that if under those circumstances he was so cruel as to carry him off, he would take away his life or lose his own. The threats were treated with contempt by the man who got him chained immediately. The fellow in order to show or convince the man of his power observed to him that he was a blacksmith by trade and was not to be kept under by such weak means and instantly broke the chain asunder. Such a lesson had no effect but another chain much stronger with an iron hook round his body was fixed and the fellow confined again; thus was he dragged as far as the Ohio. An opportunity having offered in the boat, Jack in defense of his natural rights executed his threats and killed his tyrant. But he soon returned to his natural feelings and shed tears of sorrow and pity. One of the boatmen, terrified by his actions and dreading the same fate, threw himself overboard and drowned himself, notwithstanding all Jack could say to remove his fears. When he and his fellow slaves were taken up he cleared the others immediately and declared he was the only guilty man. His conduct during his confinement has been decent, honourable, manlike, so far as to excite the pity and regard of almost every one. In vain did the heirs of the deceased offer to save his life and take him away from jail; he persisted in his resolution to attend his trial and die or be free. Since a letter was written to Gen. Carberry in his behalf which induced the Magistrates to put off his trial, he has been sat at liberty to work and maintain himself and such is his confidence in the justice of his cause that he neither attempted nor wishes to avoid a fair trial. The character given to Jack by the people who had an opportunity to know him is that of a mild, honest, sober, peaceable, industrious, fellow when treated well, but who neither would stoop to any mean acts nor bear an undeserved ill treatment. It remains with you to determine in your wisdom whether they had a right to carry off that poor fellow under the circumstances I mentioned; and if entitled to his freedom, whether the law has a right to punish a murder committed in defense of a right which no one could lawfully rob him of. If you decide in the affirmative does not justice require that as much time should be granted to him as is necessary to prepare his own defence and when you consider the situation of the poor man who can not collect himself those evidences, but must depend altogether upon a few men of feeling who having their own business to attend, can not give all their time to his. When you consider also the distance between the different places where communication must be had you will be sensible that several months will not be too much. If the fellow is guilty those delays will be no favour and will only lengthen his misery and remorse by lengthening his wretched existence and uncertainty; if, on the contrary, he has been injured, most barbarously treated, must he by an unjust precipitation be ushered into eternity when he may be a useful member of society? What happiness will it be for me, if one day I can say that the beginning of my correspondence

with you, had been a request in behalf of oppressed innocence
and to you an opportunity to save it?

> "With great respect and affection
> "I remain your most humble servant
> "J. Dubois.

"Please present my respects to Mrs.
Monroe and Miss Eliza to whom I will write in
a few days and would have written this time if I
had not feared that the least delay in this business might
be fatal to that poor black man."[1]

NUMBER V

A Communication from "Nero"

The following is a copy of a letter received by the postmaster
at Jerusalem, in Southampton county, after the publication of
the news concerning Nat Turner's insurrection. The style of the
writer leads one to believe that "Nero" may have been the Negro
author, David Walker, mentioned above. The communication
was forwarded to Richmond with the notation that it might
"give some useful hints" to the executive.

> "Boston, 1831

"Sir:

"Oppression and revenge are two prominent traits in the
human character; and as long as the former exists, the latter is
justifiable. It is the business of education and improvement to do
away with these evils; but so long as man shall task, abuse, and
act the tyrant over his fellow man, may revenge ever be cherished, and spiritedly encouraged by the injured; nor let the das-
tard scruples of conscience unnerve the muscular arm of the oppressed, till *revenge* be fully glutted. Revenge possesses some
properties in common with love—We can not enjoy either in full

[1] Executive Papers, March 13, 1802.

fruition unless the object of affection, or revenge be conscious of being loved or punished—Thus far have I moralized in order to let you know the *motive* of this communication.

"I have been informed that my worthy friend has just arrived at New York from his perilous and philanthropic enterprise at the South—Yes he has arrived and safe too, though he had many hairbreadth escapes from the bullets of the modern vandals of *Christian* Virginia. It may be somewhat interesting to you, and your community to know something of this benevolent and worthy man and his brave associate. He is a modern Leonidas, and the adored Chief of some *more* than three hundred men of colour (or Negroes as you please to denominate us) who have pledged ourselves with Spartan fidelity to avenge the indignities offered to our race from the slave holding tyrants of the United States. We have sworn in the most solemn manner that we will not shrink from our holy and laudable purpose of revenge, although we have to meet suffering and bear tortures that would have made the ghostly inquisition of Spain and Portugal feel and show pity. Indeed we expect that such sufferings await us; but know ye coward race, that each of us is a Martius who knows how to suffer and with grace too. Our beloved Chief is a native of Virginia; where he lived a slave till he was almost sixteen years old, when he found an opportunity to escape to St. Domingo, where his noble soul became warmed by the spirit of freedom, and where he imbibed a righteous indignation, and an unqualified hatred for the oppressors of his race. His person is large and athletic; his deportment and manners dignified and when enraged his eye is piercing and at pleasure, can assume a fiendish malignity which can wither anyone in his presence, and which I trust will one day have its desired effect upon the coward hearts of many a nabob who can wield the sceptre of cruel domination. He is acquainted with, and speaks fluently most of the living European languages—he is a scholar and a genius—he is acquainted with every avenue of the human heart—but more especially is he acquainted with all the feelings of a slave; for he has himself been a slave. For more than three years he has been traveling and visiting almost every Negro hut and "quarter" in the Southern States. Although he has been travelling incog, both among you and your slaves, yet he knows all about the latter, and not a little

tion the different treatment my mother received from my father's *wife*—my brothers and sisters looked upon me with contempt, for not other reason than my colour being different from their own, and they were allowed to treat me with cruel savagery, although I was their brother. I was signaled out for peculiar malignity of my pious mistress because I was the child of her husband—for this crime, however, I did not consider myself justly obnoxious to her spirit. My father died and then the full vials of vengeance were poured upon my own and my poor devoted mother's heads, from the amiable household of my mistress. After satiating their malice, I was selected to be sold to a Florida trader—The terror that one of these worse than pirates strikes upon a Virginia slave is no secret. As bad as they are treated by their savage masters in the ancient dominion, they cling to them rather than go to Florida or Georgia. I made a desperate struggle and fled; I am to New England and was happy beyond expression in breathing the air of liberty—Soon after I learned that death had emancipated my mother and sent her heaven to enjoy the society of my father never more to be annoyed by the presence of my infernal *mistress*. Since I have been here I have had but one object in view and that has been to avenge the wrongs and abuses slaves have received in the United States. I have followed every plan that possibility would suggest, or revenge could prompt and have succeeded beyond my most sanguine expectations. I do not fear to boast that our purpose in one way or another will be effected; prosperity has encouraged us to persevere, and hope has made us blind to all scruples—We have never been foiled in but one instance and that was when we confided in the ability of Basset of Georgia—Our holy cause most surely was then in jeopardy—and had it not been for a most masterful maneuver of our chief who was then in Georgia, Basset would have lost his worthless life, and our fond hopes would have been blasted—lucky for us—that Basset did not know the person of his chief—for had he most probably, he would have betrayed him. That circumstance however, has been of service to us—it has made us more circumspect —made us more cautious in making confidants—We have now many a white agent in Florida, South Carolina and Georgia but they are not Bassets. Such are some of the fond prospects on which I dwell and on which I live. I have a wife of my own colour, by whom I have seven children, and five of them boys—these I early brought to the altar of righteous retribution, and after invoking the shade of their sainted grandmother, in imitation of the great Hamilcar I made them pledge both body and soul that they would never spare either wife, child or property of a slaveholder—and that fire and sword should be their most merciful weapons—such are my deliberate sentiments—and I exult in them; I know that by some they would be styled fiendish—be it so, I care not since I am conscious of being engaged in a righteous cause and am at the same time confident of success. Do not flatter yourselves, that in consequence of our apparently *faux pas* we shall be discouraged; that was expected by us—we did not calculate upon anything of consequence—it was a mere faint—a squib to see if our piece was sure fire, or rather a starting of the machinery to see if it was in order. I say machinery, for our operatives are little more, than automatons that are moved at the will of another, or others. Fortunately not one or more than one of the men you caught in the late bustle had any knowledge of the great enterprise; that is in agitation—Your Nats and you Hanks are totally ignorant of the impulse by which they are moved— You seem to think that you will be perfectly safe for twenty years to come! My life for it if thousands of masters are not made by their servants to bit the dust within twenty years or twenty months! ! ! Our plan is to operate upon the sympathies, prejudices and superstitions of the miserable beings you at present lord it over; and above all to arouse in their feelings a religious frenzy which is always effectual; only make them think that their leaders are inspired or that they are doing God's service and that will be enough to answer our purpose. We must make them believe that if they are killed in this crusade that heaven will be their reward, and that every person they kill, who countenance slavery shall procure for them an additional jewel in their heavenly crown and we shall have volunteers enough, and such too as will fight. Of course you will debar them from religious meetings; that is exactly what we want—Our secret agents are among you, and it will be their business to inculcate a belief that they are persecuted for their religion and of all the causes that ever operated upon human beings to produce a reaction religious persecution is the most effectual—that is the grand fulcrum on which rest all hopes—I repeat it our gold to prove unfaithful—a Yankee, you know, will hazard his life for money. Later, you will see this communication in print, and in an improved edition when we get our printing establishment in operation. Little do you know how many letters in cypher pass through your post office— and others in the Southern States, though you would not be the wiser if you were to see them, for they are past your finding out. Till you hear from us in characters of blood, I remain your humble, attentive, watchful, and the Public's obedient faithful servant,

"Nero"

NUMBER VI

"House Report, No. 7, Commonwealth of Massachusetts, in the House of Representatives, Jan. 19, 1841.

"The Special Committee, to whom were referred the petition of Wm. E. Channing, and forty-two others, of Boston, and many other petitions of the same character, praying for the repeal of so much of the fifth section of the seventy-fifth Chapter of the Revised Statutes as concerns especially the intermixture of persons differing in complexion, or belonging to different races, have discharged their duty, and submit the following.

"Report

"The Law, which the petitioners ask to have repealed, is as follows:

"No white person shall intermarry with a Negro, Indian, or Mulatto." Revised Statutes, chap. 75, sec. 5.

"And all marriages between a white person and a Negro, Indian, or Mulatto, shall, if solemnized within this state, be absolutely null and void, without any decree of divorce, or other legal process." Revised Statutes, chap. 76, sec. 1.

"Your Committee are of the opinion that the prayer of the petitioners ought to be granted. They, therefore, unanimously recommend the passage of the accompanying Bill. They see many reasons for the repeal of the law but none at all for its continuance. A statement of a few only of those reasons, they cannot but hope, will make it obvious to the legislature that the law ought to be repealed.

"The law is useless. In a community supporting the atrocious system of domestic slavery, which presumes persons who have not white skins to be slaves and compels the child to follow the condition of the mother, such a law might perhaps be of use; since some, who would not be prevented, by any abhorrence of amalgamation, from forming such alliances as the law interdicts, might still be prevented by the double fear of incurring the penalty, and thrusting their offspring into a state of interminable bondage. . . . Whatever evils may be alleged to result from the intermarrying of races, your committee are satisfied, that this law is no preventive of those evils. Were it possible to regulate the course of the human affections by legislative enactments, founded on a difference of complexion, or in the contexture of the hair of our citizens, the fact might be otherwise.

"Such connections are undoubtedly as frequent in this Commonwealth as in Vermont, New Hampshire, or Connecticut, where there are no legal enactments for their prevention. By those who choose to form them, they are formed, despite the law. If the parties cannot find at home a clergyman or a justice who is willing to solemnize their nuptials, they can accomplish their purpose by stepping into a neighboring state—an obstacle quite too slight too intimidate a couple bent upon getting married. This is the course commonly adopted, at least by those who cannot afford to indemnify a justice or a clergyman, for incurring the penalty for performing the ceremony. Besides, such marriages have been solemnized by clergymen in this Commonwealth who were not at the time aware that they were violating a law of the State—not that they were ignorant of the law. The difference in complexion of the parties, though of different races and coming within the prohibition of the statute, was yet not sufficiently great to be noticed by the officiating clergyman, who perhaps might be deficient in what the new philosophy calls the organ of color. If the law were to be continued, it would seem that the case of the justices and the clergymen liable to commit such mistakes might deserve some legislative consideration. It would seem that some means should be provided, if possible, to protect from imposition those whom the state has invested with the important power of solemnizing marriages, that some mode should be devised of distinguishing, more accurately than justices or ministers have unhappily often found themselves able to do, those nice shades of coloring, which, in certain cases, determine the competency of persons for entering into the matrimonial relation.

"The law encourages vicious connections between the races. It encourages licentiousness. It does this by releasing the parties from the civil obligations of marriage. A man marries. Children are the result of the marriage. He becomes weary of the connection, which was formed, perhaps, merely for the temporary gratification of his animal feelings. He abandons both his wife and his children. The latter, whom the former was bound, by every principle of justice and benevolence, to protect, to labor for, and, if need be to die for, are exposed by his abandonment of them to all the evils of want, and, it may be starvation. And having thus seduced and ruined one woman and begotten and beggared a family of children, the miscreant may repeat his atrocities, till the number of his victims shall have equaled that of the inmates of a Turkish seraglio. And all this he may do, under the present law, with entire impunity. It is one of the effects of the law. And the case just supposed is not suppostitious merely. It is, essentially, but an example of real cases known to have occurred; some of which, perhaps, would have been introduced into this report, had the Committee been empowered to send for persons and papers. There are, within the city of Boston alone, a number of instances of such suffering, and of wrong, growing out of this legalized prostitution of the marriage covenant, as, if dragged to the light, would absolutely startle both the benevolent feelings and the moral sense of this Christian community.

"The law is unjust. Its injustice to women and children, in depriving them of the care and support of their natural protectors during the life-time of the latter, has been, incidently, already shown. But this is a part only of the injustice wrought by the law, and, unlike that which remains to be pointed out, a part which, though produced by the law, is at the same time attributable to the baseness of one of the parties to such connections. In some instances, it works equal if not greater injustice, despite of either or both of the parties, and where both of the parties are strictly virtuous. It were vain to imagine it impossible for virtuous persons to form such alliances, since facts prove they may. The Hebrew lawgiver married a colored woman. One of America's most distinguished orators and statesmen was accustomed to boast that he owed his birth to the union of Pocahontas and a certain Anglo-American,—a union from which, history tells us, have "descended some respectable families of Virginia";—Other distinguished examples, more recent and possibly more pertinent, might be cited; but the Committee would not be thought invidious. It is not to be thought that cases of this particular description are of frequent occurrence. They are not so. And here in the North, cases of amalgamation, of whatever description, are comparatively rare; the great mass of individuals of mixed blood being found in those sections of the country where woman is robbed by the law of all right to her own person, and is made the property of another. The injustice now specially alluded to as being wrought by the operation of this law, is its effects on the transmission of property. It changes what is every where deemed the natural course of property, by diverting it from those most nearly related to the deceased owner. Thus, a man dying intestate and leaving a family, his wife and children may not inherit his estate. . . . Let it not be said that the law, in this respect, is inoperative; that none are to be found so base as to take advantage of its provisions for the purpose of plundering the innocent and helpless. It is sufficient that the law authorizes the perpetration of robbery; that it offers a premium on plunder. Besides, it were not true to say that the law is inoperative. The spoliation it sanctions and rewards, miscreants have been found to commit, and have committed, in the face of day, and in defiance of the moral sense of the community, through the instrumentality of our courts of justice so called. . . . But the flagrant injustice of this law does not end in mere pecuniary spoliation, in reducing widows and orphans to beggary and starvation. It strikes a heavier blow at its victims. For what is property, what is life even, in comparison of a good name? And this law, not content with stripping virtuous citizens of their property, undertakes to filch, and, so far forth as the thing can be done by statute, does filch, from their good names also. . . .

"Your Committee have thus stated some of the reasons which have led them to the conclusion that the prayer of the petitioners ought to be granted. It were easy to multiply the reasons in favor of that conclusion; but they deem it unnecessary to do so. They know of but one objection, which has not been virtually anticipated and answered, to the granting of that prayer. The objection is, that were the legislature to repeal the law, many would infer from the act that that body had sanctioned, had pronounced to be fitting, perhaps honorable, such intermarriages as the statute was designed to prohibit. Your Committee can see no validity in such objection, admitting it to be true. They believe that it is enough that the legislature state sufficient reasons for its acts, even though some might fail of comprehending those reasons. They have too much confidence in the intelligence of the people to admit for a moment that such an inference would be drawn from the premises. . . . This last relic of the old slave code of Massachusetts, which perpetuated distinctions among citizens never contemplated by the Constitution, which slandered the innocent, which robbed widows and orphans, which trampled on the divine institution of marriage, which granted entire immunity to the most beastly licentiousness, ought to be obliterated from the statute book of this Commonwealth, as contrary to the principles of Christianity and Republicanism.

"For the Committee,

"George Brandburn, Chairman."

Bibliography

Manuscript Sources

The Archives of Virginia, Richmond, Virginia. Executive Papers, Letters Received, 1750–1835.

———. Legislative Papers, a Collection of 25,000 Petitions Sent to the Legislature of Virginia, 1775–1860.

The Archives of the Office of Indian Affairs, Washington, D.C. Letters Received.

———. Letters Sent.

FLOYD, GOVERNOR JOHN. "Slaves and Free Negroes," a Scrapbook Collection of Letters and Papers Pertaining to the Nat Turner Insurrection, the Archives of Virginia.

County Records, Virginia. Elizabeth City County, Vol. 1684–1699.

———. Henrico County, Vols. 1668–1677, 1677–1692, 1692–1701.

———. York County, Vol. 1694–1697.

Deed Books, Petersburg, Virginia, Nos. 17, 18, and 1851–1853.

Order Books, Cumberland County, 1844–1851, 1851–1857, 1858–1869.

Printed Colonial Records

BRODHEAD, JOHN R. (ed.). *Documents Relating to the Colonial History of the State of New York.* 15 vols. Albany, 1858–87.

BROWNE, WILLIAM H. (ed.). *Archives of Maryland.* Baltimore, 1883.

CHAMBERLAYNE, CHARLES G. *The Vestry Book and Register of Bristol Parish, Virginia.* Transcribed and published by C. G. Chamberlayne. Richmond, 1898.

CHANDLER, ANDREW D. (ed.). *Colonial Records of Georgia*. Vols. XXIV, XXV. Atlanta: Georgia Historical Society, 1902.

LEE, FRANCIS B. (ed.). *Archives of New Jersey*. Trenton, 1903.

MC ILLWAINE, HENRY E. (ed.). *Minutes of the Council and General Court of Colonial Virginia*. Richmond, 1924.

———. *Legislative Journal of the Council of Colonial Virginia*. Richmond, 1918.

PALMER, WILLIAM P. (ed.). *Calendar of Virginia State Papers and Other Manuscripts Preserved at Richmond*. 11 vols. Richmond, 1875–93.

SALLEY, ALEXANDER S. *Commissions and Instructions from the Lords Proprietors of Carolina as Public Officials of South Carolina, 1685–1715*. Columbia, 1916.

SAUNDERS, WILLIAM L. (ed.). *Colonial Records of North Carolina*. 16 vols. Raleigh, 1886–.

The Vestry Book of St. Peter's Parish, 1682–1721, New Kent County, Virginia. Richmond, 1905.

WHITEHEAD, A. (ed.). *Documents Relating to the Colonial History of New Jersey*. 21 vols. Newark, 1880–1902.

State Laws

ALDEN, T. J. T., and VAN HOESEN, J. A. *Digest of the Laws of Mississippi*. New York, 1839.

BACON, THOMAS. *Laws of Maryland*. Annapolis, 1765.

CLARK, H. R., COBB, T. R. R., and IRVIN, D. *The Code of Georgia*. Atlanta, 1861.

COOPER, THOMAS. *Statutes at Large of South Carolina*. Columbia, 1838–.

Delaware. *The Laws of Delaware*. New Castle, 1797.

HENING, WILLIAM W. *Statutes at Large; Being a Compilation of All the Laws of Virginia from the First Session of the Legislature in the Year 1619. Published Pursuant to an Act of the General Assembly of Virginia, Passed on the Fifth Day of February, One Thousand Eight Hundred and Eight*. Richmond, 1810–23.

Indiana. *Revised Statutes of the State of Indiana*. Indianapolis, 1852.

MARCY, VIRGIL. *The Laws of Maryland*. Baltimore, 1811.

Massachusetts. *Acts and Resolves of Massachusetts Bay*. Boston, 1869.

MITCHELL, H., and FLANDERS, E. C. *Statutes at Large of Pennsylvania*. Philadelphia, 1801.

MOORE, B. T., and BIGGS, W. *Revised Code of North Carolina*. Boston, 1835.

ORMOND, J. J., BAGBY, A. P., and GOLDWAITE, G. *The Code of Alabama.* Montgomery, 1852.

PURPLE, N. H. *A Compilation of the Statutes of the State of Illinois.* Chicago, 1856.

SCOTT, OTHO, and MC CULLOUGH, HIRAM. *The Maryland Code.* Baltimore, 1858.

Tennessee. *The Code of Tennessee.* Nashville, 1858.

THOMPSON, LAWRENCE A. *Digest of the Statute Law of Florida.* Boston, 1842.

WICKLIFFE, C. A., TURNER, C., and NICHOLAS, S. S. *The Revised Statutes of Kentucky.* Frankfort, 1852.

Records of the Courts of Appeals

Alabama

2 Porter (1835)	29 Shepherd (1856)
11 Ormond (1847)	32 Shepherd (1858)
13 Ormond (1848)	33 Shepherd (1858)
21 Shepherd (1852)	34 Shepherd (1859)
27 Shepherd (1855)	35 Shepherd (1860)

Georgia

6 Cobb (1849)
10 Cobb (1851)
20 Cobb (1856)

Louisiana

1 Martin (1810)	5 King (1850)
5 Martin (1817)	6 King (1851)
7 Martin (1820)	7 Randolph (1852)
12 Martin (1823)	8 Randolph (1854)
4 Miller (1832)	8 Randolph (1854)
9 Curry (1835)	10 Randolph (1855)
14 Curry (1840)	11 Randolph (1856)
7 Robinson (1844)	12 Ogden (1857)
10 Robinson (1845)	13 Ogden (1858)
12 Robinson (1846)	14 Ogden (1859)
13 Robinson (1847)	15 Ogden (1860)

MANNING, T. C. *Unreported Cases Heard and Determined by the Supreme Court of Louisiana.* 1877.

Maine
34 Maine Reports

Maryland
1 Harris and McHenry (1787)
2 Harris and McHenry (1808)
2 Harris and Johnson (1809)
3 Harris and Johnson (1815)

Mississippi
2 Howard (1838)
27 Mississippi Reports (1854)
30 Mississippi Reports (1855)
33 Mississippi Reports (1857)
35 Mississippi Reports (1858)
37 Mississippi Reports (1859)

New Jersey
1 Halstead (1797)

New York
69 New York Reports (1910)

North Carolina
1 Cameron and Norwood (1801)
1 Taylor (1802)
8 North Carolina Reports (1820)
2 Devereaux (1829)
3 Devereaux (1832)
3 Iredell (1843)
5 Iredell (1845)
9 Iredell (1849)
44 North Carolina Reports (1852)
2 Jones (1854)
5 Jones (1857)
7 Jones (1859)

Ohio
12 Ohio Reports (1843)

Pennsylvania
1 Dallas (1786)

South Carolina
1 Bays (1791)   2 Dudley (1838)
1 Nott and McCord (1818)   4 Strobhart (1850)
1 McCord (1821)   10 Richardson (1856)

1 Hill (1857)   2 Bailey (1858)
1 Bailey (1858)   1 Spears (1860)

Tennessee
 8 Peck (1827)   7 Humphrey (1846)
 3 Yerger (1835)   9 Humphrey (1848)
 2 Humphrey (1841)   10 Humphrey (1849)
 3 Humphrey (1842)   12 Humphrey (1850)
 5 Humphrey (1844)   3 Head (1858)

Virginia
 1 Jefferson (1769)
 1 Hening and Munford (1809)
 2 Munford (1814)
 4 Randolph (1827)

United States
   1 Wheaton (1816)
  42 Federal Reports (1890)
 162 United States Reports (1895)

Government Documents

American State Papers—Public Lands. Vol. VII. 1834–35.
Bureau of the Census. "Negroes in the United States," *Bulletin* No. 8. Washington, 1904.
————. "Negroes in the United States," *Bulletin* No. 129. Washington, 1915.
Commissioner of Indian Affairs. *Reports.* Washington, 1866.
Congressional Globe. 26th Cong., 2d sess. 1841.
Department of Interior. *Reports.* "The Five Civilized Tribes," Sm. Doc. No. 1139, 63d Cong., 3d sess. Washington, 1913.
Massachusetts. *Report of the Special Committee to Whom Were Referred the Petition of Wm. E. Channing, and Forty-Two Others, of Boston . . . Praying for the Repeal . . . of the Statutes Concerning Intermixture of Persons Differing in Complexion or Belonging to Different Races.* House Report, No. 7. Boston, 1841.
————. *Report of the Commissioners Relating to the Condition of the Indians in Massachusetts.* House Report, No. 46. Boston, 1849.
————. *Report to the Governor and Council Concerning the Indians of the Commonwealth.* Senate Report, No. 96. Boston, 1861.
MOORE, JEDIDIAH. *A Report to the Secretary of War of the United States*

on Indian Affairs, Containing a Narrative of a Tour Performed in the Summer of 1820. New Haven, 1829.

New York. Report of the Special Committee to Investigate the Indian Problem of New York. No. 51. Albany, 1889.

North Carolina. Proceedings of the Constitutional Convention of North Carolina, 1835. Raleigh, 1835.

———. Indians of North Carolina. Sen. Doc. No. 677, 63d Cong., 3d sess. Washington, 1915.

Register of the Debates of Congress, 24th Cong., 1st sess. Washington, 1836.

Virginia. Journal of the Constitutional Convention of Virginia, 1829–1830. Richmond, 1830.

———. Report of the State Librarian, 1908. Richmond, 1908.

Contemporary Writings

ARCHDALE, JOHN. A Description of the Fertile and Pleasant Province of Carolina. London, 1707.

BARTRAM, WILLIAM. Observations on the Creek and Cherokee Indians. Philadelphia: James and Johnson, 1789.

BASSETT, JOHN S. (ed.). The Writings of Colonel William Byrd. New York: Doubleday, 1901.

BEVERLY, ROBERT. History of Virginia, in Four Parts. London: R. Parker, 1722.

BIRNEY, JAMES G. James G. Birney and His Times. New York: D. Appleton, 1890.

BAINERD, D. Mirabilia Dei Inter Indicos. Philadelphia, 1746.

BRANAGAN, THOMAS. Serious Remonstrances, Addressed to the Citizens of the Northern States and Their Representatives. Philadelphia, 1805.

BRICKELL, JOHN. Natural History of North Carolina. Dublin: By Authority of Trustees of Public Libraries, 1737.

BROCK, R. A. (ed.). The Official Letters of Alexander Spotswood. Collections of the Virginia Historical Society, Vol. I. Richmond, 1882.

CAMPBELL, ALEXANDER. A Tract for the People of Kentucky. Lexington, 1849.

CAMPBELL, CHARLES (ed.). The Bland Papers; Being a Selection from the Manuscripts of Colonel Theodorick Bland, Jr. Petersburg: Edmund and Julian Ruffin, 1840.

CARR, JOHN. Early Times in Middle Tennessee. Nashville, 1857.

CHANNING, WILLIAM E. The Works of William E. Channing. Vol. V. Boston: American Unitarian Association, 1848.

DAVIS, JAMES D. *The History of the City of Memphis.* Memphis, 1873.

DEW, THOMAS R. *Review of the Debate on the Abolition of Slavery in the Virginia Legislature of 1831–1832.* Richmond: T. W. White, 1832.

DOUGLASS, THOMAS. *Autobiography of Thomas Douglas.* New York, 1856.

DOUGLAS, WILLIAM. *A Summary, Historical and Political of the Planting, Progressive Improvements, and Present State of the British Settlements in North America.* 2 vols. Boston, 1755.

DRAYTON, JOHN. *A View of South Carolina as Respects Her Nature and Civil Concerns.* Charleston: W. P. Young, 1802.

FLINT, TIMOTHY. *History and Geography of the Mississippi Valley.* Cincinnati: E. H. Flint, 1833.

FORD, PAUL L. (ed.). *The Writings of Thomas Jefferson.* 12 vols. New York: Putnam, 1892–99.

FRANKLIN, JAMES. *The Philosophical and Political History of the Thirteen United States of America.* London, 1784.

GILES, WILLIAM B. *Political Miscellanies, Political Disquisitions.* No. 3. Richmond: T. W. White.

GODWIN, MORGAN. *The Negroes and Indians Advocate Suing for Their Admission to the Church.* London, 1680.

GREGOIRE, HENRI. *An Enquiry Concerning the Intellectual and Moral Faculties and Literature of Negroes.* Brooklyn: T. Kirk, 1810.

GRUND, FRANCIS J. *The Americans in Their Moral, Social and Political Relations.* 2 vols. London, 1837.

HAMILTON, STANISLAUS M. (ed.). *The Letters and Writings of James Monroe.* New York: Putnam, 1920.

HAWKS, FRANCIS L. *History of North Carolina.* Fayetteville, N.C.: E. J. Hale and Son, 1857.

HEWATT, ALEXANDER. *Account of the Rise and Progress of the Colonies of South Carolina.* London, 1779.

HORSMANDEN, DANIEL. *The New York Conspiracy, or a History of the Negro Plot, with a Journal of the Proceedings against the Conspirators at New York in the Years, 1740–1741.* New York: Southwick and Pelsne, 1810.

HUNT, GAILLARD (ed.). *Letters and Other Writings of James Madison.* New York: Putnam, 1910.

HURD, JOHN C. *The Laws of Freedom and Bondage.* 2 vols. New York: D. Van Nostrand, 1835.

JEFFERSON, THOMAS. *Notes on the State of Virginia.* Trenton: Pennington and Gould, 1803.

JONES, HUGH. *The Present State of Virginia.* London: J. Clarke, Printer, 1724.

LAUVERS, HENRY. *South Carolina's Protest against Slavery.* New York: Putnam, 1861.

LUNDY, BENJAMIN. *The Life, Travels and Opinions of Benjamin Lundy*. Philadelphia: W. D. Parrish, 1847.

MARTINEAU, HARRIET. *Society in America*. 2 vols. London: Saunders and Otley, 1837.

MAURY, ANN. *Memoirs of a Huguenot Family*. New York: Putnam, 1872.

MEADE, WILLIAM. *Old Churches, Families and Ministers in Virginia*. Philadelphia: Lippincott, 1867.

MONETTE, JOHN W. *History of the Discovery and Settlement of the Mississippi Valley until the Year 1846*. 2 vols. New York: Harper & Bros., 1846.

OLDMIXON, JOHN. *The British Empire in America, Containing the History of the Discovery, Settlement, Progress and Present State of All the British Colonies on the Continent and Islands of America*. 2 vols. London: J. Brotherton, 1708.

The Pro-Slavery Arguments, as Maintained by the Most Distinguished Writers of the Southern States, Containing Several Essays on the Subject, by Chancellor Harper, Governor Hammond, Dr. Simms, and Professor Dew. Philadelphia: Lippincott, 1852.

A South Carolinian, A Refutation of the Calumnies Circulated against the Southern and Western States, Respecting the Existence of Slavery among Them, to Which is Added a Minute and Particular Account of the Actual Condition of Their Negro Population. Charleston: A. E. Miller, 1822.

STEWART, JAMES. *Three Years in North America*. Edinburgh, 1833.

Strictures Addressed to James Madison on the Celebrated Report of William H. Crawford; Recommending the Intermarriage of Americans with the Indian Tribes, Ascribed to Judge Cooper; and Originally Published by Mr. John Binns, in the Democratic Press. Philadelphia: John Harding, 1824.

TOCQUEVILLE, ALEXIS C. H. M. C. DE. *American Institutions and Their Influence*. Translated by H. Reeve. New York: Allyn, 1855.

TUCKER, ST. GEORGE. *A Dissertation on Slavery, with a Proposal for the Gradual Abolition of It in the State of Virginia*. New York: Mathew Carey, 1796.

WALKER, DAVID. *David Walker's Appeal*. Boston, 1830.

WOODSON, CARTER G. (ed.). *The Mind of the Negro as Reflected in His Letters Written during the Crisis*. Washington: Associated Publishers, 1926.

Diaries, Letters, and Travels

ABDY, EDWARD S. *Journal of a Residence and Tour in North America, from April 1833 to August 1834*. 3 vols. London: J. Murray, 1835.

BENWELL, JAMES. *An Englishman's Travels in America.* London: Binns and Goodwin, 1833.

BERNHARD, Duke of Saxe-Weimar Eisenach. *Travels through North America in the Years 1825 and 1826.* 2 vols. Philadelphia: Carey, Lea and Carey, 1824.

BUCKINGHAM, JAMES S. *The Slave States of America.* 2 vols. London: Fisher, Son and Co., 1842.

BULLOCK, WILLIAM. *Sketch of a Journey through the Western States of North America.* London: John Miller, 1827.

BURNABY, ANDREW. *Travels through the Middle Settlements of North America.* 3d ed. London, 1798.

CASTELLUX, FRANCOIS JEAN. *Travels in North America in the Years 1780, 1781, and 1782.* London, 1787.

CHATEAUBRIAND, VISCOUNT DE. *Travels in America and Italy.* 2 vols. London, 1828.

COFFIN, LEVI. *Reminiscences of Levi Coffin.* Cincinnati: R. Clarke & Co., 1880.

CREVECOEUR, MICHEL ST. J. DE. *Letters from an American Farmer.* London, 1783.

EDDIS, WILLIAM. *Letters from America, Historical and Descriptive: Comparing Occurrences from 1769 to 1777.* London: Printed for the author, 1782.

EVANS, ESTWICK. *A Pedestrian's Tour.* Concord, N.H.: Joseph C. Spear, 1819.

FATHER WILLIAM. *Recollections of Rambles at the South.* New York, 1854.

FAUX, U. *Memorable Days in America, Being a Journal of a Tour to the United States.* London: W. Simpkin and R. Marshall, 1823.

FEATHERSTONHOUGH, GEORGE W. *Excursion through the United States, from Washington on the Potomac to the Frontier of Mexico, with Sketches of Popular Manners and Geological Notices.* London: John Murray, 1844.

FERREL, SAMUEL A. *Ramble of Six Thousand Miles through the United States.* London, 1832.

FITHIAN, PHILIP V. *Journal and Letters, 1767–1774.* Princeton: University Press, 1900.

GRANT, MRS. ANNE. *Memoirs of an American Lady with Sketches of Manners and Customs in America as They Existed Previous to the Revolution.* 2 vols. London: Longman, 1808

HALL, JAMES. *A Brief History of the Mississippi Territory.* Salisbury: Francis Coupee, 1800.

HAMILTON, THOMAS. *Men and Manners in America.* Philadelphia: Carey, 1833.

HAPLEY, CATHERINE C. *Life in the South, by a British Subject.* London, 1863.

INGRAHAM, EDWARD D. *The Southwest, by a Yankee.* 2 vols. New York: Harper & Bros., 1834.

JENSON, CHARLES W. *The Stranger in America.* London: J. Cundee, 1807.

KALM, PETER. *Travels in North America.* 3 vols. London, 1772.

KEMBLE, FANNY A. *A Journal of a Residence on a Georgia Plantation, in 1838–1839.* New York: Harper & Bros., 1863.

KENDELL, EDWARD A. *Travels through the Northern Parts of the United States in the Years 1807 and 1808.* 3 vols. New York: I. Riley and Co., 1809.

LAMBERT, JOHN. *Travels through Canada and the United States of North America in the Years 1806, 1807, 1808.* London: Baldwin, Cradock, and Joy, 1816.

LATROBE, BENJAMIN H. *The Journey of Latrobe.* New York: D. Appleton, 1905.

LOOMIS, ANDREW W. *Scenes in the Indian Country.* Philadelphia, 1850.

LYELL, SIR CHARLES. *Second Visit to the United States of America.* 2 vols. New York: Wiley and Putnam, 1849.

MARRYAT, FREDERICK. *A Diary in America with Remarks on Its Institutions.* 2 vols. London: Green and Longmans, 1839.

MEADE, WHITMAN. *Travels in America.* New York: C. S. Van Winkle, 1820.

MURAT, ACHILLE. *A Moral and Political Sketch of the United States of North America.* London: Effingham Wilson, 1833.

NEILSON, PETER. *Recollections of a Six Years Residence in the United States of America.* Glascow: David Robinson, 1830.

NOEL, BAPTIST W. *Freedom and Slavery in the United States.* London: James Nisbet & Co., 1863.

OLMSTED, FREDERICK L. *A Journey in the Seaboard Slave States.* 2 vols. New York: Putnam, 1859.

————. *The Cotton Kingdom.* 2 vols. New York: Mason Bros., 1861.

ROBIN, ABBE. *New Travels through North America in a Series of Letters.* Boston, 1784.

ROCHEFOUCAULD, DUC DE LA. *Travels through the United States of North America.* London, 1799.

ROYALL, ANNE. *Sketches of History, Life, and Manners in the United States.* New Haven: Printed by the author, 1826.

————. *Letters from Alabama on Various Subjects.* Washington: Printed by the author, 1830.

SCHOEF, JOHANN D. *Travels in the Confederation.* London: Light & Stearns, 1784.

SINGLETON, ARTHUR. *Letters from the South and West.* Boston, 1824.

SMYTH, JOHN F. D. *A Tour in the United States; Containing an Account of the Present Situation of that Country; the Population, Agriculture, Commerce, Customs, and Manners of the Inhabitants . . . with a Description of the Indian Nations . . . Likewise Improvements in Husbandry.* 2 vols. London: G. Robinson, 1784.

SUTCLIFF, ROBERT. *Travels in Some Parts of North America in the Years 1804, 1805, 1806.* York, Eng.: C. Peacock, 1815.

TIMBERLAKE, HENRY. *Memoirs of Lieutenant Henry Timberlake.* London: I. Riley and C. Henderson, 1765.

TROLLOPE, MRS. FRANCES. *Domestic Manners of the Americans.* 2 vols. London: Gilbert and Rivington, 1832.

WARVILLE, JEAN P. BRISSOT DE. *New Travels in the United States of America, Performed in 1788.* London: J. S. Jordan, 1794.

WYSE, FRANCIS. *America, Its Realities and Resources.* 3 vols. London: T. C. Newby, 1846.

Antislavery Publications

America and Her Slave System. London, 1845.

American Slavery as It Is: The Testimony of a Thousand Witnesses. New York: American Anti-Slavery Society, 1839.

ANDREWS, ETHAN A. *Slavery and the Domestic Slave-Trade in the United States, in a Series of Letters Addressed to the Executive Committee of the American Union for the Relief and Improvement of the Colored Race.* Boston: Light & Stearns, 1836.

BOURNE, GEORGE. *Picture of Slavery in the United States.* Middletown, Conn.: Edwin Hunt, 1834.

————. *Slavery Illustrated in Its Effects upon Women and Domestic Society.* Boston: I, Knapp, 1837.

ELLIOT, CHARLES. *The Sinfulness of Slavery in the United States.* 2 vols. Cincinnati: L. Swormstedt and J. H. Power, 1857.

First Annual Report, American Anti-Slavery Society. New York, 1834.

GRIMKE, A. E. *Letters to Catherine E. Beecher, in Reply to an Essay on Slavery and Abolition.* Boston: I. Knapp, 1838.

JAY, WILLIAM. *A View of the Action of the Federal Government on Behalf of Slavery.* Utica: James C. Jackson, 1844.

PAXTON, JOHN D. *Letters on Slavery. Addressed to the Cumberland Congregation.* Lexington: Abraham T. Skillman, 1833.

RANKIN, JOHN. *Letters on American Slavery Addressed to Mr. Thomas Rankin, Merchant of Augusta County, Virginia.* Newburyport, Mass.: I. Knapp, 1836.

Slavery and the Internal Slave Trade in the United States of North America, British and Foreign Anti-Slavery Society. London, 1841.

Thirteenth Annual Report of the American and Foreign Anti-Slavery Society. New York, 1853.

TOWER, PHILO. *Slavery Unmasked.* Rochester: E. Darrow and Brother, 1856.

Secondary Sources

ABEL, ANNIE H. *The American Indian as a Slaveholder and Secessionist.* 3 vols. Cleveland: A. H. Clark, 1915.

ADAMS, ALICE D. *The Neglected Period of Anti-Slavery.* Boston: Ginn & Co., 1908.

ADAMS, JAMES T. *History of the Town of Southampton.* Bridgehampton, 1912.

ALEXANDER, ARCHIBALD. *A History of Colonization.* Philadelphia: W. S. Martien, 1846.

ALVORD, CLARENCE W. *The First Explorations of the Transallegheny Region by the Virginians, 1650–1674.* Cleveland: A. H. Clark, 1912.

AMBLER, CHARLES H. *Sectionalism in Virginia from 1776 to 1861.* Chicago: University of Chicago, 1910.

_____. *Thomas Ritchie, A Study in Virginia Politics.* Richmond, 1913.

_____. *The Life and Diary of John Floyd.* Richmond, 1918.

ANDERSON, CHARLES C. *Fighting by Southern Federals.* New York: Neale Publishing Co., 1912.

BALLAGH, JAMES C. *White Servitude in the Colony of Virginia.* Johns Hopkins University Studies in Historical and Political Science. Series XIII, Nos. 6–7. Baltimore: Johns Hopkins Press, 1895.

_____. *A History of Slavery in Virginia.* Johns Hopkins University Studies in Historical and Political Science. Extra Volume XXIV. Baltimore: Johns Hopkins Press, 1902.

BASSETT, JOHN S. *Slavery and Servitude in the Colony of North Carolina.* Johns Hopkins University Studies in Historical and Political Science. Series XIV, Nos. 4–5. Baltimore: Johns Hopkins Press, 1896.

_____. *Slavery in the State of North Carolina.* Johns Hopkins University Studies in Historical and Political Science. Series XVII, Nos. 7–8. Baltimore: Johns Hopkins Press, 1899.

BATTEN, JAMES M. *Governor John Floyd.* Randolph-Macon Historical Papers. No. 4. Richmond, 1903.

BEAUCHAMP, HELEN C. "Slavery as an Issue in Virginia Politics, 1828–1836." Unpublished Master's thesis, University of Chicago, 1930.

BEVERIDGE, ALBERT J. *The Life of John Marshall.* 4 vols. New York: Houghton Mifflin Co., 1929.

BOLTON, H. E., and ROSS, M. *The Debatable Land, a Sketch of the Anglo-Spanish Contest for the Georgia Country.* Berkeley: University of California, 1935.

BRACKETT, JEFFREY R. *The Negro in Maryland.* Johns Hopkins University Studies in Historical and Political Science. Extra Volume VI. Baltimore: Johns Hopkins Press, 1889.

BRAWLEY, BENJAMIN. *A Social History of the American Negro.* New York: Macmillan Co., 1921.

BREVARD, CAROLINE M. *History of Florida.* 2 vols. Tallahassee, 1904.

BROWN, ALEXANDER. *The Genesis of the United States.* 4 vols. Boston:' Houghton Mifflin Co., 1897.

BRUCE, PHILIP A. *Economic History of Virginia in the Seventeenth Century.* 2 vols. New York: Putnam, 1896.

BRYCE, JAMES. *Relations of the Advanced and Backward Races of Mankind.* Oxford, 1903.

CALHOUN, ARTHUR W. *A Social History of the American Family.* 3 vols. Cleveland: A. H. Clark, 1917.

CATTERALL, HELEN T. *Judicial Cases Concerning Negro Slavery.* 3 vols. Washington: Carnegie Institution Publication, 1926.

DABNEY, WENDELL P. *Cincinnati's Colored Citizens.* Cincinnati: Dabney Publishing Co., 1926.

DREWRY, WILLIAM S. *Slave Insurrections in Virginia, 1830–1865.* Washington: Neale Co., 1900.

DUBOIS, WILLIAM E. B. *The Negro.* Home University Library of Modern Knowledge. New York: Holt, 1915.

GIDDINGS, JOSHUA R. *The Exiles of Florida, or, the Crimes Committed by Our Government against the Maroons, Who Fled from Carolina and Other States, Seeking Protection under Spanish Laws.* Columbus: Follet, Foster & Co., 1858.

GOODELL, WILLIAM. *The American Slave Code.* New York: American and Foreign Anti-Slavery Society, 1853.

GRAHAME, JAMES. *History of the United States of America, from the Plantation of the British Colonies till Their Assumption of National Independence.* 4 vols. Boston, 1845.

HARRISON, FAIRFAX. *The Harrisons of Simono.* New York: De Vinne Press, 1910.

HENRY, HOWELL M. "The Police Control of the Slave in South Carolina." Doctor's dissertation, Vanderbilt University. Emory, Va., 1914.

JERNEGAN, MARCUS W. *Laboring and Dependent Classes in Colonial America.* Chicago: University of Chicago, 1931.

JERVEY, THEODORE D. *The Slave Trade, Slavery and Color.* Columbia, S.C.: State Co., 1925.

JOHNSON, ROBERT G. *An Historical Account of the First Settlement of Salem in West Jersey, by John Fenwick*. Philadelphia: Orwin Rogers, 1839.

LAUBER, ALMON W. *Indian Slavery in Colonial Times, within the Present Limits of the United States*. New York: Columbia University Press, 1913.

LAWSON, JOHN. *History of Carolina*. London: W. Taylor and J. Baker, 1709.

LOGAN, JOHN H. *History of the Upper Country of South Carolina*. Columbia: S. G. Courtney, 1859.

MC CORMAC, EUGENE I. *White Servitude in Maryland*. Johns Hopkins University Studies in Historical and Political Science. Series XXII, Nos. 3–4. Baltimore: Johns Hopkins Press, 1904.

MC CRADY, EDWARD. *Slavery in the Province of South Carolina*. Annual Report, American Historical Association. Washington, 1895.

MC DOUGAL, MARION G. *Fugitive Slaves, 1619–1865*. Boston: Ginn & Co., 1891.

MC GREGOR, JAMES C. *The Disruption of Virginia*. New York: Macmillan Co., 1922.

MC KINNON, JOHN L. *History of Walton County*. Atlanta, 1911.

MOORE, GEORGE H. *Historical Notes on the Employment of Negroes in the Army of the Revolution*. New York: W. Abbott, 1907.

————. *Notes on the History of Slavery in Massachusetts*. New York: D. Appleton, 1866.

MOORE-WILSON, MINNIE. *The Seminoles of Florida*. New York, 1911.

MORGAN, EDWIN V. *Slavery in New York*. American Historical Association Papers. New York, 1891.

MUNFORD, BEVERLY B. *Virginia's Attitude toward Slavery and Secession*. New York: Longmans, Green & Co., 1909.

PATTERSON, CALEB P. *The Negro in Tennessee, 1760–1865*. The University of Texas Bulletin, No. 2205. Austin, 1912.

PICKETT, ALBERT J. *History of Alabama*. Atlanta: Doonan, 1900.

POLLARD, JOHN G. *The Pamunky Indians of Virginia*. Bulletin 17, Bureau of American Ethnology. Washington, 1894.

REUTER, EDWARD B. *The Mulatto in the United States*. Boston: R. G. Badger, 1918.

ROBERTSON, JAMES A. *Louisiana under the Rule of Spain, France, and the United States, 1785–1807*. Cleveland: A. H. Clark, 1911.

RUSSELL, JOHN H. *The Free Negro in Virginia, 1619–1865*. Johns Hopkins University Studies in Historical and Political Science. Series XXXI, No. 3. Baltimore: Johns Hopkins Press, 1913.

SALLEY, ALEXANDER S. (ed.). *The Debatable Lands, a Sketch of the Anglo-Spanish Contest for the Georgia Country*. Berkeley, 1925.

SCOTT, ARTHUR P. "History of the Criminal Law in Virginia during the

Colonial Period." Unpublished Doctor's dissertation, University of Chicago, 1916.

SHANNON, FRED A. *The Organization and Administration of the Union Army*. Cleveland: A. H. Clark, 1928.

SHOURD, THOMAS. *History and Genealogy of Fenwick's Colony*. Bridgeton, N.J.: George F. Nixon, 1876.

SHUFELT, ROBERT W. *The Negro a Menace to American Civilization*. Boston: R. G. Badger, 1907.

STEWART, W., and STEWART, T. T. *Gouldtown*. Philadelphia: J. B. Lippincott Co., 1913.

SWANTON, JOHN R. *Indians of the Lower Mississippi Valley*. Bulletin No. 43, Bureau of American Ethnology. Washington, 1911.

TURNER, EDWARD R. *The Negro in Pennsylvania*. American Historical Association. Washington, 1911.

TYSON, ARTHUR E. *A Sketch of Benjamin Banneker*. The Maryland Historical Society Pamphlets. Baltimore, 1854.

WARMOTH, HENRY C. *War, Politics, and Reconstruction*. New York: Macmillan Co., 1930.

WENDER, HERBERT. *Southern Commercial Conventions, 1837–1859*. Johns Hopkins University Studies in Historical and Political Science. Series XLVIII, No. 4. Baltimore: Johns Hopkins Press, 1930.

WERTENBAKER, THOMAS J. *The Planters of Colonial Virginia*. Princeton: Princeton University Press, 1922.

WESLEY, CHARLES H. *Negro Labor in the United States, 1850–1925*. New York: Vanguard Press, 1927.

WEST, GERALD M. *The Status of the Negro in Virginia during the Colonial Period*. New York: W. R. Jenkins, 1889.

WHEELER, JACOB D. *A Practical Treatise on the Law of Slavery, Being a Compilation of All the Decisions Made on that Subject in the General Courts of the United States, and State Courts, with Copious Notes and References as to the Statutes and Other Authorities, Systematically Arranged*. New Orleans: B. Levy, 1837.

WHITEFIELD, THEODORE M. *Slavery Agitation in Virginia, 1829–1830*. Johns Hopkins University Studies in Historical and Political Science. Extra Volumes, New Series, No. 10. Baltimore: Johns Hopkins Press, 1930.

WILLIAMS, GEORGE W. *History of the Negro Race in America from 1619 to 1880*. 2 vols. New York: Putnam's Sons, 1882.

WISE, JENNINGS C. *Ye Kingdome of Accomacke; or the Eastern Shore of Virginia in the Seventeenth Century*. Richmond: Bell Book Co., 1911.

WOODSON, CARTER G. *A Century of Negro Migration*. Washington: Associated Publishers, 1916.

————. *Negro Owners of Slaves in the United States in 1830*. Washington: Associated Publishers, 1925.

YOUNG, CHARLES H. *The Virginia Constitutional Convention of 1829.* Randolph-Macon Historical Papers, No. 3. Richmond, 1902.

Periodicals

BAKER, HENRY E. "Benjamin Banneker, the Negro Mathematician," *Journal of Negro History,* III (April, 1918), 99–119.

BURNELL, SAMUEL W. "Notes on the Meguleons," *American Anthropologist,* II (1889), 347–49.

CROMWELL, JOHN W. "The Aftermath of Nat Turner's Insurrection," *Journal of Negro History,* V (April, 1920), 208–33.

DODGE, DAVID. "The Free Negro of North Carolina," *Atlantic Monthly,* LVII (January, 1886), 29–35.

DUNBAR-NELSON, ALICE. "The People of Color of Louisiana," *Journal of Negro History,* I (October, 1916), 361–75; II (January, 1917), 51–78.

"Eighteenth Century Slaves as Advertised by Their Masters," *Journal of Negro History,* I (April, 1916), 217–22.

FOWLEY, WILLIAM C. "The Historical Status of the Negro in Connecticut," *Historical Magazine and Notes and Queries,* III (January, 1874), 14–21.

JACKSON, LUTHER P. "Free Negroes of Petersburg, Virginia," *Journal of Negro History,* XII (July, 1927), 365–87.

————. "Religious Instruction of Negroes, 1830–1860," *Journal of Negro History,* XV (January, 1930), 72–113.

————. "Religious Development of the Negro in Virginia, 1760–1860," *Journal of Negro History,* XVI (April, 1931) 168–239.

JERNEGAN, MARCUS W. "Slavery and Conversion in the Colonies," *American Historical Review,* XXI (April, 1916), 504–27.

————. "Slavery and the Beginnings of Industrialism in the Colonies," *American Historical Review,* XXV (January, 1920), 220–40.

JOHNSTON, JAMES H. "Anti-Slavery Petitions Presented to the Virginia State Legislatures by Citizens of Various Counties," *Journal of Negro History,* XII (October, 1927), 670–90.

————. "Documentary Evidence of the Relations of Negroes and Indians," *Journal of Negro History,* XIV (January, 1929), 21–43.

————. "Participation of White Men in Virginia Negro Insurrections," *Journal of Negro History,* XVI (April, 1931), 158–67.

"Letters of Colonel William Byrd," *American Historical Review,* I (October, 1895), 60–76.

"Papers Relating to Captured Negroes," *Edinburgh Review,* LXV (March, 1827), 391–95.

PHILLIPS, ULRICK G. "Slave Crime in Virginia," *American Historical Review*, XX (January, 1915), 333–40.

PORTER, KENNETH W. "The Relation between Indians and Negroes within the Present Limits of the United States," *Journal of Negro History*, XVII (July, 1932), 287–367.

RUSSELL, JOHN H. "Colored Freemen as Slave Owners in Virginia," *Journal of Negro History*, I (July, 1916), 233–42.

SYNDOR, C. S. "The Free Negro in Mississippi," *American Historical Review*, XXXII (July, 1927).

"Traveler's Impression of Slavery in America from 1750 to 1800," *Journal of Negro History*, I (October, 1916), 442–46.

WOODSON, CARTER G. "The Beginnings of Miscegenation of Whites and Blacks," *Journal of Negro History*, III (October, 1918), 335–53.

————. "The Relations of Negroes and Indians in Massachusetts," *Journal of Negro History*, V (January, 1920), 45–57.

Newspapers

The Enquirer (Richmond), Feb. 24, 1859.

The Georgia Journal (Milledgeville), Nov. 8, 1825.

The Index-Progress (Petersburg), Oct.–Nov., 1931.

The Liberator (Boston), June 7, 1834.

The Milford Herald (Milford, Del.), June 15, 1895.

The National Intelligencer (Washington), Jan. 10, 1832.

Niles Weekly Register (Baltimore), June 9, 1821; Sept. 17, 1831; Dec. 10, 1831; March 31, 1832; Oct. 25, 1834; Dec. 10, 1837.

The Semi-Weekly Mississippian (Jackson), Jan. 11, 1859.

Index

The following includes names of notable individuals and brief descriptions of primary citations.

DATE DUE